Who's Who in the DOCTRINE & COVENANTS

SUSAN EASTON BLACK

DESERET
BOOK

Salt Lake City, Utah

Many of the photographs herein were obtained from LDS Church Archives and are used by permission. The illustration of Joseph Smith Sr. by William Whitaker is from the LDS Visual Resource Library and is also used by permission.

First printing in hardbound 1997
First printing in paperbound 2001

Library of Congress Catalog Card Number: 96-79879

ISBN 1-57008-292-8 (hardbound)
ISBN 1-57008-772-5 (paperbound)

Printed in the United States of America   3170
Alexander's Printing, Salt Lake City, UT

20   19   18   17   16   15   14   13   12   11

Key to Abbreviations Used in Notes

CHC	B. H. Roberts, *A Comprehensive History of The Church of Jesus Christ of Latter-day Saints, Century I,* 6 vols. (Salt Lake City: The Church of Jesus Christ of Latter-day Saints, 1930).
HC	Joseph Smith, *History of The Church of Jesus Christ of Latter-day Saints,* ed. B. H. Roberts, 7 vols. (Salt Lake City: The Church of Jesus Christ of Latter-day Saints, 1932–51).
JD	*Journal of Discourses,* 26 vols. (London: Latter-day Saints Book Depot, 1854–86).
Journal History	Journal History of The Church of Jesus Christ of Latter-day Saints, Church Historical Department, The Church of Jesus Christ of Latter-day Saints, Salt Lake City, Utah.
LDS Biographical Encyclopedia	Andrew Jenson, comp., *Latter-day Saint Biographical Encyclopedia,* 4 vols. (1901–36; reprint, Salt Lake City: Western Epics, 1971).

MAJOR NOBLE ASHLEY
D&C 75:17

Birth: *3 March 1798, Sheffield, Berkshire County, Massachusetts. Son of Oliver Ashley and Tabitha Baker.*

In the early 1800s parents often named their sons ennobling, honorific titles. Major was such a title and does not signify military status. Just as King Follett was never a king, neither was Major Noble Ashley a commander in the military.[1]

Little is known of Major's early years as he grew to manhood in Massachusetts. By 1831 he had joined the Church and been ordained a high priest. Pleased with his ordination, he pronounced that "it was by the help of the Lord that he had been preserved, yet his greatest fear was for those who were weak in the faith."[2] Although his testimony was meant for the backslider, it proved to be a precursor of his own weak conviction.

Confident in his faithfulness, Major submitted his name to the Prophet Joseph Smith, seeking to know the will of the Lord concerning him (see D&C 75:23). The Lord revealed on 25 January 1832, "And again, I say unto my servant Major N. Ashley, and my servant Burr Riggs, let them take their journey also into the south country" (D&C 75:17). Major, as well as other elders present when Joseph received the revelation, was promised that if faithful he would be "laden with many sheaves [meaning many baptisms], and crowned with honor, and glory, and immortality, and eternal life" (D&C 75:5).

Whether he journeyed to the "south country" is not known. Less than six months later, on 3 July 1832, he was present at the home of Edward Partridge in Independence, Missouri, and was laboring as a tanner.[3] He denied the faith after the expulsion of the Saints from Jackson County. When early minutes of the June 1831 general conference were copied into the *Far West Record,* the scribe inserted "cut off" next to Major's name, indicating a breach of Church fellowship.[4]

The Ohio federal census of 1840 reported that Major was living in Tallmadge, Summit County, with two females, one between fifty to sixty years of age and the other between eighty to ninety years. In the census his trade was listed as a miner—a "learned professional and engineer." Although recognized by worldly standards for his profession, Major forfeited his testimony and quickly became one of those for whom he had once feared: "those who were weak in the faith."

Notes

1. Every effort has been made to find a military status for the name. The census of 1840 in Ohio lists his first name as Major.

2. Donald Q. Cannon and Lyndon W. Cook, eds., *Far West Record: Minutes of The Church of Jesus Christ of Latter-day Saints, 1830–1844* (Salt Lake City: Deseret Book Co., 1983), p. 22.

3. Oliver Cowdery recognized his skills and corresponded with him about leather products.

4. See Cannon and Cook, pp. 7–8.

ALMON WHITING BABBITT
D&C 124:84

Birth: *1 October 1812, Cheshire, Berkshire County, Massachusetts. Son of Ira Babbitt and Nancy Crosier (Crasier).*
Death: *7 September 1856, near Ash Hollow, about one hundred miles northeast of Fort Kearny, Nebraska.*

Almon Babbitt received a blessing from the Prophet Joseph Smith for his willingness to march with Zion's Camp. Benjamin Johnson wrote, "Joseph . . . told [Almon] of much good he would do in preaching the gospel, and how the hearts of people would be drawn towards him, and the greatness to which he would attain."[1] Through the years this blessing was realized, even though he failed to listen to prophetic counsel.

During his first eight years in the Church, Almon struggled to comply with Church leadership. After his ordination on 28 February 1835 to the First Quorum of Seventy, he was rebuked by the Kirtland high council: "A charge was preferred . . . against Elder Almon W. Babbitt, for not keeping the Word of Wisdom; for stating the Book of Mormon was not essential to our salvation, and that we have no articles of faith except the Bible."[2]

Almon countered that "he had taken the liberty to break the Word of Wisdom, from the example of President Joseph Smith, Jun., and others, but acknowledged that it was wrong."[3] On 28 December 1835 he was charged by Joseph Smith with "traducing my character."[4] Five days later he confessed his faults and was granted fellowship.[5]

In 1838 Almon was again rebuked by the Prophet for leading a company of Canadian Saints to Missouri and settling "on the forks of Grand river . . . contrary to counsel"[6] and in 1840 for encouraging the Saints to settle in Kirtland. On 22 July 1840 Joseph wrote in a letter to Oliver Granger: "When I think that others who have lately come into the Church should be led to Kirtland instead of to this place [Nauvoo], by Elder Babbitt . . . I must say that I feel grieved in spirit, and cannot tolerate such proceedings. . . . If Brother Babbitt and the other brethren wish to reform the Church . . . they must use other weapons than lies."[7] Almon was disfellowshipped and his preaching license demanded.

By 5 September 1840 three additional charges were brought against him before the high council in Nauvoo:

> First. For stating that Joseph Smith, Jun., had extravagantly purchased three suits of clothes while he was at Washington City, and that Sidney Rigdon had purchased four suits while at the same place, besides dresses in profusion for their families.
>
> Second. For having stated that Joseph Smith, Jun., Sidney Rigdon and Elias Higbee had said that they were worth one hundred thousand dollars each, while they were at Washington. . . .
>
> Third. For holding secret councils in the Lord's House, in Kirtland, and for locking the doors of the house, for the purpose of prohibiting certain brethren in good standing in the Church, from being in the Council, thereby depriving them of the use of the house.[8]

After these charges were reconciled, Almon was called on 19 October 1840 to be president of the Kirtland Stake. In a joint letter signed by

Joseph and Hyrum Smith, they wrote: "We therefore hope that the Saints will hold up the hands of our beloved brother, and unite with him in endeavoring to promote the interests of the kingdom."[9]

Three months after this appointment the Lord revealed to the Prophet Joseph Smith: "With my servant Almon Babbitt, there are many things with which I am not pleased; behold, he aspireth to establish his counsel instead of the counsel which I have ordained, even that of the Presidency of my Church; and he setteth up a golden calf for the worship of my people" (D&C 124:84).

Benjamin Johnson recorded Almon's reaction to the revelation: "He felt hurt by the rebuke in the revelation, and he was in great temptation to complain, and to turn his heel upon the Prophet."[10] He was capable in a masterful manner of "turning his heel." He had graduated as an attorney-at-law from the State University at Cincinnati and had obtained licenses to practice law in six states.

At the October conference of 1841 Almon was disfellowshipped for "counteracting the efforts of the Presidency to gather the Saints, and in enticing them to stop in places not appointed for the gathering."[11] He persisted in rejecting the counsel of the First Presidency and even predicted that a "scourge" would hit Nauvoo in 1843. However, he removed to Illinois.

On 13 March 1843 Almon was appointed to be the presiding elder of the Ramus Illinois Branch and was restored to full fellowship on 10 April 1843. On 6 May 1844 he was called on a mission to France but did not fulfill the assignment. Seven days before the Martyrdom the Prophet Joseph Smith sent orders to Almon, who was the commander of a military unit at Ramus, to come to Nauvoo and defend the city. He refused to go, saying it was foolish, and warned his company, "If any of you go, not one will ever get to Nauvoo alive."[12] The day before the Martyrdom Patriarch John Smith visited his nephew Joseph in Carthage Jail and received instructions to "tell Almon W. Babbitt I want him to come and assist me as an attorney at my expected trial."[13] Patriarch Smith met with Almon three hours later in Macedonia and delivered the message. Almon replied, "You are too late, I am already engaged on the other side."[14]

After the Martyrdom it was reported that Almon "rendered efficient legal service to the Church during the persecutions and mobbings in Illinois."[15] Heber C. Kimball disagreed: "My house was sold for seventeen hundred dollars, intended to be used to help to gather the Saints; but Almon W. Babbitt put it in his pocket, I suppose."[16]

When more and more of the Saints fled to Iowa, Almon requested they remain in Nauvoo until after the election, as he was running for political office. In an effort to ensure his victory he "took possession of the ferry boat," refusing passage to the electorate.[17]

In 1848 Almon also left Nauvoo. After crossing the plains to the Salt Lake Valley he was selected by a joint vote of the "'General Assembly of the State of Deseret' [as a] delegate to Congress to convey the memorial [requesting Utah statehood] to Washington."[18] His actions as he traversed the nation caused Orson Hyde to write, "Mr. A. W. Babbitt is a member of our church, but professes to be no religious Mormon."[19] Even a good friend of the Latter-day Saints, Thomas L. Kane, advised Brigham Young, "Mr. A. W. Babbitt has proved himself unfit to be trusted with the care of any of your interests and this alike by an abasement of his personal character, and an unfaithfulness to his trusts."[20]

In 1852 Almon was appointed by president of the United States Franklin Pierce as secretary of the territory of Utah. Thomas L. Kane wrote to President Pierce in 1854, "It becomes my duty to warn you against this individual, known by me as an entirely untrustworthy and unprincipled person, whose word should in no extremity be relied upon."[21]

John Jacques, a member of the Martin Handcart company, described him: "A. W. Babbitt, dressed in corduroy pants, woolen overshirt and felt hat, called as he was passing west. He seemed in high glee, his spirits elastic, almost mercurial. He had started with one carriage for Salt Lake City with the mail and a considerable amount of money."[22]

While crossing the plains from Washington, D.C., to the Salt Lake Valley, Almon was killed by Cheyenne Indians near Ash Hollow, about one hundred miles northeast of Fort Kearny, Nebraska, on 7 September 1856. It was reported that he "fought like a tiger, fired all his arms, then clubbed his rifle and fought the whole twelve savages, disputing every inch."[23]

Notes

1. Benjamin F. Johnson, *My Life's Review* (Independence, Mo.: Zion's Printing and Publishing Co., 1947), p. 20.

2. *HC* 2:252.

3. Ibid.

4. *HC* 2:346.

5. See *HC* 2:354.

6. *HC* 3:62.

7. *HC* 4:166.

8. *HC* 4:187–88.

9. *HC* 4:226.

10. Johnson, p. 87.

11. Journal History, 2 October 1841.

12. *HC* 6:515.

13. *HC* 6:598.

14. *HC* 6:600.

15. *LDS Biographical Encyclopedia* 1:285.

16. Heber C. Kimball, in *JD* 8:350.

17. Linda King Newell and Valeen Tippetts Avery, *Mormon Enigma: Emma Hale Smith* (New York: Doubleday and Co., 1984), p. 235.

18. *LDS Biographical Encyclopedia* 1:285.

19. *Frontier Guardian*, 2 May 1849.

20. Letter from Thomas L. Kane addressed to Brigham Young, Willard Richards, and Heber C. Kimball, from Philadelphia, 21 February 1851, Archives Division, Church Historical Department, The Church of Jesus Christ of Latter-day Saints, Salt Lake City, Utah.

21. Letter from Thomas L. Kane to President Franklin Pierce, from Philadelphia, 3 September 1854, Archives Division, Church Historical Department, The Church of Jesus Christ of Latter-day Saints, Salt Lake City, Utah.

22. As cited in Kate B. Carter, *Our Pioneer Heritage* (Salt Lake City: Utah Printing Co., 1968), 11:552–53.

23. *CHC* 4:213.

JESSE BAKER
D&C 124:137

Birth: *23 January 1778, Charlestown, Washington County, Rhode Island. Son of Benjamin Baker and Hannah Tucker.*
Death: *1 November 1846, Mills County, Iowa.*

Leaving his native Rhode Island, Jesse Baker journeyed to Hoosick, New York, in search of adventure and fortune. Unsatisfied with his surroundings in Hoosick, he moved to Ohio in 1835. There fifty-seven-year-old Jesse worked as a shoemaker and Thomsonian doctor (a doctor who focused on healing by using herbs) before being converted to Mormonism.

By 1837 he had become an elder[1] and received his patriarchal blessing from Joseph Smith Sr.[2] A notable event during his early Church years was his receiving of a vision with journalist John Pulsipher and John's father, Elias. John recorded that vision as follows:

> One pleasant day in March [1838], while I was at work in the woods, about one mile from the Temple, with father, Elias Pulsipher and Jesse Baker, there was a steamboat past over Kirtland in the air! . . . When we first heard the distant noise, we all stopped work. . . . When it got down to the city it was seen by a number of persons. It was a large fine and beautiful boat, painted in the finest style. It was filled with people. All seemed full of joy. . . . As it arrived over the Temple a part of it broke off and turned black and went north and was soon out of sight, while the boat, all in perfect shape, went to the west more beautiful and pure than before.[3]

A few days after the vision Jesse subscribed to the constitution of the Kirtland Camp. He journeyed with the camp to Missouri, where he became a landowner until persecution forced him to leave the state. In writing his Missouri petition in 1839, he itemized the property losses he sustained:

> Illenois Quincy May th11 1839
> a bill of Damages Sustaned in the State of Missorie

for mooveing into the State	$100.00
Fo propperty lost in the State	150.00
For mooveing out of the State and loss of propprety	500.00

> I certify the a bove to Be Just and true a cording to the Best of my knowledg—   Jesse Baker

> [Sworn to before C. M. Woods, C.C.C., Adams Co., IL, 11 May 1839.][4]

Jesse never received payment for his losses.

Undaunted by adversity, and true to his religious leanings, he joined with the Saints in improving the swamplands of Nauvoo. In recognition of his faithfulness, on 19 January 1841 the Lord through his Prophet called Jesse Baker to be a counselor to John A. Hicks in the elders quorum presidency (see D&C 124:137). The assumption that

Jesse guided the quorum from 1841 to 1844 is verified by William Adams: "Thereupon a number of elders were sent out on missions to gather tithing and donations to build the temple of the Lord, and a great deal of by Jesse Baker, president of the elders quorum."[5] Service in this presidency ended when he was ordained a high priest in 1845.[6] Jesse died a faithful member of the Church on 1 November 1846 at the age of sixty-eight in Mills County, Iowa.

Notes

1. See Lyndon W. Cook and Milton V. Backman Jr., eds., *Kirtland Elders' Quorum Record 1836–1841* (Provo, Utah: Grandin Book Co., 1985), p. 31.

2. See Book of Patriarchal Blessings Index 1:101, 2:169, Archives Division, Church Historical Department, The Church of Jesus Christ of Latter-day Saints, Salt Lake City, Utah.

3. Autobiography of John Pulsipher, typescript, p. 2, Special Collections, Harold B. Lee Library, Brigham Young University, Provo, Utah.

4. As cited in Clark V. Johnson, ed., *Mormon Redress Petitions: Documents of the 1833–1838 Missouri Conflict* (Provo, Utah: Religious Studies Center, Brigham Young University, 1992), p. 130.

5. Autobiography of William Adams, typescript, p. 14, Special Collections, Harold B. Lee Library, Brigham Young University, Provo, Utah.

6. Nauvoo Temple endowment register, 1845–46, Church Historical Department, The Church of Jesus Christ of Latter-day Saints, Salt Lake City, Utah.

WHEELER BALDWIN
D&C 52:31

Birth: *7 March 1793, Albany County, New York.*
Death: *11 May 1887, Stewartsville, DeKalb County, Missouri.*

Wheeler Baldwin, a veteran of the War of 1812, was baptized at age thirty-seven. On the night of 5 June 1831, Solomon and Levi Hancock, Wheeler, and others were walking together toward the Hancock home. Levi recorded:

> We walked heavily, some said that they felt as if they would be seized by Satan. Others that they felt as though the Devil and his angels were

hanging about them. . . . When we had got against the pond which was about fourteen rods across and very deep, I said, "Let us pray." So we all kneeled down and prayed around a circle as soon as the last one got through about nine o'clock at night and the moon shown brightly. A sudden bray of a jackass was heard about twenty feet behind us. We looked and could see nothing and nothing in the way. It started toward the pond braying all the time. . . . This braying continued across the pond and ascended the high hills on the other side until it grew less and less distinct until it got out of hearing. "There," said Brother Baldwin. "This proves to me that this work is true, for we all prayed for assistance; the Devil ran away."[1]

Two days following this experience, the Prophet Joseph Smith received a revelation calling Wheeler to serve a mission with William Carter: "Let my servants Wheeler Baldwin and William Carter also take their journey" (D&C 52:31). William Carter refused the mission call, leaving Wheeler without a companion. Rather than serving the mission alone, he remained in Kirtland, strengthening the local congregations.

Church historian John Whitmer noted that during his stay in Kirtland, Wheeler was instrumental in performing mighty miracles: "An old lady who had been helpless for the space of eight years [was] confined to her bed. She did not belong to this church, but sent her request to the Elders—who immediately attended to her call . . . and laid their hands on her, and she was immediately made whole and magnified and praised God, and is now enjoying perfect health."[2]

Wheeler spoke at general conference on 25 October 1831 at the home of Sirenes Burnett in Orange, Ohio, saying that "he rejoiced while he heard those give their testimony who had been up to the land of Zion" and that "he had many times been directed by the Spirit of God, also felt to do the will of the Lord in all things."[3]

Wheeler was present at four meetings of the high priests in Independence, Missouri, held from 5 October 1832 to 11 September 1833. In 1836 he was residing in Caldwell County, Missouri, and in 1839 in Lee County, Iowa Territory. On 6 March 1840 the Iowa high council appointed him "to obtain affidavits and other documents to be forwarded to the city of Washington" regarding redress for wrongs against the Saints in Missouri.[4]

By 1853 Wheeler had denied the faith and embraced Alpheus Cutler's "True Church of Jesus Christ." He moved with the Cutlerites to Manti, Iowa, in 1854. He spoke of his brief involvement with the Cutlerites before a general conference of the Reorganized Church of

Jesus Christ of Latter Day Saints in October 1862: "[Cutler] was ordained President of the High Priesthood. I baptized some forty members. . . . Well, we took the Bible, Book of Mormon, and Doctrine [and Covenants] for our guide; those . . . are the foundation upon which we built."[5] He concluded by saying that the Cutlerites held with Joseph Smith III's leadership and were willing to join the Reorganized Church.

He affiliated with the Reorganized Church in 1863 and presided over its Iowa branches at Mills, Fremont, and Page. On 6 June 1863 at the annual conference held in the North Star Branch in Iowa,

> Wheeler Baldwin reported that his labors had been mostly confined to the branch at Manti, in Fremont County. He had preached some at Indian Creek and Farm Creek. He bore a strong testimony to the truth of this organization, and said that he had not enjoyed the Spirit and power of God so much for the past thirty years as he had since he united with this work last March. The power of God's Holy Spirit was with the people in the branch at Manti, and he looked to see many more united with them soon.[6]

Wheeler was the presiding elder of the Fremont District of the Reorganized Church of Jesus Christ of Latter Day Saints in 1867 and attended the Thurman Iowa Branch and the Pleasant Grove Missouri Branch.[7] He died at the age of ninety-four in Stewartsville, Missouri.

Notes

1. Autobiography of Levi Ward Hancock, typescript, p. 34, Special Collections, Harold B. Lee Library, Brigham Young University, Provo, Utah.

2. John Whitmer, *An Early Latter Day Saint History: The Book of John Whitmer*, ed. F. Mark McKiernan and Roger D. Launius (Independence, Mo.: Herald Publishing House, 1980), pp. 80–81.

3. As cited in Donald Q. Cannon and Lyndon W. Cook, eds., *Far West Record: Minutes of the Church of Jesus Christ of Latter-day Saints, 1830–1844* (Salt Lake City: Deseret Book Co., 1983), p. 22.

4. HC 4:94.

5. *The History of the Reorganized Church of Jesus Christ of Latter Day Saints*, 8 vols. (Independence, Mo.: Herald Publishing House, 1967–1976).

6. Ibid., 3:322.

7. See Fremont, Iowa, RLDS branch records; Thurman, Iowa, RLDS branch records; and Pleasant Grove, Missouri, RLDS branch records, as cited in Susan Easton Black, *Early Members of the Reorganized Church of Jesus Christ of Latter Day Saints*, 6 vols. (Provo, Utah: Religious Studies Center, Brigham Young University, 1993), 1:256.

HEMAN A. BASSET
D&C 52:37

Birth: *1814, Guildhall, Essex County, Vermont.*
Death: *1876, Philadelphia, Philadelphia County, Pennsylvania.*

The youngest men named in the Doctrine and Covenants were Joseph Smith and Heman Basset, both seventeen years old when first mentioned. The Prophet's name appeared in connection with the visitation of the angel Moroni (see D&C 2), and Heman's name was listed with his missionary call (see D&C 52:37).

In 1830 Heman was residing with one hundred individuals, known collectively as the "Family," sharing all things equally on the Isaac Morley farm in Kirtland.[1] In October 1830 he, along with many of the "Family," was baptized by the missionaries who had been sent to the Lamanites.

When the missionaries left the area, false spirits were detected among the new converts and "many strange visions were seen."[2] According to local historian Josiah Jones, Heman Basset had a vision that called him to "go into the world and preach."[3] Levi Hancock was one of the first to observe Heman as he taught: "Bassett would behave like a baboon. He said he had a revelation he had received in Kirtland from the hand of an angel, he would read it and show pictures of a course of angels declared to be Gods, then would testify of the truth of the work and I believed it all, like a fool."[4]

Not only was Levi deceived by Heman, but he was also robbed: "While I was in the room at 'Father Morley's' . . . this same [Heman] Bassett came to me and took my watch out of my pocket and walked off as though it was his. I thought he would bring it back soon but was disappointed as he sold it. I asked him what he meant by selling my watch. 'Oh, said he, I thought it was all in the family.' I told him I did not like such family doing and I would not bear it."[5]

Despite his shortcomings, Heman was ordained an elder in the spring of 1831. He attended the fourth general conference of the Church, held on 3 June 1831 in a schoolhouse on the Morley farm. At the conference he was sternly warned by the Prophet Joseph Smith, "Heamon Basset you sit still the Devil wants to sift you."[6] He did not heed the warning, and three days after the conference a revelation was given instructing Symonds Ryder to receive the missionary calling once meant for Heman: "In consequence of transgression, let that which was bestowed upon Heman Basset be taken from him, and placed upon the head of Simonds Ryder" (D&C 52:37).[7]

Heman Basset was among the first members of the Church to leave the fellowship of the Saints in Ohio. Little is known of his later life except that he managed a hotel at Petaluma, California, for many years before migrating across the country to Philadelphia, Pennsylvania, where he died in 1876.

Notes

1. See John Whitmer, *An Early Latter Day Saint History: The Book of John Whitmer,* ed. F. Mark McKiernan and Roger D. Launius (Independence, Mo.: Herald Publishing House, 1980), p. 37 n. 2.

2. Joseph Smith, "Try the Spirits," *Times and Seasons* 3 (1 April 1842): 747.

3. Josiah Jones, "History of the Mormonites, Kirtland, 1831," *Evangelist* 9 (1 June 1841): 135–36.

4. Autobiography of Levi Ward Hancock, typescript, p. 18, Special Collections, Harold B. Lee Library, Brigham Young University, Provo, Utah.

5. Ibid.

6. Ibid., p. 22.

7. The correct spelling of Ryder's first name is *Symonds.*

JOHN COOK BENNETT
D&C 124:16–17

Birth: *4 August 1804, Fairhaven, Bristol County, Massachusetts. Son of John Bennett and Abagail Cooke.*
Death: *5 August 1867.*

Renowned historian Hubert Howe Bancroft astutely deemed John C. Bennett a "fraud," saying, "He has ability, he has brains and fingers; but he has no soul."[1] John's duplicity and deception brought sorrow and confusion to most who made his acquaintance. Apparently he received medical training from an uncle, Dr. Samuel Hildreth, a physician in Marietta, Ohio, and his claim to be a medical doctor was accepted in the states of Ohio, Indiana, Virginia, and Illinois. He was recognized as the founder of the Illinois State Medical Society and secured professorships in midwifery, diseases of women and children, and medical jurisprudence at Willoughby University in Ohio, where he organized and served as the dean of a medical school in 1834.[2]

History has accused John of conferring medical degrees for money; the "diplomas were sold throughout the Middle West and as far east as New York."[3] The *Western Medical Reformer* in 1845 referred to John C. Bennett as "that notorious personage who, in 1833–34, traveled through New York, the north of Pennsylvania and Ohio, and peddled his New Albany diplomas to every ignoramus who could raise ten dollars to buy one. . . . He filled the diplomas and peddled them out."[4]

Despite a widespread sullied reputation, he was an unknown character to the Latter-day Saints in 1840 when he made his first formal contact with Church leaders. Joseph Smith, always cordial to the stranger, extended a warm welcome to him: "Therefore my general invitation is, Let all that will, come, and partake of the poverty of Nauvoo freely."[5] John accepted the invitation and came to the city of the Saints.

Of John C. Bennett, John Taylor said, "At one time he was a good man."6 Joseph Smith, as reported by William Clayton, compared him to the Apostle Paul: "[Paul] was a good orator, but Doctor Bennett is a superior orator, and like Paul is active and deligent, always employing himself in doing good to his fellow men."7 Thousands of other Latter-day Saints placed their confidence in him also. John was elected mayor of Nauvoo, major-general of the Nauvoo Legion, and chancellor of the Nauvoo University. In his February 1841 inaugural address as mayor-elect, he stated, "I trust that the confidence reposed in me, by my fellow citizens, has not been misplaced, and for the honor conferred they will accept my warmest sentiments of gratitude."8

In March 1841 news of his marred reputation reached Nauvoo. Convincing denials momentarily removed the speculation, and in April 1841 he was appointed assistant to Joseph Smith. Tensions soon erupted between John and the Prophet. When an animated sham battle was enacted by the Nauvoo Legion, John tried to persuade President Smith to carelessly move to an unprotected position. The Spirit whispered to the Prophet that there was "mischief concealed in that sham battle," and the Prophet did not comply with John's request.9

Eight days after the incident Joseph initiated Church court proceedings to investigate John's behavior. The investigation uncovered his unscrupulous medical practices, including his taking advantage of his close contacts with female patients and his possible performing of abortions. On 17 May 1842, after his illicit relationships had become public, John resigned as mayor. He later pleaded with Church leaders for forgiveness, "cried like a child, and . . . begged that he might be spared" punishment.10 He told William Law "that if he were exposed it would break his mother's heart—that she was old, and if such things reached her ears it would bring her down with sorrow to the grave."11 Church leaders were unconvinced.

John left Nauvoo in mid-June 1842 and, as Church member George Miller reported, soon "entered into a conspiracy . . . to bring a mob upon us, and . . . destroy and drive us from our homes."12 The bombastic speeches against Mormonism that he delivered in St. Louis, Louisville, Cincinnati, Cleveland, New York City, Boston, Salem, Philadelphia, Buffalo, Kalamazoo, and Chicago brought increased animosity against the Saints. A notice in the 26 July 1842 *Cincinnati Republican* read: "General Bennett, the distinguished seceder from the Mormon faith, was in town on Sunday, and stopped at the Broadway Hotel. He made so many startling disclosures of the iniquities practiced by Joe

Smith on the noodles congregated at Nauvoo that his life is considered in danger of the assassin's steel."[13]

To counteract the false statements, nearly three hundred Latter-day Saint volunteers hurried to the mission field to disabuse public opinion. Undaunted by the missionaries, in November 1842 John published *The History of the Saints; or, An Expose of Joe Smith and Mormonism.* The purpose of his book was "to expose the enormous iniquities which have been perpetrated by one of the grossest and most infamous imposters" on earth, to overthrow Joseph Smith, and "to save [his] country from the most dreadful evils."[14] Even after this affront, the Prophet Joseph said of him:

> I was his friend; I am yet his friend, as I feel myself bound to be a friend to all the sons of Adam. Whether they are just or unjust, they have a degree of my compassion and sympathy. If he is my enemy, it is his own fault; and the responsibility rests upon his own head; and instead of arraigning his character before you, suffice it to say that his own conduct, wherever he goes, will be sufficient to recommend him to an enlightened public, whether for a bad man or a good one.[15]

John C. Bennett never returned to faithfulness. He united momentarily with Sidney Rigdon and later with James Strang. But by the 1850s he had turned from religious endeavors and was again practicing medicine. He enhanced his career by adding dentistry and poultry breeding to his repertoire.

After residing for seven years in Iowa, John died on 5 August 1867, twenty-three years after the Martyrdom. Edward Stevenson wrote that he died "a miserable pauper [and that] like most apostates [he had] a hard fate."[16] Some have supposed, as did Aroet Hale, that his fate was a direct result of a curse pronounced by the Prophet Joseph Smith: "The Prophet Joseph . . . told him if he did not repent of his sins and sin no more, the curse of God Almighty would rest upon him, that he would die a vagabond upon the face of the earth, without friends to buy him."[17]

Notes

1. Hubert Howe Bancroft, *History of Utah* (San Francisco: The History Company Publishers, 1890), pp. 149–50.

2. See Andrew C. Skinner, "John C. Bennett: For Prophet or Profit?" *Regional Studies in Latter-day Saint Church History: Illinois* (Provo, Utah: Department of Church History and Doctrine, Brigham Young University, 1995), pp. 249–50.

3. James J. Tyler, *John Cook Bennett, Colorful Freemason of the Early Nineteenth Century* (n.p., n.d.), p. 5, as cited in Skinner, p. 251.

4. *Western Medical Reformer* 5 (Cincinnati, 1845):13, as cited in Frederick C. Waite, "The First Medical Diploma Mill in the United States," *Bulletin of the History of Medicine* 20 (Baltimore, 1946):499.

5. *HC* 4:178.

6. *HC* 5:81.

7. Joseph Smith, *The Words of Joseph Smith,* comp. Andrew F. Ehat and Lyndon W. Cook (Provo, Utah: Religious Studies Center, Brigham Young University, 1980), p. 59.

8. *HC* 4:288.

9. *HC* 5:4.

10. *HC* 5:18–19.

11. *HC* 5:76.

12. *HC* 5:47.

13. *Cincinnati Republican,* 26 July 1842, as cited in Skinner, p. 260.

14. John C. Bennett, *The History of the Saints or, An Expose of Joe Smith and Mormonism* (Boston: Leland and Whiting, 1842), preface.

15. *HC* 5:156.

16. Edward Stevenson, *Selections from the Autobiography of Edward Stevenson, 1820–1897 (1820–1846),* ed. Joseph Grant Stevenson (Provo, Utah: Stevenson's Genealogical Center, 1986), p. 88.

17. Journal of Aroet Lucious Hale, typescript, p. 7, Special Collections, Harold B. Lee Library, Brigham Young University, Provo, Utah.

EZRA T. BENSON
D&C 136:12

Birth: *22 February 1811, Mendon, Worcester County, Massachusetts. Son of John Benson Jr. and Chloe Taft.*
Death: *3 September 1869, Ogden, Weber County, Utah.*

"My parents were religiously inclined and always reverenced the Diety," said Ezra T. Benson, "yet never belonged to any religious society. They were firm believers in the Bible, and taught their children so to do, and strictly to observe the Sabbath."[1]

Ezra left home at age sixteen and moved near the town center of Uxbridge, Massachusetts, where he worked as a hotel assistant. He ended his employment there to assist his grandmother with her farm. After her death and his own marriage, twenty-year-old Ezra moved back to Uxbridge and, with the inheritance from his grandmother, purchased the hotel where he had worked.

Ezra prospered in the hotel business for two years before moving to Holland, Massachusetts, to enter a partnership with his brother-in-law in a cotton factory. This venture was short-lived and Ezra "consequently gave up that business as soon as practicable and took a hotel in the same town."[2] He was also appointed postmaster there.

Soon the lure of moving to the West became appealing. In 1838 Ezra moved his family to Quincy, Illinois, and it was there that he became acquainted with the Latter-day Saints. "The first Elder I heard preach was Sylvester B. Stoddard," penned Ezra. From Brother Stoddard's speech he concluded, "I thought the Mormons were a very peculiar people."[3] His opinion quickly changed during a debate of religious issues between the Prophet Joseph Smith and a Dr. Nelson in July 1840. Dr. Nelson tried to demean the Prophet and the Book of Mormon, but "after making another attempt to ridicule the Mormons and their doctrine, Dr. Nelson had a fit, and had it not been for his friends, would have fallen on the platform."[4]

At another gathering Ezra listened to Elder John E. Page. "[Never] heard the like before," he recorded. A collection was taken to assist him on his mission. "I threw in a half-dollar, being all I had. This was the first time I had ever helped any missionary."5

After pondering these incidents Ezra sought answers from the Lord in prayer. While praying in the winter wilderness, he heard the crust of the snow beginning to break as "though some one was walking on the frozen snow." He arose to his feet and looked in the direction of the sound "but did not see anything or anyone." The sound was repeated three times. He said aloud, "'Mr. Devil, you may break snow crust, but, I will pray!' After that, he heard nothing more."6

Ezra and his wife were baptized on Sunday, 19 July 1840 in the Mississippi River by Daniel Stanton in the presence of "some three hundred curious onlookers. When the ordinances were completed a shout went up, 'The Mormons have got them!'"7 In the fall Ezra was ordained an elder and later a high priest by Hyrum Smith. He served as second counselor in the Quincy stake presidency before moving to Nauvoo in 1841. By June 1842 he was serving the first of three missions to the eastern states. He was disheartened on the missions by religious persecution and the realization that his "most intimate acquaintances would not come to hear" him.8

Upon returning to Nauvoo in 1845, he diligently worked on the Nauvoo Temple until Brigham Young urged him to flee Nauvoo in the first company heading west. With few provisions, he wondered aloud how he could obediently follow President Young's directive. "Go down the street and ask every man you meet to give you some help," advised Brigham.9 Jared Porter loaned him a horse, a Brother Chidister sold him a wagon, and Stephen Farnsworth gave him cloth for a wagon cover. By 9 February 1846 Ezra and his family had crossed the frozen Mississippi to follow their prophetic leader.

At the Sugar Creek encampment Ezra murmured to Brigham that his team was so weak he could not proceed further with the heavily laden wagon. Brigham gladly relieved Ezra of six hundred pounds of wheat and other food, leaving him only fifty pounds of flour and a half bushel of meal. "After that, when others complained about their wagons sinking in mud to their axles, [Ezra] would respond, 'Go to Brother Brigham and he will lighten your load.'"10

At the Mount Pisgah encampment, while serving as a counselor to William Huntington, he received correspondence from Brigham Young "informing him of his appointment to the Quorum of the Twelve."[11] Thirty-five-year-old Ezra was ordained on 16 July 1846 by President Young and blessed that he should yet have "the strength of Samson."[12]

His faithfulness to that holy calling was evident throughout his life. After staying for a time in Council Bluffs, Iowa, he journeyed to the Salt Lake Valley in the vanguard company and is credited with speaking at the first sacrament meeting there. He was later appointed to preside over the Saints in Pottawattamie, Iowa, "to stir up the brethren in Pottawattamie in regard to moving and to organize them into companies."[13] He was beloved by the Latter-day Saints, and in 1849, when he was "dangerously sick on the road, and was not expected to live, the camp fasted and prayed for him and he recovered."[14]

In the Valley Ezra was noted for his industry and political leadership. He served as a member of the provisional government of the State of Deseret and several terms in the Utah Territorial House of Representatives. He played a key role in colonizing the Great Basin and in presiding over the British Mission in the 1850s. In 1860 Ezra colonized Cache Valley and organized wards and stakes in the area. During his nine years there he served as colonel of the Cache Valley militia and was instrumental in organizing the construction of homes, mills, schools, canals, and churches.

While attempting to care for a sick horse after a long ride from Logan to Ogden in September 1869, fifty-eight-year-old Ezra fell dead. It was reported that "overwork and the burden of worry had weakened his heart."[15] Four thousand attended his funeral, including all members of the Twelve and three hundred Indian braves. His testimony lives on in these words: "I testify that Joseph Smith was a Prophet of the Most High . . . My testimony is: that 'Mormonism' is the kingdom of God."[16]

Notes

1. Ezra Taft Benson, autobiography, *Instructor* 80 (February 1945): 53.

2. Ibid., p. 54.

3. Ibid., p. 55.

4. Donald Benson Alder and Elsie L. Alder, *The Benson Family* (Salt Lake City: The Ezra T. Benson Genealogical Society, 1979), p. 18.

5. As cited in Sheri L. Dew, *Ezra Taft Benson: A Biography* (Salt Lake City: Deseret Book Co., 1987), p. 3.

6. As cited in Alder and Alder, pp. 18–19.

7. As cited in Dew, p. 4.

8. As cited in ibid.

9. As cited in ibid., pp. 5–6.

10. As cited in ibid., p. 6.

11. Alder and Alder, p. 20.

12. As cited in Dew, p. 7.

13. Autobiography of David Osborn, typescript, p. 33, Special Collections, Harold B. Lee Library, Brigham Young University, Provo, Utah.

14. Alder and Alder, p. 21.

15. Ibid., p. 26.

16. As cited in Forace Green, comp., *Testimonies of Our Leaders* (Salt Lake City: Bookcraft, 1958), p. 123.

SAMUEL BENT

D&C 124:132

Birth: *19 July 1778, Barre, Worcester County, Massachusetts. Son of Joel Bent and Mary Mason.*
Death: *16 August 1846, Garden Grove, Decatur County, Iowa.*

Samuel Bent, a well-respected member of the Presbyterian and Congregationalist churches, served as a colonel in the Massachusetts militia before moving to New York and later to Pontiac, Michigan.[1] By the early 1830s he was a deacon in the Presbyterian church in Pontiac.

While visiting relatives in Pontiac, Lucy Mack Smith was introduced to Samuel's Presbyterian pastor, Mr. Ruggles, who said, "And you are the mother of that poor, foolish, silly boy, Joe Smith, who pretended to translate the Book of Mormon." Her retort to the pastor was faithfully pointed, and included the statement, "Mark my words—as true as God lives, before three years we will have more than one-third of your church; and, sir, whether you believe it or not, we will take the very deacon, too." Her remarks evoked "a hearty laugh at the expense of the minister."[2]

Within a few months Mormon elder Jared Carter was preaching in Pontiac. "He went immediately into the midst of Mr. Ruggles' church, and, in a short time, brought away seventy of his best members, among whom was the deacon, just as [Mother Smith had] told the minister."[3]

Details of Samuel Bent's conversion were recorded by his young friend Edward Stevenson: "Some, even his own wife, thought he was losing his mind. She came to my mother. . . . My mother asked, 'Does your husband continue to pray to the Lord?' 'Yes,' she said, 'more devoted than ever, but he only thinks to join this new delusion.' 'Well,' said mother, 'let us wait and see what will follow if it is of God it will stand; if not it will fall.'"[4]

In January 1833 Samuel was baptized and ordained an elder by Jared Carter, becoming the first man to join the Church and receive the priesthood in Pontiac. The day after his baptism he left on a mission to Huron, Michigan, where he organized a branch of the Church. According to the reminiscences of Lyman Littlefield, "Quite a number of people in that vicinity embraced the new faith."[5]

Many of the new converts were recruited by Samuel to join with Zion's Camp in defending the rights of the Saints in Missouri. Samuel also joined the camp, serving as a moderator or presiding officer.[6] Despite his official position, he found merriment as the recruits fought a sham snowball battle.[7]

When the camp disbanded, Samuel was called to serve another mission. Before he had finished preparing for this mission he heard a voice in the night say, "Samuel, arise immediately, and go forth on the mission which thou wast commanded to take."[8] He arose and set off without further delay.

After returning from his mission he attended the School of the Prophets and was present at the dedication of the Kirtland Temple in Ohio before joining the Saints in Liberty, Missouri. Liberty proved near fatal for Samuel, as he was a victim of religious mobocracy, being tied to a tree and whipped by a mob.[9] After the death of his wife, Mary, he left Liberty for Far West, Missouri, where he served in the Far West high council and declared before that council "that his faith [was] as ever and that he [felt] to praise God in prisons and in dungeons and in all circumstances whatever he [might] be found."[10]

Almost as if fulfilling his own prophecy, Samuel was imprisoned and confined in Richmond Jail for nearly three weeks. After being released on bail, he was warned in a vision to leave Missouri. In compliance, he left immediately, traveling through the woods on foot and just narrowly escaping pursuing mobbers.[11] Samuel's written redress petition evidences his concern not for his own suffering but for the depredations committed against other Saints in Missouri: "Saw them shoot down one of [Gad Yale's] hogs, saw them take his corn and belive they destroyed about ten acres, and likewise a small stack of Hay. . . . Saw some of the Troops in possession of Mr. Cyrus Daniel's house for several days."[12]

On 19 January 1841 the Prophet Joseph Smith appointed Samuel by revelation to serve on the Nauvoo high council (see D&C 124:132). Other assignments in Nauvoo soon followed: member of the Council of Fifty, colonel in the Nauvoo Legion, and captain of the exodus of 1846. Most notable of Samuel's contributions during the Nauvoo years was his mission in 1840 to Illinois, Indiana, and Ohio to collect needed funds for printing the Book of Mormon, Doctrine and Covenants, hymnbooks, and the new translation of the scriptures. In a signed affidavit the Prophet and other leaders wrote of their confidence in Samuel and George W. Harris to care for the collected funds. They noted that the elders' "zeal for the cause of truth, and their strict morality and honesty," enabled the leaders to "cheerfully recommend them to the Saints of the Most High."[13]

At the age of sixty-eight Samuel died while serving as the presiding officer of the small encampment of pioneers located in Garden Grove, Iowa Territory. His counselors wrote to the Council of the Twelve Apostles to inform them of his demise: "Garden Grove is left without a president, . . . and the Church has sustained the loss of an undeviating friend to truth and righteousness. The glory of his death is, that he died in the full triumphs of faith and knowledge of the truth of our holy religion, exhorting his friends to be faithful; having three days previous received intimations of his approaching end by three holy messengers from on high."[14]

Notes

1. *LDS Biographical Encyclopedia* 1:368.

2. As cited in Lucy Mack Smith, *History of Joseph Smith by His Mother*, ed. Preston Nibley (Salt Lake City: Bookcraft, 1954), pp. 215–16.

3. Ibid., p. 217.

4. Edward Stevenson, *Selections from the Autobiography of Edward Stevenson, 1820–1897 (1820–1846)*, ed. Joseph Grant Stevenson (Provo, Utah: Stevenson's Genealogical Center, 1986), p. 5.

5. Lyman Omer Littlefield, *Reminiscences of Latter-day Saints* (Logan, Utah: The Utah Journal Co., 1888), pp. 28–29.

6. See James L. Bradley, *Zion's Camp 1834: Prelude to the Civil War* (Logan, Utah: James L. Bradley, 1990), p. 33.

7. See Stevenson, p. 30.

8. Smith, p. 217.

9. See *LDS Biographical Encyclopedia* 1:368.

10. As cited in Donald Q. Cannon and Lyndon W. Cook, eds., *Far West Record: Minutes of The Church of Jesus Christ of Latter-day Saints, 1830–1844* (Salt Lake City: Deseret Book Co., 1983), p. 222.

11. See *LDS Biographical Encyclopedia* 1:368.

12. As cited in Clark V. Johnson, ed., *Mormon Redress Petitions: Documents of the 1833–1838 Missouri Conflict* (Provo, Utah: Religious Studies Center, Brigham Young University, 1992), p. 419.

13. *HC* 4:164.

14. As cited in *LDS Biographical Encyclopedia* 1:368.

TITUS BILLINGS
D&C 63:39

Birth: *25 (possibly 24) March 1793, Greenfield, Franklin County, Massachusetts. Son of Ebenezer Billings and Esther Joyce.*
Death: *6 February 1866, Provo, Utah County, Utah.*

According to family tradition, stonemason Titus Billings was the second person baptized in Kirtland, Ohio, and among the first appointed by revelation to move to Jackson County, Missouri.[1] In August 1831 the Lord said to Joseph Smith, as recorded in the Doctrine and Covenants, "Let my servant Titus Billings . . . dispose of the land, that he may be prepared in the coming spring to take his journey up unto the land of Zion, with those that dwell upon the face thereof" (D&C 63:39). In obedience Titus sold his acreage and led a small company of Saints from Kirtland to Jackson in the spring of 1832.

Upon arrival he consecrated his property to the Church:

> Be it known, that I, Titus Billings of Jackson county, . . . do, of my own free will and accord, having first paid my just debts, grant and hereby give unto Edward Partridge of Jackson county, and the state of

Missouri, Bishop of said Church, the following described property, viz.:—sundry articles of furniture valued fifty-five dollars twenty-seven cents; also two beds, bedding and extra clothing valued seventy-three dollars twenty-five cents; also farming utensils valued forty-one dollars; also one horse, two wagons, two cows and two calves, valued one hundred forty-seven dollars.

For the purpose of purchasing lands in Jackson county, Mo., and building up the New Jerusalem, even Zion, and for relieving the wants of the poor and needy.[2]

In exchange for his consecration, Titus was given a lease and a loan known as his inheritance:

> Be it known, that I, Edward Partridge, . . . do lease unto Titus Billings, of Jackson county, . . . the following described piece of parcel of land, being a part of section No. Three, township No. forty-nine. . . . And also have loaned the following described property, viz:—Sundry articles of furniture, valued fifty-five dollars twenty-five cents; also two beds, bedding and clothing, valued seventy-three dollars twenty-seven cents . . . also one horse, two cows, two calves, and two wagons. . . .[3]

Titus's first calling in Zion was issued by the First Presidency in a letter dated 25 June 1833: "Let Brother Edward Partridge choose as counselors . . . Brother Parley P. Pratt and Brother Titus Billings."[4] He was subsequently expelled from Jackson by an armed mob and was therefore unable to render any service as a counselor, but he did assist the distressed Saints fleeing across the Missouri River to Clay County.[5]

In 1834 Titus rented a small farm in Clay County. The labor of planting corn and potatoes was tedious and slow, and because of his weak physical condition "he would shake hard enough to shake himself to pieces."[6] Two years later he left Clay County after helping draft a letter of peaceful intentions to the local residents. A portion of the letter reads: "We the Mormons are grateful for the kindness which has been shown to us by the citizens of Clay County. . . . For the sake of friendship, we covenant to be in peace. We will also move to a new location from the county."[7]

Titus moved to Far West, Caldwell County, where he was able to serve as second counselor to Bishop Partridge, in fulfillment of the 1833 First Presidency letter. However, when threatened violence erupted unto mobocracy, Titus turned from counselor to defender of the Saints at the Battle of Crooked River. His son wrote: "My father, Titus, said the bullets were flying all around him but he had no fear until he saw brother [David W.] Patten fall. Then he stepped behind a large tree until the firing was over. . . . When he came home he was completely worn out as he had no rest for four or five nights. He told mother he wanted to sleep two hours. . . . He had only slept one hour when a knock came on the door."[8]

Hosea Stout had come to inform him that "all the brethren that were in the battle had to flee within two or three hours. Mother baked [Titus] as much bread as she could and he left the family without a spoonful of flour in the house." His escape from Mormon enemies was plagued with starvation and frostbite. "For three days and nights they had only slippery elm bark for food. Father's feet were frozen so badly the flesh came off in pieces."[9] In his Missouri redress petition, Titus decried the atrocities, declaring, "Never have had a writ served upon me not broken the law in one instance and now I say that these things have come upon us on account of the religion which we profess."[10]

He found safety in Lima, Illinois, where his family joined him in 1839. From 1839 to 1845 he served as president of the Lima Branch and as colonel in the Sixth Regiment of the Silver Greys.[11] In 1845 the burnings of homes and small shops in Lima forced Titus and his family to flee the settlement. They initially moved to Nauvoo, but when threats of violence increased they were compelled to leave Illinois for the unknown rigors of the Iowa wilderness.

In Iowa Titus was selected to be president of the small Running Water encampment until he migrated to the Salt Lake Valley, serving as a captain of fifty in the Heber C. Kimball company of 1848. Soon after traversing the Rockies he accepted a mission call to help settle the Sanpete Valley. He is remembered for helping build the fort and one of the first two houses in the small settlement of Manti. He served as a captain in the local militia before moving to Provo in 1863. Titus Billings died three years later at the age of seventy-two.

Notes

1. See Melvin Billings, ed., "Titus Billings, Early Mormon Pioneer" (n.p., n.d.), p. 3.
2. *HC* 1:365.

3. HC 1:366–67.

4. HC 1:363.

5. See LDS Biographical Encyclopedia 1:242.

6. Billings, p. 17.

7. As cited in ibid., p. 16.

8. Ibid., pp. 20–21.

9. Ibid., p. 21.

10. As cited in Clark V. Johnson, ed., *Mormon Redress Petitions: Documents of the 1833–1838 Missouri Conflict* (Provo, Utah: Religious Studies Center, Brigham Young University, 1992), p. 140.

11. See diary of Hosea Stout, 2 vols., typescript, 2:42, Special Collections, Harold B. Lee Library, Brigham Young University, Provo, Utah.

Lilburn W. Boggs
D&C 124: Introduction

Birth: *14 December 1792, Lexington, Fayette County, Kentucky. Son of John M. Boggs and Martha Oliver.* **Death:** *19 March 1861, Napa, Napa County, California.*

After serving with the Kentucky Volunteers in the War of 1812, Lilburn Boggs moved to St. Louis, Missouri, and worked as the head cashier in one of the first banks in that town. He then engaged in merchandising in small frontier settlements along the Missouri River—St. Charles, Franklin, and Fort Osage.

Lilburn's decision to settle in the frontier town of Independence brought him in contact with Mormons. He rented a room to Peter Whitmer Jr., one of the missionaries sent to the Lamanites. He asked Peter, a tailor, to make him a suit for the inauguration ceremonies that celebrated his reelection to the Missouri Senate. In compliance Peter made the coat, and "Mr. Boggs often came in to note the progress of the work."[1]

After serving in the state senate from 1826 to 1832, Lilburn was elected lieutenant governor of Missouri. While being recognized as a leading citizen of Independence and while serving as a state official, he was seen sitting on his horse watching mobs destroy the W. W. Phelps printing establishment on 20 July 1833. He also was seen witnessing the tarring and feathering of Bishop Edward Partridge, Charles Allen, and others in the public square near the Independence Courthouse. Lilburn was not punished for promoting mobocracy. Parley P. Pratt wrote, "The majority of the State so far countenanced these outrages that they actually elected Lilburn W. Boggs . . . [to] the executive chair, instead of suspending him by the neck, between the heavens and the earth, as his crimes justly merited."[2]

Lilburn became governor of Missouri on 30 September 1836, when Daniel Dunklin resigned. In 1838 he was reelected in a close race against William H. Ashley by only 1,260 votes out of about 27,370 votes cast. Because of his mismanagement of funds and big spending on the state capitol building, the state almost went bankrupt.[3] During the last two years of his administration, however, his fame and popularity increased because of his aggressive actions against the Mormons. He viewed it "his duty as chief executive of the state and commander-in-chief of the militia to enforce the laws and suppress insurrections" allegedly committed by the Mormons.[4] Lilburn listened to the false insinuations of the mobs and on 27 October 1838 issued an extermination order giving legal license to exterminate the Mormons or drive them from the state.[5] Chaos ensued as murder, rape, and other forms of extreme violence were legalized.

The suffering Latter-day Saints held Governor Boggs personally responsible for the atrocities. The Prophet Joseph Smith said, "All earth and hell cannot deny that a baser knave, a greater traitor, and a more wholesale butcher, or murderer of mankind ever went untried, unpunished, and unhung."[6] Brigham Young proclaimed, "If those laws [guaranteed by the Constitution] had been executed they would have hung *Governor Boggs* . . . with many others, between the heavens and the earth, or shot them as traitors to the Government."[7]

Lilburn weathered the storm of criticism because his constituents rallied behind him. As his term as governor of Missouri ended on 3 August 1840, he announced his political bid for senator, hoping to represent Missouri in the United States Congress in 1842. His hopes were threatened on 6 May 1842 when an unknown assailant fired "at the back of the Governor's head as he sat in his private family room reading his newspaper close to the front window. . . . Four balls took effect in his neck and head, two of which penetrated his skull and lodged in the left lobe of his brain, and one went through the hollow of his neck and passed through the roof of his mouth."[8] Accused of the attempted assassination were the Prophet Joseph Smith and Orrin Porter Rockwell. Neither man was convicted of the crime.

Despite the assassination attempt, Lilburn recovered and lived an additional nineteen years. He won the senate election and represented Missouri in the United States Congress from 1842 to 1846. On one occasion at the state capitol in Jefferson City,

> whilst conversing with some members of the Legislature on the portico in front of the Capitol, one of the balls that entered his neck had worked its way out, and putting up his hand to the back of his head, as was his custom long after receiving these wounds, he gently squeezed the affected part and the ball slipped into his hand, and holding it out to one of the gentlemen, said, "See here, I can pick bullets out of my head." . . . [He] was frequently spoken of as the man with his head full of bullets.[9]

After completing his senate term, Lilburn migrated to Northern California, a little in advance of the ill-fated Donner party. In California he accepted the urgent call of the United States military governor, General Bennett W. Riley, to be the alcalde of the northern district of California—an important position having jurisdiction over the territory of Northern California extending to the Oregon line.[10]

In 1849 Lilburn was elected a delegate to the state constitutional convention, but he declined the honor. His interests had turned to gold and merchandising during the California Gold Rush of 1849. In 1852 he was elected to the California State Legislature, but again he refused the honor. Simeon Ide, a historian in California, wrote that Lilburn W. Boggs was "a man of superior intelligence; [a] very competent and useful citizen—a patriotic co-worker in establishing law and order where none before existed."[11] Elder Parley P. Pratt differed dramatically in his assessment: "Lilburn W. Boggs is dragging out a remnant of existence in California, with the mark of Cain upon his brow, and the fear of Cain within his heart, lest he that findeth him shall slay him. He is a living stink, and will go down to posterity with the credit of a wholesale murderer."[12]

Lilburn retired from public life to his farm in Napa, California, where he resided until his death on 19 March 1861 at the age of sixty-seven. He is buried in Napa within the shadow of a Latter-day Saint building.

Notes

1. Mary Lightner, "Mary Elizabeth Rollins Lightner," *The Utah Genealogical and Historical Magazine* 17 (July 1926): 196.

2. Parley P. Pratt, *Autobiography of Parley P. Pratt*, ed. Parley P. Pratt Jr. (Salt Lake City: Deseret Book Co., 1985), p. 85.

3. Lilburn Boggs officiated at the laying of the cornerstone of the present Missouri State Capitol Building, and his name is engraved on a large stone over the front entrance to the capitol, where six large granite columns encircle the rotunda.

4. Leopard and Shoemaker, *Messages and Proclamations of the Governors of Missouri* 1:387, as cited in Joseph F. Gordon, *The Public Career of Lilburn W. Boggs* (n.p., 1949), p. 98.

5. *Documents, Containing the Correspondence, Orders, etc., in Relation to the Disturbance with the Mormons . . . Published by order of the General Assembly* (Fayette, 1841), p. 20, as cited in Gordon, p. 98.

6. *HC* 1:435.

7. Journal History, 25 October 1857.

8. William M. Boggs, "A Short Biographical Sketch of Lilburn W. Boggs by His Son," *Missouri Historical Review* 4 (January 1910): 107–8.

9. *History of Napa and Lake Counties, California,* pp. 381–82, as cited in L. Dean Marriot, "Lilburn W. Boggs, Interaction with Mormons following their Expulsion from Missouri," dissertation, Brigham Young University, 1979, p. 45.

10. See "A Short Biographical Sketch," p. 109.

11. Simeon Ide, *Conquest of California* (Glorieta, New Mexico: The Rio Grande Press, 1967), p. 60, as cited in Marriot, p. 101.

12. Pratt, p. 181.

EZRA BOOTH

D&C 52:23; 64:15–16; 71: Introduction

Birth: *1792, Connecticut.*

By 1831 Ezra Booth, a Methodist minister in Portage County, Ohio, was viewed as a "preacher of much more than ordinary culture, and with strong natural abilities."[1] His interest in the Restoration came from reading the Book of Mormon with John Johnson. The two men "sat up all night reading it, and were very much exercised over it."[2] They then journeyed to Kirtland to meet Joseph Smith. Luke Johnson, the son of John Johnson, recorded the details of their visit with the Prophet: "My mother had been laboring under an attack of chronic rheumatism in the shoulder, so that she could not raise her hand to her head for about two years; the prophet laid hands upon her, and she was healed immediately."[3]

After witnessing the healing miracle Ezra accepted baptism and was ordained an elder. He attended the fourth general conference in June 1831 held in Kirtland, where he required the aid of the priesthood: "Ezra Booth was bound, and his countenance was distorted, and numbers of the brethren looked at him, and thought it was a wonderful manifestation of the power of God, but to their astonishment, Joseph came forward and rebuked the foul spirit, and commanded it to depart, in consequence of which Booth was relieved."[4]

On June 7 Ezra was called by revelation to travel to Missouri with Isaac Morley for the next conference: "And again, let my servant Isaac Morley and my servant Ezra Booth take their journey, also preaching the word by the way unto this same land" (D&C 52:23). After attending the conference and returning to Ohio, Ezra was called on a mission to Missouri. On the mission Ezra lost his faith in the prophetic calling of Joseph Smith. President Joseph Fielding Smith explains, "Through the performance of a miracle he was baptized, and from that time he desired to make men believe by the performance of miracles, even by smiting them, or with forcible means."[5] George A. Smith said, "He having formerly been a Methodist minister, commenced preaching the Gospel without purse or scrip, and he did so until he found, (using a common expression,) it did not pay."[6]

When Ezra returned to Ohio in September 1831, he was an apostate. Fellowship was withdrawn from him on 6 September 1831:[7] "I, the Lord, was angry with him who was my servant Ezra Booth, . . . for [he] kept not the law, neither the commandment" (D&C 64:15). Ezra officially denounced Mormonism on 12 September 1831 and published a series of nine letters in the *Ohio Star,* a paper printed in Ravenna, Ohio, explaining the "Mormon delusion":[8] "A journey of one thousand miles to the west, has taught me far more abundantly, than I should have probably learned from any other source. It has taught me . . . the imbecility of human nature, and especially my own weakness. . . . But thanks be to God! the spell is dissipated. . . . Had my fall affected only myself, my reflections would be far less painful than they now are."[9] His letters admonish others to "look at [Mormonism] with your own eyes, and no longer suffer these strangers to blind your eyes, and daub you over with their untimpered mortar."[10]

The letters, with what Joseph Smith described as their "vain calculations to overthrow the work of the Lord," exposed the "weakness, wickedness and folly [of Ezra Booth], and left him a monument of his own shame, for the world to wonder at."[11] Yet his diatribes were so compelling that in December 1831 the Prophet and Sidney Rigdon were commanded to "temporarily" stop the revision of the Bible and to "go forth to preach in order to allay the unfriendly feelings that had developed against the Church" (D&C 71: Introduction).

Little is known of the life of Ezra Booth after his participation in the tarring and feathering of Joseph Smith in 1832. Only a brief account written in 1860 of his being found residing on a farm in Mantua, Ohio, remains.[12] Contrast his ignominious life with that of one convert, Ira V. Ames, who was attracted to the Church by reading letters from Ezra. Ira joined the Church, marched in defense of the Saints with Zion's Camp to Missouri, and remained a faithful member throughout his life.[13]

Notes

1. *HC* 1:215.

2. Marinda Johnson Hyde, as cited in Edward W. Tullidge, *The Women of Mormondom* (New York: Tullidge and Crandall, 1877), pp. 403–4.

3. Luke Johnson, "History of Luke Johnson," *Latter-day Saints' Millennial Star* 26 (31 December 1864): 834.

4. George A. Smith, in *JD* 11:4.

5. Joseph Fielding Smith, *Essentials in Church History* (Salt Lake City: Deseret Book Co., 1979), p. 116.

6. George A. Smith, in *JD* 11:5.

7. See *HC* 1:217.

8. These letters were inserted in the first major anti-Mormon book, *Mormonism Unvailed* [sic], by E. D. Howe.

9. Ezra Booth, letter I, as cited in Howe.

10. Ezra Booth, letter VII, as cited in Howe.

11. *HC* 1:217.

12. See the Ohio federal census 1860. William Kelley wrote, on p. 163 of the 1 June 1881 *Saints' Herald,* "Mr. Booth, we were told, is a Free Methodist. His address is Shortsville, Ontario County, New York." There is no reference to the first name of Mr. Booth and it would be difficult to positively identify this man as Ezra Booth.

13. Susan Easton Black, comp., *Membership of The Church of Jesus Christ of Latter-day Saints, 1830–1848,* 50 vols. (Salt Lake City: The Church of Jesus Christ of Latter-day Saints, 1990), 2:305.

JOHN FARNHAM BOYNTON
Testimony of the Twelve Apostles

Birth: *20 September 1811, Bradford, Essex County, Massachusetts. Son of Eliphalet Boynton and Susannah Nichols.*
Death: *20 October 1890, Syracuse, Onondaga County, New York.*

Of those who fell from the Church in 1837, few had excelled John Farnham Boynton in educational attainment or religious zeal. This native son of Massachusetts had been schooled at Columbia in New York City in his teens, and he had entered medical school in St. Louis by the age of twenty. His scholastic achievements far surpassed his contemporaries, most of whom knew little of letters and scarcely had even the rudiments of an elementary education. His humble acceptance of baptism by the Prophet Joseph Smith hurled against conventional norms, as revelation pierced the crust of scholastic propriety.

By age twenty-one John was ordained an elder and was serving his first mission in the eastern states and Canada. Writing on 20 January 1834 from Saco, Maine, he enthusiastically reported, "I have baptized about fourty in this section, and there are more convinced of the truth, but are still lingering on the threshold of the Church. . . . Brethren, pray for me, that I may have words of wisdom." Their prayers were answered as John, "with the stick of Joseph [the Book of Mormon] in one hand, and the stick of Judah [the Bible] in the other, labor[ed] diligently in this world" to bring the truths of the Restoration to the people of New England.[1]

John was ordained to the Quorum of the Twelve Apostles at age twenty-three. When Oliver Cowdery grasped his hand and asked, "[Will] you with full purpose of heart take part in this ministry, to proclaim the Gospel with all diligence, with these your brethren, according to the tenor and intent of the charge you have received?" Boynton responded in the affirmative.[2]

His enthusiasm for the work soared as he labored with the Twelve in the eastern states in 1835. However, in 1837, as financial speculation engulfed much of Kirtland, John became embroiled in an enticing scheme of trafficking merchandise for quick wealth. Heber C. Kimball reported, "Two of the Twelve, Lyman E. Johnson and John F. Boynton, went to New York and purchased the amount of $20,000 worth of goods, and entered into the mercantile business, borrowing considerable money."[3] Failure of the Kirtland Safety Society bank became the scapegoat for John's neglect to repay his debts. Clinging to his personal gains, he feigned losses in the speculative venture. According to Aroet Hale, "The Prophet Joseph Smith called on him for money. He had the money but refused. This was a turning point in his life."[4]

John pointed a guilt-ridden finger at the Lord's anointed. "Joseph Smith is a fallen prophet!" he proclaimed. Dubbing himself a "reformer," he joined with apostates in seeking to demean the Prophet, establish a new religion, and seize possession of the dedicated Kirtland Temple. He, Warren Parrish, and several others entered the temple before a morning service one day, armed with pistols and bowie knives, and sat in the Aaronic Priesthood pulpits. Soon after the service commenced, he and the other dissidents rushed into the congregation claiming control of the holy edifice. He threatened to "blow out the brains of the first man who dared to lay hands on him" to stop the melee.[5] Local officials were summoned and they forcibly removed John and his companions from the temple.[6]

Lucy Mack Smith described what may have been the same event. She reported that as her husband, the Patriarch Joseph Smith Sr., was publicly denouncing the dissident Warren Parrish, the angry Parrish attempted to drag Father Smith from the pulpit. William Smith grabbed Parrish, and "at this John Boynton stepped forward, and drawing a sword form his cane, presented it to William's breast, and said, 'if you advance one step further, I will run you through.'"[7]

This type of unrestrained, violent behavior, and John's continual assertion of the fallen state of Joseph Smith, led to formal recommendations that his apostleship be revoked. At a conference in Kirtland on 3 September 1837 he "endeavored to confess" before the Saints, "justifying himself in his former conduct by reason of the failure of the bank."[8] He was dismissed from the Twelve. One week later he admitted his failings and was reinstated. Unfortunately he exhibited the same quarrelsome spirit and rebellious nature, which led to his being dismissed again from the Quorum in December 1837 and excommunicated on 12 April 1838.

Mormonism and religion in general no longer held any appeal for John. He soon advertised himself as a scientific lecturer and traveled throughout the United States, becoming known as a pioneer in the field of popular science. In his lecture on "Geology and the National History of Creation" he denounced the "Cardiff Giant," an alleged prehistoric man, and graphically illustrated that it was a fake.

In the late 1840s John joined the thousands who answered the call to go west: "There's gold in them there hills." Like many frustrated miners of the California Gold Rush, he failed to make his fortune in mining. However, his fame as a scientist had spread and he was commissioned to raise a government ship that had sunk off the San Francisco port. After two years in Northern California he settled in Syracuse, New York, where he became known as a gentleman farmer and distinguished scientist. Of the many patents credited to him, the most famous was his invention of a fluid and light apparatus for the rapid generation of carbonic acid gas that could be carried by one man to extinguish small fires.[9] He also invented a soda fountain, a vacuum process method for extracting gold from ore, small electrical appliances, the process for converting cast iron into malleable steel, and a method for coloring buttons and glassware.

In 1880 John "furnished the press with daily bulletins" of the condition of Dr. Henry S. Tanner and his "famous fast."[10] He brought to the attention of the American public the Tewsbury Almshouse Horror of 1883, exposing the atrocity that human skin was being tanned into hide. Furthering his notoriety was a newspaper article detailing his second marriage, performed in a balloon over New York City.

As John neared the end of his life, his interest turned to collecting and compiling historic records of the Boynton family. Although a novice genealogist, he became president of the Boynton Association, with over six hundred members organized for the purpose of gathering, collecting, and preserving family history. Yet as death approached, John's interests again were focused on science.

John died at his home on 20 October 1890 after a brief illness, which he diagnosed as a burst blood vessel in his chest causing internal hemorrhage and interference with breathing and heart action. He was seventy-nine years old. According to his obituary, those at his bedside said he was "not depressed at the thought of death and with his characteristic zeal in the cause of science he expressed a willingness to have his body examined before the students of the Medical college to determine the cause of death." The obituary continues, "In his death the city of Syracuse lost, not only one of its oldest residents, but one of the most remarkable men who ever lived in it."[11]

Notes

1. *HC* 2:40.

2. *HC* 2:198.

3. Journal of Heber C. Kimball, as cited in Orson F. Whitney, *Life of Heber C. Kimball,* 3d ed. (Salt Lake City: Bookcraft, 1967), p. 99.

4. Journal of Aroet Lucious Hale, typescript, p. 3, Special Collections, Harold B. Lee Library, Brigham Young University, Provo, Utah.

5. Eliza R. Snow, *Biography of Lorenzo Snow,* as cited in *CHC* 1:406.

6. Milton V. Backman Jr., *The Heavens Resound: A History of the Latter-day Saints in Ohio, 1830–1838* (Salt Lake City: Deseret Book Co., 1983), p. 311.

7. Lucy Mack Smith, *History of Joseph Smith by His Mother,* ed. Preston Nibley (Salt Lake City: Bookcraft, 1954), p. 241.

8. *HC* 2:509.

9. See "John Farnham Boynton, Death of This Brilliant and Versatile Man," *Syracuse (New York) Evening Herald* 14 (20 October 1890), p. 2.

10. "Dr. John Farnham Boynton, Death of an Old and Remarkable Resident of Syracuse," *Syracuse (New York) Standard,* 21 October 1890, p. 2.

11. "John Farnham Boynton: Death of This Brilliant and Versatile Man," pp. 1–2.

&

SEYMOUR BRUNSON
D&C 75:33; 124:132

Birth: *18 September 1799, Orwell, Addison County, Vermont. Son of Reuben Brunson and Sarah (Sally) Clark.*
Death: *10 August 1840, Nauvoo, Hancock County, Illinois.*

By 1830 Seymour Brunson, a veteran of the war of 1812, had migrated from New York to Ohio. In Ohio he was baptized by Solomon Hancock in January 1831 and ordained an elder by John Whitmer that same month. His first mission assignment followed in 1832 (see D&C 75:33). With companions Daniel Stanton and Luke Johnson he shared the gospel with new acquaintances in Virginia, Ohio, and Kentucky. His brief accounting of the mission appeared in *The Evening and the Morning Star,* part of which reads:

> Dear brethren in Christ, I, for the first time, take up my pen to give you a general account of my travels. On the eleventh of March, 1832, I started with brother Luke Johnson unto the south country, and on the twenty second, we left our brethren at Shalersville, and began to preach and baptize, and arrived at Windsor, Lawrence county, Ohio, on the ninth of May, having witnessed several instances of the Lord's healing power. At this place we built up a church, which made in all that we had baptized, fifty three members.[1]

The December 1834 *Messenger and Advocate* reported, "Seymour Brunson writes . . . that during the past summer, the church in Lawrence Co. in the south part of this State, have received some persecution, such as attempts to injure persons, and destroy some property."[2] This witnessing of violent hatred against the Saints was but a prelude to the personal struggles that would beset Seymour.

In Kirtland, where he became the first elder in the Church to solemnize a marriage,[3] his struggles were heightened when he submitted charges against Oliver Cowdery and David Whitmer that led to the excommunication of both men. In 1838 he was physically attacked and captured by mobbers and only narrowly escaped by putting his shoes on backward to mislead his pursuers and treading lightly through the snow.[4] As he and other men were being chased from Missouri by other mobbers seeking their lives they journeyed through the wilderness and were "five days lost" before finding safety in Illinois.[5]

On 8 May 1839 Seymour wrote a redress petition detailing his suffering in Missouri:

> Account against the state of Missouri for actual survace rendered by my Self and Company being Called uppon by judge King the Circuit judge. . . .
> $240.00
> . . . and allso for the arms and aquipments of my Company whoo ware Called uppon to . . . defend the State in unison with others from Savage barbarity Called out by the order of Lilburn W. Boggs. . . .
> $1,000.00
> . . . total amount $3,020.00
> I certify the above account to just and true according to the best of my Knowledge[6]

He was never compensated for any of the itemized losses.

Although safe in Illinois, Seymour chose to return to Missouri to help Parley P. Pratt escape from prison, but was unsuccessful.[7] However, he did succeed in assisting the Joseph Smith Sr. family in ferrying to safety across the Mississippi to Illinois.[8]

Seymour lived for only two years following the persecution he experienced in Missouri. During those years he resided in Nauvoo and served on the high council (see D&C 124:132), as lieutenant-colonel in the Nauvoo Legion, as colonel in the Hancock County militia, and, more important, as a bodyguard for the Prophet Joseph Smith.[9]

In July 1840 he became overly chilled after herding cattle. According to family tradition, "for awhile he desired to live and help put over the work of the Lord but gave up and did not want to live. After calling his family together, blessing them and bidding them farewell" on 10 August, he died at the Prophet's home at the age of 40.[10] Heber C. Kimball descriptively wrote of his death: "Semer Bronson is gon. David Paten came after him. the R[o]om was full of Angels that came after him to waft him home."[11]

On 15 August 1840 the Prophet, while speaking at Seymour's funeral, declared, "He has always been a lively stone in the building of God and was much respected by his friends and acquaintances. He died in the triumph of faith, and in his dying moments bore testimony to the Gospel that he had embraced."[12] He then introduced the doctrine of baptism for the dead.[13]

According to Heber C. Kimball, following the funeral the remains of Seymour Brunson were buried "under arms. the Procession, that went to the grave was judged to be one mile long, and a more joyfull Season [Vilate Kimball] Ses She never Saw be fore on the account of the glory that Joseph set forth."[14] In a revelation given to the Prophet four months later, on 19 January 1841, the Lord said, "Seymour Brunson I have taken unto myself; no man taketh his priesthood, but another may be appointed unto the same priesthood in his stead" (D&C 124:132).

Notes

1. *The Evening and the Morning Star* 2 (June 1833), p. 100.

2. *Messenger and Advocate* 1 (December 1834): 46.

3. See Benjamin F. Johnson, letter to George S. Gibbs, 1903, as cited in E. Dale LeBaron, "Benjamin Franklin Johnson: Colonizer, Public Servant, and Church Leader," M. A. thesis, Brigham Young University, 1967, p. 341.

4. Arlene Bishop Hecker, "History of Seymour Brunson" (n.p., n.d.), p. 2.

5. Autobiography of Sarah DeArmon Pea Rich, typescript, p. 26, Special Collections, Harold B. Lee Library, Brigham Young University, Provo, Utah.

6. As cited in Clark V. Johnson, ed., *Mormon Redress Petitions: Documents of the 1833–1838 Missouri Conflict* (Provo, Utah: Religious Studies Center, Brigham Young University, 1992), pp. 146–47.

7. See Amasa Lyman, "Amasa Lyman's History," *Millennial Star* 27 (1865): 536.

8. See Lucy Mack Smith, *History of Joseph Smith by His Mother,* ed. Preston Nibley (Salt Lake City: Bookcraft, 1954), p. 297.

9. See Peter L. Brunson, "Seymour Brunson" (n.p., n.d.), p. 2, in author's possession.

10. Hecker, p. 4.

11. As cited in Joseph Smith, *The Words of Joseph Smith,* comp. Andrew F. Ehat and Lyndon W. Cook (Provo, Utah: Religious Studies Center, Brigham Young University, 1980), p. 49 n.1.

12. HC 4:179.

13. See HC 4:231. There is no known contemporary text for this discourse.

14. As cited in Smith, *The Words of Joseph Smith,* p. 49 n. 1.

STEPHEN BURNETT
D&C 75:35; 80:1–2

Birth: *1814, Ohio. Son of Sirenes and Jane Burnett.*

Stephen Burnett was residing in Orange, Ohio, when he first heard the gospel preached by journalist John Murdock, who recorded in his journal:

> I preached in great plainness to the people, and baptized three . . . [including] Steven Burnet. . . . I confirmed them by the laying on of hands, and the two last [one being Stephen] received the outpouring of the spirit so that their strength was taken from them. . . . [The next morning] Brother Steven was carried away of the spirit, and said he must go to see his uncle Warren Thorp, and family, before he went home for so the spirit directed him. I went with him, and he bore testimony to them of the work, but they would not believe.[1]

John, Stephen, and others then went to the home of Stephen's parents and were invited for supper: "Mr. Burnet asked me to give thanks, and while I was doing so, Brother Steven was overcome with the spirit, so as to lose his strength. . . . His father and mother sat in tears."[2]

John Murdock's missionary labors helped bring more than sixty individuals into the Church. The newly baptized members often met at the home of Stephen's parents. It was at one such meeting, on 25 January 1832, that eighteen-year-old Stephen was called by revelation to serve a mission with Ruggles Eames (see D&C 75:35). It is assumed that this mission was aborted, for in March 1832 Stephen was called to be a missionary companion to Eden Smith: "Verily, thus saith the Lord unto you my servant Stephen Burnett: Go ye, go ye into the world and preach the gospel to every creature that cometh under the sound of your voice. And inasmuch as you desire a companion, I will give unto you my servant Eden Smith." (D&C 80:1–2.)

Only a few of Eden Smith's missionary entries are preserved, one of which states: "We traveled on north two miles and Cald with A presbyterian Priest and told him Concerning the Bok of mormon and Concerning the Gosple of Jesus Christ and he Cald for proof of the Book of

Mormon and we cited him to the bible and he said he did not Receive that and we told the Cituation he was in and what he must do left him and went on our way."[3]

An extract from a letter by Levi B. Wilder of Dalton, New Hampshire, states, "A small church was formed in this place in the July of 1833, consisting of 15 members: brother Stephen Burnet was the first one that sounded the glad tidings of the everlasting gospel in this place."[4]

Unfortunately, when Stephen returned to Ohio he became disaffected with the Church. By 1837 he had united with apostate Warren Parrish and others in opposition to the Prophet. Dubbing themselves "reformers," they insisted that the "regular authorities in Kirtland had departed from the true order of things by calling the church 'The Church of the Latter-day Saints.'" They publicly "rejected the Prophet, and denounced those who adhered to him as heretics."[5]

Joseph Smith in the *Elders' Journal* denounced Stephen's irrational conduct:

> A little ignorant blockhead, by the name of Stephen Burnet, whose heart was so set on money, that he would at any time, sell his soul for fifty dollars; and then think he had made an excellent bargain; and who had got wearied of the restraints of religion, and could not bear to have his purse taxed . . . ran to Kirtland, got into the temple, and tried with all his powers to bring forth something, nobody knows what, nor did he know himself; . . . after some terrible gruntings, and finding nothing coming but an abortion, rose up in his anger, proclaimed all revelation lies, and ran home to his daddy with all his might, not leaving even an egg behind, and there sat down, and rejoiced in the great victory he had obtained, over the great God and all the holy angels, how he had discovered them liars and [impostors].[6]

The 1850 Ohio federal census reveals that Stephen was residing in Orange on his father's family estate at that time, just as Joseph had stated.[7]

Notes

1. Journal of John Murdock, typescript, pp. 8–9, Archives and Manuscripts, Harold B. Lee Library, Brigham Young University, Provo, Utah.

2. Ibid., p. 9.

3. Journal of Eden Smith (25 September 1831–21 August 1832), p. 5, in author's possession.

4. *Messenger and Advocate* 1 (February 1835): 76.

5. *CHC* 1: 405.

6. *Elders' Journal* 1 (August 1838): 57.

7. See the Ohio federal census 1850.

PHILIP BURROUGHS
D&C 30:10

Birth: *1795, New Hampshire. Son of Jonathan Burroughs.*

Before becoming a gentry farmer in Fayette, Seneca County, New York, Philip Burroughs fought in the War of 1812 with the New York militia and was elected "overseer of the highways and fence viewer" for Junius, Seneca County, New York, in April 1819.[1]

In September 1830 his neighbor, twenty-eight-year-old John Whitmer, was directed by the Lord to "proclaim my gospel, as with the voice of a trump. And your labor shall be at your brother Philip Burroughs', and in that region round about." (D&C 30:9–10.) A Church meeting was held at the Burroughs's home on 5 September 1830. Parley P. Pratt, ordained an elder only a few days before, addressed a large audience at the home. "The Holy Ghost came upon me mightily," penned Parley. "I spoke the word of God with power, reasoning out of the Scriptures and the Book of Mormon. The people were convinced, overwhelmed in tears, and four heads of families came forward expressing their faith, and were baptized."[2] A record of John Whitmer's preaching at the home has not been found.

Whether Philip Burroughs was converted remains a mystery. The Honorable Diedrich Willers, writer and Seneca County historian, believed that Philip was "at one time, attracted to the LDS Church, but did not become a member."[3] Samuel Smith and Orson Hyde may not have concurred. In 1832 they visited with the Burroughs family, and Samuel wrote, "He was glad to see us & Sister Buroughs was strong in the faith held a meeting in the school house a considerable number of people came to hear & paid good attention."[4] Orson Hyde noted, "Brother B. [was] rather low, but left him about persuaded to go to Zion."[5]

In June 1860 Philip was still residing in New York with his wife, Anna, and five other family members. He was a farmer by trade, owning acreage valued at five thousand dollars.⁶

Notes

1. "Junius Town Meeting Records," Utah Genealogical Society, as cited in Lyndon W. Cook, *The Revelations of the Prophet Joseph Smith* (Salt Lake City: Deseret Book Co., 1985), pp. 42, 127.

2. Parley P. Pratt, *Autobiography of Parley P. Pratt,* ed. Parley P. Pratt Jr. (Salt Lake City: Deseret Book Co., 1985), p. 27.

3. See letter of Lee Yost to the Honorable Diedrich Willers, 18 May 1897, as cited in Larry C. Porter, "A Study of the Origins of The Church of Jesus Christ of Latter-day Saints in the States of New York and Pennsylvania, 1816–1831," dissertation, Brigham Young University, August 1971, p. 262.

4. Journal of Samuel H. Smith, 1831–33, microfilm, Church Historical Department, The Church of Jesus Christ of Latter-day Saints, Salt Lake City, Utah.

5. Journal of Orson Hyde, 1831–32, microfilm, Church Historical Department, The Church of Jesus Christ of Latter-day Saints, Salt Lake City, Utah.

6. See the New York federal census 1860.

JOSIAH BUTTERFIELD
D&C 124:138

Birth: *13 March 1795, Dunstable, Middlesex County, Massachusetts. Son of Abel Butterfield and Mary Farnsworth.*
Death: *3 March 1871, Watsonville, Santa Cruz County, California.*

Josiah Butterfield enthusiastically accepted the covenant of baptism on 1 October 1833 and within the year was laboring as a missionary with Sylvester Stoddard in his locality of Buxton, Maine. By 1835 he had migrated with other converts from Maine to Kirtland and was working on the Kirtland Temple.[1] His devotion, whether in the mission field of Maine or Vermont or in constructing the Lord's house, was impeccable. It was not surprising that on 6 April 1837 he was called to be one of the first Seven Presidents of the Seventies.[2]

In 1837 the Kirtland Safety Society bank collapsed, and in the dark days that followed, Josiah emerged as a strong, faithful leader. He assisted the poor who left Ohio with the Kirtland Camp of 1838. On the journey he was arrested for alleged involvement with "Kirtland Safety Society money" and was committed to jail, but he was discharged the next day.[3]

Josiah was then able to continue the journey with others in the Kirtland Camp and settle in Daviess County, until further religious bigotry forced his exodus once again. Before fleeing from his enemies he covenanted to assist the poor in their removal from Missouri. Of his own sufferings, he penned an itemized account:

To expences of journey & time in moveing from Ohio to Mo. in the summer of 1838	$200.00
Loss of time while in the State of Mo. Six months at 35 dollars per month	210.00
To Loss of horse & waggon taken by the mob & malitia	100.00
To one musket taken by the malitia in Daviss Co.	8.00
To loss of furniture at Richmond landing	16.00
For being driven out of Daviss Co. in the month of November and being thereby exposed to the inclemency of the weather which has caused the sickness of my wife during the winter from which She has not yet recovered	1,000.00
For being driven out of the State of Mo. by the authorities there of & being deprived of citizenship	2,000.00
To loss on a Note due me in consequence of being driven out of the State of Mo.	240.00
	$3,774.00

. . . In addition to the above I was taken prisner from my dwelling without any cause & shamefully treated by the malitia in Daviss Co. Mo.[4]

He never received recompense for the above stated violations.

Hoping to settle down to a more peaceful existence, Josiah joined the Saints in Nauvoo. Unfortunately, the Nauvoo era proved to be some of his most difficult days. He was tried "for a number of criminal charges" but acquitted:

> Nauvoo Nov. 1st, 1840.
>
> TO THE SAINTS SCATTERED ABROAD.
>
> Be it known that Elder Josiah Butterfield, (one of the Presidents of the Quorum of Seventies,) was arraigned before the Quorum on the 4th of Oct. last and tried for a number of criminal charges. But the Quorum are happy, publicly to announce, that after a patient and candid investigation, the charges were unsustained, and Pres't Butterfield stands acquited by the counsel and Quorum.
>
> Z. PULCIPHER, Chair.
>
> A. P. ROCKWOOD, Clerk.[5]

On 19 January 1841 Josiah was acknowledged again as one of the Seven Presidents of the Seventies (see D&C 124:138–39). However, his status in the quorum was questioned a second time in 1843. Joseph Smith recorded in his journal on 28 March 1843: "Josiah Butterfield came to my house and insulted me so outrageously that I kicked him out of the house, across the yard, and into the street."[6] Watching the incident was young Joseph F. Smith, who shared his impression:

> I was one day playing marbles in front of the Mansion with my cousin Alexander Smith. We were amusing ourselves on the sidewalk . . . playing at the gate just outside the stone steps, when all of a sudden the door flew open and I looked, and there came a great, big man right off the end of Joseph Smith's foot, and he lit on the sidewalk just by the gate. . . . Since I grew to be a man, I learned that this man was there insulting the Prophet, and abusing him in his own house.[7]

Josiah's service as one of the Seven Presidents ended on 7 October 1844, when he was excommunicated because "he had got a little money, and was lifted up."[8]

A few years later he rejoined the Church and received his endowment in the Nauvoo Temple.[9] However, when the Saints began migrating to the Rockies he remained in the Midwest until 1853. Instead of gathering with his fellow Saints, he settled in Northern California. He was baptized a member of the Reorganized Church of Jesus Christ of

Latter Day Saints on 1 May 1865 at Watsonville, California, and later served as RLDS president of the local branch.[10]

It appears that Josiah Butterfield did not renounce his testimony of Mormonism. Several years after his excommunication his nephew, Thomas Butterfield, heard him explain to relatives in the Salt Lake Valley that his faith in Mormonism was as strong as ever.[11]

Notes

1. See Lyndon W. Cook and Milton V. Backman Jr., eds., *Kirtland Elders' Quorum Record 1836–1841* (Provo, Utah: Grandin Book Co., 1985), p. 75.

2. See *CHC* 1:376–77.

3. See *HC* 3:108–9.

4. As cited in Clark V. Johnson, ed., *Mormon Redress Petitions: Documents of the 1833–1838 Missouri Conflict* (Provo, Utah: Religious Studies Center, Brigham Young University, 1992), p. 151.

5. *Times and Seasons* 2 (1 November 1840): 207.

6. *HC* 5:316.

7. Joseph F. Smith, in Brian H. Stuy, comp., *Collected Discourses* (Burbank, California: B.H.S. Publishing, 1987).

8. *HC* 7:297.

9. See Nauvoo Temple endowment register, 1845–46, Church Historical Department, The Church of Jesus Christ of Latter-day Saints, Salt Lake City, Utah.

10. See Susan Easton Black, *Early Members of the Reorganized Church of Jesus Christ of Latter Day Saints,* 6 vols. (Provo, Utah: Religious Studies Center, Brigham Young University, 1993), 1:784–85.

11. See *LDS Biographical Encyclopedia* 1:192.

REYNOLDS CAHOON
D&C 52:30; 61:35; 75:32; 94:14

Birth: *30 April 1790, Cambridge, Washington County, New York. Son of William Cahoon Jr. and Mehitable Hodge.*
Death: *29 April 1861, South Cottonwood, Salt Lake County, Utah.*

At the outbreak of the War of 1812, Reynolds Cahoon left his young bride in Harpersfield, Ohio, to enlist in the United States militia. When the British retreated from the American forces, Reynolds returned home to Harpersfield. In 1825 he moved closer to Kirtland, where he labored as a farmer and opened a small enterprise for tanning leather and making shoes.

Reynolds was one of the first in Kirtland to accept the gospel as taught by the missionaries sent to the Lamanites. He was baptized on 12 October 1830 by Parley P. Pratt. Less than a year later, forty-one-year-old Reynolds was called by revelation to travel to Missouri: "Let my servants Reynolds Cahoon and Samuel H. Smith also take their journey" (D&C 52:30). Of their journey Samuel wrote, "Preached the gospel without purse or script, enduring much for want of food and rest."[1] Yet to Reynolds, once they arrived in Missouri it all seemed worth it: "My mortal eyes beheld great and marvelous things such as I had not ever expected to see in this world."[2]

Reynolds and Samuel returned to Kirtland in obedience to the Lord's command: "Let my servant Reynolds Cahoon, and my servant Samuel H. Smith, with whom I am well pleased, be not separated until they return to their homes" (D&C 61:35). On their journey they "found the region of the country in a state of excitement over the Book of Mormon. People were searching the scripture and came to hear what further testimony we had to give."[3]

In Ohio, Reynolds served in many positions of trust. Although diligent in fulfilling these assignments, he wished to return to Missouri. "The question which I wish settled is, whether it is the will of the Lord that I should go to Zion in the spring," he said.[4] The answer, poignantly, was no. Reynolds was needed in Kirtland to serve on the temple building committee (see D&C 94:14–15), as a counselor to Bishop Newel K. Whitney, and later as a counselor in the stake presidency.

Perhaps of equal significance was the privilege to be the first to learn from the Prophet the name of the brother of Jared. In 1834 the Prophet named and blessed Reynolds's seventh child, Mahonri Moriancumer. The Prophet explained, "The name I have given your son is the name of the brother of Jared; the Lord has just shown (or revealed) it to me."[5]

In 1838 Reynolds's family fled from persecution in Kirtland. Reynolds's son William F. Cahoon wrote, "We turned the key and locked the door of our homes, leaving our property and all we possessed in the hands of enemies and strangers, never receiving a cent for anything we owned."[6] The family journeyed to Missouri and settled among the Saints in the Adam-ondi-ahman Stake, until Governor Lilburn Boggs's extermination order forced them to flee to Illinois.

In Nauvoo, Illinois, Reynolds served on the building committees for the Nauvoo House, the Mansion House, and the Nauvoo Temple. Of his temple assignment he lamented, "I think I never was placed in so critical a position since I was born. . . . I call upon the brethren, if they have anything against me, to bring it forward and have it adjusted."[7]

On 22 June 1844 Reynolds was asked by the Prophet to guard the Mansion House:

> About 9 p.m. Hyrum came out of the Mansion and gave his hand to Reynolds Cahoon, at the same time saying, "A company of men are seeking to kill my brother Joseph, and the Lord has warned him to flee to the Rocky Mountains to save his life. . . ." In a few minutes afterwards Joseph came from his family. His tears were flowing fast. He held a handkerchief to his face, and followed after Brother Hyrum without uttering a word.[8]

The next day Reynolds, Lorenzo D. Wasson, and Hiram Kimball advised the Prophet that he would be a coward if he did not return and surrender to the law at Carthage.[9] When the Prophet made the decision to return, he instructed Reynolds to gather documents for the promised trial.[10] The hoped-for trial never materialized, as the Prophet was martyred in Carthage Jail. However, false accusations soon rose against Reynolds. He was arrested on a charge of treason, as Joseph had been just several months before. The case against Reynolds was dismissed on failure to substantiate the rumors.[11]

Soon after the proceedings Reynolds fled from his enemies to Iowa and then trekked across the plains to the Salt Lake Valley. In the Valley he held several responsible positions: supervisor of road repair, manager of the Church farm, superintendent of the armory construction, and sergeant-at-arms of the Utah territorial legislature.

In his declining years Reynolds moved to Cottonwood, Utah, to live with his son. He died of dropsy on 29 April 1861 in South Cottonwood at the age of seventy-three. A *Deseret News* obituary states that Reynolds was "a true friend to the prophet of God while he was living; full of integrity and love for the truth and always acted cheerfully the part assigned him in the great work of the last Days."[12]

Notes

1. As cited in Stella Cahoon Shurtleff and Brent Farrington Cahoon, eds., *Reynolds Cahoon and His Stalwart Sons* (Salt Lake City: Stella Cahoon Shurtleff, 1960), p. 10.

2. As cited in ibid., p. 10.

3. As cited in ibid., p. 11.

4. As cited in ibid., p. 12.

5. As cited in ibid., p. 21.

6. As cited in ibid., p. 28.

7. HC 5:338.

8. HC 6:547.

9. See HC 6:549.

10. See HC 6:599.

11. See Shurtleff and Cahoon, p. 47.

12. As cited in Erma Cahoon Nelson, "History of Reynolds Cahoon" (n.p., n.d.), p. 5, in author's possession.

GIDEON HAYDEN (HADEN) CARTER

D&C 75:34

Birth: *1798, Benson, Rutland County, Vermont. Son of Gideon Carter and Johanna Sims.*
Death: *25 October 1838, Battle of Crooked River, Ray County, Missouri.*

Newly ordained priest Gideon Carter was told by the Prophet Joseph Smith that he "had one tallent and if after being ordained [he] should hide it God would take it."[1] Heeding the admonition, Gideon concluded that the talent given him was to preach the gospel. He served several short missions in Ohio in 1831 before being ordained an elder and being commanded by revelation to labor in the ministry with Sylvester Smith (see D&C 75:34).

On 5 April 1832 Gideon and Sylvester began their mission to the East. In northeastern Pennsylvania they held four meetings and administered to a "sick sister, who recovered immediately."[2] Continuing north, they journeyed through New York and baptized several persons. Then, with Gideon's brother Jared Carter, they extended their mission to Vermont, "where it appeared to us the greater part of our labors would be for this season," as Jared later wrote.[3] In Gideon's hometown of Benson he expressed some fears about Jared's prophesying. His negative expressions led Jared to part company with the other missionaries.[4] Gideon returned to Kirtland on 24 August 1832.

In Kirtland he helped lay the cornerstones of the temple and was mentioned in the Prophet's writings on 6 December 1835 as having preached "a splendid discourse."[5] He actively participated in the Mormon culture in the area by becoming a charter member of the Kirtland Safety Society and serving for a season on the Kirtland high council. As troubles escalated against the Kirtland Saints in 1838, Gideon moved to Far West, Missouri.

During the evening of 24 October 1838, news reached Far West of depredations committed against the Saints by mobocrats, including the imprisonment of two or possibly three men. Captain David W. Patten, Parley P. Pratt, Charles C. Rich, and many others, including Gideon Carter, resolved to rescue the imprisoned Saints. Early in the morning of 25 October 1838, when Captain Patten and his men neared Crooked River and saw the enemy, orders were given to charge, and "the two parties engaged in a hand to hand fight."[6] Gideon Carter lost his life during the battle, and Patrick O'Banion, their non-Mormon guide, and David Patten were mortally wounded.[7]

Parley P. Pratt saw Gideon in his last moments: "I turned to Gideon Carter, who was lying on his face, and saw him die. His face was so marred and disfigured with wounds and blood that I did not recognize him then, but learned afterwards that we had mistaken him for one of the enemy, and left him on the ground in mistake."[8]

Oliver Huntington recorded seeing Gideon's remains brought back to Far West for burial:

> One day I saw a crowd around a wagon not far from our house, so I ran up to see what was going on; I climbed up and stuck my head over the edge of the box and the first thing my eyes met was the familiar face of Gideon Carter, and although the cursed, worse than inhuman mob, had dug his eyes out with sticks he still looked like himself. Gideon was killed in the [Crooked] River Battle, had a ball hole in his breast and a large gash of a sword in the back side of his head. He lay on the battle ground until the next day or two when the mob came and buried their own dead, dug his eyes out and kicked the dirt over him where he had laid until now, the brethren not daring to go that far from home or for some other cause I know not what.[9]

In recollection of the religious martyr, Daniel Tyler said that Gideon Carter had "sealed [his] testimony with [his] blood."[10]

Notes

1. As cited in Donald Q. Cannon and Lyndon W. Cook, eds., *Far West Record: Minutes of The Church of Jesus Christ of Latter-day Saints, 1830–1844* (Salt Lake City: Deseret Book Co., 1983), p. 25.

2. *LDS Biographical Encyclopedia* 3:615.

3. Autobiography of Jared Carter, typescript, p. 11, LDS Archives Division, Church Historical Department, The Church of Jesus Christ of Latter-day Saints, Salt Lake City, Utah. Spelling has been standardized.

4. See ibid., p. 15.

5. *HC* 2:326.

6. Newel Knight, "Newel Knight's Journal," in *Scraps of Biography*, p. 97, as published in *Classic Experiences and Adventures* (Salt Lake City: Bookcraft, 1969).

7. See James B. Allen and Glen M. Leonard, *The Story of the Latter-day Saints*, 2nd ed. (Salt Lake City: Deseret Book Co., 1992), p. 136.

8. Parley P. Pratt, *Autobiography of Parley P. Pratt,* ed. Parley P. Pratt Jr. (Salt Lake City: Deseret Book Co., 1985), p. 154.

9. Autobiography of Oliver B. Huntington, typescript, p. 40, Special Collections, Harold B. Lee Library, Brigham Young University, Provo, Utah.

10. As cited in "Recollections of the Prophet Joseph Smith," *Juvenile Instructor* 27 (1 February 1892): 95.

JARED CARTER
D&C 52:38; 79; 94:14; 102:3

Birth: *14 June 1801, Benson, Rutland County, Vermont. Son of Gideon Carter and Johanna Sims.*
Death: *July 1855, DeKalb County, Illinois.*

In January 1831 twenty-nine-year-old Jared Carter, younger brother of Gideon Carter, left Chenango, New York, on a business journey. About twelve miles from his home, he stopped to visit John Peck, who, though opposing the Book of Mormon, shared it with him. He read the sacred writ and "became immediately convinced that it was a revelation of God and it had such an influence on my mind that I had no mind to pursue my business."[1]

He returned home and told his wife about the Book of Mormon. At first she "thought it was delusion" but later encouraged her husband to investigate the new religion. The investigation led to their conversion. Jared wrote, "I felt it my duty to separate from Babylon and be baptized. Accordingly I was baptized by Hyrum Smith about the 20th of February, for the remission of sins. As I was baptized I felt the influences of the spirit of God, for as I stepped out of the water I was wrapped in the spirit both soul and body, even so that the chill of the cold water was taken from me."[2]

After Jared returned to Chenango and shared his enthusiasm for sacred truths, "some of my best friends, as I had formerly supposed became now my worst enemies." They mocked his faith and promised him land if he would renounce Mormonism. His reaction: "Not for fifteen of the best farms in the place would I stay in Chenango one year. . . . I commenced immediately to see my things and to make preparation to go on to the West."[3]

Jared and his family moved with the Colesville Saints to Thompson, Ohio, which he described as "one of the most trying scenes that I ever experienced, for the grand adversary of all souls gained great power over some of my brethren."[4] His experience in Thompson contrasted with his experience at the fourth general conference in June 1831. In describing the Prophet on this occasion, Jared wrote, "Notwithstanding he is not naturally talented for a speaker yet he was filled with the power of the Holy Ghost so that he spoke as I never heard man speak for God, by the power of the Holy Ghost spoke in him."[5]

At the conference he met his brother Simeon, a member of the Church, whom he had not seen for eight years. He joined Simeon in the brotherhood of the priesthood on 7 June 1831: "And again, verily I say unto you, let Jared Carter be ordained a priest" (D&C 52:38). He then moved his family to Amherst, Ohio, so he could be near his brother. Together they attended many Church meetings in the area, where Jared was blessed with the gift of healing. His journal is replete with examples of this: "I found [Almon Babbitt] very sick with a fever. Soon after I came there, I bade him to arise, in the name of Jesus Christ, and walk and he arose and his fever left him and he walked in my company for three miles."[6]

Jared is most remembered for his missions to the eastern states. From 1831 to 1834 his missionary labors were examplary. The Lord revealed through the Prophet Joseph Smith the source of Jared's missionary power: "And I will send upon him the Comforter, which shall teach him the truth and the way whither he shall go; and inasmuch as he is faithful, I will crown him again with sheaves" (D&C 79:2–3).

Of preaching in his hometown of Benson, Jared wrote, "I commenced holding meetings and the Lord was with me. . . . Baptised 27 in number."[7] His missionary labors in New York, Ohio, Pennsylvania, and Vermont led to the baptism of seventy-nine people. Mother Smith encouraged Joseph to send Jared to Michigan, where he succeeded in establishing the first branch of the Church there, as he had done in Vermont.

Upon returning to Ohio he penned, "I met with some of my brethren and heard them read revelations which caused my heart to rejoice. . . . I have seen many marvelous manifestations of the power of God in more than eighty instances, by the instrumentality of myself and other elders in this Church of Christ."[8] Unfortunately, not all of his missionary labors had proven fruitful. "It appears that the wide world is ignorant," wrote Jared, "unapprised of the great work the God of heaven has commenced."[9] He recognized that "there are hundreds that are ready to declare in the name of the Lord that they know the Book of Mormon is of divine origin, and I, myself, am one of the hundreds."[10]

It caused great distress among the Saints when seeds of apostasy became apparent in the life of Jared Carter. He also noted the change, reporting that "the spirit of God in a measure has left me,"[11] but he failed to completely rectify the problem. While struggling to regain his testimony he was assigned an inheritance in Kirtland and appointed to a Church building committee (see D&C 94:14–15). Heber C. Kimball wrote that the committee members "used every exertion in their power to forward the work" on the Kirtland Temple.[12] Jared assisted in laying the foundation stones of the temple on 23 July 1834.

Despite Jared's overt diligence, he reportedly told some Saints that "he had power to raise Joseph Smith to the highest heavens, or sink him down to the lowest hell."[13] The Patriarch Joseph Smith Sr. "warned Jared to repent of the injudicious course that he was taking, and speedily confess his sins to the Church, or the judgments of God would overtake him."[14] Mother Smith recorded, "The next morning he was seized with a violent pain in his eyes and continued in great distress for two days. On the evening of the second day, he arose from his bed, and, kneeling down, besought the Lord to heal him, covenanting to make a full confession to the Church at meeting the next Sunday."[15] The following Sunday at church Jared arose and asked for forgiveness.

His conviction did not remain steadfast. On 19 September 1835 he was tried by the Kirtland high council for preaching false doctrine. He was told that if he would make a public apology, "in full faith, and . . . truly humble before God," he would be forgiven.[16] Apparently he complied with this directive.

Unfortunately, by 1838 Jared had again become disaffected. He supported the "Brothers of Gideon," later called Danites, and was nicknamed "the terrible Brother of Gidean [sic] [Carter]."[17] In 1843 he was accused of conspiring with John C. Bennett, Sidney Rigdon, and George W. Robinson against the Prophet. In a letter to Sidney Rigdon dated 27 March 1843, Joseph wrote, "Jared Carter, is as deep in the mire, as you, Sir, are in the mire, in your conspiracies."[18] In September 1844 Jared was disfellowshipped for not following counsel.[19] Jared confessed his errors and promised abiding faithfulness.[20]

He did not stay true to his promise. When the Saints fled from Nauvoo to the rigors of Iowa's wilderness, he settled in Chicago and by 1848 in DeKalb County, Illinois. He died at the age of fifty-four in

DeKalb County.[21] In 1861 George A. Smith reflected on Jared Carter: "I remember, when in Kirtland, having heard Jared Carter say that he had sacrificed everything that ever would be required of him. He said, I have sacrificed all my property once, but I will never do it again. Where is that man? He is numbered in the long catalogue of apostates."[22]

Notes

1. Autobiography of Jared Carter, typescript, p. 1, Archives Division, Church Historical Department, The Church of Jesus Christ of Latter-day Saints, Salt Lake City, Utah. Spelling has been standardized.

2. Ibid., p. 1.

3. Ibid., p. 2.

4. Ibid., p. 3.

5. Ibid., p. 4.

6. Ibid., p. 7.

7. Ibid., p. 8.

8. Ibid., p. 23.

9. Ibid., p. 26.

10. Ibid., p. 32.

11. Ibid., p. 28.

12. Heber C. Kimball, "Extracts from H.C. Kimball's Journal," *Times and Seasons* 6 (15 April 1845): 868.

13. Lucy Mack Smith, *History of Joseph Smith by His Mother,* ed. Preston Nibley (Salt Lake City: Bookcraft, 1954), p. 242.

14. Ibid.

15. Ibid.

16. *HC* 2:277, 280.

17. John Whitmer, *An Early Latter Day Saint History: The Book of John Whitmer,* ed. F. Mark McKiernan and Roger D. Launius (Independence, Mo.: Herald Publishing House, 1980), p. 176 n. 3.

18. Joseph Smith, *The Personal Writings of Joseph Smith,* comp. Dean C. Jessee (Salt Lake City: Deseret Book Co., 1984), p. 555.

19. See *Times and Seasons* 5 (15 October 1844): 687.

20. See *HC* 7:271.

21. See *The Biographical Record of DeKalb County, Illinois* (S. J. Clarke Publishing Co., 1898), p. 116, microfilm: 0496841, Family History Library, The Church of Jesus Christ of Latter-day Saints, Salt Lake City, Utah.

22. George A. Smith, in *JD* 9:72.

JOHN SIMS CARTER
D&C 102:3

Birth: *1796, Killingworth, Middlesex County, Connecticut. Son of Gideon Carter and Johanna Sims.*
Death: *26 June 1834, Clay County, Missouri.*

John Sims Carter was the last of the Carter brothers to unite with the Saints. He was baptized and ordained an elder and a high priest in 1832. In that same year he was appointed to preach the gospel with his brother Jared Carter in Vermont.[1] Joining them on their journey was Harrison Burgess, who wrote, "I started in company with Brother John S. Carter to the state of Vermont where we labored about two months."[2]

John led his newly baptized converts from Vermont to Kirtland. In Kirtland his speech at the funeral of David Johnson in November 1833 was described as "a discourse suited to the occasion."[3] He used as his scriptural text Revelation 14:13: "And I heard a voice from heaven saying unto me, Write, Blessed are the dead which die in the Lord from henceforth: Yea, saith the Spirit, that they may rest from their labours; and their works do follow them."

On 17 February 1834 John was asked whether he would accept an appointment to serve on the Kirtland high council and whether he "would act in that office according to the law of heaven" (D&C 102:4). He responded in the affirmative "according to the grace of God bestowed upon [him]" (D&C 102:4). His service was brief, for three days later he and Jesse Smith were called to go to the East "as soon as they can."[4]

Most of what is known about John occurred in May and June of 1834 in Zion's Camp. Levi Hancock journalized that Sylvester Smith "lost the spirit of peace and became dissatisfied with John Carter and called him an old jackass and many other names which soon brought dissatisfaction in our tent. Some dared to express their feelings until Joseph rebuked them and told [Sylvester Smith] that he was guilty of sowing the seeds of discord."[5]

Nathan Baldwin wrote of a "mimic battle" within the camp on 19 May 1834 "which afforded a little fun to the lovers of such sport. Our army was divided into two or three divisions with a commander to each. . . . A general engagement was brought on which was soon decided by a hand to hand encounter in which I was confronted by John S. Carter." Carter was victorious, for, as Nathan Baldwin reported, he "ordered us to surrender and our arms stacked, and we were marched off as prisoners of war."[6]

Heber C. Kimball penned that on Sunday, 1 June 1834, while encamped about one mile from Jacksonville, Illinois, "we preached all day, and many of the inhabitants of the town came out to hear. Brother John Carter preached in the morning."[7] George A. Smith recorded that Carter "delivered a very eloquent discourse on 'Practical Piety.' "[8]

Thirty-eight-year-old John Carter was the first to succumb to cholera in Zion's Camp. His friend Harrison Burgess wrote, "Among the number that I attended upon, and helped to bury, was my Brother John S. Carter. My feeling on this occasion can never be described."[9] Heber C. Kimball's journal states, "I was left at the camp in company with three or four of my brethren in care of those who were sick. We staid with, and prayed for them, hoping they would recover, but all hope was lost, for about 6 o'clock p.m., John S. Carter expired, he being the first that died in the camp."[10] The Prophet Joseph Smith recorded, "When the cholera made its appearance, Elder John S. Carter was the first man who stepped forward to rebuke it, and upon this, was instantly seized, and became the first victim in the camp. He died about six o'clock in the afternoon."[11]

Notes

1. See autobiography of Jared Carter, typescript, p. 12, Archives Division, Church Historical Department, The Church of Jesus Christ of Latter-day Saints, Salt Lake City, Utah.

2. Autobiography of Harrison Burgess, as cited in Kenneth Glyn Hales, ed., *Windows: A Mormon Family* (Tucson, Arizona: Skyline Printing, 1985), pp. 100–101.

3. *The Evening and the Morning Star* 2 (December 1833): 117.

4. *HC* 2:35.

5. Autobiography of Levi Ward Hancock, typescript, p. 53, Special Collections, Harold B. Lee Library, Brigham Young University, Provo, Utah.

6. Autobiography of Nathan Baldwin, typescript, p. 9, Archives Division, Church Historical Department, The Church of Jesus Christ of Latter-day Saints, Salt Lake City, Utah.

7. *HC* 2:78.

8. George A. Smith, "Autobiography of George A. Smith," *Millennial Star* 27 (1865): 2.

9. Burgess, p. 101.

10. Heber C. Kimball, extract from journal, *Times and Seasons* 6 (15 March 1845): 838–39.

11. *HC* 2:115.

SIMEON CARTER
D&C 52:27; 75:30

Birth: *7 June 1794, Killingworth, Middlesex County, Connecticut. Son of Gideon Carter and Johanna Sims.*
Death: *3 February 1869, Brigham City, Box Elder County, Utah.*

Simeon Carter was the oldest of the Carter brothers mentioned in the Doctrine and Covenants and in the writings of Parley P. Pratt. Elder Pratt, who had been called on a mission to Indian territory in 1830, wrote of meeting with Simeon:

We were in the act of reading to [Simeon] and explaining the Book of Mormon, when there came a knock at the door, and an officer entered with a warrant from a magistrate . . . to arrest me on a very frivolous charge. I dropped the Book of Mormon in Carter's house. . . .
. . . He read it with attention. It wrought deeply upon his mind, and he went fifty miles to the church we had left in Kirtland, and was there baptized and ordained an Elder. He then returned to his home and commenced to preach and baptize. A church of about sixty members was soon organized.[1]

On 3 June 1831 Simeon attended the fourth general conference, where he was ordained a high priest by Lyman Wight. Four days later he was called by revelation to journey to Missouri with Solomon Hancock (see D&C 52:27). They traveled through Ohio, Illinois, and Indiana; baptizing, preaching, and instructing the Saints along the way.

Simeon later acknowledged that "he was thankful that he had been spared & preserved to go to the land of Zion . . . & also thanked the Lord that his feet had troden upon the consecrated ground which was the inheritance of the saints."[2]

In January of 1832, four months after returning to Ohio, he was called by revelation to serve a mission: "Wherefore, let my servant Simeon Carter and my servant Emer Harris be united in the ministry" (D&C 75:30). Accompanying Simeon and his companion was his brother Jared Carter. The *Evening and the Morning Star* describes their success:

> Brothers Simeon and Jared Carter, we understand, have done wondrous works in Vermont, in breaking down prejudice in a wonderful manner. Better than one hundred have been brought into the kingdom, in a few months past, by their instrumentality.[3]

> I [Simeon] have baptized in all about seventy, and the Lord has kept me and supported me. The church at this place [Cincinnati, Ohio] is expecting to go up to Zion next summer.[4]

> Brother Simeon Carter built up a new church in Hanover, Indiana, while on his way to this place last winter, containing twenty seven members.[5]

A letter from convert Robert Culbertson also reveals their success:

> May 2, 1834.
> DEAR BROTHER . . . Last winter, one year ago, brother Simeon Carter came through our section of country, preaching the everlasting gospel of our blessed Savior, which made a great ado. . . . Our preacher was chosen to refute him; but when he came to appose truth with error, he found that a *mole* could as soon upset the Rocky Mountains, or a *popgun* blow down the Pyramids of Egypt, as his system stand against the system of truth. He became converted, and is now preaching the everlasting gospel to perishing sinners.[6]

Jared wrote of Simeon's power of healing:

> [My daughter] to every appearance was mortally bruised and she was not expected to live but a very short time. . . . I spoke to my brother Simeon and told her that he was one that was endowed with power from on high and that she might be healed if she had faith. . . . He took her by the hand and said: "I command you in the name of

Jesus Christ to rise up and walk" and she arose and walked from room to room.[7]

By late 1833 the celebrated missionary Simeon Carter had moved to Jackson County, Missouri, and was presiding over Branch Number Nine. He wrote to Jared of escalating mobocracy, as reported in the *Messenger and Advocate:*

> Elder [Simeon] Carter writes that he has met with some persecution. . . . A gang of about 20 men, armed, came to escort him before a court; but after a hearing he was discharged, though not without being threatened by the rabble that if he did not leave the country immediately, he would be dealt with in a different manner. He however appointed meetings, and continued to proclaim the gospel of our Lord, and hold up the truth to a dying people with as much zeal as before. This was honorable, it was commendable.[8]

As mobocracy raged, Simeon was forced to flee from Jackson to Clay County and then to Kirtland, where he joined Zion's Camp in 1834. After the march on 7 July 1834 he was appointed to the Clay high council. He and John Corrill, Parley P. Pratt, and Orson Pratt were assigned "to teach the disciples how to escape the indignation of their enemies, and keep in favor with those who were friendly disposed."[9]

Simeon moved to Far West in 1836, where he again served on a high council. He was wounded at the Battle of Crooked River while defending the Saints. Despite his personal sufferings, he said in December 1838 that "he did not think that Joseph was a fallen Prophet, but he believed in every revelation that had come through him. . . . He did not think that Joseph would be removed and another planted in his stead. . . . He was still determined to persevere and act in righteousness in all things, so that he might at last gain a crown of glory, and reign in the kingdom of God."[10]

Simeon remained true to the gospel throughout his life. From 1846 to 1849 he served a mission in England. In 1850 he migrated with English converts in Orson Hyde's company to the Salt Lake Valley. In 1851 he was called by Brigham Young to settle at Box Elder Creek, about fourteen miles north of Ogden. Family tradition purports that he "plowed with a hand plow and cleared some land, hiding his plow as they expected to return to Salt Lake City . . . because of the hostility of the Indians."[11] Simeon Carter died in 1869 at the age of seventy-four in the settlement he helped found—Brigham City.

Notes

1. Parley P. Pratt, *Autobiography of Parley P. Pratt*, ed. Parley P. Pratt Jr. (Salt Lake City: Deseret Book Co., 1985), pp. 36, 39.

2. As cited in Donald Q. Cannon and Lyndon W. Cook, eds., *Far West Record: Minutes of The Church of Jesus Christ of Latter-day Saints, 1830–1844* (Salt Lake City: Deseret Book Co., 1983), p. 22.

3. *The Evening and the Morning Star* 1 (February 1833): 69.

4. Ibid., p. 70.

5. *The Evening and the Morning Star* 1 (March 1833): 84.

6. *The Evening and the Morning Star* 2 (May 1834): 156.

7. Autobiography of Jared Carter, typescript, p. 3, Archives Division, Church Historical Department, The Church of Jesus Christ of Latter-day Saints, Salt Lake City, Utah. Spelling has been standardized.

8. *Messenger and Advocate* 1 (March 1835): 93.

9. *HC* 2:137.

10. *HC* 3:225.

11. Georgia Ellen Winkler, "Simeon Daget Carter" (n.p., n.d.), p. 4, in author's possession.

WILLIAM CARTER
D&C 52:31

Birth and death: *Unknown.*

There were at least four William Carters in the early days of the Church. The one mentioned in the Doctrine and Covenants is the least known. This William Carter was baptized and ordained an elder by June 1831 and attended the fourth general conference of the Church.[1] The day after the conference, William, although blind, was called by revelation to serve a mission: "Let my servants Wheeler Baldwin and William Carter also take their journey" (D&C 52:31). Church historian John Whitmer recorded, "Three of the elders commanded to undertake the mission by this revelation, Jacob Scott, Edson Fuller, and William Carter, apostatized following the command and refused to go on the venture."[2]

According to the Far West Record of 1 September 1831, "Edison

Fuller and William Carter [were] silenced from holding the office of Elders in this Church."[3] William's uncle, Jared Carter, sought to bring him back to the faith. After speaking with him about the Book of Mormon in 1832, Jared penned:

> He said he was convinced that it was the work of the Lord but he did not as yet feel prepared to obey the work. I then told him that was an impropriety in putting off obedience to the Lord. I also felt with my own soul as though his situation was very dangerous for he had some time grieved the Spirit by his disobedience and I having a sense felt to cry mightily to my Heavenly Father for him. I, at length, felt the power of prophecy to him and expressed to him that this was the very day that he would obey the commands if ever. I then commanded him to repent and be baptized in the name of Jesus Christ for the remission of sins. Soon after this, he knelt down with me and entreated the Lord to have mercy on him. He, the same day, was baptized and received the Spirit of the Lord to his soul.[4]

Rejoicing, William Carter threw his energies into the work of the Lord. He helped with construction of the Kirtland Temple and received a blessing for his sacrifice in which he was "promised a restoration of sight, if faithful."[5] Whether he met the conditions of this blessing is unknown.

Notes

1. This conference numbered "two thousand souls." In 1838, when minutes from the conference were copied from loose pages into the Far West Record, the recorder inserted a notation in parentheses next to the name of William Carter: "denied the faith." See Donald Q. Cannon and Lyndon W. Cook, eds., *Far West Record: Minutes of The Church of Jesus Christ of Latter-day Saints, 1830–1844* (Salt Lake City: Deseret Book Co., 1983), p. 6.

2. John Whitmer, *An Early Latter Day Saint History: The Book of John Whitmer*, ed. F. Mark McKiernan and Roger D. Launius (Independence, Mo.: Herald Publishing House, 1980), p. 73.

3. As cited in Cannon and Cook, p. 11.

4. Autobiography of Jared Carter, typescript, p. 17, Archives Division, Church Historical Department, The Church of Jesus Christ of Latter-day Saints, Salt Lake City, Utah. Spelling has been standardized.

5. *HC* 2:207.

❧

JOSEPH COE
D&C 55:6; 102:3

Birth: *12 November 1784, Genoa, Cayuga County, New York. Son of Joel Coe and Huldah Horton.*
Death: *17 October 1854, Kirtland, Lake County, Ohio.*

Joseph Coe, an early convert from New York, was aided in his preparation to move to Ohio in January 1831 by Orson Pratt and Samuel H. Smith. Pratt wrote, "Elder Samuel H. Smith and myself commenced laboring for one of the Saints, by the name of Joseph Coe, to assist him in making preparations to remove to Ohio according to the revelation given at the conference on the 2nd of January."[1]

Joseph arrived in Kirtland in time to attend the fourth general conference of the Church on 3 June 1831. A few days later he was called by revelation to serve a mission to Missouri (see D&C 55:6). Traveling with him to Missouri was the Prophet Joseph Smith, Sidney Rigdon, and other Church leaders. He was privileged to be one of eight elders present when Sidney Rigdon dedicated Missouri for the land of inheritance and when the Prophet "laid a stone at the Northeast corner of the contemplated Temple."[2]

Unresolved difficulties arose between the Prophet and Joseph Coe in 1831. A debt of four hundred dollars had accrued on the Frederick G. Williams farm, where the Prophet was living, and needed to be paid within a specific time or the farm would revert to its former owner. Joseph Coe, who was responsible for raising the needed funds, excused himself from paying any portion of the debt, "for his wife held the money and she did not belong to the Church."[3] The excuse was accepted but not appreciated.

Joseph Coe was subsequently appointed general agent of the Church and as such was responsible for superintending land purchases in Kirtland in 1833, including 103 acres of the Peter French farm on which the temple was later built. Joseph also served on the Kirtland high council from 1834 to 1837 (see D&C 102:3). It appears that he was a man of few words, for, in accounts of two different high council meetings, "Councilor Joseph Coe stood up on the part of the accused, but could say but a few words"; "Joseph Coe commenced twenty minutes before nine o'clock and spoke five minutes."[4] In one of his few recorded expressions he defended Jared Carter, who was being tried in a Church court after delivering a controversial sermon. Joseph said that "Elder Carter had a small degree of the Spirit in his discourse, and a greater degree in his remarks afterwards, but was awkward in expressing his views, not having much of the Spirit, and that the feelings of his heart were not as expressed by his words."[5]

Joseph participated in many activities in Kirtland, but he is perhaps best remembered for his interest in and eight-hundred-dollar contribution for the purchase of Egyptian mummies. The Prophet wrote, "This evening Elder Coe called to make some arrangements about the Egyptian records and the mummies, he proposes to hire a room at J[ohn] Johnsons Inn and exhibit them there from day to day at certain hours, that some benefit may be derived from them—I complied with his request, and only observed that they must be managed with prudence and care especially the manuscripts."[6]

In June 1837 Joseph Coe ended his affiliation with the Church by attempting to overthrow the leadership of the Prophet in favor of the newly organized Church of Christ, alleging that Joseph Smith was a fallen prophet and that he taught false doctrines. Joseph Coe's own leadership in the new organization soon became tentative: "Last Sabbath a division arose among the Parrish party about the Book of Mormon; John F. Boyington, Warren Parrish, Luke S. Johnson, and others said it was nonsense. Martin Harris then bore testimony of its truth and said all would be damned if they rejected it. Cyrus Smalling, Joseph Coe and others declared his testimony was true."[7] Before the year's end Joseph had moved from a leader to a "lackey," as the *Elders' Journal* noted: "Granny Parrish had a few others who acted as lackeys, such as Martin Harris, Joseph Coe, Cyrus P. Smalling, etc., but they are so far beneath contempt that a notice of them would be too great a sacrifice for a gentleman to make."[8] Joseph was excommunicated from the Church in December 1838.

When the Saints left Kirtland he remained in the rural community and rented the Joseph Smith farm for ninety dollars per year plus taxes. In 1842 he failed to pay the tax and half of the rent. Although he promised to settle the account, by 1843 he had paid nothing, claiming, in January 1844, that "his part in the purchase of the mummies had never been repaid and that an agreement to do so with Joseph's father through a gift of land had been ignored."[9]

On 18 January 1844 the Prophet wrote to Joseph Coe:

I have received a letter from you . . . concerning some pretended claim you seem to think you have on the Mummies, and also requesting me to let you have the use of my farm for a longer Season &c, as a recompense for your interest in the Mummies. . . .

. . . I am satisfied that you know you wrong me when you thus expose my property for sale for the Taxes, and at the same time are reaping the fruits of it. . . .

. . . I have got your Deed, executed by your own hand, in due form, for all the interest you ever held in the Mummies, and consequently dont feel under the necessity of listening to such unjust claims.10

The Prophet further denounced Coe's actions by stating, "It is astonishing that any man can be so wicked and corrupt as to suffer the property of his benefactor and best friend to be sold in order to defraud him out of it by getting a Sheriffs Deed, surely the shades of darkness prevail over such a man; his heart must be hard as the nether-mill-stone, and virtue have no place in him."11

Joseph Coe lived in Kirtland until his death in 1854 at the age of sixty-nine.

Notes

1. Orson Pratt, *The Orson Pratt Journals,* comp. Elden J. Watson (Salt Lake City: Elden Jay Watson, 1975), p. 10.

2. John Whitmer, *An Early Latter Day Saint History: The Book of John Whitmer,* ed. F. Mark McKiernan and Roger D. Launius (Independence, Mo.: Herald Publishing House, 1980), p. 80.

3. Philo Dibble, "Philo Dibble's Narrative," in *Early Scenes in Church History* (Salt Lake City: Juvenile Instructor Office, 1882), p. 78, as published in *Four Faith Promoting Classics* (Salt Lake City: Bookcraft, 1968).

4. *HC* 2:34, 158.

5. *HC* 2:278–79.

6. Joseph Smith diary, 17 February 1836, as cited in Joseph Smith, *The Personal Writings of Joseph Smith,* comp. Dean C. Jessee (Salt Lake City: Deseret Book Co., 1984), p. 161.

7. Journal History, 30 March 1838.

8. *Elders' Journal* 1 (August 1838): 59.

9. Dean C. Jessee, in Smith, p. 567.

10. Letter of Joseph Smith to Joseph Coe, 18 January 1844, as cited in Jessee, pp. 569, 570.

11. Ibid., p. 570.

ZEBEDEE COLTRIN
D&C 52:29

Birth: *7 September 1804, Ovid, Seneca County, New York. Son of John Coltrin and Sarah Graham.* **Death:** *2 July 1887, Spanish Fork, Utah County, Utah.*

In 1814 Zebedee Coltrin moved with his parents to the small community of Strongsville, Ohio, and grew to manhood accepting the Methodist faith of his father. Then on 8 January 1831 he and his father listened to the preaching of Solomon Hancock, a Mormon elder. That evening Zebedee "resolved to be baptized and as I lay meditating the room became lighted up with a brilliant light and I saw a number of men dressed in white robes."[1] The next day he was baptized in a pond near his father's farm by Elder Hancock and twelve days later was ordained an elder by John Whitmer.

The first of the revelations calling him to labor in Missouri is found in Doctrine and Covenants 52:29. Other subsequent missionary assignments were recorded in his journal.

In Zebedee's most quoted account from the Kirtland era, he describes his sacred remembrances of the School of the Prophets: "I saw a personage passing through the room as plainly as I see you now [high priests in Spanish Fork]. Joseph asked us if we knew who it was and answered himself, that is Jesus, our elder brother, the Son of God."[2] As the vision closed, Zebedee reported, "Again I saw passing through the same room, a personage whose glory and brightness was so great, that I can liken it to nothing but the burning bush that Moses saw, and its power was so great that had it continued much longer I believe it would have consumed us."[3] The Prophet announced that the personage was the Father of Jesus Christ. "I saw him," said Zebedee. He also testified of seeing the Prophet come from the translating room after receiving the revelation known as the Word of Wisdom. "His face shone with brilliance," Zebedee later said.[4]

Zebedee possessed an unusual spiritual nature that the Prophet recognized: "President Zebedee Coltrin . . . saw the Savior extended before him, as upon the cross, and a little after, crowned with glory upon his head above the brightness of the sun."[5] On another occasion the Prophet recorded, "President Zebedee Coltrin, one of the Seven [meaning the Seven Presidents of the Seventies], saw a vision of the Lord's host."[6]

Zebedee's spirituality contrasted with the religious bigotry in Kirtland that caused him and other Saints to flee to Missouri and then to Illinois. In 1839 he settled in Nauvoo but soon accepted an opportunity to return to Kirtland. Misfortune followed his move to Ohio, as his wife, Julia Ann, died, saying, "Let me go! Let me go! Come Lord Jesus and take me."[7]

Zebedee served briefly as second counselor to Almon W. Babbitt of the Kirtland Stake before returning to Nauvoo. From Nauvoo he journeyed on a mission assignment to Wisconsin, where he met Mary Mott and said to himself, "There is my future wife."[8] They were married on 5 February 1843 in Nauvoo. Zebedee supported his family as a merchant during the Nauvoo years amid missions to Illinois and Michigan.

As religious persecution flared again, he fled with his family and joined the exiled Saints in Iowa and, later, Winter Quarters. Zebedee was in the vanguard company that journeyed to the Salt Lake Valley in 1847. In August 1847 he returned to the Camp of Israel and seved as a high councilman and, later, as a missionary in Iowa and Wisconsin. Almost four years passed before Zebedee returned to the Valley. He settled on Main Street in Salt Lake City, where the Joseph Smith Memorial Building now stands, before accepting a settlement call to Palmyra near the Spanish Fork Canyon in 1852. There he helped pioneer the community, assisting in building schools, bridges, meetinghouses, and roads. He was elected to the Utah County branch of the Deseret Manufacturing Society and served as a city councilman for Spanish Fork. For several years he was a home missionary, president of the Utah Stake high priests quorum, and a frequent speaker at pioneer celebrations and reunions.

On 31 May 1873 Zebedee was ordained a patriarch by John Taylor. He served in this office for fourteen years and gave over one thousand patriarchal blessings, including blessings to Melvin J. Ballard and George Albert Smith. He spent the last years of his life traveling and doing temple work in the Logan Temple—the temple in which he had offered the benediction at the dedication.

After a brief illness Zebedee died in 1887 in Spanish Fork at the age of eighty-two. He had been scheduled to give the July twenty-fourth oration, but his funeral was held that day instead. He is buried in the Spanish Fork Cemetery, and on his tombstone is written:

> A friend of Joseph Smith lies here
> A patriarch and pioneer
> His life was marked by faith and zeal
> His mission was to bless and heal.

Notes

1. Minutes of a high priest meeting in Spanish Fork, Utah, 5 February 1878, Archives Division, Church Historical Department, The Church of Jesus Christ of Latter-day Saints, Salt Lake City, Utah.

2. Ibid.

3. Ibid.

4. Ibid.

5. *HC* 2:387.

6. *HC* 2:392.

7. *Times and Seasons* 3 (15 January 1842): 669.

8. Interview with Mary Marcusen, 13 February 1974, as cited in Calvin Robert Stephens, "The Life and Contribution of Zebedee Coltrin," M.A. thesis, Brigham Young University, August 1974, p. 10.

LEMAN COPLEY
D&C 49; 54: Introduction

Birth: *1781, Connecticut. Son of Samuel Copley.*
Death: *December 1862, Thompson, Geauga County, Ohio.*

Leman Copley, a member of the United Society of Believers in Christ's Second Appearing (Shakers), converted to Mormonism in March 1831. However, the Prophet Joseph Smith thought his conversion seemed tenuous. He said that Leman was "apparently honest-hearted, but still retain[ed] the idea that the Shakers were right in some particulars of their faith."[1]

Perhaps in hope of strengthening his religious convictions or sharing the gospel with his old acquaintances, Leman "was anxious that some of the elders should go to his former brethren [the Shakers] and preach the gospel" in North Union, Ohio.[2] The Prophet wrote, "In order to have a more perfect understanding on the subject, I inquired of the Lord" for clarification of the truth pertaining to the Shaker doctrine. The resulting revelation, received in May 1831 and recorded in Doctrine and Covenants 49, "refuted some of the basic concepts of the Shaker group." (D&C 49: Introduction.)

The revelation was taken to the Shaker settlement in North Union by Leman, Sidney Rigdon, and Parley P. Pratt. Leman and Sidney arrived in the village on a Saturday evening and discussed religion with Ashbel Kitchell, a Shaker of some prominence, who wrote in his journal that Leman "had taken up with Mormonism as the easier plan."[3]

The next morning Parley P. Pratt arrived and the three attended a Shaker service. At the end of the service Sidney received permission to read Joseph's revelation to the congregation, but the Shakers did not accept the message. "We fulfilled this mission, as we were commanded," wrote Parley, "in a settlement of this strange people, near Cleveland, Ohio; but they utterly refused to hear or obey the gospel."[4]

This visit with the Shakers may have influenced the problems that soon developed on Leman Copley's 759 acres in Thompson, Ohio, about sixteen miles northeast of Kirtland.[5] Leman had contracted with Church leaders to allow newly arriving Saints from Colesville, New York, to occupy and improve his land. He reneged on the promise in June 1831. In answer to the broken promise, the Prophet received Doctrine and Covenants 54: "Wo to him by whom this offense cometh, for it had been better for him that he had been drowned in the depth of the sea" (verse 5).

Fellowship was withdrawn from Leman Copley in the summer of 1831 but was extended again by October 1832. Nevertheless, Leman's faith continued to waver. In 1834 he testified against Joseph Smith at a trial instigated by the Prophet against Philastus Hurlburt for threatening his life. On 1 April 1836 he sought forgiveness from the Prophet for his false testimony:

[Leman Copley] confessed that he bore a false testimony against me in that suit, but verily thought, at the time, that he was right, but on calling to mind all the circumstances connected with the things that happened at that time, he was convinced that he was wrong, and humbly confessed it, and asked my forgiveness, which was readily granted. He also wished to be received into the Church again, by baptism, and was received according to his desire. He gave me his confession in writing.[6]

Leman did not gather with the Saints to Missouri, but chose to remain in Ohio. In 1849 he joined apostates James C. Brewster and Hazen Aldrich in their Church of Christ (Brewsterites). He left that church to join another religious organization led by Austin Cowles.[7] Even though his religious leanings changed dramatically through the years, his interest in land did not. By 1850 he was viewed as a successful farmer, having real estate valued at $3,500.[8] Leman died a wealthy landlord in December 1862 at about eighty-one years of age.

Notes

1. *HC* 1:167.
2. John Whitmer, *An Early Latter Day Saint History: The Book of John Whitmer,* ed. F. Mark McKiernan and Roger D. Launius (Independence, Mo.: Herald Publishing House, 1980), p. 60.
3. Ashbel Kitchell, "A Mormon Interview," as cited in Lawrence R. Flake, "A Shaker View of a Mormon Mission," *BYU Studies* 20 (Fall 1979): 97.
4. Parley P. Pratt, *Autobiography of Parley P. Pratt,* ed. Parley P. Pratt Jr. (Salt Lake City: Deseret Book Co., 1985), p. 47.
5. See Joseph Knight, "Manuscript of the Early History of Joseph Smith," as cited in Dean Jessee, "Joseph Knight's Recollection of Early Mormon History," *BYU Studies* 17 (Autumn 1976): 37.
6. *HC* 2:433.
7. See *The History of the Reorganized Church of Jesus Christ of Latter Day Saints* 8 vols. (Independence, Mo.: Herald Publishing House, 1967–1976), 3:73–74.
8. See the Ohio federal census 1850.

JOHN CORRILL
D&C 50:38; 52:7

Birth: *17 September 1794, Bone, Worcester County, Massachusetts.*

John Corrill was residing in Harpersville, Ohio, in 1830 when the missionaries to the Lamanites stopped at his home for a night's lodging.

He attended one of their meetings and heard members speaking in tongues: "I was obliged to acknowledge in my own mind, that the meeting had been inspired by some supernatural agency."[1] He was baptized in January 1831 and soon ordained an elder.

John's zeal for his newfound faith was made evident by the many converts he brought into the Church in New London, Ohio, amid bitter opposition. He had a willingness to serve, as shown by his acceptance of the calling of second counselor to Bishop Edward Partridge in Jackson County, Missouri, and the calling of president of the Independence branch. On 23 July 1833 he illustrated resolute determination when he and five other Saints offered themselves to the mob "as a ransom for the Church, expressing . . . willing[ness] to be scourged or to die if that would appease the anger of the mob against the Saints." The offer was not accepted.[2]

Even his imprisonment in Jackson County by Judge Samuel Weston on a trumped-up charge was met with characteristic faith. During a mob attack he and other brethren had observed a man breaking into a store and demolishing property. Their complaint against the man was dismissed, but they were jailed based on false accusations. "Although [we] could not obtain a warrant against him for breaking open the store," wrote John, "yet he had gotten one for us for catching him at it."[3]

After being expelled from Jackson County, John was recognized as a Church leader for the next five troubled years. His name is attached to nearly all correspondence passing between the Saints and Missouri governor Daniel Dunklin and other officials. He became one of the founders and surveyors of Far West, the keeper of the Lord's storehouse, and a Church historian "to write and keep the Church history."[4]

Almost overnight the tenor of John's faith faltered. In 1838 he became disillusioned with other Church leaders and penned, "I felt it was necessary for me to look out for my own safety."[5] Joseph Smith recorded on 30 August 1838:

> I spent considerable time to day in conversation with Brother John Corrill. . . . Brother Corrill's conduct for some time had been very unbecoming, especially in a man in whom so much confidence had been placed. He said he would not yield his judgment to anything proposed by the Church, or any individuals of the Church, or even the Great I Am, given through the appointed organ, as revelation, but would always act upon his own judgment, let him believe in whatever religion he might.[6]

John's dissension led to his betrayal of the Prophet. At the Richmond hearings in November 1838, John testified with bitterness against the Prophet and former friends and associates in the priesthood. He was excommunicated from the Church on 17 March 1839 in Quincy, Illinois.[7]

John remained in Missouri after the Saints fled, representing Caldwell County in the Missouri legislature. Esquire Mann, a nonmember who had also been a member of the Missouri legislature, said, "If ever I felt like fighting any man," it was John Corrill. He then explained, "He never once raised his voice, nor even his hand, in behalf of that abused people, once while the House was in session."[8]

Most remembered from John's apostasy was a pamphlet he wrote, *A Brief History of the Church of Latter-day Saints (commonly called Mormons), Including an Account of Their Doctrine and Discipline, with the Reasons of the Author for Leaving the Church.* In the pamphlet he stated, "Much exertion has been used to confute and put down their [Mormon] doctrine, but as foolish as it is, their elders have been able to compete with and baffle their opponents."[9]

His bitterness against the Church had not abated by 1841. In a letter to Samuel A. Arthur of Liberty, Missouri, he wrote:

> Sir I have just returned from Nauvoo. . . . The Mormons are naturely poor and what property there is among them Jo and his associates contrives to make use of for public or Church uses. . . . They keep the work a going on but this only serves to reduce and enslave these people. . . . You would not be safe for he [Joseph Smith] had boys there that would put a ball through you quick as he would snap his thumb. . . . I must confess that I found their feelings much more hostile than I expected.[10]

Notes

1. John Corrill, *A Brief History of the Church of Latter-day Saints (commonly called Mormons), Including an Account of Their Doctrine and Discipline, with the Reasons of the Author for Leaving the Church* (St. Louis: John Corrill, 1839), pp. 7–9.

2. *HC* 1:394.

3. *HC* 1:428 n.

4. *HC* 3:13; see also *HC* 2:524; Donald Q. Cannon and Lyndon W. Cook, eds., *Far West Record: Minutes of The Church of Jesus Christ of Latter-day Saints, 1830–1844* (Salt Lake City: Deseret Book Co., 1983), p. 158.

5. Corrill, p. 37.

6. *HC* 3:65–66.

7. See *HC* 3:284.

8. As cited in Lucy Mack Smith, *History of Joseph Smith by His Mother,* ed. Preston Nibley (Salt Lake City: Bookcraft, 1954), p. 296.

9. Corrill, p. 45.

10. Letter of John Corrill to Samuel A. Arthur, 21 March 1841, in author's possession.

JAMES COVILL
D&C 39; 40

Birth and death: *Unknown.*

Little is known of James Covill. Some biographers have concluded that he was James Covell, son of James and Sarah Grover Covell, who was born 1 March 1756 at Dover, New York.[1] This is not the case, however. All that is known of James Covill is that on 5 January 1831, three days after the third conference of the Church at Fayette, New York, the Prophet Joseph Smith received a revelation directed to him.[2] He had been a Baptist minister for about forty years and had made a covenant with the Lord that he would obey any command that the Lord gave to him through the Prophet (see D&C 39: Introduction). In the revelation he was told:

> I say unto you, my servant James, I have looked upon thy works and I know thee.
>
> . . . Thine heart is now right before me at this time. . . .
>
> . . . Arise and be baptized, and wash away your sins, calling on my name, and you shall receive my Spirit, and a blessing so great as you never have known.
>
> And if thou do this, I have prepared thee for a greater work. Thou shalt preach the fulness of my gospel. . . .
>
> . . . Thou art called to go to the Ohio. (D&C 39:7, 8, 10–11, 14.)

James received the word of the Lord through his prophet with "gladness" (D&C 40:2). One biographer indicates, "He may have united with the Church at Fayette in January 1831 as 'Reverand James Civill.'"[3] However, LDS Church records do not indicate that he was baptized.[4]

Whether he was baptized is conjecture, but what is known is that he was tempted by Satan, and "the fear of persecution and the cares of the world caused him to reject the word" (D&C 40:2). As James "rejected the word of the Lord, and returned to his former principles and people" (D&C 40: Introduction), the Lord gave the Prophet and Sidney Rigdon a revelation. This was the first revelation given to Sidney Rigdon, who, like Covill, had been a Baptist preacher. The focus of the revelation is once again directed to James Covill: "Wherefore he broke my covenant, and it remaineth with me to do with him as seemeth me good" (D&C 40:3).

Notes

1. See Lyndon W. Cook, *The Revelations of the Prophet Joseph Smith* (Salt Lake City: Deseret Book Co., 1985), p. 57.

2. See *HC* 2:143–45.

3. Larry C. Porter, "A Study of the Origins of The Church of Jesus Christ of Latter-day Saints in the States of New York and Pennsylvania, 1816–1831," dissertation, Brigham Young University, August 1971, pp. 266–67.

4. See Diedrich Willers Notebook #1, Seneca Falls Historical Society, Seneca Falls, New York, as cited in Porter, p. 266.

OLIVER COWDERY

D&C 6–9; 13; 17–18; 20:3; 21: Introduction, 10, 12; 23–24;
26; 28; 30:5; 32:2; 55:4; 57:13; 58:58; 61:23, 32; 63:
Introduction, 46; 67: Introduction; 68:32; 70:3; 82:11; 102:
Introduction, 3, 34; 104:28–29, 34; 110; 111:
Introduction; 124:94–95

Birth: *3 October 1806, Wells, Rutland County, Vermont. Son of William Cowdery Jr. and Rebecca Fuller.*
Death: *3 March 1850, Richmond, Ray County, Missouri.*

Oliver Cowdery became a teacher after receiving his rudimentary education in Vermont and New York. While teaching school in Manchester, New York, he learned of the prophetic calling of Joseph Smith. In April 1829 he accompanied Samuel Smith to Harmony, Pennsylvania, to meet the Prophet: "Near the time of the setting of the sun, Sabbath evening, April 5th, 1829, my natural eyes, for the first time beheld this brother. . . . On Tuesday the 7th, commenced to write the Book of Mormon."[1]

The name of Oliver Cowdery was intertwined with the Prophet's during the early days of the Church. The two men were privileged to receive the Aaronic Priesthood from John the Baptist on 15 May 1829 (see D&C 13; 27:8) and the Melchizedek Priesthood from the ancient Apostles Peter, James, and John.[2] Several of the early revelations in the Doctrine and Covenants are instructions to Oliver Cowdery, the second elder of the Church.

He shared his testimony from New York to the western border of the frontier in the early 1830s. Wilford Woodruff wrote of his preaching: "I have seen Oliver Cowdery when it seemed as though the earth trembled under his feet. I never heard a man bear a stronger testimony than he did when under the influence of the Spirit."[3] On 5 December 1834 Oliver was ordained an assistant to the President of the Church by the Prophet, who said these words: "I lay my hands upon thee and ordain thee an assistant-president to the High and Holy Priesthood, in the Church of the Latter-day Saints."[4] On 3 April 1836 he received priesthood keys from Elijah, Elias, and Moses (see D&C 110:11–16).

Despite the glorious revelations, Oliver did not remain faithful. Pride led to his chastisement of the Prophet. In the summer of 1830 he wrote in a letter to Joseph, referring to words now found in Doctrine and Covenants 20:37, "I command you in the name of God to erase those words, that no priestcraft be amongst us!"[5] In a letter to his brothers, Warren and Lyman Cowdery, written on 4 February 1838 from Far West, he complained about Church leaders' supposed efforts to control his land in Jackson County: "I told them if I had property, while I lived and was sane, I would not be dictated, influenced or controlled, by any man or set of men by no tribunal of ecclesiastical practices whatever."[6]

On 7 April 1838 nine formal charges were drawn against Oliver Cowdery, including charges that he persecuted the brethren "by urging on vexatious law suits against them" and that he sought "to destroy the character of Joseph Smith Jr., by falsely insinuating that he was guilty of adultery."[7] He refused to attend the high council meeting where the charges were presented. At one point he wrote, *"Give me my freedom or take my life!* I shall no longer be bound by the chains of hell. I shall speak out when I see a move to deceive the ignorant."[8] Oliver was excommunicated on 12 April 1838 in Far West.

The Prophet continued to reach out to his friend. He told members of the Quorum of the Twelve, "Write to Oliver Cowdery and ask him if he has not eaten husks long enough? If he is not almost ready to return, be clothed with robes of righteousness, and go up to Jerusalem?"[9] But Oliver rejected the fellowship of the Prophet as his attentions turned to his vocation.

He practiced law in Ohio, and said of his employ, "My business is steadily increasing—nothing operates against me, except the fact that I have formerly been connected with what is now an important church."[10] Perhaps to dispel the impact of his former Mormon affiliation, Oliver became a charter member of the Methodist Protestant Church in Tiffin, Ohio. During his years of allegiance to the Methodist doctrine, he remembered his family and friends in the Mormon faith. On 14 February 1847 he wrote to Phineas Young, "No day passes without our thoughts being turned toward our relatives and loved friends, who are toiling and struggling in the far off wilderness, during a cold and pitiless winter."[11]

By the spring of 1847 Oliver had moved to Elkhorn, Wisconsin, where he made an unsuccessful bid for the state legislature. It was while in Wisconsin that news of his interest in rejoining the Church was conveyed to the Quorum of the Twelve Apostles. On 22 November Brigham Young wrote to him:

> Return to our father's house, from whence thou hast wandered, and partake of the fatted calf and sup and be filled, . . . and renew thy testimony to the truth of the Book of Mormon with a loud voice, and faithful heart and you will soon feel the Holy Ghost burning your bones like fire in the dry stubble . . . and the Saints, His sons and daughters will with open arms hail thee as their long lost brother found in the New and Everlasting Covenant.[12]

Ill health prevented Oliver from joining the Saints in the West. However, eleven years after leaving the Church—during which time he had been plagued by financial difficulties and illness—Oliver left his law practice in Elkhorn and traveled to Kanesville, Iowa. At a conference held on 21 October 1848 he addressed the assembled congregation: "Friends and Brethren,—My name is Cowdery—Oliver Cowdery. In the early history of this Church I stood identified with her, and one in her councils, . . . not because I was better than the rest of mankind. . . . I wrote, with my own pen, the entire Book of Mormon (save a few pages) as it fell from the lips of the Prophet Joseph Smith. . . . That book is true."[13]

Early the next month Oliver appeared before the high council at Kanesville and formally requested fellowship in the Church, saying, "Brethren, for a number of years, I have been separated from you. I now desire to come back. . . . I seek no station. I only wish to be identified with you."[14] After his case was considered, and upon the motion of Orson Hyde, he was received by baptism.

His first assignment in the Church was to remain in Iowa and help Orson Hyde with publishing a newspaper. He did so until April 1849, when he and his wife traveled to Richmond, Missouri, to visit her extended family. He wrote in a letter from Richmond of his struggles with his "old difficulty of the lungs."[15] His chronic lung condition advanced to consumption, and on 3 March 1850 at David Whitmer's home, with his family assembled near his bed, he spoke to those present. He admonished his loved ones to live the teachings of the Book of Mormon, and promised that if they did, they would meet him in heaven.[16]

Notes

1. Oliver Cowdery, *Messenger and Advocate* 1 (October 1834): 14.
2. See *HC* 1:40 n.
3. "Testimony of Wilford Woodruff," *Deseret News Weekly* 35:391, as cited in Stanley R. Gunn, *Oliver Cowdery* (Salt Lake City: Bookcraft, 1962), p. 73.
4. *HC* 2:176.
5. *HC* 1:105.
6. Huntington Library Letters, no. 83, as cited in Gunn, p. 148.
7. As cited in Gunn, pp. 151–52.
8. Huntington Library Letters, microfilm #87, as cited in Gunn, p. 230.
9. *HC* 5:368.
10. Letter to Phineas H. Young, Kirtland, Ohio, written from Tiffin, Ohio, 19 August 1842, as cited in Gunn, p. 169.
11. Letter to Phineas H. Young from Tiffin, Ohio, 14 February 1847, as cited in Gunn, p. 187.
12. Letter from Brigham Young to Oliver Cowdery, 22 November 1847, as cited in Gunn, pp. 191–93.
13. As cited in *LDS Biographical Encyclopedia* 1:249.
14. Ibid., 1:250.
15. Letter of Oliver Cowdery, 24 June 1849, from Richmond, Mo., as cited in Gunn, p. 207.
16. See Gunn, pp. 208–9.

Warren A. Cowdery
D&C 106

Birth: *17 (possibly 5) October 1788, Poultney, Rutland County, Vermont. Son of William Cowdery and Rebecca Fuller.*
Death: *23 February 1851, Kirtland, Lake County, Ohio.*

Warren Cowdery, a successful farmer, physician, and apothecary entrepreneur in Freedom, New York, seemed less inclined to new religious leanings than other contemporaries. However, when he received some of the Book of Mormon proof sheets from his younger brother Oliver Cowdery, he perused them with faith and belief.[1] He entered the waters of baptism in late 1831, and by 1834 was called by the Lord to preside over the Church in his local community:

It is my will that my servant Warren A. Cowdery should be appointed and ordained a presiding high priest over my church, in the land of Freedom and the regions round about;

And should preach my everlasting gospel, and lift up his voice and warn the people, not only in his own place, but in the adjoining counties;

And devote his whole time to this high and holy calling, which I now give unto him, seeking diligently the kingdom of heaven and its righteousness, and all things necessary shall be added thereunto; for the laborer is worthy of his hire (D&C 106:1–3).

The Lord promised that if Warren would humble himself and continue to be faithful, "I have prepared a crown for him in the mansions of my Father" (D&C 106:8).

Warren's position as high priest over the Freedom branch led him to boast in his priesthood power. In September 1835 he wrote a letter that was "derogatory to the character and teaching" of the Twelve,[2] and the Twelve countered with "a charge against Dr Cowdery for his unchristian conduct."[3] In March 1836, after Warren had moved from New York to Kirtland, the Prophet met with him and others in the upper room of the printing office regarding the Twelves' charges. Warren admitted that he was wrong and "was willing to publish that they [the Twelve] were not in the fault."[4] His public apology was accepted.

Possessing many of the same talents as his brother Oliver, Warren acted as a scribe and an assistant recorder for the Church from 1836 to 1837 and served on the Kirtland high council in May 1837. He kept Kirtland council minutes, made entries in the Prophet's diary, penned the historical record of the Church from 1835 to 1836, and scribed patriarchal blessings. He assisted in writing the dedicatory prayer for the Kirtland Temple in 1836 (see D&C 109). He was an agent or manager for the Prophet and Sidney Rigdon in the printing office and book bindery.[5] He succeeded his brother in serving as editor of the *Messenger and Advocate* until February 1837. Warren edited the paper through its final edition in September 1837.[6]

He did not remain with the Church after 1838. His disaffection with Church leaders corresponded with that of his brother Oliver. Warren continued to reside in Kirtland, and in the Ohio federal census of 1850 he was listed as living with his wife and six children and possessing assets of seven hundred dollars.[7] He died in 1851 at the age of sixty-two.

Notes

1. See autobiography of William Hyde, typescript, p. 6, Special Collections, Harold B. Lee Library, Brigham Young University, Provo, Utah.

2. *HC* 2:283.

3. Joseph Smith, *The Personal Writings of Joseph Smith*, comp. Dean C. Jessee (Salt Lake City: Deseret Book Co., 1984), p. 137.

4. Oliver Cowdery diary, 5 March 1836, as cited in Smith, p. 664 n. 198.

5. See Dean C. Jessee, "The Writings of Joseph Smith's History," *BYU Studies* 11 (Summer 1971): 449.

6. During these years of heightened Church activity Warren kept a journal, which is located in the Church Historical Department in Salt Lake City, Utah.

7. See the Ohio federal census 1850.

ALPHEUS CUTLER
D&C 124:132

Birth: *29 February 1784, Plainfield, Sullivan County, New Hampshire. Son of Knight Cutler and Elizabeth Boyd.*
Death: *10 August 1864, Manti, Mills County, Iowa.*

Alpheus Cutler, a veteran of the War of 1812, was first introduced to the Church by David W. Patten and Reynolds Cahoon in 1833. He listened to one of the two elders preach about the sticks of Judah and Joseph and witnessed him clap the Bible and the Book of Mormon together, saying, "And they shall be one in the Lord's hands." To Alpheus's surprise, his sick daughter Lois clapped her hands and said, "And I believe it." She then received a healing blessing from Elder Patten and Elder Cahoon and was immediately restored to health.[1]

News of the miraculous healing of Lois Cutler spread, and many listened to the gospel message and joined the Church. Among those baptized was Alpheus, on 20 January 1833, by David W. Patten. He and his family moved from western New York to Kirtland to be with others of the Mormon faith.

In Kirtland, Alpheus attended the School of the Prophets, worked on the temple, and served on the high council.[2] In March 1836 he beheld a glorious vision during the Kirtland Temple dedication, in which he saw "a gold chain, suspended or draped, across the room and saw the Lord descending on a long strip, which resembled a carpet. This Being seemed to move toward him and he spoke to him."[3]

In contrast to the peaceful scene of the vision, hatred and bigotry soon forced Alpheus to flee from his home in Ohio to Missouri. There he again faced persecution and suffered the loss of crops, livestock, and property before finally leaving for Nauvoo. In his redress petition he stated his grievances:

A Bill of Damage Sustained By Alpheus Cutler in Consequence of the Unlawful Conduct of the Inhabitants thereof & the Unconstitutional Decrees of the Governor

Damage on Land	$600.00
Do. Do. on Personal Property	400.00
Do. Do. for being obliged to remove with a large family & an old aged mother the Inconveniences & the Exposure to the weather & being thrown out of Business &c &c	350.00
Do. Do. Expences for Journey	100.00
	$1,450.00

Alpheus Cutler

I do hereby Certify the within Statements to be true according to the Best of my knowledge.[4]

Alpheus was never recompensed for the losses. Yet he willingly returned to Missouri to lay the foundation of the Far West Temple under the direction of the Quorum of the Twelve Apostles.[5] The minutes of a Church council meeting on 24 April 1839 read: "Elder Alpheus Cutler then placed the stone . . . in its regular position, after which, in consequence of the peculiar situation of the Saints, he thought it wisdom to adjourn until some future time, when the Lord shall open the way; expressing his determination then to proceed with the building; whereupon the conference adjourned."[6]

Alpheus joined the Saints in Illinois, where he served on the high council (see D&C 124:131–32), the Council of Fifty, and the temple committee. After the death of Joseph Smith, he was assigned by Brigham Young to be a captain over the third company of Saints to leave Nauvoo.[7] As his company reached a campsite near Nebraska, the site was named Cutler's Park in honor of him. He became the presiding member of the municipal high council in Cutler's Park until he found the more favorable campsite—Winter Quarters.

Alpheus Cutler's apostasy was most unusual after his years of faithful service. He withdrew from the Church claiming that Joseph Smith, before his death, had assigned him to fulfill missionary labors among the Indians in Kansas Territory.[8] After a brief mission to the Indians, Alpheus settled in Manti, Iowa, where he formed the Church of Jesus Christ (Cutlerites). Claiming to be Joseph Smith's successor, he denounced tithing, plural marriage, and Brigham Young. On 19 September 1853 Alpheus—or Father Cutler, as he was known to his followers—was "chosen our head or chief Councilor and sustained by a unanimous vote."[9]

The thrust of his leadership was to confer priesthood authority, for he believed that he alone was authorized to do this important work. His belief was based on his ordination to the "Quorum of Seven, . . . with all the rights, keys, powers, privileges, and blessings," and that "he would not sever the tie between himself and Joseph Smith, or in other words the authority which now rested upon him alone."[10]

Near the end of his life Alpheus suffered from a stroke, which resulted in paralysis of his legs and blurred speech, "making it difficult to understand him, which for him was very embarrassing and frustrating." He also suffered from a form of tuberculosis that greatly damaged his lungs. During the last years of his life he was an invalid, completely unable to care for himself. Since he was "a large heavy man, nursing care for him was a burden that required strength and stamina."[11] It was while in this condition that he acknowledged his apostasy to his grandson, Abraham Kimball: "I know that Joseph Smith was a Prophet of God, and I know that Brigham Young is his legal successor and I always did know it. But, the trouble with me was, I wanted to lead, and could not be lead and I have run my race and sealed my doom, and I know what I have got to meet. . . . One favor I wish to ask of you—namely—that you will not divulge this confession to those whom I lead while I live."[12]

Since the days of Alpheus Cutler, the church he founded has been plagued by apostasy and an "inability to retain the natural increase, failure to achieve unity, and a variety of other mistakes. . . . The little church, reorganized by Cutler, has barely managed to keep enough members to ensure continuity of the organization."[13] A small group still exists in Manti, Iowa.

Notes

1. Inez Smith Davis, *The Story of the Church* (Independence, Mo.: Herald Publishing House, 1959), pp. 186–88; see also Daisy Whiting Fletcher, "Alpheus Cutler and the Church of Jesus Christ" (n.p., 1970), p. 4.

2. See *HC* 2:151–52.

3. As cited in Fletcher, p. 8.

4. As cited in Clark V. Johnson, ed., *Mormon Redress Petitions: Documents of the 1833–1838 Missouri Conflict* (Provo, Utah: Religious Studies Center, Brigham Young University, 1992), pp. 181–82.

5. See *HC* 3:337.

6. *HC* 3:339.

7. See *HC* 7:481.

8. See Danny L. Jorgensen, "Building the Kingdom of God: Alpheus Cutler and the Second Mormon Mission to the Indians 1846–1853," *Kansas History* 15 (Autumn 1992): 192, 200.

9. As cited in Fletcher, p. 32.

10. As cited in ibid., pp. 36–37.

11. Ibid., pp. 42–43.

12. "Alpheus Cutler's Testimony Bore to Grandson Abraham Kimball Who Recorded It As Follows," p. 1, in author's possession.

13. Fletcher, p. 54.

AMOS DAVIES
D&C 124:111–14

Birth: *20 September 1813, Hopkinton, Rockingham County, New Hampshire. Son of Wells Davis and Mary John.*
Death: *22 March 1872, Big Mound, Hancock County, Illinois.*

Amos Davies[1] was the postmaster, a merchant, and a landowner in Commerce (Nauvoo) when the Latter-day Saints located in the area. He welcomed the new Mormon settlers and employed several in his business ventures. Nancy Tracy journalized: "My husband had been in the employ of Amos Davis, a merchant in Nauvoo, for one year. . . . At this time, my husband was one who was chosen to go and preach the Gospel. . . . My husband went to Mr. Davis and got his wages, and besides, Mr. Davis made him a present of a nice suit of clothes, a hat, and fine boots and gave to me a dress pattern."[2]

Amos was baptized a member of The Church of Jesus Christ of Latter-day Saints in April 1840. Two months after his baptism he journeyed to Vermont to visit relatives and remained in the East from June to September. After his return Joseph Smith received a revelation on 19 January 1841 directing Amos to "pay stock into the hands of those whom I have appointed to build a house for boarding, even the Nauvoo House" (D&C 124:111). The revelation continues:

> This let him do if he will have an interest; and let him hearken unto the counsel of my servant Joseph, and labor with his own hands that he may obtain the confidence of men.
>
> And when he shall prove himself faithful in all things that shall be entrusted unto his care, yea, even a few things, he shall be made ruler over many;
>
> Let him therefore abase himself that he may be exalted. Even so. Amen. (D&C 124:112–14.)

It is assumed that Amos followed this counsel, for soon thereafter he was ordained an elder and appointed to be a first lieutenant in the Nauvoo Legion.[3]

Difficulties arose between the Prophet and Amos Davies in 1842. On 10 March 1842 the Prophet Joseph Smith attended the trial of "the City of Nauvoo versus Amos Davis, for indecent and abusive language about me while at Mr. Davis' the day previous. The charges were clearly substantiated by the testimony of Dr. Foster, Mr. and Mrs. Hibbard, and others. Mr. Davis was found guilty by the jury, and by the municipal court, bound over to keep the peace six months, under $100 bond."[4]

On 30 November 1842 the Prophet had "Amos Davis brought before the municipal court for slander; but, in consequence of the informality of the writ drawn by Squire Daniel H. Wells, I was non-suited."[5] Two days later Joseph Smith sat in on the trial of "Amos Davis, who was fined in the sum of $25 for breach of city ordinance for selling spirits by the small quantity."[6] Amos, unhappy with the judgment, appealed his case before the municipal court, but the earlier judgment was confirmed.[7]

After these court cases, Amos left Nauvoo and was reported to be in Philadelphia from April through September 1843. Two months after his return the Prophet wrote, "Attended Municipal Court on 'habeas corpus, John M. Finch at suit of Amos Davis.' Finch discharged, Davis to pay costs, it being a vexatious and malicious suit."[8] Another case was pending against Amos in the circuit court in April 1844.

Amos's character was revealed in case after case to those who attended the trials, and even to the lurking apostates. Conspirator Robert D. Foster wrote on 20 June 1844 from Carthage, Illinois, "Tell Amos Davis to keep his eyes open, as we learn that consecration law will soon commence on him. This we know, and he had better look out sharp."[9] To his credit he did not leave Nauvoo to join the conspirators in Carthage or to join the mob at the Carthage Jail.

He remained in Nauvoo with his interest focused on his merchandising enterprises. When the Saints left the area in 1846, Amos journeyed to visit them in their extremities in Winter Quarters. The wife of one former employee wrote: "In the early part of winter, my husband's old employer, Amos Davis, came along through our settlement with a load of goods from his store in Nauvoo. He stopped with us for a day. When he left, he gave us some tea, sugar, and coffee, which was highly appreciated and was a luxury in those hard times."[10]

In 1850 he journeyed to California with others lured by the Gold Rush. By 1853 he had returned to the Midwest and was residing in Michigan, and by 1858 he was again living in Illinois. Amos died on 22 March 1872 in Illinois at the age of fifty-eight.

Notes

1. His name on all preserved historical records appears as Amos Davis.

2. Autobiography of Nancy Tracy, typescript, p. 27, Special Collections, Harold B. Lee Library, Brigham Young University, Provo, Utah.

3. See *HC* 4:295.

4. *HC* 4:549.

5. *HC* 5:197.

6. *HC* 5:198.

7. See *HC* 5:200.

8. *HC* 6:80.

9. *HC* 6:520.

10. Tracy, p. 35.

Asa Dodds
D&C 75:15

Birth: *1793, New York.*

Soon after joining the Church in the 1830s, Asa Dodds accepted a call to preach the gospel from Ohio to Missouri with Orson Pratt. Orson wrote, "About the first of October [1831] . . . I started on foot for Ohio, in company with Asa Dodds, preaching by the way, as commanded of the Lord through the Prophet. Brother Dodds stopped in Indiana, but I continued my journey, although suffering much from the ague."[1]

Asa later returned to Ohio and by January 1832 was appointed by revelation to journey "unto the western countries": "And again, I say unto my servant Asa Dodds, and unto my servant Calves Wilson, that they also shall take their journey unto the western countries, and proclaim my gospel, even as I have commanded them" (D&C 75:15). It is not known if this mission was fulfilled by either man.

Eight days after the January 1832 revelation Asa was ordained a high priest by Hyrum Smith. Little is known of his whereabouts following the ordination. However, in 1850 he was residing in Farmington, Ohio, and working as a stonemason.[2]

Notes

1. Orson Pratt, *The Orson Pratt Journals*, comp. Elden J. Watson (Salt Lake City: Elden Jay Watson, 1975), p. 11.
2. See the Ohio federal census 1850.

DAVID D. DORT

D&C 124:132

Birth: 6 January 1793, Surry, Cheshire County, New Hampshire. Son of John Dort and Elishaba Briggs.
Death: 10 March 1841, Nauvoo, Hancock County, Illinois.

David Dort married Joseph Smith's cousin Mary Mack on 2 June 1813, when she was twenty years old. After her death he married her sister Fanny Mack. Both of his wives were daughters of Joseph Smith's maternal uncle and aunt, Stephen and Temperance Bond Mack.

David resided with his family in Gilsum, New Hampshire, in 1820, and in Pontiac, Michigan Territory, from 1822 to 1835. It was in Michigan that he was introduced to the Church by his aunt, Lucy Mack Smith. Lucy wrote that when she learned that her son Hyrum would be traveling in the Detroit vicinity, "I thought it would be a good opportunity to visit the family of my brother, General Mack. . . . I remained in this section of country about four weeks, during which time I labored incessantly for the truth's sake, and succeeded in gaining the hearts of many, among whom were David Dort and his wife."[1]

Thirty-eight-year-old David was baptized in 1831. He attended the Huron Michigan Branch until 5 May 1834, when he joined the Zion's Camp recruits from Michigan who were led by Hyrum Smith. After the camp was disbanded he returned to Pontiac before moving with his family to Kirtland in 1836.

David served on the Kirtland high council in 1837 and on the Far West high council in 1838, until religious persecution forced him to flee from Missouri to Illinois. Recognizing the suffering of other Latter-day Saints, he covenanted to assist fellow Saints in their forced exodus from Missouri.[2]

David and his family were among the first to settle in Nauvoo in 1839. In a revelation given to the Prophet Joseph Smith on 19 January 1841 he was called to serve on the Nauvoo high council (see D&C 124:131–32). Two months later, after faithfully serving on three high councils, David died at the age of forty-eight.

Notes

1. Lucy Mack Smith, *History of Joseph Smith by His Mother,* ed. Preston Nibley (Salt Lake City: Bookcraft, 1954), pp. 211, 216.

2. See *HC* 3:253.

RUGGLES EAMES
D&C 75:35

Birth: *Son of Benjamin Eames and Julia Bacon.*

Ruggles Eames, a resident of Medina, Ohio, joined the Church and was ordained a priest in his hometown in 1831. On 25 January 1832 he was one of twenty-four called by revelation to serve a mission. His senior companion was teenager Stephen Burnett, who had joined the Church ten months before Ruggles was baptized (see D&C 75:35).

It does not appear that either man accepted the call to serve. In March 1832, approximately six weeks later, the Prophet received another revelation calling Stephen to serve a mission with Eden Smith.

Ruggles withdrew his Church membership in 1832. The Iowa federal census of 1840 reveals that at that time he was residing in Van Buren County, Iowa. He declared himself to be married with two living children—a male child under five and a female child between five and ten—and to be the owner of three slaves.[1] By 1850 he had moved from Iowa, but his whereabouts were unknown. In contrast to Ruggles, his brother Ellis Eames remained faithful to the Church and was selected by Brigham Young to be in the vanguard pioneer company of 1847.[2]

Notes

1. See the Iowa federal census 1840.

2. See *CHC* 3:163.

JAMES FOSTER

D&C 124:138

Birth: *1 April 1775, Morgan County, Indiana.*
Death: *21 December 1841.*

In the summer of 1834, about a year after his baptism, James Foster marched with Zion's Camp. On the journey he became very ill, and the Prophet Joseph Smith suggested he stay behind to recover. James replied, "Brother Joseph, let me go with you [even] if I die on the road." The Prophet said, "I told him in the name of the Lord, that if that was his faith, to go on his bed in the wagon, and he should get better every day until he recovered, which was literally fulfilled."[1]

On 12 June 1834 the camp heard the "crack of a rifle": "Men came running from all directions in answer to the signal. When they had gathered, they were surprised to see Joseph Smith holding a squirrel he had shot. He explained that James Foster was ill and that he had shot the squirrel as a delicacy for the sick brother. Joseph Smith closed the incident by asking that the men pray for their friend."[2] James recovered and completed the march as the Prophet had said.

In 1837, at the age of sixty-two, James was chosen as one of the seven Presidents of the Seventies. His leadership in that quorum was most evident when the Kirtland poor were being organized to journey from Ohio to Missouri in 1838: "He declared that he saw a vision in which was shown unto him a company (he should think of about five hundred) starting from Kirtland and going up to Zion. That he saw them moving in order, encamping in order by the way, and that he knew thereby that it was the will of God that the quorum should go up in that manner. The Spirit bore record of the truth of his assertions for it rested down on the assembly in power."[3]

As the camp journeyed, difficulties arose over decisions made by James. For example, when Henry Herriman and James expelled Charles Wood from the camp, it was perceived that the two men acted without a majority of the Council being present. Later, on 26 September 1838, "Elder James Foster at a late hour proposed to disband and break up the camp in consequence of some [disturbing] rumors he had heard from the west which he said he believed."[4] His proposal was rejected after assurances of continued safety. Nevertheless, James left the camp and sought his own safety.

He settled with family members in DeWitt until religious persecution forced him to flee. Instead of gathering with the Saints to Nauvoo, he settled in Jacksonville, Illinois. It is believed that he did not have direct communication with his brethren for the next two years.

On 19 January 1841 the Lord reaffirmed through the Prophet Joseph Smith that James still held his position as a President of the Seventies (see D&C 124:138–39). However, within three months James answered charges of impropriety that had been made against him, "after which it was resolved that Elder James Foster continue his standing in the Church."5

James became very ill after the resolution and died on 21 December 1841 at the age of sixty-six. At an October conference in 1844 Brigham Young said that "the Seventies had dropped James Foster, and cut him off, and we need not take an action upon his case."6

Notes

1. *HC* 2:88.
2. James L. Bradley, *Zion's Camp 1834: Prelude to the Civil War* (Logan, Utah: James L. Bradley, 1990), p. 157.
3. *HC* 3:88–89.
4. *HC* 3:144.
5. *HC* 4:342.
6. *HC* 7:297.

ROBERT D. FOSTER
D&C 124:115–18

Birth: *14 March 1811, Braunston, Northampton County, England. Son of John and Jane Foster.*

Robert D. Foster rose to Church prominence when he journeyed with the Prophet Joseph Smith and Sidney Rigdon to the nation's capital in 1839 to seek redress for the wrongs the Saints had suffered in Missouri. On the journey the Prophet reproved him for his conduct toward "certain females."[1] Robert was next reproved by the Nauvoo high council for "lying, slandering the authorities of the Church, profane swearing, etc.," but after lengthy deliberation he was acquitted of all charges.[2] Freed from both the censure of the Prophet and the reproach of the high council, Robert became a prominent citizen in Nauvoo. He served as a regent of the University of Nauvoo, as a member of the Agricultural and Manufacturing Association, as surgeon-general of the Nauvoo Legion, and as the Hancock County magistrate.

However, in January 1841 the Lord chastised him for his unscrupulous actions, also giving him specific commandments:

> If my servant Robert D. Foster will obey my voice, let him build a house for my servant Joseph, according to the contract which he has made with him, as the door shall be open to him from time to time.
>
> And let him repent of all his folly, and clothe himself with charity; and cease to do evil, and lay aside all his hard speeches;
>
> And pay stock also into the hands of the quorum of the Nauvoo House, for himself and for his generation after him, from generation to generation;
>
> And hearken unto the counsel of my servants . . . and it shall be well with him forever and ever. Even so. Amen. (D&C 124:115–18.)

According to his own words, Robert did buy stock in the Nauvoo House and did assist Joseph in building a house: "If any man accuses me of exchanging Nauvoo stock for rags, &c., he is mistaken. I gave a thousand dollars to this house . . . and fifty dollars to the Relief Society, and some to Fullmer to get stone to build Joseph a house; and I mean to build Joseph a house, and you [the Nauvoo House committee] may build this, and I will help you. I mean to profit by this."[3] It is assumed that the financial issues between these two men were solved as the Prophet wrote that he "settled with Dr. Robert D. Foster, and gave him a note to balance all demands."[4]

Despite the settlement Robert continued to conflict with Church leaders. In 1844 Robert revealed himself to be an ardent opponent of the Prophet. In April 1844 the Prophet preferred charges against Robert before the high council "for unchristianlike conduct in general, for abusing my character privily, for throwing out slanderous insinuations against me, for conspiring against my peace and safety, for conspiring against my life, for conspiring against the peace of my family, and for lying."[5]

Robert was fined for gambling in April 1844, excommunicated for immorality and apostasy on the eighteenth of that month, and court-martialed in May by the Nauvoo Legion for "unofficer-like and un-becoming conduct."[6] In April he was also tried civilly "for resisting the authorities of the city" and refusing to come to the aid of Marshal John P. Greene. The marshal testified that Robert "swore by God they would see the Mayor [Joseph Smith] in hell" before he and his companions would submit to arrest. He was fined one hundred dollars and ap-pealed the case to the municipal court.[7]

The Prophet said of the rebellious Dr. Robert Foster, "The skirts of my garments were free from his (Foster's) blood; I had made the last overtures of peace to him; and then delivered him into the hands of God, and shook my garments against him as a testimony thereof."[8]

Robert became one of the "twelve apostles" of an apostate church organized by William and Wilson Law.[9] As such, he joined in the con-spiracy to murder Joseph Smith and coauthored an anti-Mormon newspaper, the *Nauvoo Expositor.* However, for a time Robert appeared reluctant to support the planned murder. In an affidavit Marshal John P. Greene testified that on approximately 27 May 1844 Robert said to him, "For God's sake, don't suffer that man, Joseph Smith, to go out of doors; for if he steps outside of the door his blood will be spilt."[10] On 27 May the Prophet recorded, "Robert D. Foster told some of the brethren (with tears in his eyes) that there was evil determined against me; and that there were some persons who were determined I should not go out of Carthage alive."[11] However, the die was cast.

On 7 June 1844, the very day the inflammatory *Expositor* was is-sued, Robert "wanted a private interview" with Joseph Smith. The Prophet declined the interview.[12] But as they spoke he put his hand on Robert's vest and said, "What have you concealed there?" Robert stam-mered, "It's my pistol."[13]

After the deaths of Joseph and Hyrum on 27 June 1844, Robert was ordered by nine women to leave the city: "Mrs. Hyrum Smith, Mrs. John Taylor [and others] waited upon Mr. R. D. Foster, and told him they would not bear his taunts and insults any longer. They or-dered him to leave the city forthwith. . . . These ladies having good reason to believe that Foster was accessory to the murder of their rela-tives, the Prophets, took liberty of pursuing this course towards him."[14] In fear, Robert fled from Nauvoo that evening.

Eventually he was charged with the murders, but unsubstantiated evidence led to his acquittal. Was he guilty? In conversation with

Abraham C. Hodge in 1845, he said, "I am the most miserable wretch that the sun shines upon. If I could recall eighteen months of my life I would be willing to sacrifice everything I have upon earth, my wife and child not excepted. I did love Joseph Smith more than any man that ever lived, if I had been present I would have stood between him and death." To this Hodge then asked, "Why did you do as you have done? You were accessory to his murder." Robert replied, "I know that, and I have not seen one moment's peace since that time. I know that Mormonism is true, and the thought of meeting (Joseph and Hyrum) at the bar of God is more awful to me than anything else."[15]

Notes

1. *HC* 6:440.
2. *HC* 4:239, 250.
3. *HC* 5:287.
4. *HC* 5:308.
5. *HC* 6:333.
6. *HC* 6:355.
7. *HC* 6:344–45.
8. *HC* 6:345.
9. Edward Stevenson, *Selections from the Autobiography of Edward Stevenson, 1820–1897 (1820–1846),* ed. Joseph Grant Stevenson (Provo, Utah: Stevenson's Genealogical Center, 1986), p. 99.
10. *HC* 6:522.
11. *HC* 6:413.
12. *HC* 6:430.
13. George Q. Cannon, *Life of Joseph Smith the Prophet* (Salt Lake City: Deseret Book Co., 1958), p. 484.
14. *HC* 7:176.
15. *HC* 7:513.

EDSON FULLER
D&C 52:28

Birth: *1809, New York.*

Edson Fuller, a carpenter by trade, was residing with his family in Chardon, Ohio, when he accepted baptism in 1831. He was called by revelation on 7 June 1831 to journey from Ohio to Jackson County, Missouri (see D&C 52:28). Apparently he didn't go to Missouri but remained in Ohio. According to historian Josiah Jones, he claimed that visions had called him to preach the gospel in Ohio.[1]

His preaching was accepted by a few of the local residents. Joel Johnson wrote that Edson Fuller and another Mormon elder, Harvey Whitlock, "preached upon the first principles of the Gospel. . . . This preaching filled me with astonishment, it being the first discourse that I had ever heard that corresponded with the New Testament."[2]

Josiah Jones described Edson's sometimes unusual preaching style: "E. Fullers while lying on the floor has been seen to jump up and cling to a beam for a while and then drop like a log on the floor."[3] Early Church members viewed this manner of preaching to be false and even claimed that Edson was possessed by false spirits. "Edson Fuller would fall and turn black in the face," penned Levi Hancock.[4]

One of his converts, David Johnson, desired to be "rebaptized for he felt dissatisfied with his former baptism, he having been baptized by Edson [Fuller], who, while baptizing him was under the influence of an evil spirit. It was a short time before Edson was cut off from the Church of Christ."[5]

In 1840 Edson was still residing at Chardon, where his household consisted of himself, his wife, two boys between five and ten, and one girl under five. He was employed as a farmer before moving to Grand Rapids, Michigan, prior to 1850.[6]

Notes

1. See Josiah Jones, "History of the Mormonites, Kirtland, 1831," *The Evangelist* 9 (1 June 1841): 135.

2. Joel Johnson, excerpts from autobiography (1802–1868), p. 3, Special Collections, Harold B. Lee Library, Brigham Young University, Provo, Utah.

3. Jones, p. 136.

4. Levi Hancock Autobiography, typescript, p. 27, Special Collections, Harold B. Lee Library, Brigham Young University, Provo, Utah.

5. Autobiography of Jared Carter, typescript, p. 12, Archives Division, Church Historical Department, The Church of Jesus Christ of Latter-day Saints, Salt Lake City, Utah. Spelling has been standardized.

6. See the Ohio federal census 1840.

DAVID FULLMER
D&C 124:132

Birth: *7 July 1803, Chillisquaque, Northumberland County, Pennsylvania. Son of Peter Fullmer and Susannah Zerfoss.*
Death: *21 October 1879, Salt Lake City, Salt Lake County, Utah.*

David Fullmer moved from a rented hotel in Plymouth, Pennsylvania, "on account of dullness in business," to Richland, Ohio, in the 1830s. In Richland he accepted the gospel and was baptized on 16 September 1836.[1] This singular event changed his life dramatically from that of financial entrepreneur to church and civil servant. He was soon ordained an elder and joined the beleaguered Saints in Missouri.

By September 1837 David was residing near Far West and by spring 1838 was living in Adam-ondi-Ahman. Religious persecution forced him to flee for safety at a time when he "had a severe sickness and was reduced nigh unto death."[2] His wife added, "Before he recovered, the mob came and ordered us to leave our homes and go away in 24 hours or they would come and burn our homes and destroy our property."[3]

David and his family found safety in Illinois, where his service to the Church and community was noteworthy. He was elected a city councilman and chosen to be on the high council and the council of Fifty before serving a mission in Michigan (see D&C 124:132).[4] His stay in Nauvoo was terminated because of mobocracy: "We were not permitted to enjoy our home long, for the mobs burned and otherwise destroyed our property and finally drove us from the state of Illinois."[5]

In 1846 David was presiding over the Saints' encampment in Iowa called Garden Grove. He recorded, "There were many poor among us who were almost destitute both of food and clothing."[6] Rumors of misconduct in Garden Grove caused Church leaders to disfellowship the entire Garden Grove branch. On 19 July 1847 Orson Hyde wrote from

Winter Quarters: "The High Council here did yesterday withdraw the hand of fellowship from the branch of the Church at Garden Grove, until a proper investigation can be had as to the real causes of the division and contentions that appear to exist in that branch."[7] David and other brethren from Garden Grove journeyed to Winter Quarters and appeared before the high council to answer the charges. The council's conclusions were set forth in a letter dated 8 August 1847. "Misrepresentations had been made . . . without foundation in truth," the letter stated, and full fellowship was restored.[8]

David journeyed on to the Salt Lake Valley in 1848 in Willard Richards's company. Once again he served his community and church. Most interesting was his service of five months as a counselor to Parley P. Pratt on a southern Utah expedition. Of this exploring expedition David wrote, "I was with this company for five months during the winter season, until we could dig our way out of the snow."[9]

Civically, David's talents were used to help draft a constitution for the provisional State of Deseret, and he also served as chief judge of the county court. He served in the territorial legislature, representing Salt Lake County in 1851, and was treasurer of the University of Deseret, Salt Lake City, and Salt Lake County. Due to his prominent civic positions he was often called upon to give speeches in public meetings on Temple Square. On one such occasion he said, "I would not give my experience in the gospel for all the gold and riches of the world, for it is worth much more to me."[10]

David's greatest contribution to the building of the West was his service as acting president of the Salt Lake Stake from 1852 to 1856, while President Daniel Spencer was on a mission in England. Daniel Spencer resumed his duties as president upon his return, and David became his counselor, as he had been prior to President Spencer's mission call. David served under President Spencer until poor health necessitated his release.[11] In 1870 he was ordained a patriarch.

David died on 21 October 1879 in Salt Lake City. He was buried in the Salt Lake Cemetery according to a request in his last will and testament: "That my body be deasently entombed but without ostentation." He added in his will, "I do not forgit my Love for President Bygham Young and the Saints."[12]

Notes

1. See Elvira Fullmer Hickenlooper, "Experiences in the Life of Rhoda Ann Fullmer" (n.p., n.d.), p. 1, in author's possession.
2. Autobiography of David Fullmer (n.d., n.p.), p. 1, in author's possession.
3. Hickenlooper, p. 2.
4. See HC 7:296.
5. Fullmer, p. 2.
6. Ibid., p. 3.
7. Journal History, 19 July 1847.
8. Ibid., 7 August 1847.
9. Fullmer, p. 4.
10. *Deseret News,* 3 May 1857.
11. See Fullmer, p. 4.
12. Will of David Fullmer, in author's possession.

ISAAC GALLAND
D&C 124:78–79

Birth: *15 May 1791, Somerset County, Pennsylvania. Son of Matthew Galland and Hannah Fenno.*
Death: *27 September 1858, Fort Madison, Lee County, Iowa.*

In his youth Isaac Galland was confined for a year in an adobe prison in Sante Fe by Mexican officials. Upon his release he quickly journeyed to Ohio and then to Indiana, announcing himself to be a doctor and a lawyer. At the outbreak of the War of 1812 he moved to Edgar County, Illinois, where locals claimed that he was a horse thief and engaged in "counterfeiting until driven out by authorities."[1] This view contrasts with that of Dr. C. F. Wahrer, former president of the Iowa Medical Association, who wrote:

[Isaac Galland] was a brilliant physician and was specially successful in the treatment of cholera, as well as the prevention of the epidemic. One of his contributions was a medicine chest or box about one foot cubic, on which was printed in red letters, "Dr. Isaac Galland's Family Medicines." This box contained the usual and ordinary remedies used by the doctors in those days, and was placed in nearly every cabin in his wide field of practice.[2]

Isaac's medical practice spread as he journeyed through the frontier. He traveled by canoe down the Mississippi River to Fort Madison and then on to Nashville, Iowa Territory—later known as Galland, Iowa, in honor of him. In Nashville he opened a fur trade with the Indians and learned to fluently speak their language and made a study of their habits. He is credited with establishing the first schoolhouse in Iowa Territory in 1830.[3]

Despite his pioneering efforts in Iowa, for safety reasons Isaac moved his family to Fort Edwards in Illinois during the Black Hawk War of 1832. At the fort he enlisted in the military and attained the rank of colonel before entering the political arena. When his notorious past was spoken of by his political opponent, Isaac said, "Yes, siree, I've been found guilty of most everything except hog stealing—and I never owned a hog."[4] His bid for the legislature was unsuccessful.

In Illinois he turned his attention to land speculation. He held claim as a trustee for the New York Land Company to extensive acreage in Commerce and vicinity and also held claims on land (119,000 acres) in Iowa called the "Half-Breed Tract." In 1839 he offered to sell the Latter-day Saints twenty thousand acres of the Half-Breed Tract (between the Des Moines and Mississippi Rivers) for two dollars an acre, to be paid in twenty annual payments without interest.

The Prophet Joseph Smith wrote from Liberty Jail on 25 March 1839: "It still seems to bear heavily on our minds that the Church would do well to secure to themselves the contract of the land which is proposed to them by Mr. Isaac Galland, and to cultivate the friendly feelings of that gentleman, inasmuch as he shall prove himself to be a man of honor and a friend to humanity."[5] Later that year, land was purchased from Isaac for approximately fifty thousand dollars in credit. Isaac later accepted the Saints' lands in Missouri as payment.[6]

As Isaac's acquaintance with the Mormons grew, so did his interest in their new religion. He was baptized on 3 July 1839 by Joseph Smith, confirmed at the water's edge by the Prophet, and ordained an elder about two hours later.[7] After two years he was appointed a land agent for the Church. On 25 August 1841 Joseph wrote, "I delegated my brother Hyrum and Dr. Isaac Galland to go east and negotiate for lands."[8] They arrived in Pennsylvania in March 1841, but because of illness Hyrum remained only a couple of weeks. This unexpected change in plans left the responsibility of land exchanges to Isaac. This proved to be a fiasco. The Prophet wrote to Isaac on 19 January 1842:

> I have become embarrassed in my operations to a certain extent, and partly from a presentation of notes, which you, as my agent, had given for lands purchased in the eastern states, they having been sent to me. I have been obliged to cash them, and having no returns from you to meet those demands, or even the trifling expenses of your outfit, it has placed me in rather an unpleasant situation. . . .
>
> And now, sir, . . . I think we had better have a settlement, and if I am owing you, I will pay you as soon as I can, and if you owe me, I shall only expect the same in return, for it is an old and trite maxim, that short reckonings make long friends.[9]

Isaac returned to Nauvoo and met in council with the Prophet on 2 February 1842. The last known interaction between Joseph Smith and Isaac is a letter dated 11 March 1843, in which Isaac expressed his outrage at John C. Bennett's anti-Mormon lectures and the arrest of Porter Rockwell.[10]

Isaac resided in Keokuk County, Iowa, from 1842 to 1853. In 1851 he ran for the legislature on the "Possum" ticket but once again was unsuccessful. During the last decade of his life he was "a firm and zealous believer in Spiritualism, and was heard to say that Joe Smith was the dupe of his own impostures; that Smith was simply a so-called spiritual medium."[11] In April 1853 he journeyed from Iowa to Sacramento, California. After learning in 1856 that a lawsuit against the New York Land Company had netted him eleven thousand dollars, Isaac returned to Iowa. His last two years were spent among friends in Fort Madison. To "his dying breath, Galland felt the Mormons cheated him by non-payment of money owed for the land he purportedly sold them."[12]

Isaac died in 1858 in Fort Madison at the age of sixty-seven. His son, Washington Galland, a member of the Iowa legislature, was instrumental in placing a beautiful marble monument over his remains.[13]

At the time of his death Isaac was writing a book on Indian life, manners, and customs. His manuscript was published posthumously in 1869 in *Annals of Iowa*. His other publications include *The Western Adventurer and Herald of the Upper Mississippi*, the second newspaper printed in Iowa; *Galland's Iowa Emigrant: Containing a Map and General Description of Iowa Territorys* in 1840; and a seventeen-page pamphlet, *Dr. Galland's Reply to Various Falsehoods, Misstatements, and Misrepresentations Concerning the Latter Day Saints, Reproachfully called Mormons* in July 1841.

Notes

A portrait of Isaac Galland hangs in the Iowa Historical Society building in Iowa City, Iowa. The painting was done by Charles Caleb Bingham and donated by a relative to the museum. The original is 28" x 32" and was painted in 1830 at a cost of one hundred dollars.

1. "Keokuk's First Citizen Was a Doctor!" *Keokuk (Iowa) Shoppers Free Press* (10 January 1979): 2.

2. Ibid.

3. The site of the old school is now covered with water backed up by the Keokuk dam, but a log replica was built on the bluff by the Lee County Schoolmasters Association.

4. "A Man of Conflicting Aspect—That was the Famous Dr. Galland," *Keokuk (Iowa) Daily Grate City* (13 April 1960).

5. *HC* 3:298.

6. See Lyndon W. Cook, "Isaac Galland-Mormon Benefactor," *BYU Studies* 19 (Spring 1979): 274–77.

7. See Edward Stevenson, *Selections from the Autobiography of Edward Stevenson, 1820–1897 (1820–1846)*, ed. Joseph Grant Stevenson (Provo, Utah: Stevenson's Genealogical Center, 1986), p. 59.

8. *HC* 4:406.

9. *HC* 4:499–500.

10. See letter of Isaac Galland to Joseph Smith, 11 March 1843, Archives Division, Church Historical Department, The Church of Jesus Christ of Latter-day Saints, Salt Lake City, Utah.

11. John M. Madsen, "Study of Dr. Isaac Galland" (n.p., 18 August 1964), p. 10, Special Collections, Harold B. Lee Library, Brigham Young University, Provo, Utah.

12. "Keokuk's First Citizen," p. 2.

13. Madsen, p. 11.

JESSE GAUSE
D&C 81: Introduction

Birth: *1785 (possibly 1784), East Marlborough, Chester County, Pennsylvania.[1] Son of William Gause and Mary Beverly.*

In 1806, as a young man in his twenties, Jesse Gause was received into membership of the Society of Friends (Quakers). During the next twenty-three years he actively participated in Quaker life and taught at the Friends' school in Wilmington, Delaware. On 30 January 1829 he resigned from the Society of Friends and soon affiliated with the United Society of Believers in Christ's Second Appearing (Shakers). He settled in the Shaker community of North Union, Ohio, about fifteen miles from Kirtland.

It is not known when Mormon missionaries contacted Jesse Gause. On 8 March 1832 the Prophet wrote, "Chose this day and ordained brother Jesse Gause and Broth Sidney [Rigdon] to be my counsellors of the ministry of the presidency of the high Priesthood."[2] Both men were simply called "counselors," but Jesse may rightfully have been the first counselor to the Prophet Joseph Smith—he was eight years older than Sidney Rigdon, and twenty years older than the Prophet. One week after Jesse was chosen as a counselor, the Prophet received a revelation confirming him in the Presidency and giving further direction to his office and calling (see D&C 81: Introduction).

Jesse functioned in his calling for only a brief six months, in the spring and summer of 1832. In April 1832 he accompanied the Prophet Joseph, Newel K. Whitney, and Peter Whitmer Jr. to Jackson County, Missouri. Upon returning to Kirtland he was called on a mission with Zebedee Coltrin on 1 August 1832. On their missionary journey they traveled to North Union. There Jesse petitioned his wife, Minerva, to unite with him and with Mormonism. She refused. An elder of the Shaker community, Matthew Houston, wrote a letter to Seth Y. Wells about Jesse's vain attempt to reunite with his wife:

> I presume you was acquainted with Jesse Gause from Hancock he was here a few days since after his wife Minerva—she utterly refused being his slave any longer—he had to go away without her. altho he

tryed what the law could do for him he was very much inraged threatened to take away Minerva's child—she presented it to him but he went away without it and her—he is yet a Mormon—& and is second to the Prophet or Seer—Joseph Smith—this state of exaltation may tend to steady him or keep him away from us a little longer—for which I am heartily glad for he is certainly the meanest of men.[3]

Jesse left North Union discouraged and reportedly feeling his sorrow "to his gizzard."[4]

He continued his journey with Elder Coltrin until illness caused Coltrin to desire to return to Kirtland. After praying the two men "parted in the fellowship of the gospel of our Lord and Savior Jesus Christ."[5] It is believed that Jesse Gause did continue his journey to the East, but his whereabouts after 1832 are unknown.[6]

In September 1836 his brother was appointed legal guardian of the orphaned "children of Jesse Gause late of the County of Chester deceased." Nearly forty years later, his sister Hannah said that Jesse "died away from his family when [his son Owen, born 1825] was a little boy, and no record seems to have been found."[7]

The name Jesse Gause does not appear in pre-1981 editions of the Doctrine and Covenants. In section 81 of the earliest written record of the Doctrine and Covenants, the name of Jesse Gause has been crossed out and Frederick G. Williams's name written above it. All published copies of this revelation list Frederick G. Williams as the one to whom the revelation was directed.

Notes

1. See D. Michael Quinn, "Jesse Gause: Joseph Smith's Little Known Counselor," *Brigham Young Studies* 23 (Fall 1983): 487; surname originally spelled *Goss* and pronounced like "house."

2. Kirtland Revelation Book, p. 10, as cited in Robert J. Woodford, "Jesse Gause, Counselor to the Prophet," *BYU Studies* 15 (Spring 1975): 363.

3. Letter of Matthew Houston to Seth Y. Wells, 10 August 1832, North Union, Ohio, as cited in Woodford, p. 364.

4. Ibid.

5. Zebedee Coltrin diary, 20 August 1832, as cited in Quinn, p. 491.

6. According to some historians Jesse Gause apostatized from the Church and was excommunicated on 3 December 1832. See Lyndon W. Cook, *The Revelations of the Prophet Joseph Smith* (Salt Lake City: Deseret Book Co., 1985), p. 172.

7. As cited in Quinn, p. 492.

ALGERNON SIDNEY GILBERT
D&C 53; 57:6, 8–10; 61:7, 12; 64:18–19, 26; 82:11; 90:35

Birth: *28 December 1789, New Haven, New Haven County, Connecticut.*[1]
Son of Eli Gilbert and Lydia Hemingway.
Death: *29 June 1834, near Fishing River, Clay County, Missouri.*

Algernon Sidney Gilbert was reared in Huntington, Connecticut, twelve miles west of New Haven. Family tradition suggests that he was college-educated in the East.[2] By 1817 he was a resident of Painesville, Ohio, where he owned a small store. From 1820 to 1827, newspaper advertisements reveal that Sidney was an entrepreneur, buying and selling properties in Ohio and Michigan, and that he had commercial interests in trading centers near Lake Ontario and the Erie Canal.

By 1827 Sidney and Newel K. Whitney had entered a mercantile partnership and opened a small store under the name of N. K. Whitney and Company in Kirtland, Ohio. It was while engaged in this business enterprise that both men accepted Mormonism in 1830.

Sidney lived only four years after his baptism. During these years the Lord recognized his talents and the unique contribution he would make to the Church: "I have heard your prayers. . . . Take upon you mine ordination, even that of an elder, . . . and also to be an agent unto this church. . . . Take your journey with my servants." (D&C 53:1, 3–5.)

He was ordained an elder on 6 June 1831, and fourteen days later left Kirtland in company with the Prophet to journey to Independence, Missouri. After he arrived the Lord said in a revelation: "Let my servant Sidney Gilbert plant himself in this place, and establish a store, that he may sell goods without fraud. . . . And thus provide for my saints, that my gospel may be preached unto those who sit in darkness and in the region and shadow of death." (D&C 57: 8, 10.) In obedience Sidney established a branch store of dry goods and groceries in Independence for the blessing of "the affairs of the poor" (D&C 82:12).

Some of Sidney's most noteworthy contributions were his personal handwritten copies of sections of the Doctrine and Covenants: sections 20, 22, 42, 50, 51, 53, 57, 61, 63, 64, 72, 76, 83, 86, 87, 88, 89, and 91, plus Matthew 24 and biblical notes. The consistent theme of the sections centers on governing the Church and keeping the commandments of God. It is presumed that these sections would be most valued by Sidney as he served as one of the seven presiding high priests in Missouri. His handwritten copies of sections 22, 57, and 61 are the earliest known copies of these sections.

A difficulty arose in Church circles over a letter Sidney wrote to Mormon leaders in Kirtland. Unfortunately, the letter is not extant and only the reaction of Orson Hyde and Hyrum Smith, as recorded in a letter to the Saints, remains: "Brother Gilbert's letter of December 10th, has been received and read attentively, and the low, dark, and blind insinuations, which were in it, were not received by us as from the fountain of light, though his claims and pretensions to holiness were great."[3]

In a revelation to the Prophet Joseph Smith on 8 March 1833 the Lord said, "I am not well pleased with my servant . . . Sidney Gilbert" (D&C 90:35). Although rebuked severely by both his brethren and the Lord, Sidney remained in the Church.

When violent mob action erupted in Independence, the brick portion of Sidney's home was demolished and the windows were broken. The doors of the Gilbert and Whitney store were split open and goods tossed into the street. On 4 November 1833 Sidney was arrested and imprisoned on pretended charges of assault. Seven days later he fled to Clay County. The only known possessions he took with him were his Bible and the revelations of the Doctrine and Covenants that he had copied.

A month after Sidney's escape, the Lord instructed him through the Prophet to not sell his store in Independence (see D&C 101:96). Sidney was obedient even though he was now residing in Liberty, Missouri. He built a new store in Liberty for the purpose of caring for the needs of the Saints. Parley P. Pratt described an encounter with him:

> "Well," says he, "brother Parley, you certainly look too shabby to start a journey; you must have a new suit; I have got some remnants left that will make you a coat," etc. A neighboring tailoress and two or three other sisters happened to be present on a visit, and hearing the conversation, exclaimed, "Yes, brother Gilbert, you find the stuff and we'll make it up for him." This arranged, I now lacked only a cloak; this was also furnished by brother Gilbert.[4]

A further example of Sidney's generosity was his opening of his home and lands to the men of Zion's Camp. A few days after their arrival, thirteen men and one woman had died from cholera. Five of the deaths occurred at his home, and on 29 June 1834, cholera took the life of Algernon Sidney Gilbert. He was rolled in a quilt and buried with the others who had succumbed.[5]

B. H. Roberts eulogized the contributions of Gilbert but added, "He was once heard to say, when informed that he had been called to preach the gospel, that he 'would rather die than go forth to preach the gospel to the Gentiles.'" According to Elder Roberts, this comment "did not arise out of any lack of faith in the truth of God's great latter-day work, but from a . . . lack of confidence in his ability to preach." But Sidney's death led Heber C. Kimball to say, "The Lord took him at his word."[6]

Notes

1. Algernon Sidney Gilbert's Holy Bible, 1831, in possession of Geraldine Hamblin Bangerter, Alpine, Utah.

2. See Geraldine Hamblin Bangerter and Susan Easton Black, *My Servant Algernon Sidney Gilbert: Provide for My Saints (D&C 57:10)* (Salt Lake City: Rollins, Hamblin and Bangerter Families, 1989), p. 2.

3. *HC* 1:319.

4. Parley P. Pratt, *Autobiography of Parley P. Pratt*, ed. Parley P. Pratt Jr. (Salt Lake City: Deseret Book Co., 1985), p. 108.

5. See Bangerter and Black, p. 40.

6. *CHC* 1:360 n. 7; see also *HC* 2:118–19.

JOHN GOULD
D&C 100:14

Birth: *11 May 1808, Ontario, Canada. Son of Seth E. Gould.*
Death: *9 May 1851, Cooley's Mill, Pottawattamie County, Iowa.*

In 1831 John Gould was presiding over a Free Will Baptist congregation in Spafford, New York: "In the year 1831 [Spafford] was struck by the proselyting wave of the newly established Mormon religion, and a large share of its members, led by their pastor, Elder Gould, was carried from the fold of the church into the embraces of the new faith. . . . It was not possible for the church to recover from such an exodus of membership. The church building was deserted."[1] John journeyed with members of his former congregation to Kirtland to be with the Prophet Joseph Smith.

In the fall of 1833 he and Orson Hyde were sent with instructions from the Prophet to the Saints in Missouri. Of this assignment Orson Hyde wrote:

> We started on foot with our valises on our backs, a distance of about one thousand miles. We travelled about forty miles per day through a sickly fever and ague country, swimming rivers, and pushing our clothes over on a log or raft before us. We arrived in Jackson County about the beginning of the Saints' troubles there [September 1833]. We delivered our letters and documents, and were sometimes surrounded by the mob, who threatened to wring our heads off from our shoulders. Several little skirmishes took place while there, and some few were killed and wounded.[2]

On 12 October 1833 the Prophet and Sidney Rigdon received a revelation in Perrysburg, New York, acknowledging the Lord's awareness of the persecuted missionaries: "Thy brethren, my servants Orson Hyde and John Gould, are in my hands; and inasmuch as they keep my commandments they shall be saved" (D&C 100:14). They returned unharmed to Kirtland on 25 November 1833.[3]

In March 1834 John accompanied the Prophet to western New York, seeking volunteers for Zion's Camp. "We proceeded on our journey," wrote Joseph Smith, ". . . leaving Brothers Gould and Matthews to prepare and gather up the companies in the churches in that region, and meet us in Ohio, ready to start for Zion on the first of May."[4] John not only helped in recruitment but also in spreading the gospel. His missionary labors were briefly described in the *Messenger and Advocate:*

> [Warren A. Cowdery] informs us that an addition of about 20 members has recently been made to a small church of 13, raised up in Grove, Allegany Co. by elder J. Gould; and that the prospects are flattering.[5]
>
> A new church has been recently raised up by the instrumentality of Elders Gould and Babcock in Woodhull, in Steuben co. consisting of six members, represented by J. Gould, Elder.

The church in Grove, Allegany co. consists of eighteen members, two of whom have been added since last conference, reported by J. Gould, Elder.[6]

In August 1835 "John Gould gave his testimony in favor of the [Doctrine and Covenants] . . . and acknowledge[d] it as the doctrine and covenants of [his] faith."[7] Two months later, the tenor of his faith was tested. Reynolds Cahoon preferred charges against him "for making expressions calculated to injure the cause we have espoused, and manifesting a strong dissatisfaction with the teachings of the Presidency." The accuser and defendant agreed the matter should be discussed, "by which all difference of feeling was allayed."[8] John confessed before the Kirtland high council and was forgiven.

At age twenty-eight John was chosen as one of the Seven Presidents of the Seventies. He served in the presidency for only five months. Nathan Tanner wrote that during these months,

> an article was drawn up by Brother Goold . . . and presented to the Seventies assembled in the upper story of the Temple for their sanction. It declared that the Seventies disapproved of the circulating of Kirtland money in any way, or the passing of it; and that they would disfellowship, disapprove of, and raise their hand against all such parties whoever or wherever they may be. This article was to be printed and sent out the next day to the four winds.[9]

However, when the article proposed by him was presented, it was rejected as being a vote "against the Heads of the Church."[10]

On 3 September 1837 John Gould was "objected to" as a President of the Seventies.[11] He was dropped from the quorum. He remained associated with the Saints and united with them in Nauvoo. He was residing in Cooley's Mill, Iowa, at the time of his death in 1851, two days before his forty-third birthday.

Notes

1. As cited in Everett Ellsworth Roundy, *The Roundy Family in America* (Dedham, Mass.: Everett Ellsworth Roundy, 1942), pp. 215–16.

2. As cited in ibid.

3. See *LDS Biographical Encyclopedia* 1:191.

4. *HC* 2:42.

5. *Messenger and Advocate* 1 (December 1834): 45.

6. *Messenger and Advocate* 1 (April 1835): 101.

7. *HC* 2:246.

8. *HC* 2:286.

9. Autobiography of Nathan Tanner, typescript, p. 55, Special Collections, Harold B. Lee Library, Brigham Young University, Provo, Utah.

10. Ibid.

11. *HC* 2:510.

OLIVER GRANGER

D&C 117: Introduction; 117:12–13

Birth: *7 February 1794, Phelps, Ontario County, New York. Son of Pierce Granger and Clarissa Trumble.*
Death: *25 August 1841, Kirtland, Lake County, Ohio.*

At age thirty-three Oliver Granger lost most of his eyesight due to extreme cold and exposure. In spite of his handicap he was able to serve as the sheriff of Ontario County, New York, and as a colonel in the New York militia. He was a licensed exhorter in the local Methodist congregation before reading the Book of Mormon in 1830.[1] Oliver recounted to his daughter, Sarah Granger Kimball, a heavenly visitation that led to his conversion to Mormonism. Sarah stated, "My father was told by a person who said his name was Moroni, that the Book of Mormon, about which his mind was exercised, was a true record of great worth." Moroni instructed Oliver to testify of the truthfulness of the Book of Mormon and prophesied that if he would so testify, he "should hereafter be ordained to preach the everlasting Gospel to the children of men." The angel instructed him to offer a prayer while kneeling. As he did so, "Moroni and another personage knelt with him by the bedside. Moroni repeated words and instructed [Oliver] to repeat them after him."[2]

Oliver was baptized and ordained an elder at Sodus, New York, by Brigham Young and his brother, Joseph Young. He moved to Kirtland to be with the Saints in 1833. In Kirtland he served on the high council and labored on the temple before fleeing from religious persecution to Missouri in 1838.

One month after Oliver arrived in Missouri, the Prophet received a revelation instructing him to return to Kirtland and represent the First Presidency in settling the Church debts (see D&C 117:12–15). "As I was driven away from Kirtland without the privilege of settling my business," wrote Joseph Smith, "I had . . . employed Colonel Oliver Granger as my agent, to close all my affairs in the east."[3]

He performed this assignment with such satisfaction to the creditors that one wrote, "Oliver Granger's management in the arrangement of the unfinished business of people that have moved to the Far West, in redeeming their pledges and thereby sustaining their integrity, has been truly praiseworthy, and has entitled him to my highest esteem, and ever grateful recollection."[4]

Oliver eventually settled in Commerce, Illinois, where he was again appointed to be a land agent. A letter signed by the First Presidency on 13 May 1839 attested to his business skills: "We have always found President Oliver Granger to be a man of the most strict integrity and moral virtue; and in fine, to be a man of God. . . . We have entrusted vast business concerns to him, which have been managed skilfully to the support of our characters and interest as well as that of the Church."[5]

Oliver purchased lands in Montrose, Iowa, in the name of the Church before being sent to Kirtland in 1840 as the Prophet's attorney-in-fact to cancel his outstanding debts, "free the Lords House from all incumbrances," and look after other affairs of the Church.[6]

The only known contrary statement about Oliver's behavior in Kirtland is found in the writings of Benjamin F. Johnson: "[Oliver] was a man of eminent capability, but had suffered greatly by intemperance, which habit, after obtaining money, overcame him again, and so the money was squandered. He took dropsy and soon died."[7] Oliver Granger died in 1841 in Kirtland at the age of forty-seven. His funeral was "attended by a vast concourse of people from the neighboring towns."[8]

Notes

1. See *HC* 4:408.
2. As cited in Augusta Joyce Crocheron, *Representative Women of Deseret* (Salt Lake City: J. C. Graham and Co., 1884), p. 24.
3. *HC* 3:164.

4. *HC* 3:174.

5. *HC* 3:350.

6. Joseph Smith to Oliver Granger, July 1840, as cited in Lyndon W. Cook and Milton V. Backman Jr., eds., *Kirtland Elders' Quorum Record 1836–1841* (Provo, Utah: Grandin Book Co., 1985), p. 62.

7. Benjamin F. Johnson, *My Life's Review* (Independence, Mo.: Zion's Printing and Publishing Co., 1947), p. 85.

8. *HC* 4:409.

SELAH J. GRIFFIN
D&C 52:32; 56:5–6

Birth: *17 March 1799, Redding, Fairfield County, Connecticut. Son of Joseph Griffin Jr. and Eunice Hamilton.*

Selah J. Griffin resided in Morgan, Ohio, before moving to Kirtland, where he worked as a blacksmith and served the community in 1827 as a supervisor of highways.[1] He united with the Church during the early days in Kirtland and was ordained an elder on 6 June 1831 by Joseph Smith.[2] The day following his ordination Selah was called by revelation to journey to Jackson County, Missouri, with Newel Knight: "And let my servants Newel Knight and Selah J. Griffin both be ordained, and also take their journey" (D&C 52:32). Newel Knight was unable to fulfill the mission call and so Selah was given Thomas B. Marsh as a missionary companion (see D&C 56:5–6).

It appears that their initial missionary journey was successful in some respects as they traveled through Ohio, Indiana, and Illinois, but it seemed to lack focus. "Many believed our testimony," wrote Elder Marsh, "but we did not wait to baptize any."[3] At a conference in Jackson County on 24 August 1831, Bishop Edward Partridge requested that Selah "tarry a while after arriving in this land if the Spirit so direct him."[4] Being so directed, Selah moved with his family to Jackson County. Unfortunately, there he suffered with his fellow Saints from persecution and was driven from his home by mobs in November 1833. He penned, "In November they Strip us of guns and Drive us a crost the river in to Clay County the lose of property susstained in Jackson County [$150.00] dollars of book a counts Lost worth [$200.50] of Crops and two guns worth 75 dollars hous and Black Smith Shop and tools to the amount of thre hundred Dollars Lost in the hol amounted was Seven hundred And Seventy five dollars is My los Buy the mob."[5]

He journeyed to Kirtland to report on conditions in Missouri and was noted by W. W. Phelps to be "in a good spirit."[6] In Kirtland he received his anointing, elder's license, and ordination to the office of a seventy in 1836. He returned to Missouri, true to the faith, and joined with the Saints in Caldwell County. It was the Extermination Order of 1838 that again forced his expulsion. In an affidavit filed on 6 January 1840 he itemized personal property losses: "I was obliged to leave hom which I had paid the govement for Being a Blacksmith i had five hundred dollars of Book a counts taken from me and one Set of Blacksmith toals worth on hundred Forty akers of land in Calwell County The improvements thare or worth fore hundred dollars."[7]

Selah never recouped his losses in Missouri. Angered by the governmental affront and by the persecution he had suffered for his religious conviction, Selah weighed the cost and concluded that the price of faithfulness was too great. He settled in Knox, Illinois, in 1840 and apparently was still living in the area years later, when other Latter-day Saints fled to the Rockies.

Notes

1. See Lyndon W. Cook, *The Revelations of the Prophet Joseph Smith* (Salt Lake City: Deseret Book Co., 1985), p. 76.

2. See ibid.

3. Thomas B. Marsh, "History of Thomas Baldwin Marsh," *Millennial Star* 26 (11 June 1864): 376.

4. As cited in Donald Q. Cannon and Lyndon W. Cook, eds., *Far West Record: Minutes of The Church of Jesus Christ of Latter-day Saints, 1830–1844* (Salt Lake City: Deseret Book Co., 1983), p. 14.

5. As cited in Clark V. Johnson, ed., *Mormon Redress Petitions: Documents of the 1833–1838 Missouri Conflict* (Provo, Utah: Religious Studies Center, Brigham Young University, 1992), p. 454.

6. Letter of William Phelps, 11 September 1835, Archives Division, Church Historical Department, The Church of Jesus Christ of Latter-day Saints, Salt Lake City, Utah.

7. As cited in Johnson, p. 454.

THOMAS GROVER
D&C 124:132

Birth: *22 July 1807, Whitehall, Washington County, New York. Son of Thomas Grover Sr. and Polly Spaulding.*
Death: *20 February 1886, Farmington, Davis County, Utah.*

Thomas Grover was reared by his mother and his stepfather, David Young, in a canal town near Lake Champlain, a lake on the border of New York and Vermont. By age twelve he was a cabin boy on a barge on Lake Erie and in later years was a captain of a freighter vessel that traversed the waterways from southern Quebec to New York City and westward to Buffalo.

According to family tradition he was a Methodist preacher when he first heard Joseph Smith preach. After listening to Joseph, he abandoned his Methodist belief and was baptized in September 1834 by Warren A. Cowdery.[1] Less than a year later he sold his farm for five hundred dollars and moved to Kirtland. "If ever God sent a man he sent you," remarked the Prophet as he greeted Thomas in Kirtland. "I want every dollar . . . that you have got in the world."[2] The money, freely proffered, was used to purchase building materials needed for the construction of the Kirtland Temple.

Thomas's faithfulness to gospel truths led to his call to the high councils in Kirtland, Far West, Nauvoo (see D&C 124:131–32), Cutler's Park, Salt Lake, and Farmington. In Nauvoo his service to the Church and community was particularly noteworthy—he was called to be captain and an aide-de-camp on the general staff of the Nauvoo Legion, personal bodyguard to the Prophet, and missionary to Mississippi, Michigan, and Canada. Although he was extremely ill when called to serve in Canada, the Prophet promised him: "Brother Grover you are very feeble but God will bless you and you shall be blessed and strengthened from this very hour."[3] The promise was fulfilled. Another promise given to him by Hyrum Smith in a patriarchal blessing was also fulfilled: "Your name will be written in the chronicles of your brethren and perpetuated by your posterity unto the latest generation."[4]

Thomas was among the first to leave Nauvoo in February 1846. While crossing the Mississippi River on a flatboat, most of his possessions were lost or damaged. Brigham Young described the scene: "A filthy wicked man squirted some tobacco juice into the eyes of one of the oxen attached to Thomas Grover's wagon, which immediately plunged into the river, dragging another ox with him, and as he was going overboard he tore off one of the side boards which caused the water to flow into the flatboat."[5] The generosity of other pioneers enabled Thomas to proceed across Iowa and join the vanguard company of pioneers in 1847.

Thomas is remembered for advertising his willingness to ferry pioneers across the Platte River. One sign read, "The ferry good and safe maned by experienced men black Smithing horse and ox shoing done all so a wheel right."[6] By mid-July he closed this venture and divided the profits equally among the Latter-day Saints.

Thomas arrived in the Salt Lake Valley in October 1847 and settled his family first in Centerville and later in Farmington. At the request of Brigham Young he left Farmington to settle disturbances among the Saints in California. According to his son, some of his adventures in California involved Indians and gold: "While camping in Lower California the Indians stole their horses and they had to walk to Sacramento, depending on what game they could find for food. Gold having been discovered in California, he joined in mining until 1849 when he returned to his family in Salt Lake Valley in connection with Thomas Rhodes, he turned over to the church one hundred lbs. of Gold."[7] According to family tradition, he gave five hundred dollars for the construction of the Salt Lake Temple. The gold Thomas kept for his personal use helped him buy 150 cattle.

Through his means and ingenuity Thomas became prosperous. During the 1850s he was prominent in civic affairs, serving as a representative of Davis County in the Utah legislature, a member of the Counties and Public Works Committee, a member of the Deseret Agricultural and Manufacturing Society, and a probate judge for Davis County.

An unusual situation developed in December 1863 that led to his being disfellowshipped from the Church "until he makes satisfaction [for] . . . refusing to pay . . . a small debt due for school teaching, in wheat, flour or corn."[8] It is assumed that "satisfaction" was made, for within the month the First Presidency stayed in Thomas's home and dedicated the new Farmington chapel, built on land he had donated.

In 1887, when a marshal sought his arrest in his own home, Thomas exclaimed, "Get me Brother Joseph's sword . . . and watch while I cut this man's head off!" Biographer Mark Grover writes: "The prospect of the sword in the hand of Thomas . . . a large, powerful and firm-speaking man . . . was admittedly frightening. At any rate, the stranger quickly departed . . . without making his arrest."[9]

On 16 February 1887 Thomas attended sacrament meeting in the Farmington ward. As the closing prayer ended, "Thomas suddenly raised his hand and said: 'Wait a minute, Bishop.' Then he added, that he could not go home until he had borne testimony that the Gospel was true and that Joseph Smith was a true Prophet of God."[10]

By Thursday of that week he had died from pneumonia. His daughter eulogized: "My father was loved by all who knew him. He never spoke evil of anyone; he did not boast, and he did not take honor unto himself. Many times he has divided his last meal with a sufferer. His word was as good as his bond. He could neither be bought nor sold."[11]

Notes

1. See autobiography of Joseph Holbrook, typescript, p. 69, Special Collections, Harold B. Lee Library, Brigham Young University, Provo, Utah.

2. As cited in Mark Grover, "The Life of Thomas Grover, Utah Pioneer" (n.p., n.d.), p. 10, in author's possession.

3. As cited in ibid., pp. 19–20.

4. Patriarchal blessing in author's possession. As I wrote to the posterity of those mentioned by name in the Doctrine and Covenants the greatest response came from the Thomas Grover family.

5. *HC* 7:582.

6. This sign is located in the Fort Casper Museum in Wyoming.

7. Grover, p. 32.

8. As cited in ibid., p. 40.

9. As cited in ibid., p. 43. The Prophet Joseph Smith gave him a sword that is now in the hall of relics at the Utah State Capitol.

10. *LDS Biographical Encyclopedia* 4:142.

11. As cited in ibid., p. 141.

LEVI WARD HANCOCK
D&C 52:29; 124:138

Birth: *7 April 1803, Springfield, Hampden County, Massachusetts. Son of Thomas Hancock and Amy Ward.*
Death: *10 June 1882, Washington, Washington County, Utah.*

Levi Ward Hancock attributed much of his unusual youthful interest in religion to his mother, who taught him that "I must love God, or he would let the devil have me; this would frighten me so much I could not sleep nights." He claimed, "At the age of four I began to call upon the Lord seriously."[1]

Although his prayers were fervent, the need to improve his family's economic plight soon crowded his thoughts. He opened his first hand-crafted furniture shop at age fourteen. Stories of prosperity in Ohio led him to close shop and venture to the Western Reserve, where by age nineteen he was an accomplished carpenter and had enough money to purchase his father's property in New York: "The whole land of my Fathers had now become mine save about sixty dollars and no brother could say but what I came honestly by it."[2]

In the fall of 1830 Levi's brother Alvah asked him if he had heard the news. "What news?" asked Levi. "Why," said he, "four men have come and have brought a book with them that they call history and a record of the people that once inhabited this land. . . . They lay hands on those they baptize and bestow on them the Holy Ghost." As Alvah said these words, Levi "gathered faith and there seemed to fall on me something pleasant and delightful. It seemed like a wash of something warm took me in the face and ran over my body which gave me a feeling I cannot describe. The first word I said was, 'It is the truth, I can feel it.' "[3]

Levi was baptized on 16 November 1830 by Parley P. Pratt after assuring Parley that he "believed that Jesus is the son of God, and felt within my heart that the things he had told us were the truth."[4]

After his baptism he "preached from place to place where the folks were well acquainted with me."[5] In a revelation given through the Prophet on 7 June 1831 he was commanded to journey to Missouri with Zebedee Coltrin (see D&C 52:29).

In Jackson County, Levi helped construct the Gilbert and Whitney store and the printing office. Returning to Kirtland, he discovered that "all my property was scattered to the four winds, tools and all for pretended claims, where I owed not one cent justly."[7] He paid the false claims by selling his property and working at his painting and carpentry trade until the Prophet sent for him. In his journal he penned, "I did all I could do to hold up that good man. My heart would ache for him. He had to stand against thousands of his pretended friends seeking to overthrow him. It was terrible the abuse he suffered."[8]

Although subjected to abuse himself, Levi shared his time and talents with the Saints. On 29 March 1833, at age thirty, he married Clarissa Reed, and within a year he was approached by the Prophet, who asked, "Now that you have a wife, don't say you can't go [on the Zion's Camp march]."[9] Levi told the Prophet that his wife would not hinder him. On the march he is remembered for making a flag for the camp that had a white background, an eagle, and in large letters the word *Peace*.[10] Upon returning home, he found that "my wife had managed to get along with the baby without running me in debt. . . . I felt thankful for this and loved her dearly."[11]

Levi was chosen to be one of the Seven Presidents of the Seventy in February 1835 (see D&C 124:138–39).[12] He faithfully fulfilled this assignment for the next forty-seven years. During these years he also was a fife major in the Nauvoo Legion, was a police officer in Nauvoo, and played the fife in the Mormon Battalion. Levi, the only General Authority in the battalion, was revered as a father figure and a spiritual leader by the men. His zeal led some officers to wrongfully accuse him of being officious. Yet, true to his principles, he sought to do what was right. One day, after baptizing a stranger, he exclaimed, "If I have baptized a murderer, it will do him no good."[13] His words had such an effect upon the man that he soon confessed that he had killed his brother.

After his discharge from the battalion in 1847, Levi joined the Saints in the Rockies. Continuing his responsibilities as a President of the Quorum of the Seventy, he traveled extensively, strengthening the Saints in small pioneering settlements. He settled in Payson, Utah County, before moving to Manti in 1853. For three terms he represented that small community in the Utah legislature. In 1872 he was ordained a patriarch. Ten years later he died in Washington County, Utah, at the age of seventy-nine.

Notes

1. Autobiography of Levi Ward Hancock, typescript, p. 1, Special Collections, Harold B. Lee Library, Brigham Young University, Provo, Utah.
2. Ibid., p. 21.
3. Ibid., p. 24.
4. Ibid., p. 25.
5. Ibid., p. 26.
6. Ibid.
7. Ibid., p. 50.
8. Ibid., p. 51.
9. Ibid., p. 53.
10. Ibid., p. 55.
11. Ibid., p. 57.
12. He was released by mistake because it was erroneously presumed that he had been ordained a high priest.
13. As cited in *LDS Biographical Encyclopedia* 1:189.

SOLOMON HANCOCK
D&C 52:27

Birth: 14 (possibly 5) August 1793, Springfield, Hampden County, Massachusetts. Son of Thomas Hancock and Amy Ward.
Death: 2 December 1847, Council Bluffs, Pottawattamie County, Iowa.

Solomon Hancock joined the Methodist Church in 1814 and, "having inherited a good talent for vocal music became their favorite singer in camp meetings, which were frequent in those days."[1] He often sang duets with Alta Adams, whom he married. He and his family resided in Springfield, Massachusetts, from 1817 to 1819; in Wolcott, New York, in 1820; in Columbia, Ohio, in 1823; and in Chagrin Falls, Ohio, in 1828. At these various locations Solomon adhered to the Methodist faith until he received evasive answers from a minister about "the place in heaven for children and infants who died."[2]

Observing the preaching and baptizing of Parley P. Pratt in the Kirtland vicinity, he dismounted from his horse and asked Parley "if he would baptize me. He said he would if I believed. I told him that I believed that Jesus is the son of God, and felt within my heart that the things he had told us were the truth. He then baptized me."[3]

Solomon composed a poem in remembrance of his baptism:

> Once I was Methodist, Glory Hallelujah,
> Then I thought it was best, Glory Hallelujah,
> But when I read my Bible right, Glory Hallelujah,
> I found myself a Mormonite, Glory Hallelujah![4]

In June 1831 he was called to serve a mission with Simeon Carter (see D&C 52:27). They journeyed through Ohio, Illinois, and Indiana, organizing branches of the Church.

Solomon became a resident of Jackson County, Missouri, in 1832. He witnessed the violence of mobs, as related by George A. Smith: "Solomon Hancock, an eye witness [to the atrocities], . . . with the assistance of two or three others, protected one hundred and twenty women and children for the space of ten days, who were obliged to keep themselves hid from their pursuers, while they were hourly expecting to be massacred, and who finally escaped into Clay County, by finding a circuitous route to the ferry."[5]

On 7 July 1834 he was appointed to the high council in Clay County. He was serving a second mission to the East when he received word of his wife's death. The Prophet Joseph penned in his journal, "May the Lord bless him and comfort him in this hour of affliction."[6]

Solomon returned to Missouri and settled with his children in Far West in 1836, where he purchased property and again served on the high council. He married Phoebe Adams, the niece of his first wife, on 28 June 1836. He is remembered in Far West for his defense of the Presidency: "Elder Solomon Hancock pleaded in favor of the Presidency, stating that he could not raise his hand against them."[7] He is also remembered for singing a song by Levi W. Hancock at the Independence Day festivities of 1838:

> Come lovers of freedom together
>   And hear what we now have to say,
> For surely we ought to remember
>   The cause which produced this great day.
> Oh, may we remember while singing
>   The pains and distresses once borne
> By those who have fought for our freedom
>   And oftimes for friends called to mourn.[8]

Minutes of the Far West high council on 13 December 1838 contain his testimony: "Solomon Hancock says he is a firm believer in the Book of Mormon and Doctrine and Covenants, and that Brother Joseph is not a fallen prophet, but will yet be exalted and become very high."9

Before fleeing to safety in Illinois, Solomon covenanted to assist poor refugees in their escape from Missouri. His nephew Mosiah Hancock reported, "The Hancock brothers, Levi, Joseph, and Solomon, with their guns guarded and fed 600 men, women, and children while camped in the woods after they had been driven from their homes."10

In the spring of 1841 Solomon moved to Lima, Illinois, where he again served on the high council until violence forced him to flee to Nauvoo for protection. As the fear of mobocracy lessened, Solomon was appointed president of the Yelrome Illinois branch in 1845. When mobs again threatened, Brigham Young wrote to Solomon, advising, "It is wisdom for you to remove the women and children from Yelrome as fast as you can. . . . We think it best to let them burn up our houses while we take care of our families. . . . Employ the best scribe you have, or half a dozen of them, if necessary, to pen minutely all the movements of the enemy."11

In his reply to Brigham Young, Solomon reported that the mob burned all the houses on the south side of the branch, including his own home, and that they had vowed to destroy everything from Yelrome to Nauvoo.12 He fled to Nauvoo, where he was appointed to the "Utility Committee."

By April 1846 he had migrated to Iowa Territory and had verbalized that his "greatest desire was to go west."13 Unfortunately, poverty necessitated his seeking employment before beginning the trek. While engaged in the manual labor of clearing timber, he became critically ill. As only two-thirds of the land was cleared, his employer refused to pay him until the work was finished. Solomon returned to the Camps of Israel just as poor as when he had left.

His health rapidly declined, and on 2 December 1847 near Council Bluffs, he died at the age of fifty-four. A walnut headboard was used as a grave marker. Erastus H. Rudd composed a poem in remembrance of Solomon:

> Thou art gone to the grave, we'll no longer behold thee
> Till mortal shall put on their clothing of glory,
> Then, then thou will come thy kingdom to save

Oh, then thou will rise from thy cold prison grave
Oh, then thou will rise from thy cold prison grave![14]

Notes

1. Charles Brent Hancock, "Sketch of Solomon Hancock by His Son," p. 24, in author's possession.
2. "A Brief Outline on Solomon Hancock of D&C 52:27" (n.p., n.d.), p. 2, in author's possession.
3. As cited in "Biographical Note, Solomon Hancock" (n.p., n.d.), p. 2, in author's possession.
4. Solomon Hancock, as cited in "Grandfather" (n.p., n.d.), p. 48, in author's possession.
5. George A. Smith, in *JD* 13:107.
6. *HC* 2:406.
7. *HC* 3:4.
8. Levi W. Hancock, as cited in "Grandfather," p. 55.
9. *HC* 3:225.
10. Autobiography of Mosiah Hancock, typescript, p. 13, Special Collections, Harold B. Lee Library, Brigham Young University, Provo, Utah.
11. *HC* 7:440–41.
12. See *HC* 7:441.
13. "Grandfather," p. 55.
14. Erastus H. Rudd, as cited in ibid.

EMER HARRIS
D&C 75:30

Birth: *29 May 1781, Cambridge, Washington County, New York. Son of Nathan Harris and Rhoda Lapham.*
Death: *28 November 1869, Logan, Cache County, Utah.*

In 1793 twelve-year-old Emer Harris moved with his parents to Palmyra, New York, where his father purchased a six-hundred-acre farm for three hundred dollars. His father sold Emer fifty acres of his holdings for two hundred dollars on 2 January 1806 and another parcel of land on 17 February 1807.[1] Within a few years Emer sold his acreage and moved to Luzerne County, Pennsylvania, where he purchased shares in a sawmill.

It is assumed that his younger brother Martin Harris told him of the coming forth of the Book of Mormon as early as 1828. Family tradition purports that "Emer walked twenty-five miles to hear more about the new 'golden Bible' from his brother" in Harmony, Pennsylvania.[2] He and Martin were together when the first bound copy of the Book of Mormon came off the Grandin Press in 1830. It is said that Martin picked up the book and presented it to Emer.[3]

Emer read the book and was baptized on 10 February 1831 by Hyrum Smith. He soon rented his property in Pennsylvania and moved to Ohio to be with the Saints. He was ordained a high priest on 25 October 1831 by the Prophet and said on that occasion that "he was determined to be for God & none else & with his assistance to do his will."[4] Two days later he was appointed "scribe for Joseph Smith, while they are employed writing and copying the fullness of the scriptures."[5]

On 25 January 1832 he was called to preach the gospel with Simeon Carter (see D&C 75:30). It appears that the two men initially left together but that Simeon later joined Jared Carter while Emer went with his brother Martin. Of this mission Emer penned, "Brother Martin is with me & has been the grater part of the time since we left Kirtland. We have traveled mutch & Preached mutch. Eighty two have been baptised and many more have believed. We find no end to the call for our labours."[6] The *Evening and Morning Star* reported that "brothers Martin and Emer Harris have baptized 100 persons at Chenango point, New York [south of Oneida Lake], within a few weeks."[7] They also organized a branch of the Church with seventy members in Springville, Susquehanna County, Pennsylvania.[8]

In midsummer 1833 Emer returned from his mission, having preached the gospel and, to the joy of his family, having sold his land in Pennsylvania for $550. The money was used to purchase a farm in Florence township, Ohio. When not working on the farm, Emer labored as a carpenter and a joiner on the Kirtland Temple. He created the window sash in the temple and other intricate details within the sacred building.

In 1838 he moved his family to Missouri. They arrived in October, the same month Governor Lilburn Boggs issued the Extermination Order. Among his "meager possessions was a chest containing copies of the Book of Mormon. Emer had fitted the books under a false bottom, lined with Fuller's cloth, in case they were searched by the mobs."[9] They were searched and the books were preserved by his advance preparation.

Exhaustion and exposure as a result of the violence in Missouri caused Emer's health to fail. After a year of recovery in Quincy, Illinois, he moved to Nauvoo and "bought a claim of 40 acres in the timber."[10] He worked on the Nauvoo Temple, using the same tools he had used on the Kirtland Temple, and is credited with building the winding stairway.

In 1848 Emer received his patriarchal blessing from John Smith in Iowa Territory. He was told, "Thou has not fainted in times of disease and persecution when every evil thing has [been] spoken against the church of the Living God. Thou hast endured in faith. The Lord is well pleased with thee because of the integrity of thy heart."[11] His faithfulness continued throughout his life.

Emer migrated west in 1850 with the Wilford Woodruff company. He settled first in Ogden and then in Provo in 1855. Among his Church callings was that of patriarch. He also gave many healing blessings. One of the young men he blessed was John Henry Smith, who said, "When old Father Emer Harris came to bless me as a child, no matter what the ailment might be, I never had the least doubt but that health would be my portion."[12]

In 1862 Brigham Young advised Emer to move to Dixie for his health. He resided with his children in southern Utah but preferred to live in Logan. In 1867 he returned to northern Utah, where he died in 1869 at the home of his son Alma Harris at the age of eighty-eight.

Notes

1. County records show that Nathan Harris and his sons Emer and Martin bought and sold land to each other several times.

2. Madge Harris Tuckett and Belle Harris Wilson, *The Martin Harris Story with Biographies of Emer Harris and Dennison Lott Harris* (Provo, Utah: Vintage Books, 1983), p. 118.

3. This book is now in a vault at Deseret Book Company in Salt Lake City.

4. As cited in Donald Q. Cannon and Lyndon W. Cook, eds., *Far West Record: Minutes of The Church of Jesus Christ of Latter-day Saints, 1830–1844* (Salt Lake City: Deseret Book Co., 1983), p. 21.

5. Tuckett and Wilson, p. 120.

6. Ibid., p. 121.

7. *The Evening and the Morning Star* 1 (February 1833): 70.

8. See Tuckett and Wilson, p. 121.

9. Ibid., p. 127.

10. Ibid., p. 129.

11. Patriarchal Blessing Book Index 9:303, Church Historical Department, The Church of Jesus Christ of Latter-day Saints, Salt Lake City, Utah.

12. John Henry Smith, "Unquestioned Integrity," in Brian H. Stuy, comp., *Collected Discourses* (Burbank, Calif., and Woodland Hills, Utah: B.H.S. Publishers, 1987–92), p. 183.

GEORGE WASHINGTON HARRIS
D&C 124:132

Birth: *1 April 1780, Lanesboro, Berkshire County, Massachusetts. Son of James Harris.*
Death: *1857, Council Bluffs, Pottawattamie County, Iowa.*

After his marriage to the widow of Masonic martyr William Morgan, George W. Harris moved from Batavia, New York, to Terre Haute, Indiana. There he was baptized in the fall of 1834 by Orson Pratt. By 1836 he had moved to Far West, Missouri, and on 3 March 1838 he was called to serve on the high council there. The Prophet noted that on 14 March he, his family, and others were "received under the hospitable roof of Brother George W. Harris, who treated us with all possible kindness."[1]

George was active in the fight against violence in Missouri, even though he believed that "the scourge which has come upon us [has] the hand of God" in it.[2] George itemized his personal suffering in a Missouri redress petition:

Quincy Illinois May 8th, 1839
    The State of Missouri to Geo W Harris Dr

to one lot in Far West with hous and barn and frute trees on the Same	$1,000.00
to another lot in Far West unocupied	600.00
to a wood lot of forty acres Joining the City	1,000.00
To a lot of land in Adam on Diammon Joining Square	1,000.00
To three Sections of land that I improved on for my Self and famely in Daves County	3,000.00
To fals imprisonment for rising of thre weeks in an unfinished Coart hous with the windows broken out of about avery window and very Coald wether	

Say worse than laying out in the woods in the
same kind of weather   3,000.00

                                                    $9,600.00
                                                    Geo W Harris

[Not sworn.][3]

He was not reimbursed for his personal losses.

In Illinois, George served on the Nauvoo high council (see D&C 124:131–32) and was president of the Nauvoo Coach and Carriage Manufacturing Association. He was an alderman and president pro tem of the Nauvoo City Council at the time of the Martyrdom and signed the document on 10 June 1844 declaring the *Nauvoo Expositor* a "public nuisance."[4]

George was appointed commissary of the first encampment of pioneers to leave Nauvoo in 1846.[5] He journeyed with the Saints to Council Bluffs, Iowa Territory, where he was appointed bishop and later high councilman. George failed to continue migrating to the Salt Lake Valley. Brigham Young explained:

> There are a great many who profess to be still in the faith, neglecting to gather, and waiting for the time when Zion will be redeemed. George W. Harris, whom many of you remember, was going to wait in Kanesville until we returned. Brother George A. Smith told him that the nearest way to the centre Stake of Zion was through Great Salt Lake City. Harris has gone to the spirit-world, and where his circuit will be I neither know nor care.[6]

George died in 1857 in Council Bluffs at age seventy-seven.

Notes

1. *HC* 3:9.

2. As cited in Donald Q. Cannon and Lyndon W. Cook, eds., *Far West Record: Minutes of The Church of Jesus Christ of Latter-day Saints, 1830–1844* (Salt Lake City: Deseret Book Co., 1983), p. 222.

3. As cited in Clark V. Johnson, ed., *Mormon Redress Petitions: Documents of the 1833–1838 Missouri Conflict* (Provo, Utah: Religious Studies Center, Brigham Young University, 1992), p. 226.

4. *HC* 6:448.

5. See *HC* 7:586.

6. Brigham Young, in *JD* 8:198.

MARTIN HARRIS

D&C 3: Introduction, 12–13; 5: Introduction, 1, 24–25, 28;
10:6–7; 17: Introduction; 19: Introduction, 26–27, 35; 52:24;
58:35, 38–39; 70:1–3; 82:11; 102:3, 34; 104:24, 26

Birth: *18 May 1783, Easttown, Saratoga County, New York. Son of Nathan Harris and Rhoda Lapham.*
Death: *10 July 1875, Clarkston, Cache County, Utah.*

At age twenty-five Martin Harris married his sixteen-year-old cousin Lucy Harris. They resided for over twenty years in Palmyra, New York, on property given to them by Martin's father. During these years Martin became known as a "gentleman and a farmer of respectability"[1] as well as a patriot. He was the first sergeant in the 39th New York Militia during the War of 1812.

It was not until 1824 that his reputation in the community became tarnished. It began when he hired Father Smith and his son Hyrum. During their employ Martin learned of the prophetic calling of young Joseph. Historian Willard Bean writes: "Each day while they were there Martin would find excuse to bring up the matter and would ask many questions, referring frequently to the Bible to prove that heavenly messengers visiting the earth was not a new doctrine. . . . Martin was thrilled beyond expression. He requested that he be kept posted on any new developments."[2]

He was not only curious but supportive of Joseph Smith. He gave fifty dollars to help defray expenses when Joseph journeyed to Harmony, Pennsylvania. He hand-carried transcribed characters from the Book of Mormon to linguists Charles Anthon and Dr. Mitchell in New York City, afterwards testifying, "The translation that I carried to Professor Anthon was copied from these same plates; also, that the professor did testify to it being a correct translation. I do firmly believe and do know that

Joseph Smith was a prophet of God; for without I know he could not have had that gift; neither could he have translated the same."[3]

Martin was the scribe to the book of Lehi translation. Joseph wrote, "Mr. Harris . . . arranged his affairs, and returned again to my house about the 12th of April, 1828, and commenced writing for me while I translated from the plates, which we continued until the 14th of June following, by which time he had written one hundred and sixteen pages of the manuscript on foolscap paper."[4]

Unfortunately, through carelessness the manuscript pages were lost (see D&C 3, 10). Historical recountings of the loss of the manuscript differ in detail, but scholars agree that Martin's wife played a central role in its falling into the hands of designing men.

Martin's repentance and remorse was sincere, and in June 1829 he became one of three witnesses to the Book of Mormon (see D&C 5:23–29). The Prophet Joseph wrote that after seeing an angel and the Book of Mormon plates, "Martin Harris cried out . . . , ''Tis enough; mine eyes have beheld . . . ;' and jumping up, he shouted, 'Hosannah,' blessing God, and otherwise rejoiced exceedingly."[5]

Martin mortgaged his farmland to ensure the publication of the Book of Mormon. Eighteen months later when the mortgage fell due, he was without funds to pay the debt. Near the time he defaulted on his mortgage he and Lucy separated.[6] Despite these personal tragedies he never lost sight of the value of the Book of Mormon (see D&C 19).

Martin was baptized on 6 April 1830 in the Seneca River by Oliver Cowdery. On 22 February 1831 he received a letter from Joseph Smith, who wrote, "I send you this to inform you that it is necessary for you to come here [Kirtland] as soon as you can."[7] He arrived in Kirtland in June 1831 and by 7 June was directed by revelation to journey to Missouri (see D&C 52:24). By mid-July 1831 he was in Independence and in August 1831 was told through the Prophet that he should "be an example unto the Church, in laying his moneys before the bishop of the Church. . . . And let him repent of his sins, for he seeketh the praise of the world." (D&C 58:35, 39.)

He endeavored to be an example. He served a mission with his brother Emer Harris in 1832 and "baptized 100 persons at Chenango Point, New-York"; in Pennsylvania, he said, "Eighty-two have been baptized and many more have believed."[8] While on his mission Martin was taken prisoner on a false charge until bail was obtained. His brother Emer wrote poetic verses of his incarceration:

Dear Brother though you are bound in jail
Yet never fear the powers of hell
Your God he will deliver you
Therefore fear not what men can do.

Let all the hosts of hell engauge
With all their mallice spite and rage
The Mormonites God will defend
Who are so called by wicked men.[9]

After his release he returned to Ohio, where he volunteered to march with Zion's Camp to Missouri. After the march he was privileged to be one of three to choose the Quorum of the Twelve Apostles. On 17 February 1835 Martin became a member of the first high council in Kirtland (see D&C 102:3). Despite the appointment he continued to struggle with desires for fortune and fame. He failed to heed the warnings in his patriarchal blessing to "be humble and meek in heart or Satan will seek to raise thee up to pride and boasting."[10]

At a conference in the Kirtland Temple in September 1837, Martin was rejected as a member of the high council. According to one account he was disfellowshipped "for speaking against the Prophet." Brigham Young stated, "He was never tried for his fellowship; he was never excommunicated."[11] However, he chose to estrange himself from the Church for the next thirty-two years. During these years he vacillated from one dissenting sect to another—the Strangites, the Whitmerites, and even the group led by William Smith. Amid his vacillations, he maintained a residence in Kirtland and became the self-appointed caretaker of the Kirtland Temple. Latter-day Saint missionaries were guided through the temple by Martin and reported his continuing bitterness and discord with Church leaders. "I never did leave the Church; the Church left me," he remarked.[12]

At age eighty-six he requested that Brigham Young be told of his impoverished circumstances and his desire to visit Utah: "Tell him I should like to visit Utah, my family and children—I would be glad to accept help from the church, but I want no personal favor. Wait! Tell him that if he sends money, he must send enough for the round trip. I should not want to remain in Utah."[13]

Upon hearing of this request President Young replied, "I want to say this: I was never more gratified over any message in my life. Send for him! Yes, even if it were to take the last dollar of my own."[14]

Although in his eighty-eighth year, Martin ventured to the West. In

Des Moines, Iowa, the Saints gave him a suit of clothes, for which he was very grateful.[15] He was rebaptized on 17 September 1870 by Edward Stevenson in the presence of five Apostles. The *Deseret News* of 31 August 1870 reported, "He is remarkably vigorous for one of his years, his memory being very good, and his sight, though his eyes appear to have failed, being so acute that he can see to pick a pin off the ground. . . . We are glad to see Martin Harris once more in the midst of the Saints."

Martin strengthened the faith of the Saints as he visited congregations in Utah. Upon gazing at the temple and tabernacle and the beautiful Salt Lake City, he exclaimed, "Who would have thought that the Book of Mormon would have done all this?"[16]

The final testimony of Martin Harris was recorded by his grandson William Pilkington: "On the 9th day of July 1875, while he was dying, I knelt by his cot. . . . I wanted to get what I thought would be his last words, but he could not talk audibly." Pilkington then prayed that his grandfather's last words could be understood. He reported, "Strength was given to him and he bore his testimony as he had done many times before and I understood every word. He then bore the same testimony to the whole world and then laid back exhausted."[17] Martin died on 10 July 1875 in Clarkston, Utah. He was buried with his Book of Mormon in his right hand and the Doctrine and Covenants in his left.[18]

Notes

1. Madge Harris Tuckett and Belle Harris Wilson, *The Martin Harris Story with Biographies of Emer Harris and Dennison Lott Harris* (Provo, Utah: Vintage Books, 1983), p. 10.

2. Willard Bean, *History of Palmyra* (Palmyra, New York: P. Courier Co., 1937), p. 35, as cited in Tuckett and Wilson, pp. 15–16.

3. Letter of Martin Harris, 23 November 1870, as cited in Tuckett and Wilson, p. 23.

4. *HC* 1:20–21.

5. *HC* 1:55.

6. The home and eighty-eight acres of the original farm were purchased by the Church in 1937.

7. Letter of Joseph Smith to Martin Harris, 22 February 1831, as cited in Tuckett and Wilson, p. 52.

8. Tuckett and Wilson, p. 121.

9. As cited in ibid., pp. 55–56.

10. As cited in ibid., p. 59.

11. Ibid., p. 63. According to Donald Q. Cannon and Lyndon W. Cook, Martin was excommunicated in 1837 and rebaptized in 1842. See *Far West Record: Minutes of*

The Church of Jesus Christ of Latter-day Saints, 1830–1844 (Salt Lake City: Deseret Book Co., 1983), p. 266.

    12. As cited in Tuckett and Wilson, p. 75.

    13. As cited in William Harrison Homer Jr., "The Passing of Martin Harris," *Improvement Era* 29 (1926): 470.

    14. As cited in ibid., p. 471.

    15. See *LDS Biographical Encyclopedia* 1:271.

    16. Journal History, 1 June 1877.

    17. William Pilkington, testimony sworn before Joseph W. Peterson, 3 April 1934, typescript, Archives and Manuscripts, Harold B. Lee Library, Brigham Young University, Provo, Utah.

    18. See *LDS Biographical Encyclopedia* 1:276.

PETER HAWS
D&C 124:62, 70

Birth: *17 February 1795, Young Township, Leeds County, Ontario, Canada. Son of Edward and Polly Haws.*
Death: *1862, California.*

Peter Haws was baptized in Canada before migrating to Kirtland and then to Illinois. He was a prominent property owner in the Nauvoo area: "[He] bought considerable property. It was a short time after the Church had been driven out of Missouri, and had arrived in this place. The families having been robbed of all in Missouri, were in a starving condition. By the counsel of the Presidency, [Peter Haws] converted his funds to feeding the poor, bringing in meat and flour, &c."[1] His charity did not leave him destitute, for he owned and operated a steam-driven sawmill near Nauvoo.[2]

During the Nauvoo era Peter was a member of the Nauvoo Agricultural and Manufacturing Association from 1841 to 1845 and a member of the Nauvoo House building committee (see D&C 124:62). The official pronouncement of the Nauvoo House association read: "Be it enacted by the people of the state of Illinois, represented in the general assembly, that George Miller, Lyman Wight, John Snider, and Peter Haws, and their associates, are hereby declared a body corporate, under the name and style of the 'Nauvoo House Association;' and they are hereby authorized to erect and furnish a public house of entertainment, to be called the 'Nauvoo House.'"[3]

The zeal with which Peter accepted this assignment was recorded by the Prophet on 21 February 1843: "At eleven I went to the Temple, and found a large assembly, and Brother Haws preaching about the Nauvoo House."[4] On another occasion Peter called for "twenty-five hands to go with him to the Pine country, to get lumber for the Nauvoo House."[5] He even served a mission to collect needed funds for the construction of the Nauvoo House and the Nauvoo Temple in 1843. His missionary companion, Amasa Lyman, recorded, "During the winter I went, in company with Peter Haws, on a mission to secure means to build the temple and Nauvoo House, we went as far east as Indiana."[6]

Peter testified that "when he returned he found his family must have starved, if they had not borrowed money to get food."[7] Despite his personal and family sacrifice he continued to give valiant service in Nauvoo as an alternate on the Nauvoo high council from 1840 to 1844[8] and as a member of the Council of Fifty in 1844.

It was not until his years in Iowa that Peter Haws exhibited his disaffection with Church leaders. In 1848 he journeyed to Texas to visit Lyman Wight's apostate colony. Upon returning to Iowa he publicly criticized the leadership of the Twelve, arguing that revelation was not binding on the Church without the sanction of the Council of Fifty. He was tried by the Pottawattamie high council for speaking against Brigham Young and for selling whiskey to the Indians and was cut off from the Church.

By 1854 Peter had moved near the Humboldt River in Nevada, where he raised grain, vegetables, and cattle for overland emigrants. From 1855 to 1862 he was living in California. He died in 1862 at the age of sixty-seven.

Notes

1. *HC* 6:440.
2. See Lyndon W. Cook, *The Revelations of the Prophet Joseph Smith* (Salt Lake City: Deseret Book Co., 1985), p. 260.
3. *HC* 4:301.
4. *HC* 5:283.
5. *HC* 5:369.
6. Amasa Lyman, "Amasa Lyman's History," *Millennial Star* 27 (2 September 1865): 552.
7. *HC* 6:441.
8. See Donald Q. Cannon and Lyndon W. Cook, eds., *Far West Record: Minutes of The Church of Jesus Christ of Latter-day Saints, 1830–1844* (Salt Lake City: Deseret Book Co., 1983), p. 227.

HENRY HERRIMAN
D&C 124:138

Birth: *9 June 1804, Rowley, Essex County, Massachusetts. Son of Enoch Herriman and Sarah Brocklebank.*
Death: *17 May 1891, Huntington, Emery County, Utah.*

According to family tradition, "it was the Parting of the Ways" with Henry Herriman's twin, Hiram, and kinfolk when he became a Mormon in 1832.[1] "Feeling my weakness," he wrote, "but having confidence in the promises of the Lord," he remained steadfast in his new religious commitment. He moved to Kirtland in the fall of 1833 to be with other Saints, but found "I was under necessity of arming myself to protect the Saints and the Prophet Joseph."[2] He volunteered to march with Zion's Camp because "I felt constrained to perform this mission by the Spirit of God to expose my life for the welfare and salvation of the Saints."[3]

Henry's nobility of soul was also shown toward a gravely ill Mrs. Waltham in Dover, New York. Henry wrote that he "prayed for her, took her by the hand and said in the name of Jesus Christ, according to your faith, be it done unto you in a moment her countenance changed from death to life, she arose from her bed forth with and gave praise to God."[4]

In January 1838 Henry became one of the Seven Presidents of the Seventies (see D&C 124:138). One of his first assignments in that council was to help organize the Kirtland Camp.[5] "The Lord in mercy made known to us by Vision and prophesy that we gather together," explained Henry, "going to the Land of Zion pitching our Tents by the way." The Kirtland poor followed his direction and traversed from Kirtland to Caldwell County. Henry continued his journey to Daviess County, where he "was made a prisoner by an armed force."[6] He was one of few Saints authorized by the Missourians to travel in Daviess County after the Extermination Order was issued.[7]

In Nauvoo the Prophet revealed to Henry the doctrine of plural marriage. According to Henry's nephew Aroet Hale, the Prophet told him:

> "Henry, your wife Clarisa[?] is barren; she never will have any children. Upon your shoulders rests great responsibilities. You have a great work to perform in the temple of our God. You are the only Harriman that will ever join this Church." He even told him . . . that he must take another wife and raise up a family to assist him in his great work, and to honor and revere his name. The Prophet also told Aunt Clarisa[?] that if she would consent to this marriage and not try to hinder Henry, that she should share a portion of the glory that would be derived from this marriage. Uncle Henry Harriman was finally convinced that the command that the Prophet Joseph had given him was right.[8]

In a short time he was sealed to a young woman, Eliza Elizabeth Jones, by the Prophet.[9]

Henry served two missions during the Nauvoo era, one to the eastern states and the other to Canada. In Cape Cod, to his "sorrow and gloom" he learned of the Martyrdom.[10] He soon returned to Nauvoo and then joined the Saints in their westward movement. He crossed the plains in the Heber C. Kimball company in 1848, as captain of the first hundred.[11] In the spring of 1849 he helped build a fort in the Salt Lake Valley, named Herriman in his honor.

On 21 December 1856 in a speech delivered by Heber C. Kimball, Henry and others in the Presidency of the Seventies were admonished to release certain men from their callings: "And here are brother Pulsipher, Herriman and Clapp, members of the first Presidency of the Seventies, sitting here as dead as door nails, and suffering these poor curses to live in our midst as Seventies. As the Lord God Almighty lives, if you do not rise up and trim your quorums, we will trim you off, and not one year shall pass away before you are trimmed off."[12] Henry's affirmative response to the public reprimand was immediate.

Henry led the only handcart company of missionaries to cross the plains in an eastbound direction from Salt Lake City in 1856. He proceeded on to England but returned early to help protect the Saints from the invasion of Johnston's army.

Brigham Young called Henry to settle in southern Utah after the threat of war had abated. He remained in Dixie for the next twenty-five years and, according to Aroet Hale, had "done a good work in the St. George temple."[13] In 1890 it was reported that Henry was blind and a monogamist. He died in 1891 at the age of eighty-six, having served as a General Authority for over fifty-three years, longer than any other Church leader up to that time.

Notes

1. Alta Harrington, "Life History of Henry Harriman, Pioneer 1848" (n.p., n.d.), p. 1.

2. Henry H. Herriman, "A Short History of Henry H. Herriman," typescript, pp. 2–3, in author's possession.

3. Ibid., p. 4.

4. Ibid., p. 5.

5. See *HC* 3:97.

6. Herriman, p. 7.

7. See *HC* 3:210.

8. Autobiography of Aroet Hale, typescript, pp. 8–9, Special Collections, Harold B. Lee Library, Brigham Young University, Provo, Utah.

9. Ibid.

10. Herriman, p. 10.

11. See *HC* 7:626.

12. Heber C. Kimball, in *JD* 4:140.

13. Hale, p. 8.

JOHN A. HICKS

D&C 124:137

Birth: *1810, New York.*

John A. Hicks struggled from the beginning with his commitment to the faith. After joining the Church in Upper Canada, he moved to Nauvoo. He is first mentioned in historical records for being charged with slandering the good reputation of John P. Greene and lying on 19 April 1840. His confession and promise to make restitution was accepted by the Nauvoo high council on 2 May 1840.

The forgiveness of the Lord was evident as John was appointed by revelation to preside over the elders quorum in Nauvoo on 19 January 1841 (see D&C 124:137). In March, anxious to learn about those in his quorum, he wrote an epistle "to the elders scattered abroad," seeking to "know how many are on the Lord's side, how many there are laboring in the vineyard . . . [for] it is necessary that every one should render an account of his stewardship."[1]

His own stewardship was questioned and even objected to one month later, on 8 April 1841.[2] The congregation gathered for the April 1841 general conference voted to reject John's appointment as elders quorum president. He was subsequently tried by his quorum for stating falsehoods, engaging in schismatical conversation, and breaching Nauvoo city ordinances. At the general conference on 5 October 1841 Brigham Young presented an appeal, but "after hearing the testimony in the case it was voted that Elder John A. Hicks be cut off from the Church."[3]

John associated with apostates in Nauvoo after 1841. On 22 June 1844 Governor Ford wrote to Joseph Smith and the Nauvoo City Council, directing them to release the persons and property that had been "forcibly imprisoned and detained" in Nauvoo: "The following-named persons are reported to me as being detained against their will by martial law: John A. Hicks. . . . It will tend greatly to allay excitement if they shall be immediately discharged and suffered to go without molestation."[4]

On 24 June 1844, three days before the Martyrdom, John, with a company of apostates, was quartered at the Hamilton Hotel in Carthage. Hicks stated to Cyrus H. Wheelock "that it was determined to shed the blood of Joseph Smith . . . whether he was cleared by the law or not." Wheelock told Governor Ford what "Hicks had said, but he treated it with perfect indifference, and suffered Hicks and his associates to run at liberty and mature their murderous plans."[5]

Notes

1. *Times and Seasons* 2 (1 March 1841): 340.
2. See *HC* 4:341.
3. *HC* 4:428.
4. *HC* 6:534, 537.
5. *HC* 6:560.

ELIAS HIGBEE
D&C 113:7–10

Birth: *23 October 1795, Galloway, Gloucester County, New Jersey. Son of Isaac Higbee and Sophia Somers.*
Death: *8 June 1843, Nauvoo, Hancock County, Illinois.*

Soon after joining the Church in Cincinnati, Ohio, Elias Higbee moved his family to Jackson County, Missouri. Mobocracy in 1833 forced their removal to Clay County, where Elias was given his first of several leadership assignments in the Church. He was a high councilor in Clay County before serving as a clerk, historian, recorder, and high councilor in Far West.[1] His only elected position in Missouri was that of judge of Caldwell County. In this capacity he ordered "the sheriff of said county to call out the militia" to disperse the mobs and retake Mormon prisoners near Richmond.[2] The Battle of Crooked River was a direct result of this official order.

In March 1838 Elias asked the Prophet Joseph Smith to explain the meaning of several verses in Isaiah 52. The answers given are contained in Doctrine and Covenants 113. In 1838 he was driven from Missouri by mobbers and lost all that he had owned.[3]

In Illinois, Elias continued to take a prominent role in civil and ecclesiastical affairs. On 9 March 1839 he was appointed to determine which properties in Illinois and Iowa should be purchased for the Saints. On 6 October 1839, "because of his legal training," he was appointed to accompany the Prophet Joseph Smith to Washington, D.C., to present grievances before Congress and the president of the United States.[4] President Martin Van Buren, after listening to the grievances, said, "Gentlemen, your cause is just; but I can do nothing for you!"[5]

Elias remained at the nation's capital to lobby for redress of Missouri wrongs long after the Prophet's departure. He wrote letters to the Prophet about the discussions of redress presented to a senate committee. In a 20 February 1840 letter Elias stated:

> I have just returned from the Committee Room, wherein I spoke about one hour and a half. . . .

I told them first, that I represented a suffering people, who had been deprived, together with myself, of their rights in Missouri. . . .

. . . I went on to prove that the whole persecution, from beginning to end, was grounded on our religious faith. . . .

I demanded from them a restitution of all our rights and privileges as citizens of the United States, and damages for all the losses we had sustained.[6]

In his third letter Judge Higbee admonished the Prophet, "If the Missourians should send for you, I would say consult God about going."[7] In the fourth letter, written on 26 February 1840, Judge Higbee lamented, "I feel now that we have made our last appeal to all earthly tribunals; that we should now put our whole trust in the God of Abraham, Isaac, and Jacob. We have a right now which we could not heretofore so fully claim—that is, of asking God for redress and redemption, as they have been refused us by man."[8]

Elias left Washington, D.C., and returned to Nauvoo. His most important assignment in Nauvoo was his service on the Nauvoo Temple committee. However, he was reproved by the Prophet for his failings on that committee: "Elias Higbee, of the temple committee, came into my office, and I said unto him: The Lord is not well pleased with you; and you must straighten up your loins and do better, and your family also; for you have not been as diligent as you ought to have been, and as spring is approaching, you must arise and shake yourself, and be active, and make your children industrious, and help build the Temple."[9]

Joseph's friendship and respect for Elias was unchanged, despite the rebuke. On 7 June 1843 he wrote, "Visited Elias Higbee, who was very sick."[10] He had been ill only five days from cholera morbus and inflammation when he died on 8 June 1843 at his home at the age of forty-seven.[11]

The Prophet wrote, "His loss will be universally lamented, not only by his family, but by a large circle of brethren who have long witnessed his integrity and uprightness, as well as a life of devotedness to the cause of truth."[12] Eliza R. Snow also penned about the death of Elias, "It is to us a mysterious providence at this time, when every talent and exertion are peculiarly needed for the erection of the Temple; that one of the Committee should be so suddenly cal'd from time to eternity."[13]

Joseph Smith preached at Elias's funeral sermon on 13 August 1843: "We are called this morning to mourn the death of a just and good man—a great and mighty man. . . . Where has Judge Higbee gone? Who is there that would not give all his goods to feed the poor, and pour out his gold and silver to the four winds, to go where Judge Higbee has gone?"[14]

Notes

1. See Donald Q. Cannon and Lyndon W. Cook, eds., *Far West Record: Minutes of The Church of Jesus Christ of Latter-day Saints, 1830–1844* (Salt Lake City: Deseret Book Co., 1983), pp. 114, 123.

2. *HC* 3:425.

3. See autobiography of Orange Wight, typescript, p. 5, Special Collections, Harold B. Lee Library, Brigham Young University, Provo, Utah.

4. John Whitmer, *An Early Latter Day Saint History: The Book of John Whitmer*, ed. F. Mark McKiernan and Roger D. Launius (Independence, Mo.: Herald Publishing House, 1980), p. 153 n.5.

5. As cited in Lyman Omer Littlefield, *Reminiscences of Latter-day Saints* (Logan, Utah: The Utah Journal Co., 1888), p. 116; Lucy Mack Smith, *History of Joseph Smith by His Mother*, ed. Preston Nibley (Salt Lake City: Bookcraft, 1954), p. 305.

6. *HC* 4:81–82.

7. *HC* 4:87.

8. *HC* 4:88.

9. *HC* 4:503.

10. *HC* 5:420.

11. See *HC* 5:421.

12. Ibid.

13. As cited in Maureen Ursenbach, ed., "Eliza R. Snow's Nauvoo Journal," *BYU Studies* 15 (Summer 1975): 405–6.

14. *HC* 5:529–30.

SOLOMON HUMPHREY
D&C 52:35

Birth: *23 September 1775, Canton, Hartford County, Connecticut. Son of Solomon Humphrey Sr. and Lucy Case.*
Death: *September 1834, Clay County, Missouri.*

The "Baptist exhorter" Solomon Humphrey was residing in Stockholm, New York, when he first heard of the Book of Mormon. "Being impressed with the truth of the Work," he left Stockholm and journeyed to Manchester "to see cousin Joseph, and was baptized and ordained an elder." Upon returning to his hometown he "commenced preaching the word to the people, although constantly hissed at by the ministers of all denominations and their followers."[1]

Discouraged but resolute in his faith, Solomon chose to migrate from New York to Kirtland to be with the Saints of God. In June 1831, soon after his arrival in Kirtland, he was called to return to the East and attempt again to share the gospel with his relatives: "And again, I say unto you, let my servants Joseph Wakefield and Solomon Humphrey take their journey into the eastern lands; let them labor with their families, declaring none other things than the prophets and apostles, that which they have seen and heard and most assuredly believe, that the prophecies may be fulfilled" (D&C 52:35–36).

In obedience he returned to Stockholm and shared again the truths of the gospel. This second attempt proved successful and Solomon was able to baptize several family members—including John Smith, a future patriarch of the Church—and to confirm George A. Smith, a future Apostle.[2]

In between a number of like missions, Solomon labored on the Kirtland Temple and attended the School of the Prophets. Zebedee Coltrin spoke of one meeting in the school that Solomon attended:

> About the time the school was first organized some wished to see an angel, and a number joined in the circle and prayed. When the vision came, two of the brethren shrank and called for the vision to close or they would perish; they were Brothers Hancock and Humphries. When the Prophet came in they told him what they had done and he said the angel was no further off than the roof of the house, and a moment more he would have been in their midst.[3]

In 1834, ever faithful to the call of the Prophet, Solomon volunteered to march with Zion's Camp to Missouri. On the march his love for wildlife was recorded:

> [One] afternoon, Elder Solomon Humphreys, an aged brother of the camp, having become exceedingly weary, lay down on the prairie to rest himself and fell asleep. When he awoke he saw, coiled up within one foot of his head, a rattlesnake lying between him and his hat, which he had in his hand when he fell asleep. The brethren

gathered around him, saying, "It is a rattlesnake, let us kill it;" but Brother Humphreys said, "No, I'll protect him; you shan't hurt him, for he and I had a good nap together."[4]

When the camp disbanded most of the volunteers returned to their homes, but Solomon chose to remain in Clay County, Missouri, accepting a call in August 1834 to further missionary service.[5] This final mission was never completed, as Solomon died in September 1834 at the age of fifty-nine. A notice of his death appeared in the *Messenger and Advocate,* stating, "He was an elder in the church of Latter day Saints, and had done much good in the cause of our Lord."[6]

Notes

1. George A. Smith, "Sketch of the Auto-Biography of George Albert Smith," *Millennial Star* 27 (1 July 1865): 407.

2. See ibid., p. 438.

3. Zebedee Coltrin, Minutes of the Salt Lake City School of the Prophets, 11 October 1883, p. 66, Church Historical Department, The Church of Jesus Christ of Latter-day Saints, Salt Lake City, Utah.

4. *HC* 2:73–74.

5. See Journal History, 6–7 August 1834.

6. *Messenger and Advocate* 1 (August 1835): 176.

WILLIAM HUNTINGTON SR.
D&C 124:132

Birth: *28 March 1784, New Grantham, Cheshire County, New Hampshire. Son of William Huntington and Prescinda Lathrop.*
Death: *19 August 1846, Mount Pisgah, Harrison County, Iowa.*

William Huntington Sr. resided in Watertown, New York, and, in his words, "prospered In the things of the world untill 1811," when "one sene of Misfortune after Another rolls Uppon me untill I was reduced Lo as to property."[1] In 1816 "providence Smiled on me a gain" and he "united with the presbyterians walked with them some fourteen years In good standing." In 1832 his allegiance to the Presbyterian faith faltered: "I was moved uppon by the spirit of god to Look into the situation of the churches I found the ordinances changed the Covenants broken the fear of god was Taught by precepts of men." True to his convictions, he withdrew from Presbyterianism and "stood alone."2

In 1833 William "found the book of Mormon I read the book believed in the book." He "preached it almost every day, to his neighbors and everybody he could see."3 At the time of his conversion he owned a two-hundred-acre farm, 130 improved acres, a stone house, two barns, and was "nearly out of debt in comefertable Situation as I could ask for to Make us comefertable in life."4

In August 1836 he sold his farm for $3,500, disposed of other possessions, and joined the Saints in Kirtland. There his home was used as the hiding place for the Egyptian mummies and for Joseph Smith Sr.'s family. William was harassed with noxious lawsuits that led to the loss of his home and the knowledge that "his children often go to bed crying for bread."5 Reduced to poverty, he was loaned an ox and a wagon to journey to Missouri in 1838, and "when we Arived in far west I had not one Cent to help my self."6

He was persecuted by mobs in Missouri: "I slept in my clothes with my rifle in my arms nearly one Month. . . . Our case now become alarming It appeared the inhabitants Were determined to strip us of All means of getting out of the State."7 Despite the alarming situation he succeeded in helping his family and others leave Missouri and settle in Illinois. He petitioned for redress of his losses in Missouri, but was given none.

In Illinois his wife, Zina Baker, died from chills and fever. William also became ill and was nurtured in the Prophet's home. Of these sorrows William wrote, "I had passed from a State of affluence worth thousands Down to the lowest state of poverty. . . . Through all our trials and Scens of afflictions . . . never murmerd."8 He married Lydia Partridge, the widow of Edward Partridge, in September 1840.

During his Nauvoo years William served on the high council (see D&C 124:131–32), was a captain of the Silver Greys, a member of the Nauvoo Legion Band, and a member of the Nauvoo Agricultural and Manufacturing Association. He supported his family as a stonemason and assisted in laying the first stone of the Nauvoo Temple. He was privileged to bury the bodies of Joseph and Hyrum Smith: "A day of as great mourning as was every seen on earth I was one of the sixteen who ware appointed Bury their bodies."9

After the Martyrdom William continued to labor on the Nauvoo Temple day after day. On 25 February 1845 he penned, "I finnished Cutting stones for the body of the temple I finished one of the stars."[10] Two months later he witnessed the last stone being placed on the temple and heard the congregation shout hosanna.

He left Nauvoo on 9 February 1846 and was one of a few men who kept journals of their struggles in the wilderness:

> The rain increased the roads soon become impassable teams were stauled in every direction. . . . Many families remained on the pararie over the night with out fire with their clothing wet and cold—high wind all night. . . . I am now out of provision or I have none of con-ciquence have no meat no flower no meal save a few quarts of pearched Corn meal no milk have a few crackers how I shall be provided for the Lord knows I do not.[11]

William presided over the Mount Pisgah encampment until his death on 19 August 1846 from fever and chills at the age of sixty-two.

Notes

1. Journal of William Huntington, book 1, p. 2, in author's possession.
2. Ibid., p. 4.
3. "Huntington Genealogy," (n.p., n.d.), p. 372, in author's possession.
4. Journal, book 1, p. 6.
5. "Huntington Genealogy," p. 373.
6. Journal, book 1, p. 12.
7. Ibid., pp. 13, 26.
8. Ibid., p. 36.
9. Ibid., pp. 51–52.
10. Ibid., p. 77.
11. Ibid., book 2, p. 14.

ORSON HYDE

Testimony of the Twelve Apostles,
D&C 68: Introduction, 1–3; 75:13; 100:14; 102:
Introduction, 3; 103:40; 124:129

Birth: *8 January 1805, Oxford, New Haven County, Connecticut. Son of Nathan Hyde and Sally Thorpe.*
Death: *28 November 1878.*

Of his younger years Orson Hyde wrote, "In our early childhood, we were left an orphan. We grew up to manhood, a stranger to a father's protection and to a mother's care; . . . few seemed to care for us, or take any interest in our welfare."[1] Youthful Orson migrated to Ohio in 1819 and supported himself by accepting menial work in a small iron foundry, in a woolen mill, and in the Gilbert and Whitney store in Kirtland.

In 1827 he joined the Methodist Church and soon became a class leader. It was Sidney Rigdon's logical arguments that convinced him to affiliate with the Campbellite movement. He served as a Campbellite pastor in the Elyria and Florence, Ohio, congregations. However, the Book of Mormon changed his religious course, though his first impression of the book was unfavorable. While preaching against it, "for the first time, [I] thought that the 'Mormon Bible' might be the truth of heaven . . . [and I became] pretty strongly convicted in my own mind that I was doing wrong."[2] On 30 October 1831 Orson was baptized by Sidney Rigdon in the Chagrin River.

On 1 November 1831 the Lord commanded Orson and all the faithful elders of the Church to "go ye into all the world, preach the gospel to every creature" (D&C 68:8). Orson wrote of his first mission with Samuel Smith to the East: "Wherever we were received and entertained, we left our blessing; and wherever we were rejected, we washed our feet in private against those who rejected us."[3] When he returned to Kirtland he was appointed to teach in the School of the Prophets. Of his scholarship he said, "I have once memorized the Bible, and when any one quoted one verse, I could quote the next. I have memorized it in English, German, and Hebrew."[4] On 6 June 1833 he was called to be a clerk to the First Presidency of the Church and is credited with recording the Kirtland revelations from 1831 to 1834, the Book of Commandments, the Kirtland council minutes, Joseph Smith's letter book, and patriarchal blessings.

In 1834 Orson served on the first high council in Kirtland until enlisting in Zion's Camp to help redeem the exiled Saints in Missouri (see D&C 102:3; 103:40). At the conclusion of the Camp he returned to Ohio and was called to the Council of the Twelve Apostles and promised that he "shall go forth according to the commandment, both to Jew and Gentile, and to all nations, kingdoms and tongues."[5] In fulfillment of this blessing Orson was one of the first Apostles to serve a mission to the British Isles. "When we came in sight of Liverpool, the Spirit of God rested down upon us to a very great degree," wrote Orson. "Let me assure you . . . that the Lord God Omnipotent is with us."[6] Of his preaching with Heber C. Kimball and John Goodson in England, the Reverend James Fielding penned, "Kimball bored the holes, Goodson drove the nails, and Hyde clinched them."[7]

It was on this mission that Orson was attacked by evil spirits who rushed "upon me with knives, threats, [and] hellish grins."[8] Despite the satanic attack, he and his companion were successful in sharing the gospel. Heber wrote, "Brother Hyde and myself have labored all the time, night and day, so that we have not had much time to sleep. There are calls on the right and left. . . . There are ten calls where we can only fill one."[9]

When Orson returned to the States, his testimony faltered and he was numbered among the apostates. On 24 October 1838 he affixed his signature to a slanderous affidavit of Thomas B. Marsh that villified the Prophet. As a result, his fellowship was withdrawn.

By the spring of 1839 Orson felt sorrowful and later lamented, "Few men pass through life without leaving some traces which they would gladly obliterate. Happy is he whose life is free from stain and blemish. . . . I sinned against God and my brethren; I acted foolishly. . . . I seek pardon of all whom I have offended, and also of my God."[10] His confession was accepted and he reunited with the Saints in faith and in the Apostleship.

Orson was privileged to receive a blessing from the Prophet: "In due time thou shalt go to Jerusalem, the land of thy fathers, and be a watchman unto the house of Israel; and by thy hand shall the Most High do a great work, which shall prepare the way and greatly facilitate the gathering together of that people."[11] The opportunity for fulfilling this blessing came in the 1840s. Orson journeyed from Nauvoo to England and from there through Europe to Palestine. On 24 October 1841 he climbed the Mount of Olives and dedicated Jerusalem for the return of the Jews and the building of the temple. In the prayer he petitioned the Lord to "remove the barrenness and sterility of this land, and let springs of living water break forth to water its thirsty soil. Let the vine and olive produce in their strength, and the fig-tree bloom and flourish. Let the land become abundantly fruitful when possessed by its rightful heirs."[12] He then erected a pile of stones as a witness "according to ancient custom."[13]

Upon returning to Nauvoo, it was publicly announced that Orson had been called on a mission to St. Petersburg, Russia. This mission was never fulfilled, as Orson was sent instead to Washington, D.C., to present a memorial reviewing the persecution of the Saints in Missouri. While in the East on 27 June 1844, "he felt very heavy and sorrowful in spirit, and knew not the cause. . . . He retired to the further end of the hall alone, and walked the floor; tears ran down his face. . . . He never felt so before, and knew no reason why he should feel so then."[14]

Days later he learned the cause of the depression was the martyrdom of the Prophet Joseph Smith and his brother Hyrum. Speaking of their deaths and the future of the Church before a crowd in Boston, he declared, "I will prophesy that instead of the work dying, it will be like the mustard stock that was ripe, that a man undertook to throw out of his garden, and scattered seed all over it, and next year it was nothing but mustard. It will be so by shedding the blood of the Prophets—it will make ten saints where there is one now."[15]

As the leadership of the Church fell to the Quorum of the Twelve, Orson Hyde was responsible for supervising the completion of the Nauvoo Temple before joining the Saints in the small encampments in Iowa Territory. In 1852 he migrated to the Great Salt Lake Valley, where he served as an associate judge of the supreme court, a member of the territorial legislature, president of the senate in 1870, and a regent of the University of Deseret. He presided ecclesiastically and civically over the Sanpete-Sevier district from 1860 to 1877. During these same years he continued to serve as the senior member of the Quorum of the Twelve Apostles, which he had done since 1847.

In June 1875 Brigham Young adjusted the seniority of the Twelve because of Orson Hyde's and Orson Pratt's prior estrangement from the Church. As a result, Orson was removed as president of that quorum, and John Taylor assumed the position. If Orson felt any disappointment or resentment at the change, it is not recorded. Orson died on 28 November 1878 and is buried in the Spring City cemetery. The inscription on his tombstone reads, "Orson Hyde, apostle of the Lord Jesus Christ, Defender of truth, preacher of righteousness."

Notes

1. *Frontier Guardian*, 26 December 1851, p. 2, as cited in Howard H. Barron, *Orson Hyde: Missionary, Apostle, Colonizer* (Bountiful, Utah: Horizon Publishers, 1977), p. 16.

2. Orson Hyde, "History of Orson Hyde," *Millennial Star* 26 (19 November 1864), 760–61.

3. Hyde, pp. 774–75; see also D&C 75:13.

4. Orson Hyde, in *JD* 2:81–82.

5. *HC* 2:189.

6. Letter from Orson Hyde to his wife, Marinda Hyde, 1837, as cited in Barron, pp. 91–92.

7. As cited in Heber C. Kimball, "Synopsis of the History of Heber Chase Kimball," *Millennial Star* 26 (24 September 1864), 614.

8. As cited in Barron, p. 96.

9. As cited in ibid., p. 99.

10. *CHC* 1:474.

11. *HC* xxxi.

12. *HC* 4:457.

13. *HC* 4:459.

14. *HC* 7:132.

15. *HC* 7:198.

VIENNA JACQUES
D&C 90:28–31

Birth: *10 June 1787, Beverly, Essex County, Massachusetts. Daughter of Henry and Lucinda Jaques.*
Death: *7 February 1884, Salt Lake City, Salt Lake County, Utah.*

Vienna Jacques (or Jaques) was described as possessing self-reliance, "patient toil and strict economy."[1] It has been assumed that she worked as a nurse in the Boston area. She attended Methodist services at the Bromfield Street church in Boston until dissatisfaction with her religion led her to investigate other Christian denominations.[2]

Upon learning of the Book of Mormon, she sent for a copy. After glancing through it she laid it aside, until one evening she received a vision of the book, which convinced her to diligently search this new scripture. She did so until her mind was "illuminated."[3] Convinced of its truth, forty-three-year-old Vienna traveled alone by canal boat and then by stagecoach to Kirtland to meet the Prophet. After being further instructed by him she accepted baptism.

Vienna remained in Ohio about six weeks before returning to Boston, where she was instrumental in converting several family members. Then, again alone, she rejoined the Saints in Ohio. She brought with her precious valuables, including fourteen hundred dollars in savings. On 8 March 1833 the Prophet directed Vienna to consecrate her monies to the Church. In obedience, she gave all that she had.

Vienna was to receive needed funds from the Church for her journey to Missouri (see D&C 90:28). In a revelation the Lord promised her that for her consecration she would "be rewarded in mine own due time. . . . It is meet in mine eyes that she should . . . receive an inheritance from the hand of the bishop; that she may settle down in peace inasmuch as she is faithful, and not be idle in her days from thenceforth." (D&C 90:29–31.)

She intended to leave Kirtland immediately but was advised on 20 April 1833 that she should wait and journey with William Hobart. Once again, in obedience she waited until Hobart was ready to travel. On 2 July 1833 the Prophet wrote, "We rejoiced greatly to hear of the safe arrival of Sister Vienna Jaques and Brother William Hobert, and thank our Heavenly Father that their lives have been spared them till their arrival."[4]

She was given the inheritance she had been promised. Unfortunately, escalating persecution led Vienna to abandon her inheritance and flee to safety in northern Missouri. Near Fishing River she attended the sick in Zion's Camp. Heber C. Kimball penned, "I received great kindness . . . from sister Vienna Jaques, who administered to my wants and also to my brethren—may the Lord reward [her] for [her] kindness."[5] On 4 September 1833 the Prophet wrote to Vienna:

> I have often felt a whispering since I received your letter, like this: "Joseph, thou art indebted to thy God for the offering of thy Sister Vienna, which proved a savor of life as pertaining to thy pecuniary concerns. Therefore she should not be forgotten of thee, for the Lord hath done this, and thou shouldst remember her in all thy prayers and also by letter, for she oftentimes calleth on the Lord, saying, O Lord, inspire thy servant Joseph to communicate by letter some word to thine unworthy handmaiden."[6]

The Prophet then added that he had had a foreknowledge of the struggles she had endured, and he promised eternal blessings:

> I was aware when you left Kirtland that the Lord would chasten you, but I prayed fervently in the name of Jesus that you might live to receive your inheritance. . . . I am not at all astonished at what has happened to you. . . . Therefore let your heart be comforted; live in strict obedience to the commandments of God, and walk humbly before Him, and He will exalt thee in His own due time.[7]

Before being driven from Missouri, Vienna married Daniel Shearer, a widower who was a whipmaker and blacksmith by trade. Together they fled from further mobocracy to Illinois. By 1839 Vienna was residing in Nauvoo, where Joseph Smith III remembered her as "a frequent visitor in our home" until religious persecution forced her to flee to the West.[8]

The westward exodus to the Rockies presented difficulties and hardships for her, as her marriage ended. At age sixty Vienna drove her own wagon across the plains in the Charles C. Rich company, arriving in the Salt Lake Valley on 2 October 1847. She was given a city lot in the Salt Lake Twelfth Ward.

At age ninety she traveled with General Authorities from Salt Lake City to Provo to speak to a gathering of over six hundred "old folk."[9] At ninety-one she was interviewed by a reporter from the *Woman's Exponent,* who penned that she "milked her own cow" and had made sixty-one pounds of butter that spring. The reporter observed, "She lives entirely alone, . . . does all her own housework, including washing, ironing and cooking, writes many letters, and does a great deal of reading. Sister Vienna is very familiar with the Scriptures."[10] When Vienna was ninety-four another reporter commented, "The erectness of her carriage is sufficient to fill many of the Misses of the nineteenth century with envy."[11]

Vienna died on 7 February 1884 in her own home at the age of ninety-six. In her obituary her faithfulness was extolled: "She was true to her covenants and esteemed the restoration of the Gospel as a priceless treasure."[12]

Notes

1. *Woman's Exponent* 7 (1 July 1878): 21.
2. Ibid. 12 (1 March 1884): 152.
3. Ibid.
4. *HC* 1:368.
5. Heber C. Kimball, Extract from Journal, *Times and Seasons* 5 (15 March 1845): 839–40.
6. *HC* 1:408.
7. Ibid.
8. As cited in Jerrie W. Hurd, *Our Sisters in the Latter-day Scriptures* (Salt Lake City: Deseret Book Co., 1987), p. 68.
9. Ibid., p. 69.
10. *Woman's Exponent* 7 (1 July 1878): 21.
11. Ibid. 9 (15 June 1880): 13.
12. Ibid. 12 (1 March 1884): 152.

GEORGE FITCH JAMES
D&C 52:38

Birth: *1797, Massachusetts. Son of Stephen James.*
Death: *November 1864, Brownhelm, Lorain County, Ohio.*

By 1820 George James was residing in Ohio and by 1830 was a resident of Brownhelm, Ohio. He was an early convert to the Church, having been baptized in 1831. A revelation received by the Prophet Joseph Smith on 7 June 1831 instructed him to see that "George James be ordained a priest" (D&C 52:38). From priest to elder to traveling companion of the Prophet on one of his "tours" from Kirtland, George evidenced his faithfulness.[1]

However, on 4 April 1834 the minutes of the Kirtland high council reveal that George was charged with not attending his meetings, not going on an assigned mission, and treating "lightly some of the weak."[2] In his confession before the council:

> Brother George said that he had often promised to take up his cross and magnify his calling, but had failed, and ought to have written to the President ere this time and given him the information that his pecuniary affairs called his attention at home, which prevented his fulfilling the promise he made to President Joseph Smith, in going out to proclaim the Gospel; and he sincerely asked pardon of the Lord, and of his brethren, and particularly of Brother Joseph. He also said he was willing to ask the forgiveness of this Church.[3]

After listening to his explanation the Prophet said that "he had no hardness; he only wished Brother George to consider this as a chastisement, and . . . if Brother George was willing to walk according to the new covenant, he should have his hand of fellowship."[4]

Seven months later, on 10 November 1834, Joseph Smith and Sidney Rigdon co-signed a letter to George admonishing him to come again to Kirtland and face additional charges. In the letter he was informed that his priesthood authority was suspended until the matter was resolved.[5] Although not recorded, apparently resolution was reached, for on 26 March 1836 at the age of thirty-nine, George James was anointed in the Kirtland Temple.

His conviction wavered again and again. When the call came for the Saints to gather to Missouri and later to Illinois, George hesitated. In 1844 Elder Simeon Carter sought him out on his old estate in Brownhelm and encouraged him to move immediately to Nauvoo. Despite promises and assurances to do so, George remained in Ohio.[6] In the 1850 census he is listed as a farmer with assets of one thousand dollars.[7] George died in November 1864 in his hometown of Brownhelm at the age of sixty-seven, outside the fellowship of the Saints.

Notes

1. See *HC* 1:369.
2. *HC* 2:47.
3. Ibid.
4. Ibid.
5. See *HC* 2:170.
6. See Lyndon W. Cook, *The Revelations of the Prophet Joseph Smith* (Salt Lake City: Deseret Book Co., 1985), p. 78.
7. See the Ohio federal census 1850.

AARON JOHNSON
D&C 124:132

Birth: *22 June 1806, Haddam, Middlesex County, Connecticut. Son of Didymus Johnson and Rahuma Stevens.*
Death: *10 May 1877, Springville, Utah County, Utah.*

It was not until 1836 that Aaron Johnson, a blacksmith and a gunsmith and a Methodist by persuasion, "heard several sermons on Mormonism, and being convinced of its truth he concluded to join the Church."[1] He was baptized on 5 April 1836 by Daniel Spencer. In spring 1837 he and his family migrated to Kirtland to be near the

Prophet. Upon meeting him, Aaron laid forty-five hundred dollars on his desk and proclaimed, "There is all the wealth I possess, what shall be done with it?" Joseph took him to the window, pointed to an eighty-acre piece of land, and said, "Take your money and buy that piece of land, build you a house and it shall be yours for an inheritance, and may the Lord bless you."[2]

In obedience Aaron followed the Prophet's instructions and prospered in Ohio until mob threats forced his removal from Kirtland. With the poor he migrated to Far West, where he is remembered as one of "the defenders, and when the town fell, he was also among the prisoners of war."[3] Despite these hardships Aaron remained faithful.

By 1839 he was residing in Nauvoo, two blocks from Joseph Smith's property. "During the first year at Nauvoo, he and his family suffered from chills and fever. . . . For nine months he did not miss the shakes of this disease for a single day."[4] Despite failing health Aaron served the community as a member of the city council, a commissioned officer in the Nauvoo Legion, a high councilor (see D&C 124:131–32), and a municipal court judge. He went to Carthage in June 1844 as "one of the bondsman for the Prophet Joseph Smith and his brother Hyrum when they were placed in Carthage Jail."[5] After the Martyrdom several court cases were tried in Aaron's court against participants in the Carthage mob. The charges against the accused men could not be substantiated.

Aaron migrated west with the Saints, leaving behind his Nauvoo "real estate which cost him over $4000, but for which he only received $150."[6] In Iowa, as in Nauvoo, he gave service to the Saints—as a high councilor, bishop, and member of a stake presidency—before journeying to the Salt Lake Valley in 1850 as captain of nearly six hundred pioneers. When he arrived in the Valley, Brigham Young invited him to "choose a number of families, go into Utah Valley, and make a settlement, establish homes, and be united."[7] To Aaron the most beautiful area in Utah County was near Hobble Creek: "We gazed with admiration upon the vast meadows spread before us, while the bunch grass along the foothills brushed the horses breasts. Never before had I beheld a grander prospect."[8] The official Church record simply states, "Springville, Utah Co., was settled by Aaron Johnson and others."[9]

Aaron served as the first bishop of Springville, helping new settlers spiritually and temporally. He built water ditches, dams, and roads into the canyons. He helped establish the city square and an academy with a stage for learning and theatrical productions, and built a thirty-room home referred to as Springville's first hotel. He served as a probate judge of Utah County and in 1861 as a chief justice of the county. Aaron was also a legislator in the House of Representatives and served on a number of committees, including the Elections Committee, the Judiciary Committee, Public Domain and School Lands Committee, and the Roads, Bridges, Ferries, and Canyons Committee. In 1856 he was commissioned a brigadier general of the Utah militia. He fought in three armed confrontations: the Walker, Tintic, and Blackhawk Indian Wars.

Aaron's demanding ecclesiastical and civic responsibilities continued from 1851 to 1870, a period of nineteen years. Seven years before his death he tended to become an average citizen. It was recorded in January 1871, "Bp. A. J. left home for parts unknown. He returned again shortly but kept out of public notice."[10] Yet it appears that his influence in Springville continued. His last Church calling was that of patriarch. Whether Aaron gave any patriarchal blessings is not known.

In April 1877 he became ill with a cold and was confined to his home. He died early in the morning of 10 May 1877 at the age of seventy. His obituary in the *Deseret News* reported that the cause of death was "nervous exhaustion from cold," and it contained a few of his final words: "I feel that my work is done, and if it be the will of the Lord that I should die I am fully resigned and willing to go."[11]

Notes

1. "Aaron Johnson, First Judge of Utah County," *Tullidge's Quarterly Magazine* 3 (October 1883), p. 410, as cited in Alan P. Johnson, *Aaron Johnson, Faithful Steward* (Salt Lake City: Publishers Press, 1991), p. 4.

2. Luke William Gallop, "Biographical Sketch of Aaron Johnson's Life," unpublished typescript, as cited in Johnson, p. 5.

3. "Aaron Johnson," p. 411, as cited in Johnson, p. 20.

4. Gallop, p. 2, as cited in Johnson, p. 30.

5. Mozelle Braithwaite and Wayne Braithwaite, comp., "History of Annie Rachel Johnson," *Aaron Johnson, Sr.* (n.p., n.d.), p. 251, as cited in Johnson, p. 68.

6. "Aaron Johnson," p. 413, as cited in Johnson, p. 97.

7. Gallop, as cited in Johnson, p. 190.

8. Ibid.

9. Journal History, October 1850.

10. Gallop, as cited in Johnson, p. 602.

11. *Deseret News* 26:234, as cited in Johnson, pp. 607–8.

JOHN JOHNSON
D&C 102:3; 104:24, 34

Birth: *11 April 1778, Chesterfield, Cheshire County, New Hampshire. Son of Israel Johnson and Abigail Higgins.*
Death: *30 July 1843, Kirtland, Lake County, Ohio.*

John Johnson, or "Father Johnson," as he was affectionately called by the Saints, was a farmer by trade and "noted for paying his debts and living independently."[1] He resided in various locations in the East including Pomfret, Vermont, a small town a few miles from the Prophet's birthplace, from 1803 to 1818.

In 1818 the Johnson family moved to Hiram, Ohio, where Father Johnson purchased one hundred acres. Through the ensuing years he bought additional land and by 1830 owned a 304-acre estate and a newly constructed farmhouse.[2] His prosperity and religious affiliation with the "Methodist Church for about four or five years" before learning of Mormonism is well-documented.[3]

Soon after the Prophet's arrival in Ohio, fifty-three-year-old Father Johnson, his wife, Elsa, and Methodist minister Ezra Booth journeyed to Kirtland to investigate Mormonism. While discussing the tenets of the new faith Elsa was healed of chronic rheumatism. A historical record recounts details of the miraculous healing: "During the interview the conversation turned on the subject of supernatural gifts, such as were conferred in the days of the apostles. Some one said, 'Here is Mrs. Johnson with a lame arm; has God given any power to man now on the earth to cure her?' A few moments later, when the conversation had turned in another direction, Smith rose, and walking across the room, taking Mrs. Johnson by the hand, said in the most solemn and impressive manner: 'Woman, in the name of the Lord Jesus Christ I command thee to be whole,' and immediately left the room." Elsa was instantly healed, and the next day she did her washing "without difficulty or pain."[4] The healing led directly to the conversion of Father and Mother Johnson and their baptism by the Prophet.

On 12 September 1831 the Prophet and his family moved into the Johnsons' home in Hiram, viewing their hospitality as the answer to the Lord's directive to "seek them a home, as they are taught through prayer by the Spirit" (D&C 63:65). For six months Joseph enjoyed uninterrupted spiritual outpouring in the Johnson home. However, violence displaced peace on 24 March 1832, when Joseph Smith was tarred and feathered. Father Johnson, "hearing the outcry of the family," attempted to help. He "went to the door, but finding it held by some one on the outside, he called for his gun, when those who held the door left; he pursued, and was knocked down; his collarbone was broken." He was taken back to his home and blessed by David Whitmer and immediately healed.[5]

Soon after the terrible incident Father Johnson moved to Kirtland and opened an inn near the Newel K. Whitney Store. In Kirtland on 17 February 1833 he was ordained an elder, and on 4 June 1833 he was ordained a high priest by Joseph Smith and given a "promise of eternal life inasmuch as he keepeth my commandments from henceforth—for he is a descendant of Joseph and a partaker of the blessings of the promise made unto the fathers" (D&C 96:6–7). On 17 February 1834 he became a member of the Kirtland high council (see D&C 102:3). Father Johnson is remembered for displaying in his inn the mummies and papyri obtained from Michael Chandler and also for his work on the Kirtland Temple and for receiving an inheritance and blessing for his labors on 8 March 1835 (see D&C 104:34–38).

Financial difficulties plagued him in 1836. He was a defendant in a number of lawsuits for various sums of money owed on unpaid notes. Five of the suits were for nonpayment of private loans. According to family tradition, one lawsuit was for selling "spiritous liquors" contrary to existing laws. The prosecution discontinued this suit when Father Johnson agreed to mend his ways.[6] The failure of the Kirtland Safety Society, of which he was a charter member, added to his troubles.

His legal and financial problems, combined with a loss of commitment to eternal truths, led to his apostasy in 1837. Procedural difficulties developing during his Church trial were never resolved, as the meeting ended in confusion. However, on 3 September 1837 his continuing service on the high council was "objected to," giving rise to the impression later held by some of his descendants that he was excommunicated from the Church.[7]

Father Johnson died on 30 July 1843 in Kirtland at the age of sixty-five. He is buried in the cemetery near the Kirtland Temple near his daughters, Emily and Mary.

Notes

1. Luke Johnson, "History of Luke Johnson," *Millennial Star* 26 (31 December 1864): 834.

2. See Larry C. Porter and Susan Easton Black, eds., *The Prophet Joseph Smith: Essays on the Life and Mission of Joseph Smith* (Salt Lake City: Deseret Book Co., 1988), p. 173. The John Johnson farm and home in Hiram was purchased by the Church Historic Cities Committee in 1956. The farmhouse was dedicated by Elder James A. Cullimore. In 1984 a branch of the Church was organized in Hiram and began meeting in the John Johnson home. Less than two years later, on 22 March 1986, President Ezra Taft Benson broke ground for a meetinghouse on the historic John Johnson farm. The building was dedicated in 1987.

3. See Johnson, p. 834.

4. *HC* 1:215–16.

5. Johnson, p. 835.

6. Virginia Tims, quoted in Max E. Aycock, letter to author, 22 January 1992, Ephraim, Utah.

7. *HC* 2:510.

LUKE S. JOHNSON

Testimony of the Twelve Apostles,
D&C 68; 75:9; 102:3

Birth: *3 November 1807, Pomfret, Windsor County, Vermont. Son of John Johnson and Elsa Jacobs.*
Death: *9 December 1861, Salt Lake City, Salt Lake County, Utah.*

The conversion of Luke Johnson's parents to Mormonism led directly to Luke's baptism on 10 May 1831 by the Prophet Joseph Smith. During the first six years of his membership he faithfully adhered to gospel principles and often sought occasions for service (see D&C 68:8). His mission with Sidney Rigdon to New Portage, Ohio, led to the baptism of about fifty people and the organization of a branch. His labors with Seymour Brunson in the southern states led to the baptism of over one hundred individuals and the formation of two branches.

His zeal to serve was mingled with a sense of humor:

> Passing by the home of Ezekial on his way home from a council meeting, late at night, he sighted a ladder leaning against the side of Ezekial's house—it happened to be close to the window of Ezekial's upstairs bedroom. [Luke] immediately seized upon the thought that this would be an opportune time to have Ezekial's wish of a voice from the unknown fulfilled. Climbing up the ladder, he proceeded, thusly; in a low pitched voice; EZEKIAL! EZEKIAL!! EZEKIAL!!! REPENT! REPENT!!! REPENT!!!! . . . It is said that Ezekial did his best to do as the voice had commanded—so was never informed of its true source.[1]

In May 1834 Luke joined Zion's Camp, making "a declaration before I started that I would go into Jackson Co., or die in the attempt."[2] On the journey he acted as a scout, going before the camp and marking the signs and noting the situation of the enemies. When cholera struck the camp, he dug the graves. Heber C. Kimball recorded: "While brother Luke Johnson was digging, the cholera attacked him with cramping and blindness; brother Brigham laid hold of him and pulled him out of the grave, and shook him about, talked to, and prayed for him, and exhorted him to jump about and exercise himself, when it would leave him for a few moments, then it would attack him again; and thus we had the greatest difficulty to keep the destroyer from laying us low."[3]

When the camp dispersed, Luke returned to Kirtland, where on 17 February 1834 he was chosen to be in the first high council of the Church (D&C 102:3). Two days later his father, John Johnson, gave him a blessing, saying, "Bless this my son, according to the blessings of his forefathers; that he may be strengthened in his ministry, according to his holy calling."[4]

For a time, Luke was a strong defender of the Prophet. When a Baptist clergyman from New York called the Prophet "a hypocrite, a liar, an imposter, . . . [Joseph] kicked him into the street." Luke followed the man to the edge of town, "making him travel pretty lively until he got a few rods over the line when I overtook him and said, 'Sir, you are lucky to have got over the line, and out of my jurisdiction, or I should have arrested you.'"[5]

In February 1835 Luke was ordained to the Quorum of the Twelve Apostles. His spiritual resolve weakened as financial speculation took precedence in 1837: "My mind became darkened, and I was left to pursue my own course. I lost the Spirit of God, and neglected my duty; the consequence was, that at a Conference held in Kirtland, September 3, 1837, . . . I was cut off from the Church."[6] The following Sunday, Luke confessed his faults and was received into fellowship. His repentance was brief. By December 1837 he joined apostates in publicly denouncing the Church. Luke was excommunicated for apostasy the next year in Far West.

During these difficulties it is most interesting that his love and concern for the Smith family did not waver. When he learned of a plan to present the Prophet with a serious charge that could have resulted in an expensive lawsuit, Luke arrested Joseph on a trivial charge, which prevented the carrying out of the former plan. "Joseph settled the execution, and thanked me for my interference," Luke penned.[7] He also aided the imprisoned Joseph Smith Sr.:

> I put him in a small room adjoining the entrance from the office. . . .
> I took a nail out from over the window sash, left the room and locked
> the door, and commenced telling stories in the courtroom, to raise a
> laugh, for I was afraid they would hear father Smith getting out of the
> window; when the court called for the prisoner, I stepped into the
> room in the dark and slipped the nail into its place in the window, and
> went back and told the court that the prisoner had made his escape.[8]

When the Saints moved to Missouri and then to Illinois, Luke chose to remain in Ohio, except for one year when he resided in Cabal County, Virginia, where he taught school and studied medicine. He pursued additional medical training in Ohio by attending lectures at the Botanical College in Cincinnati. For eight years he had a medical practice in Kirtland and, according to family tradition, "did not officiate in any religious duties."[9]

It was not until 1846 that Luke and his family returned to the fellowship of the Saints: "I have stopped by the wayside and stood aloof from the work of the Lord. But my heart is with this people. I want to be associated with the saints; go with them into the wilderness and continue with them to the end."[10] He was rebaptized by his brother-in-law Orson Hyde on 8 March 1846.

Luke journeyed to the Salt Lake Valley with the original company of pioneers in 1847. He settled in Taylorsville, Utah, before moving to Rush Creek, Tooele County. The small community at Rush Creek was renamed Johnson's Settlement, later St. John, in honor of Luke. In

1856 he was appointed by Wilford Woodruff as the presiding elder and in 1858 he was named bishop of the Church in St. John.

His life in the settlement was laced with kindness to those in need. The wife of George Burridge recalled that one winter, when she came to his home seeking milk, "my feet [were] wrapped in gunny-sacks, to keep them warm. Luke looked at my feet and laughed and said, 'Hannah, is that the best you can do for shoes?' I told him they were all I had. The next morning when I called for the milk Luke presented me with a good substantial pair of shoes."[11]

Another recorded incident depicts Luke's bravery. After a quarrel erupted between Luke and a rogue in the settlement named Jake, the rogue drew his gun and said, according to one source, "'Now, Johnson, I'm going to kill you.' [Luke], without the slightest fears or agitation calmly said, 'Jake, you're not fool enough to try to shoot a man with a gun without a cap?' The cap was on the gun, but Jakes eyes fell and [Luke] gave him an upper-cut to the chin and over-powered him."[12]

On 9 December 1861, while in Salt Lake City on business, Luke Johnson died at the home of Orson Hyde. He was fifty-four years old. Brigham Young eulogized, "Since his return to the church he has lived up to the truth to the best of his ability, and he died in the faith."[13]

Notes

There exists uncertainty about Luke S. Johnson's middle name. Several questions have arisen as to what the initial *S* represents. Some assume it stands for Samuel, while others conclude it stands for Safford.

1. Darrel K. Loosle, "Luke S. and Lyman E. Johnson—Apostles" (n.p., n.d.), p. 2, in author's possession.

2. Luke Johnson, "History of Luke Johnson," *Millennial Star* 26 (31 December 1864): 836; 27 (1865): 5–7.

3. Heber C. Kimball, "Extract from the Journal of Heber C. Kimball," *Millennial Star* 26 (27 August 1864): 551.

4. *HC* 2:32.

5. Johnson, *Millennial Star* 27:5.

6. Ibid., p. 6.

7. Ibid., pp. 5–6.

8. Ibid., p. 6.

9. Ibid., p. 7.

10. As cited in "Deposed Church Official Won Reinstatement," *Church News,* 19 November 1960, p. 16.

11. As cited in Loosle, p. 13.

12. As cited in ibid.

13. *CHC* 5:143.

LYMAN EUGENE JOHNSON
Testimony of the Twelve Apostles,
D&C 68; 75:14

Birth: *24 October 1811, Pomfret, Windsor County, Vermont. Son of John Johnson and Elsa Jacobs.*
Death: *20 December 1856, near Prairie Du Chien, Crawford County, Wisconsin.*

In November 1831, nine months after Lyman Johnson's baptism, the Prophet received a revelation directing him and the other faithful elders of the Church to be missionaries: "Go ye into all the world, preach the gospel to every creature, acting in the authority which I have given you" (D&C 68:8). In obedience he accepted the call. Another revelation given on 25 January 1832 directed him to serve a mission to the East with Orson Pratt (see D&C 75:14). Lyman left penniless and with one change of clothing, walking from Ohio to Pennsylvania and then on to New Jersey and New York.

Upon returning to Ohio he attended the School of the Prophets before recruiting volunteers for Zion's Camp in Vermont. On the camp march Lyman is remembered for speaking on "the necessity of men being upright in their walk, and keeping the Sabbath day holy."[1]

Lyman Johnson was called to the Quorum of the Twelve Apostles on 14 February 1835. He was the first Apostle chosen in this dispensation but did not become President of the Quorum, because age rather than ordination determined seniority. Since Lyman was only twenty-three years old and the youngest member called to the Twelve, he served in the twelfth position. In his apostolic blessing he was promised that "he should bear the tidings of salvation to nations, tongues, and people, until the utmost corners of the earth shall hear the tidings."[2] The promise began to be fulfilled when he labored with his brethren in New Brunswick and along the eastern seaboard.

Lyman's apostasy began in 1837 over a merchandising venture in Kirtland. He claimed his loss of six thousand dollars was the fault of the Prophet Joseph Smith. He and Orson Pratt preferred charges against the Prophet "for lying and misrepresentation—also for extortion—and for speaking disrespectfully, against his brethren behind their backs."[3]

These charges were dismissed; however, Lyman was charged with misrepresentation and disfellowshipped on 3 September 1837.[4] One week later he confessed his wrongdoings and was reinstated.

But it appears his heart was not entirely right. Heber C. Kimball recalled speaking with Lyman about his forthcoming mission to England and hearing him say, "'Brother Heber, . . . I am sorry you are going, and consider you are foolish; but if you are determined to go, I will help you all that is in my power'; and he took from his shoulders a good, nice camlet cloak and put it onto mine. . . . That cloak I wore three times across the sea, and Parley P. Pratt wore it four times; and in all it crossed the sea seven times."[5]

On 13 April 1838 Lyman was excommunicated for bringing distress to the innocent, assaulting Phineas Young, not attending Church meetings, failing to observe the Word of Wisdom, and unrighteous conduct. Although no longer adhering to the Mormon faith, Lyman remained friendly to the Saints and often lamented with them about his spiritual downfall. He stated: "I would suffer my right hand to be cut off, if I could believe it again. Then I was full of joy and gladness. My dreams were pleasant. When I awoke in the morning my spirit was cheerful. I was happy by day and by night, full of peace and joy and thanksgiving. But now it is darkness, pain, sorrow, misery in the extreme. I have never since seen a happy moment."[6]

Lyman was an attorney in Davenport and Keokuk, Iowa, in the 1840s and 1850s. He died in a sleighing accident in 1856 at the age of forty-five. An obituary notice detailed the tragedy: "He was in a sleigh with others, when it went through an air-hole in the ice, of the Mississippi" near Prairie Du Chien, Wisconsin.[7]

Notes

1. Darrell K. Loosle, "Luke S. and Lyman E. Johnson—Apostles" (n.p., n.d.), p. 3, in author's possession.

2. *HC* 2:188.

3. As cited in Chad J. Flake, "The Newell K. Whitney Collection," *BYU Studies* 11 (Summer 1971): 327.

4. See *HC* 2:484, 509.

5. Heber C. Kimball, in *JD* 6:65.

6. As cited by Brigham Young, in *JD* 19:42.

7. *Prairie Du Chien (Wis.) Cousier,* 22 December 1859.

HEBER CHASE KIMBALL
Testimony of the Twelve Apostles,
D&C 124:129

Birth: *14 June 1801, Sheldon, Franklin County,
Vermont. Son of Solomon Farnham Kimball and
Anna Spaulding.*
Death: *22 June 1868, Salt Lake City, Salt Lake
County, Utah.*

Financial reverses within the Kimball family forced nineteen-year-old Heber to venture from his home and seek his fortune: "I found myself cast abroad upon the world, without a friend to console my grief." After several weeks of suffering "for want of food and the comforts of life," he accepted an offer from his brother to board with him and learn the potter's trade.[1]

An unusual evening was spent by this apprentice potter on 22 September 1827 in Mendon, New York. With his young bride, Vilate, and neighbors, Heber beheld an army marching in the sky and engaging in combat with opposing military forces. The vision was symbolic of the final great struggle between the forces of good and evil. Heber later learned that on that very evening the Prophet Joseph Smith had received the plates from the angel Moroni.[2]

Heber and his family joined the Prophet in Kirtland. He wrote of the perilous events of those early days: "[We] were obliged to lay with our firelocks in our arms, to preseve Brother Joseph's life."[3] On 4 June 1837 Joseph said, "Brother Heber, the Spirit of the Lord has whispered to me: 'Let my servant Heber go to England and proclaim my Gospel, and open the door of salvation to that nation.'" In obedience to the prophetic promptings, Heber "felt a determination to go at all hazards."[4]

He journeyed from Ohio to New York and then sailed on the ship *Garrick* to Liverpool. When the ship anchored, a small boat took him to shore: "When we were within six or seven feet of the pier, I leaped on shore, . . . and for the first time in my life I stood on British ground, among strangers. . . . I put my trust in God, believing that He would assist me in publishing the truth, give me utterance, and be a present help in time of need."[5] The success he enjoyed on English shores was remarkable.

After preaching to a gathering in Chatburn, he wrote, "I felt someone pulling at my coat, exclaiming, 'Maister, Maister.' I turned round and asked what was wanted, Mrs. Elizabeth Partington said, 'Please sir, will you baptize me?' 'And me?' 'And me?' exclaimed more than a dozen voices. Accordingly I went down into the water and baptized twenty-five."[6]

Of the many converts to Mormonism Heber humbly expressed, "Blessed be the name of the Lord, who has crowned our labors with such success!"[7]

Upon returning to Kirtland he found his family in good health and "our joy was mutual." They journeyed to Far West, Missouri, where he met with friends, "some of whom were so glad to see us, that tears started in their eyes when we took them by the hand." Unfortunately, his joy was dampened as his family and friends were subjected to the atrocities of mobocracy. When the Prophet was incarcerated in Liberty Jail, Heber was a frequent visitor: "I went to Liberty almost every week to visit the brethren."[8]

In 1840 Heber left on his second mission to England with companion Brigham Young. They reached Liverpool on 6 April 1840. After strengthening the Saints and baptizing hundreds of new converts, Heber returned to Nauvoo and penned, "There were about three hundred Saints there to meet us, and a greater manifestation of love and gladness I never saw before."[9]

In Nauvoo he struggled to accept the doctrine of plural marriage. He fasted for three days, wept, and prayed. When the answer came, he was strongly supportive.

Heber's strength did not lessen at the Martyrdom, for he knew the Twelve held "the keys to open up the authority of [the Lord's] kingdom upon the four corners of the earth" (D&C 124:128). He pressed forward through additional trials of threatened mobocracy, the rigors of the Iowa wilderness, and the trek to the Great Salt Lake Valley.

In December 1847 he was chosen as First Counselor to Brigham Young in the Presidency of the Church. Five years before, this calling had been prophesied by Hyrum Smith: "You shall be blest with a fulness and shall be not one whit behind the chiefest; as an Apostle you shall stand in the presence of God to judge the people; and as a Prophet you shall attain to the honor of the three!"[10] Though he did not profess to be a prophet, he manifested the gift of prophecy, and Brigham Young said of him, "Heber is my prophet."[11]

During the remaining two decades of Heber's life, his history is inseparably interwoven with the pioneer development of the intermountain region. He was chief justice and lieutenant governor of the provisional government of Deseret. "Brother Heber" traveled through the pioneer settlements strengthening the Saints, and was everywhere honored and beloved. His testimony of the truth was loudly proclaimed from settlement to settlement: "The Gospel and plan of salvation that I have embraced, is music to me; it is sweet to my body, and congenial to my spirit; and it is more lovely than anything else I have ever seen since I have been in the world. I love it."[12]

At the death of his wife, Vilate, on 22 October 1867, Heber lamented, "I shall not be long after her."[13] Eight months later, on 22 June 1868, Heber died. His death was linked to a severe fall from a wagon. His funeral was held on 24 June 1868 in the Salt Lake Tabernacle, and the eulogy offered by Brigham Young, who said: "We can say truly that the day of this man's death was far better to him than the day of his birth. . . . I have been personally acquainted with him forty-three years and I can testify that he has been a man of truth, a man of benevolence, a man that was to be trusted. . . . Brother Heber C. Kimball has been my first counselor for almost twenty-four years. I am happy to state, it is a matter of great joy to me."[14]

Notes

1. Heber C. Kimball, "Synopsis of the History of Heber Chase Kimball," *Millennial Star* 26 (23 July 1864): 471.

2. See Orson F. Whitney, *Life of Heber C. Kimball*, 3d ed. (Salt Lake City: Bookcraft, 1967), pp. 15–17.

3. Kimball, "Synopsis," p. 535.

4. Whitney, p. 104.

5. As cited in ibid., p. 119.

6. As cited in ibid., p. 171.

7. As cited in ibid., p. 174; see also p. 187.

8. As cited in ibid., pp. 202, 203.

9. As cited in ibid., p. 313.

10. Patriarchal blessing, 9 March 1842, Archives Division, Church Historical Department, The Church of Jesus Christ of Latter-day Saints, Salt Lake City, Utah.

11. As cited in Lawrence R. Flake, *Mighty Men of Zion* (Salt Lake City: Karl D. Butler, 1974), p. 83.

12. As cited in Whitney, p. 457.

13. As cited in ibid., p. 473.

14. As cited in ibid., pp. 495–96.

Spencer Woolley Kimball
Official Declaration—2

Birth: *28 March 1895, Salt Lake City, Salt Lake County, Utah. Son of Andrew Kimball and Olive Woolley.*
Death: *5 November 1985, Salt Lake City, Salt Lake County, Utah.*

In his youth Spencer W. Kimball worked hard feeding the hogs raised on the family farm in Thatcher, Arizona. He quipped that carrying an endless succession of large cans of slop to the pigs had stunted his growth. "Those blamed hogs are enough to worry one bald-headed," he once wrote.[1] Spencer's father remarked about his quick-witted son, "I have dedicated him to the Lord and to His service. He will become a mighty man in the Church."[2]

At age twelve Spencer was ordained a deacon and at fourteen he was teaching his first Sunday School class. By fifteen he "took down the family Bible, climbed the stairs to his attic room, . . . and began [reading] at Genesis." He read nightly for about a year "until he could shut the book with great pride, finished."[3]

His schooling in Thatcher was at the LDS Academy. He served as president of each of his classes and played forward on the academy basketball team. "I would rather play this game than eat," he said.[4] After completing his schooling at the Academy, Spencer served a mission in the central states. He was enthusiastic about proselyting, but as a junior companion he was subject to his partner, who "tried my soul."[5] On the mission he baptized five individuals, though disclaiming any personal credit: "They were probably more the fruits of the work of other missionaries who preceded me."[6]

Upon returning home he saw a picture of Camilla Eyring, the new home economics teacher at Gila Academy, in a local newspaper. "There's my wife. I am going to marry her," said Spencer.[7] For thirty-one days he courted Camilla. On their wedding day in 1917, Spencer possessed less than ten dollars and Camilla owed fifty dollars. To better their financial situation Spencer played the piano for two orchestras, wrote columns for a weekly newspaper, and kept books for a department store. His financial success came when he accepted work at a bank and then with an insurance company.

When the Mount Graham Stake was formed, Spencer was selected as president. To visit each ward in his stake, he had to travel 1,750 miles. He is remembered in the area for coordinating the emergency response for the Gila River flood.

On 8 July 1943 Elder J. Reuben Clark telephoned him and said, "The brethren have just chosen you to fill one of the vacancies in the Quorum." His response was, "I am so weak and small and limited and incapable. Of course, there could be only one answer to any call from the Brethren."[8]

As he shared the news with others, friends congratulated him and one said, "It's clear the Lord must have called you—no one else would have thought of you."[9] He was ordained by President Heber J. Grant and told, "Set your heart upon the service of the Lord thy God."[10]

Throughout his years in the Twelve Spencer was known for his kindness. For example, one time when his host insisted on shining his shoes, Spencer agreed. As the man pronounced "Finished!" Spencer replied, "Oh, no! Not yet! You sit here and I'll shine yours."[11]

Much of Spencer's service in the Quorum was with the posterity of Father Lehi. In 1965 he said to President David O. McKay, "I think the time of the Lamanite has come for them to hear the Gospel." President McKay remarked, "Yes, it is time and . . . you are the one of the Twelve who has the vision of it."[12]

Despite his fast pace and energetic mannerisms, Spencer suffered much from physical ailments: heart pains, insomnia, facial paralysis, Bell's palsy, and cancer of the throat, to name just a few. His many illnesses led Harold B. Lee to remark, "Spencer lives from blessing to blessing."[13]

Spencer's travels led him to far-off places throughout the world. Everywhere he went, members were anxious to shake his hand. He remarked once in South Africa, on receiving a comment about his strong handshake, "I milked cows the first half of my life so I could shake hands the other half."[14] Of the sites he saw on his travels, the most memorable for him was the tomb where the body of Jesus was laid. His love for the Savior and recognition of the Atonement led to his writing of *The Miracle of Forgiveness* and *Faith Precedes the Miracle*.

On 30 December 1973 Spencer became President of The Church of Jesus Christ of Latter-day Saints. His phrase "Lengthen your stride" became an important slogan in spurring Church members to greater efforts. Under his energetic leadership the First Quorum of the Seventy was organized and additional scriptures were added to the Pearl of Great Price.[15] The Church moved forward at an unprecedented rate, and temples began to dot the earth. Spencer is best remembered for the announcement on 9 June 1978 of a revelation entitling all worthy male members of the Church to hold the priesthood (see Official Declaration—2).

Spencer's testimony was sure: "I know this work is true and the work will roll on and God is at the helm."[16] He died on 5 November 1985 in his apartment in Salt Lake at the age of ninety.

President Ezra Taft Benson said his life was characterized by his "humble dependence on the Lord," "his great love for the sons and daughters of Lehi," and "the quiet miracle of forgiveness that has come to many as a result of President Kimball's counseling, interest in, caring for, and loving those souls who have been tainted by sin."[17]

Notes

1. As cited in Edward L. Kimball and Andrew E. Kimball Jr., *Spencer W. Kimball* (Salt Lake City: Bookcraft, 1977), p. 37.
2. As cited in ibid., p. 196.
3. Ibid., pp. 56–57.
4. As cited in ibid., p. 65.
5. As cited in ibid., p. 75.
6. As cited in ibid., p. 79.
7. As cited in ibid., p. 83.
8. As cited in ibid., p. 189.
9. As cited in ibid., p. 198.
10. As cited in ibid., p. 205.
11. As cited in ibid., p. 233.
12. As cited in ibid., p. 361.
13. As cited in ibid., p. 401.

14. As cited in ibid., p. 407.

15. These scriptures are now found in Doctrine and Covenants 137 and 138.

16. As cited in Kimball, p. 269.

17. As cited in Don L. Searle, "President Ezra Taft Benson, Ordained Thirteenth President of the Church," *Ensign* 15 (December 1985): 4.

JOSEPH KNIGHT SR.
D&C 12; 23

Birth: *3 November 1772, Oakham, Worcester County, Massachusetts. Son of Benjamin and Hannah Knight.*
Death: *2 February 1847, Mount Pisgah, Harrison County, Iowa.*

In 1808 Joseph Knight Sr. and his family moved to Bainbridge, New York, and two years later to Colesville, New York, where they resided for nineteen years. Father Knight, as Joseph was affectionately known by the Saints, purchased a farm on the Susquehanna River and built a gristmill. Biographer William G. Hartley wrote that he was "not rich, yet he possessed enough of this world's goods to secure to himself and family, not only the necessaries, but also the comforts of life." His religious orientation was the Universalist doctrine.[1]

Father Knight first became acquainted with Joseph Smith in 1826. While lodging at the Knight home Joseph spoke of his glorious visitations. "My father and I believed him," wrote Joseph Knight Jr., "and I think we were the first to do so, after his own family."[2] When Joseph Smith obtained the Book of Mormon plates, he used Father Knight's horse and carriage as his means of conveyance.

Joseph Knight wrote of assisting the young prophet on another occasion: "I let him have some little provisions and some few things out of the store, a pair of shoes, and three dollars in money to help him a little." He also wrote, "I gave . . . Joseph a little money to buy paper to translate."[3] Joseph Smith praised Father Knight for his donations that "enabled us to continue the work when otherwise we must have relinquished it for a season."[4]

As others sought baptism into the Church, Father Knight hesitated: "I had some thots to go forrod, But I had not red the Book of Mormon and I wanted to [examine] a little more I Being a Restorationar and had not [examined] so much as I wanted to."[5] Aware of his hesitation, the Prophet Joseph prayed for him and received a revelation in April 1830: "Joseph Knight, . . . you must take up your cross, in the which you must pray vocally before the world as well as in secret. . . . It is your duty to unite with the true church, and give your language to exhortation continually." (D&C 23:6–7.)

In obedience Father Knight was baptized on 28 June 1830 by Oliver Cowdery. Soon after his baptism religious persecution was directed against him. Rather than deny his new faith Father Knight left New York and settled with others from Colesville in the small Ohio community of Thompson. "We all went to work and made fence and planted and sowed the fields," wrote Father Knight. His stay in Thompson was brief: "We was Commanded to take up our Jorney to the Regions westward to the Boarders of the Lamanites."[6]

He moved with the Saints to Jackson County, Missouri, in 1831. There the Knight family suffered from poverty. According to William G. Hartley, "A stranger staring at them would not see in them the prosperous Yankees they had once been in New York before embracing Mormonism."[7]

In 1839 the Knight family settled in Nauvoo. There Father Knight was feeble and unable to work. His son Newel wrote, "My father, as my own family, depended on me for bread and the necessities of life." He added, "It was a pleasure to me to supply his wants and add to his comforts."[8] Aware of his faithfulness and poor health, the high council donated a house and lot to him.[9] One day the Prophet Joseph saw his elderly friend hobbling along without a cane. The Prophet approached him and, putting his arm around him, pressed Father Knight's fingers onto the top of his cane and said, "Brother Knight, you need this cane more than I do." The Prophet then told him to keep it as long as he needed it, and then to pass it on to descendants with the first name Joseph. The cane has been passed down through several descendants until the present day.

On 22 January 1842 the Prophet Joseph wrote a tribute to Joseph Knight:

> Joseph Knight . . . was among the number of the first to administer to my necessities. . . . For fifteen years he has been faithful and true, and even-handed and exemplary, and virtuous and kind, never deviating to the right hand or to the left. Behold he is a righteous man, may God Almighty lengthen out the old man's days; and may his trembling,

tortured, and broken body be renewed, . . . and it shall be said of him, by the sons of Zion, while there is one of them remaining, that this man was a faithful man in Israel; therefore his name shall never be forgotten.[10]

Father Knight left Nauvoo and, with the aid of his son Joseph Knight Jr., gathered with the poor in Mount Pisgah, Iowa. Father Knight died in February 1847 at Mount Pisgah at the age of seventy-four.

Notes

1. William G. Hartley, *"They Are My Friends": A History of the Joseph Knight Family, 1825–1850* (Provo, Utah: Grandin Book Co., 1986), pp. 11–12.
2. Joseph Knight Jr., "Joseph Knight's Incidents of History from 1827–1844," compiled 16 August 1862, film of holograph, Archives Division, Church Historical Department, Salt Lake City, Utah, as cited in Hartley, p. 18.
3. As cited in Hartley, p. 30.
4. As cited in ibid., p. 35.
5. Joseph Knight, "Manuscript of the Early History of Joseph Smith," in Dean C. Jessee, "Joseph Knight's Recollections of Early Mormon History," *BYU Studies* 17 (Autumn 1976): 37.
6. Ibid., p. 39.
7. Hartley, p. 135.
8. As cited in Hartley, p. 143.
9. See *HC* 4:76.
10. *HC* 5:124–25.

NEWEL KNIGHT
D&C 52:32; 54; 56:6–7; 72; 124:32

Birth: *13 September 1800, Marlborough, Windham County, Vermont. Son of Joseph Knight and Polly Peck.*
Death: *11 January 1847, Knox County, Nebraska.*

Newel Knight settled near his father in Colesville, New York, and operated a carding machine business and a gristmill. "Peace, prosperity and plenty, seemed to crown our labors, and indeed we were a happy family, and my father rejoiced in having us around him," wrote Newel.[1]

In 1826 young Joseph Smith boarded with the Knight family. "I was particularly attached [to Joseph]," penned Newel. "We were very deeply impressed with the truthfulness of his statements concerning the Plates of the Book of Mormon which had been shown him by an Angel of the Lord."[2]

As the Prophet visited with the Knight family in April 1830, he noticed Newel's hesitation to vocally pray. Joseph encouraged him, but Newel's attempt while alone in the woods was unsuccessful. When he returned home, the experience triggered a violent physical struggle. The Prophet Joseph, who was summoned to the scene by Newel's alarmed wife, found that Newel's facial appearance and limbs had become "distorted and twisted in every shape," and his body was finally "caught up off the floor . . . and tossed about most fearfully." Newel pleaded with the Prophet to cast the devil out of him, to which the Prophet replied, "If you know that I can, it shall be done." He commanded the devil in the name of Jesus Christ to depart, and miraculously Newel's body returned to normal. Newel saw the devil leave him and vanish from sight.[3]

As he rested from the ordeal, a vision of the heavens caused him to levitate: "I now began to feel a most pleasing sensation resting upon me, and immediately the visions of heaven were opened to my view. I felt myself attracted upward, . . . I found that the Spirit of the Lord had actually caught me up off the floor, and that my shoulder and head were pressing against the beams."[4]

Newel was baptized in May 1830 at the Whitmer farm. He declared that during the first conference of the Church, held the next month, "I saw the heavens opened, I beheld the Lord Jesus Christ seated at the right hand of the Majesty on High."[5] As the year of 1830 ended he wrote, "Great things have transpired, too great for pen to paint."[6]

In obedience to the Lord's command given in January 1831 to gather in Ohio, Newel and other Saints, "having made the best arrangements we could for the journey, . . . bade adieu to all we held dear on this earth" except the few who had embraced the gospel.[7] Soon after arriving in Thompson, near Kirtland, he was called to serve a mission with Selah J. Griffin (see D&C 52:32). The mission was canceled when difficulties arose in Thompson, where Newel was serving as branch president. The Lord instructed Newel and the Saints in the branch to "go to now and flee the land, lest your enemies come upon you; and take your journey . . . into the regions westward, unto the land of Missouri, unto the borders of the Lamanites" (D&C 54:7–8).

In compliance with the revelation Newel Knight led the branch members to Jackson County, Missouri. In April 1833 he was called to be a counselor to Bishop Isaac Morley. This call was brief, as mobocracy forced him to flee to Clay County. There, in September 1834, his wife, Sally, died. Newel wrote, "Truly she died a martyr to the gospel of our Lord and Savior, Jesus Christ. She was of a frail constitution, and the hardships and privations she had to endure were more than she could survive."[8]

In sorrow Newel returned to Kirtland in May 1835. During his months in Kirtland he developed a romantic interest in Lydia Goldthwaite Bailey. She refused his advances as she was still married to Mr. Bailey. Newel apologized but explained that legally she was no longer married since her husband had deserted her over three years before. Lydia believed that to marry under the circumstances, if legally right, was morally wrong. The Prophet intervened and married Lydia and Newel on 24 November 1835.

Newel and his bride remained in Kirtland until the temple was dedicated, and he "received my anointings, and was also a witness to the great manifestations of God's power in that sacred edifice."[9] They then migrated to Far West, where Newel was called to serve on the high council. Persecution grew in intensity, and Newel wrote, "We calmly submitted to the numerous indignities heaped upon us. . . . Our people made many concessions to the mob in the hope of pacifying them, but it was useless."[10] He joined in the defense of Far West but to no avail, as it was overrun by men he labeled "Boggs Butchers."

Amid these trying times he was privileged to greet the Prophet after his return from Missouri jails. "I can never describe my feelings on meeting with him," he wrote, "and shaking hands with one whom I had so long and so dearly loved, his worth and his sufferings filled my heart with mingled emotions."[11] In January 1843 the Prophet wrote about "Newel Knight and Joseph Knight, junior, whose names I record in the Book of the Law of the Lord with unspeakable delight, for they are my friends."[12]

After the Martyrdom Newel penned his feelings for the Prophet and his brother Hyrum: "O how I loved those men, and rejoiced under their teachings! it seems as if *all* is gone, and as if my very heart strings will break, and were it not for my beloved wife and dear children I feel as if I have nothing to live for, and would rejoice to be with them in the Courts of Glory."[13] One year and a day after their deaths Newel and

Lydia visited Carthage Jail to see the room where the Martyrdom took place. Blood still stained the floor and bullet holes pocked the walls.

Continuing bigotry and mobocracy forced Newel and his family to abandon Nauvoo and join the migrating Saints in Iowa Territory. On 1 January 1847 he seemed to sense that his death was near: "I scarcely know why I am thus anxious, why this world appears so trifling, or the things of the world. I almost desire to leave this tenement of clay, that my spirit may soar aloft and no longer be held in bondage, yet my helpless family seem to need my protection."[14]

Three days later Newel wrote his last diary entry. He described his preaching in church that day of the Saints' need to purify themselves so that "the Lord's presence [will] go before us, while we are journeying in the wilderness."[15] He died on 11 January 1847 from lung inflammation. His remains were placed in a lumber coffin fashioned from a wagon box. Because of the cold, the fingers and feet of the men digging his grave froze.

Lydia, a widow with seven young children, wondered why he had left her. According to her history:

> As she spoke, he stood by her side, with a lovely smile on his face, and said: "Be calm, let not sorrow overcome you. It was necessary that I should go. I was needed behind the vail to represent the true condition of this camp and people. You cannot fully comprehend it now; but the time will come when you shall know why I left you and our little ones. Therefore, dry up your tears. Be patient, I will go before you and protect you in your journeyings. And you and your little ones shall never perish for lack of food."[16]

Notes

1. Newel Knight, "Newel Knight's Journal," in *Scraps of Biography,* p. 48; as published in *Classic Experiences and Adventures* (Salt Lake City: Bookcraft, 1969).

2. As cited in William G. Hartley, *"They Are My Friends": A History of the Joseph Knight Family, 1825–1850* (Provo, Utah: Grandin Book Co., 1986), p. 19.

3. HC 1:82–83.

4. Ibid.

5. Knight, p. 53.

6. As cited in Hartley, p. 64.

7. Knight, pp. 68–69.

8. Ibid., p. 94; see also Hartley, p. 102.

9. Knight, pp. 94–95.

10. Ibid., p. 97.

11. As cited in Hartley, p. 138.

12. As cited in *LDS Biographical Encyclopedia* 2:772.

13. As cited in Hartley, pp. 153–54.

14. As cited in ibid., p. 177.

15. As cited in ibid.

16. Susa Young Gates, *Lydia Knight's History* (Salt Lake City: Juvenile Instructor Office, 1883), pp. 71–72.

VINSON KNIGHT

D&C 124:74, 141

Birth: *14 March 1804, Norwich, Hampshire County, Massachusetts. Son of Rudolphos Knight and Rispah Lee.*
Death: *31 July 1842, Nauvoo, Hancock County, Illinois.*

By age twenty Vinson Knight had inherited an estate located in Perrysburgh, New York, and had cleared a beautiful farm, built a large frame home, and was purported to be prosperous. A housekeeper "complained of a large sack of money that was always in the way on the top shelf of the cupboard."[1]

His life dramatically changed in March 1834 when two strangers, Joseph Smith and Parley P. Pratt, arrived at his home. Vinson and his wife listened to their message and "became convinced that he was no false prophet but an instrument in the hands of the Lord."[2] They were baptized in the spring of 1834 and soon sold their holdings in New York and journeyed 135 miles to Kirtland, Ohio.

Vinson wrote to his mother from Kirtland on 24 June 1835, "I feel that the Lord has blessed me in all my undertakin[g]s since I left there, both in spiritual and temporal blessings. Our children are blessed with the privilege of school and are blessed with the privilege of going to meetings such as we never had before. I can say to you that I am strong in the faith that I have embraced. . . . I am willing to stand and proclaim it to all that I see."[3] He remained with the Saints in Kirtland and worked as a druggist. Vinson was told in his patriarchal blessing, "The Lord loves thee; he has looked upon all thy ways and brought thee thus far that He might make thee useful in His church. . . . Thou art a chosen vessel unto the Lord, and if thou art faithful before Him, thou shalt be sanctified and enjoy a fullness of glory."[4]

In partial fulfillment of the blessing Vinson was ordained an elder on 2 January 1836. Eleven days later he was ordained a high priest and a counselor to Bishop Newel K. Whitney. The Prophet recorded on that occasion, "This has been one of the best days I ever spent; there has been an entire union of feeling expressed in all our proceedings this day and the spirit of the God of Israel has rested upon us in mighty power."[5]

Vinson's complete immersion in the ecclesiastical affairs of Kirtland was evidenced by his attendance at the School of the Prophets and the dedication of the Kirtland Temple and his charter membership in the Kirtland Safety Society. His defense of the Prophet was noted when an apostate declared he would throw Joseph Smith out of the temple. The Prophet turned to Vinson and simply stated, "Brother Knight, take this man out."[6] Vinson caught the man by the legs and tossed him head downward over his shoulder and then carried him, struggling and bawling, out of the building.

His loyalty to the Prophet was also manifest in Missouri. He traveled with Joseph to Far West in the fall of 1837 and was selected as acting bishop in Adam-ondi-Ahman in 1838. As religious persecution escalated Vinson left his holdings in Missouri rather than deny the Prophet. In his redress petition he presented claims against Missouri for damages totaling ten thousand dollars. Of those trying days he penned on 3 February 1839 to William Cooper of Perrysburgh, New York:

> I was at Far West while the troups were there and I did not go home as they threatened my life. . . . What the final end will be I am not able to say. . . . Now sir, I ask you and every republican in these U. States how you would like to be brought up and compelled to lay down your arms. I think that you would feel the same as I did, that death would be a welcome messenger. . . . I was placed in as good a situation as any man in this state to get a living, but now am deprived of it all except my health and the faith I have in that God that has created and preserved me thus far through life.[7]

Vinson temporarily located at Quincy, Illinois, in 1839 and was appointed a Church agent, being authorized to purchase thousands of acres in Illinois and Iowa Territory in behalf of the Church. On 4 May 1839 he was appointed to assume the full title of bishop. He served as bishop of the Lower Ward in Nauvoo and on 19 January 1841 was designated Presiding Bishop of the Church (see D&C 124:75).

In addition to his Church responsibilities, Vinson served on the Nauvoo City Council, as a member of the Nauvoo Agricultural and Manufacturing Association, and as a regent of the University of Nauvoo. On 14 February 1842 he wrote his mother, "The cause why I am separated so far from my relatives is well known to you and to all my relatives. . . . I think we have no reason to complain but on the other hand rejoice and praise that God who has ever been willing to hear the prayers of the righteous, notwithstanding we have been persecuted."[8]

Six months after reaffirming his faithfulness, Vinson's health began to fail. Joseph Smith penned on 31 July 1842, "In council with Bishops Miller and Whitney, Brigham Young, John Taylor, &c., concerning Bishop Vinson Knight's sickness. Brother Knight has been sick about a week, and this morning he began to sink very fast until twelve o'clock when death put a period to his sufferings."[9]

Vinson was thirty-eight when he passed away. While speaking at his funeral the Prophet declared, "There lies a man that has done more for me than my own brother would do."[10]

Notes

1. "Biographies of Vincent Knight and Abigale Meade McBride and Copies of Letters Obtained from a Descendant of Rispah Lee Knight," typescript, 1962, p. 1, Harold B. Lee Library, Brigham Young University, Provo, Utah.

2. Ibid., p. 3.

3. Letter of Vinson Knight to his mother, Rispah Knight, 24 June 1835, Kirtland, Ohio, in author's possession.

4. As cited in "Biographies," p. 4.

5. As cited in ibid., p. 6.

6. As cited in ibid., p. 8.

7. Letter of Vinson Knight to William Cooper, Esq., 8 February 1838, Spencerburg, Missouri, in author's possession.

8. Letter of Vinson Knight to his mother, Rispah Knight, 14 February 1842, Nauvoo, Illinois, in author's possession.

9. HC 5:84.

10. As cited in "Biographies," p. 15.

WILLIAM LAW
D&C 124:82, 87–91, 97–101, 107, 126

Birth: *8 September 1809, Tyrone County, Ireland. Son of Richard Law and Mary Wilson.*
Death: *12 January 1892, Shullsburg, LaFayette County, Wisconsin.*

In 1836 William Law abandoned his Presbyterian leanings for Mormonism, in spite of his father's opposition: "My father is much opposed to [Mormonism] from evil reports &c. which he has heard," he wrote.[1] In November 1839 he moved from Canada to Nauvoo to be with the Saints. From his vantage point as a near neighbor of the Prophet he observed: "I have carefully watched his movements since I have been here, and I assure you I have found him honest and honourable in all our transactions which have been very considerable. I believe he is an honest upright man, and as to his follies let who ever is guiltless throw the first stone at him, I shant do it."[2]

William was called as the Second Counselor in the First Presidency of the Church in 1841 (see D&C 124:91, 126). From 1842 to 1843 he faithfully fulfilled this office by vigorously defending the Prophet's character against the anti-Mormon sentiments of John C. Bennett and offering to risk his own life to rescue the Prophet from Missouri captors. But his loyalty faltered by the winter of 1843.

On 2 January 1844 he journalized, "This day I learn from remarks made by J. Smith before the city council and police, I am suspected of being a Brutus, and consequently narrowly watched, and should any misconceive my motives my life would be jeopardized."[3] On 8 January 1844 he wrote, "I was passing along the street near my house, when call'd to by Joseph Smith, he said I was injuring him by telling evil of him, he could not name any one that I talked to." When the Prophet informed him that he was no longer in the First Presidency, "I confess I feel annoyed very much by such unprecedented treatment for it is illegal, inasmuch as I was appointed by revelation." However, he penned, "I feel relieved from a most embarrassing situation I cannot fellowship the abominations which I verily know are practiced by this man, concequently I am glad to be free from him."[4]

On 18 April 1844 William Law was excommunicated. Angered at the decision, he requested a review of his case at the forthcoming general conference. His request was denied. Embittered, on 1 June 1844 he wrote of his intent to publish the *Nauvoo Expositor:* "Our enemies rage, and publish slander about us, but we cease not to vindicate the cause of truth, and oppose crime. To this end we have purchased a printing press and intend issuing in a few days a paper to be entitled the Nauvoo Expositor. This course has caused great alarm in the camp of our enemies."[5]

On 7 June 1844 the first edition of the anti-Mormon newspaper was published: "This day the Nauvoo Expositor goes forth to the world, rich with facts, such expositions as make the guilty tremble and rage. 1000 sheets were struck and five hundred mailed forthwith. If the paper is suffered to continue it will set forth deeds of the most dark, cruel and damning ever perpetrated by any people under the name of religion since the world began."[6]

The printing and destruction of the fraudulent newspaper led to the arrest, imprisonment, and martyrdom of Joseph and Hyrum. Although denying his complicity in the tragedy William wrote:

> The judgment of an offended God had fallen upon them. During the latter part of their lives they knew no mercy, and in their last moments they found none. Thus the wicked may prosper for a time, but the hour of retribution is sure to overtake them. . . .
>
> . . . [Joseph] was one of the false prophets spoken of by Christ who would come in sheep's clothing but inwardly be a ravelling wolf. . . . He claimed to be a god, whereas he was only a servant of the Devil, and as such met his fate.[7]

By the fall of 1844 William had moved to Hampton, Illinois. On 29 September 1844 he was taken into custody on charges of contributing to the Martyrdom, but he was released the following day. In a letter to the newspaper *The Upper Mississippian* he wrote: "Our lives are yet threatened by a band of desperate men, who have sworn with a solemn oath to shed our blood, even to the third generations.—Our homes here in your peaceful county are to be given to the burning flames, and our wives to be left widows in our midst." However, even during this precarious situation he wrote in the letter of his belief in the early teachings of the Prophet: "We verily believe, and many of us know of a surety, that the religion of the Latter Day Saints, as originally taught by Joseph Smith, which is contained in the old and new Testaments, book of Covenants, and book of Mormon, is verily true."[8]

In Hampton William was employed for a decade as a merchant before turning his professional attention to medicine. For nearly forty years he was acknowledged as a physician and surgeon near Apple River, Illinois, and in Shullsburg, Wisconsin.

After the death of his wife William resided with his son, Judge "Tommy" Law, in Shullsburg. He wrote in 1885 that the Church "never was a Church of Christ, but a most wicked blasphemous humbug gotten up for the purpose of making money."[9] In 1887 William confessed, "The great mistake of my life was my having anything to do with Mormonism."[10]

> Have never read any of the books published about the Mormons; never read Bennett's book, have kept no papers published in Nauvoo; haven't a scrap of any kind; the only number of the Expositor I had some one carried off. My wife (at an early day) burned up the Book of Mormon and the Doctrine and Covenants. She said no Mormon work could find a place in her house. We have lived down in a great measure the disgrace following our unfortunate association with the Mormons. We committed a great error, but no crime. This is my consolation, that we only erred in judgment.[11]

He died on 12 January 1892 in Shullsburg at the age of eighty-two.

Notes

1. William Law to Isaac Russell, 17 January 1839, Archives Division, Church Historical Department, Salt Lake City, Utah, as cited in Lyndon W. Cook, *William Law* (Orem, Utah: Grandin Book Co., 1994), p. 8.

2. William Law to Isaac Russell, 29 November 1840, Archives Division, Church Historical Department, Salt Lake City, Utah, as cited in Cook, p. 11.

3. William Law's Nauvoo diary, as cited in Cook, p. 38.

4. Ibid., p. 46.

5. Ibid., pp. 54–55.

6. Ibid., p. 55.

7. William Law's Nauvoo diary, as cited in Cook, pp. 60–61.

8. Letter of William Law, published in the *Upper Mississippian,* 7 September 1844, as cited in Cook, pp. 91, 94.

9. "1885 Affidavit of William Law," as cited in Cook, p. 29 n. 91.

10. William Law to Wilheim Wyl, 7 January 1887, in *The Daily Tribune,* 3 July 1887, as cited in Cook, p. 104.

11. William Law to Wilheim Wyl, 20 January 1887, in *The Daily Tribune,* 3 July 1887, as cited in Cook, pp. 105–6.

ANN LEE
D&C 49: Introduction

Birth: *29 February 1736, Manchester, England. Daughter of John Lees.* [1]
Death: *8 September 1784, Watervliet, Schenectady County, New York.*

As a child Ann Lee worked twelve hours a day cutting velvet, preparing cotton for looms, and shearing fur for hatmakers. She later worked as a cook in a Manchester infirmary, where "she was distinguished for her neatness, faithfulness, prudence, and good economy."[2] She never received any formal education and could not read or write. To compensate, Ann developed memory skills and could recite verbatim many passages from the Bible.

At age twenty-two her life was dramatically changed when she attended a series of revival meetings conducted by James and Jane Wardley. She united with the Wardleys' Shaking Quakers, a name first used to ridicule the group's mode of religious worship. Followers of the Wardleys believed that chanting, dancing, shaking, clapping, and whirling caused sin to fall from the believers. They professed that Christ was coming to reign on earth and that his second appearance would be in the form of a woman.[3]

Sharing in that belief, Ann confessed her sins and joined in the frenzy of the dance. She then felt endowed "with great power over sin" and vowed to take up the cross against evil. "I love the day that I first received the Gospel," Ann said. "I call it my birthday."[4]

Ann was married on 5 January 1762 to Abraham Standerin, an illiterate local blacksmith, at her father's insistence. In rapid succession she gave birth to four children; three died as babies and the fourth, Elizabeth, died at age six. The loss of her children caused her much grief and directly led to her conviction that sexual relations and marriage were the root of all evil. According to historian F. W. Evans, she convinced herself that "only a total denial of the body could purify her tortured soul."[5] Although married to Abraham for the next six years, she became an avowed celibate.

Public denunciations of her blasphemous religious convictions led local authorities to imprison her, but this did not thwart her stance. By 1777 she was the recognized leader of the Shakers. Her vision of Adam and Eve became the cornerstone of the Shakers' belief. Biographer Nardi Reeder Campion writes: "She watched them defy God and commit the forbidden sexual act. Then she witnessed their expulsion from the garden by an enraged Deity. All at once it became crystal clear to Ann Lee there was one single cause for humanity's separation from God: sex."6

Ann "took up her cross against the carnal gratifications of the flesh" and pronounced herself the long-sought-for "female Christ." She purported that she was Christ's anointed successor on earth and chosen to carry his truth to the world. She became known by her followers as Ann the Word or, more affectionately, Mother Ann. "I feel the blood of Christ running through my soul and body!" she declared.7

To escape heightened persecution, Ann and her followers, six men and two women, set sail aboard the *Mariah* in 1774, bound for America. Soon after arriving in New York, her husband ended their thirteen years of marriage by marrying another woman. Distraught but true to her convictions, forty-year-old Ann and her followers moved to the Niskeyuna wilderness near Albany, New York. There they established a communal form of living, forbidding the touching of the opposite gender—even the shaking of hands.

Ann was imprisoned for her religious beliefs in the Old Court at Albany, but even while she was in confinement her eloquent speeches through the grates of the prison window attracted crowds. After her release her proselyting venture in Massachusetts and Connecticut was termed "a triumphal tour and a march to the cross," as the Shaker society was established in six areas in New England.8 Later, however, Ann, who was suspected of being a man because of her large frame, was kidnapped in Petersham, Massachusetts, and stripped of her clothing to determine her gender. The traumatic experience broke her health.

Her last days were spent among followers in Niskeyuna, one of whom reported, "Mother sat in a chair almost all day and sang in unknown tongues the whole time, and seemed to be wholly divested of any attention to material things."9 She told her disciples that Shakerism, or the United Society of Believers in Christ's Second Appearing, would spread into Ohio. Ann Lee died in September 1784 in Watervliet, New York, at the age of forty-eight. In the *Albany Gazette* obituary of 9 September 1784 she was called an "elect lady or Mother of Zion."10

Her teachings and the societies she established continued after her demise. A stronghold of Shakerism was established in Ohio, just as Ann had predicted. In 1831 the Prophet Joseph Smith received a revelation refuting the teachings of Shakerism (see D&C 49).

Notes

1. Ann Lees later modified her surname to Lee.

2. F. W. Evans, *Shakers. Compendium of the Origin, History, Principles, Rules and Regulations, Government, and Doctrines of the United Society of Believers in Christ's Second Appearing: With Biographies of Ann Lee . . .* (New York: D. Appleton and Co., 1859), p. 121.

3. See Nardi Reeder Campion, *Mother Ann Lee, Morning Star of the Shakers* (Hanover and London: University Press of New England, 1990), p. 9.

4. As cited in Evans, pp. 123–24.

5. Campion, p. 15.

6. Ibid., p. 24.

7. As cited in ibid., pp. 25, 33–35.

8. Ibid., p. 114.

9. As cited in Evans, p. 140.

10. As cited in ibid., p. 145.

AMASA MASON LYMAN
D&C 124:136; 136:14

Birth: *30 March 1813, Lyman, Grafton County, New Hampshire. Son of Roswell Lyman and Martha Mason.*
Death: *4 February 1877, Fillmore, Millard County, Utah.*

Amasa Lyman "was born to no patrimony but poverty, no home but the world."[1] At age six his father left the family and never returned, and was dead two years later in the Southwest. When his mother remarried, Amasa resided with his grandparents. After the death of his grandparents he was raised by a strict uncle, Parley Mason, for seven years. During his turbulent youth he "became thoughtful on the subject of religion and found peace with God and my soul in striving to break off my sins in righteousness and my iniquities by turning to the Lord."[2]

Mormon elders taught him the gospel and he was baptized on 27 April 1832. His embrace of Mormonism was viewed by his uncle as unbearably offensive. Ten days later he left his uncle's home, and "no one offered a word to dissuade him."3 He journeyed over seven hundred miles to join with the Saints in Ohio, with only a knapsack containing his belongings and $11.13.

In Kirtland he met the Prophet Joseph Smith and later recalled, "There was nothing strange or different from other men in his personal appearance, yet when he grasped my hand in that cordial way (known to those who have met him in the honest simplicity of truth), I felt as one of old in the presence of the Lord."4

The Prophet called Amasa on his first mission to the East. He preached the gospel in West Virginia, Pennsylvania, and New York before returning to Ohio. Disappointment plagued him during his mission when family members refused to adhere to his preaching.

After returning to Ohio he joined Zion's Camp in 1834 and marched with other brethren to Missouri: "We pursued our anomalous and strange journey, the vicissitudes of which afforded us ample opportunity to evince our faith by offering our lives for the truth."5

When the encampment ended his attention turned to courtship. In a letter written on 31 May 1835 to "Miss L. M. Tanner," he explained: "Having been a wanderer, and desiring to enjoy the blessings that would result from the society of a companion who would participate with me in the changing scenes of life, if you desire or feel willing to converse with me on the subject of matrimony, please write your answer below. . . . Please answer this tomorrow."6 Eleven days later, on 10 June 1835, Amasa and Louisa Maria Tanner were married.

Marriage did not alter his missionary zeal. Amasa continued to preach throughout the East and served several short missions in Ohio before moving to Far West, Missouri, in the fall of 1837. He was imprisoned in Richmond, released, and then threatened with mobbing. "Several times in the course of the day," he wrote, "I met with parties of the mob whom I learned, about sundown, were searching for me to take me back to prison."7 He evaded his enemies by fleeing to Quincy, Illinois. He wrote to a friend, "Of our sufferings in Missouri I have nothing to say, only let silence cover them till the Avenger of our wrongs shall reward our enemies according to their works."8

He settled in Nauvoo and served as a counselor in the high priests quorum (see D&C 124:136) and was recognized by Church leaders as a powerful preacher. In August 1842 he was called to fill the vacancy left by Orson Pratt in the Quorum of the Twelve Apostles, but due to Orson's repentance, his call was uncertain for six months. In January 1843 the Prophet said, "I can take Amasa into the First Presidency." It was his intention that Amasa take the place of Sidney Rigdon. However, Rigdon was upheld in his office by the Saints. The Prophet then appointed Amasa as a Counselor to the Presidency until a vacancy occurred.

After the Martyrdom, question arose as to Amasa Lyman's right to claim the leadershp of the Church. With unswerving devotion he supported the leadership of the Twelve: "I do not rise to electioneer. I am gratified with the open, frank and plain exposition of President Young. . . . I have been at the back of Joseph Smith, and will be at the back of the Twelve forever, and then we will be saved."[9]

Amasa became a member of the Twelve on 12 August 1844. He urged the Saints, "Whether I rise or fall . . . heed the advice of President Young; he is the one to look to for counsel in all things pertaining to the kingdom of God."[10] He was faithful to the Church for many years. Unfortunately, he did fall from the Twelve and lose his standing in the Church on 12 January 1870.

The remaining seven years of his life were most peculiar. He espoused the doctrine that the more one comprehends universal truth, the closer he or she is to salvation. He spoke of Jesus as a holy man who attained perfection through years of learning. He believed that the shedding of Christ's blood had no effect on the salvation of man.[11] His oldest son, Francis Marion Lyman, wrote of his father's confused doctrinal stance: "Father's death would have been a pleasure compared with what we suffered at this terrible announcement."[12] The only explanation for many was that Amasa Lyman was "diseased of the mind."[13] He died on 4 February 1877 at Fillmore, Utah, at the age of sixty-three.

Notes

1. Albert R. Lyman, *Amasa Mason Lyman, Trailblazer and Pioneer from the Atlantic to the Pacific*, ed. Melvin A. Lyman (Delta, Utah: Melvin A. Lyman, 1957), p. 7.

2. As cited in ibid., p. 11.

3. Ibid., p. 16.

4. *HC* 1:332.

5. Writings of Amasa M. Lyman, as cited in Lyman, p. 43.

6. Letter of Amasa M. Lyman to Maria Tanner, 31 May 1835, Kirtland, Ohio, as cited in Lyman, p. 61.

7. As cited in Lyman, p. 94.

8. As cited in ibid, p. 102.

9. *HC* 7:236–37.

10. Lyman, p. 249.

11. See Loretta L. Hefner, "From Apostle to Apostate: The Personal Struggle of Amasa Mason Lyman," *Dialogue: A Journal of Mormon Thought* 16 (spring 1983): 100, 104; see also Hefner, "Amasa Mason Lyman, the Spiritualist," *Journal of Mormon History* 6 (1979): 80.

12. As cited in ibid., p. 102.

13. Hefner, "From Apostle to Apostate," p. 103.

WILLIAM MARKS
D&C 117; 124:79

Birth: *15 November 1792, Rutland, Rutland County, Vermont. Son of Cornwall (Cornell) Marks and Sarah Goodrich.*
Death: *22 May 1872 at Plano, Kendall County, Illinois.*

At age forty-nine William Marks was baptized and ordained a priest in New York. He soon moved his family to Kirtland, where he established a book and stationery store. His advertisement in the *Latter Day Saints' Messenger and Advocate* read:

WILLIAM MARKS
DEALER IN
BOOKS, STATIONERY,
CAP, LETTER,
AND WRAPPING PAPER.
Plain and Ornamental
JOB PRINTING.[1]

On 3 September 1837 he was called to the Kirtland high council, and two weeks later he was called to be an "agent" to Bishop Newel K. Whitney.[2]

On 29 March 1838 the Prophet recorded seeing William in a vision, being closely pursued by enemies that sought to devour him. When it appeared that the enemies had the advantage, "a chariot of fire came, and near the place, even the angel of the Lord put forth his hand unto Brother Marks and said unto him, 'Thou art my son, come here,' and immediately he was caught up in the chariot, and rode away triumphantly out of their midst. And again the Lord said, 'I will raise thee up for a blessing unto many people.'"[3]

In a revelation given to the Prophet on 8 July 1838 William was commanded to settle his business in Kirtland and move to Missouri: "Let him preside in the midst of my people in the city of Far West" (D&C 117:10). Before he could obey the directive the Saints were driven by mobocracy from Missouri. William joined the exiles in Quincy, Illinois.

At a conference on 5 October 1839 at Commerce (later Nauvoo), William was appointed to preside over the stake there. He also served as a city alderman, regent of the University of Nauvoo, associate justice of the municipal court, member of the Nauvoo Agricultural and Manufacturing Association, and bodyguard for the Prophet. However, by 1844 his faith faltered. The Prophet, noting his failings, classified him with apostate William Law: "What can be the matter with these men [Law and Marks]? Is it that the wicked flee when no man pursueth, that hit pigeons always flutter, that drowning men catch at straws, or that Presidents Law and Marks are absolutely traitors to the Church."[4]

After the martyrdom of Joseph and Hyrum Smith, William helped wash the bodies of the slain leaders, despite his association with the conspirators. Afterwards, according to Hosea Stout, William attempted to hide conspirator John C. Elliot in his home, but John "was found out and arrested." William used his "influence to notify the mob and raise an excitement," and one of Elliot's lawyers "gave the court to understand that if they committed him to jail, that it might cause some of our best men to be slain, thus threatening us with a mob if we attempted to put the law in force against willful murderers." The court, however, "took a bold and decided stand in favor of the Laws," and Elliot was jailed.[5] However, justice failed as Elliot later escaped and was never brought to trial.[6]

The Saints recognized William as an enemy and on 7 October 1844 at general conference rejected him as the Nauvoo stake president for supporting the claims of Sidney Rigdon to the Presidency. On 9 December 1844 he publicly acknowledged his error in the *Times and Sea-*

sons: "After mature and candid deliberation, I am fully and satisfactorily convinced that Mr. Sidney Rigdon's claims to the Presidency of the church of Jesus Christ of Latter-day Saints, are not founded in truth. . . . The twelve are the proper persons to lead the church."[7] After his confession he returned to the fellowship of the Saints, but did not return to his former position.[8]

At a Strangite conference on 6 April 1846 William made a motion that the "Church receive, acknowledge, and appoint JAMES J. STRANG as President of this Church, Prophet, Seer, Revelator, and Translator." William became president pro tempore of the Strangite high priest's quorum as well as bishop, apostle, and counselor to Strang.[9]

However, in January 1849 Strang wrote, "WILLIAM MARKS, has gone far ASTRAY in departing from me."[10] William withdrew from the Strangites and joined with Charles B. Thompson in organizing a new church in 1852. He left that church in 1853 and by 1855 was associated with apostate John E. Page. On 11 June 1859 he was received into the Reorganized Church. He became a prominent figure in the history of the RLDS Church, being one of three to ordain Joseph Smith III as president. In March 1863 he was called to be first counselor to President Smith. He was ordained to the position on 8 April 1863. William Marks died on 22 May 1872 at Plano, Illinois, at the age of seventy-nine.

On the records of the Reorganized Church of Jesus Christ of Latter Day Saints, William is eulogized: "President Marks was a man of sterling integrity, true to his convictions, faithful and courageous in the discharge of duty. . . . He maintained his honor intact, and his record was unstained by immoral acts. . . . The last years of his life he spent in peace, satisfied in the possession of what he long had sought among the factions in vain."[11]

Notes

1. *Messenger and Advocate* 3 (April 1837): 496.

2. *The History of the Reorganized Church of Jesus Christ of Latter Day Saints,* 8 vols. (Independence, Mo.: Herald Publishing House, 1967–76), 3:721.

3. Letter of Joseph Smith to the First Presidency, 29 March 1838, Far West, Missouri; in *HC* 3:12.

4. *HC* 6:170.

5. Diary of Hosea Stout, 2 vols., typescript, 1:23, Special Collections, Harold B. Lee Library, Brigham Young University, Provo, Utah.

6. Dallin H. Oaks and Marvin S. Hill, *Carthage Conspiracy* (Urbana and Chicago: University of Illinois Press, 1979), p. 67.

7. *Times and Seasons* 5 (15 December 1844): 742.

8. Patriarch John Smith was chosen as his successor. According to RLDS records William Marks was never legally expelled from the LDS Church. See C. J. Hunt, *Priesthood, Rebaptisms and Reordinations in the Utah Mormon Church, William Marks Retained the Holy Priesthood, Isaac Sheen Opposes Brigham Young* (Independence, Mo.: n.d.), p. 2.

9. "Cornerstones of Reorganization: A Few Facts Concerning its Founders. . . . Compiled from Early Church History" (n.p., n.d.), p. 4, in author's possession.

10. Ibid.

11. *History* 3:725.

THOMAS BALDWIN MARSH

Testimony of the Twelve Apostles,
D&C 31; 52:22; 56:5; 75:31; 112; 118:2

Birth: 1 *November 1799, Acton, Middlesex County, Massachusetts. Son of James Marsh and Mary Law.*
Death: *January 1866, Ogden, Weber County, Utah.*

Thomas B. Marsh ran away from home at age fourteen and wandered for years from one large city to another until entering the grocery business in New York. He failed in this enterprise and soon moved to Boston and secured work in a type foundry. In Boston he joined the Methodist Church. He wrote, "[I] tried for two years to be a genuine Methodist, but did not succeed any better in getting Methodist religion than I did in the grocery business." He and several friends "kept aloof from sectarians, and were called by them Quietists" because they resembled a sect of that name in France.[1]

After leaving the Methodist Church, Thomas felt led by the Spirit to journey to western New York. There he heard rumors of a "golden book, that had been found by a youth named Joseph Smith." His search to learn more about the matter led him to E. B. Grandin's printing office in Palmyra.[2] "Highly pleased with the information I had obtained concerning the new found book,"[3] Thomas took sixteen pages of the text and returned to Boston. Within the year he had moved his family to Palmyra.

Thomas was baptized on 3 September 1830 in Cayuga Lake by David Whitmer. A few days later he was ordained an elder and called by revelation to preach the gospel: "Lift up your heart and rejoice, for the hour of your mission is come; and your tongue shall be loosed, and you shall declare glad tidings of great joy unto this generation. . . . Govern your house in meekness, and be steadfast. Behold, I say unto you that you shall be a physician unto the church, but not unto the world, for they will not receive you." (D&C 31:3, 9–10.) This was the first of many missionary opportunities for Thomas (see D&C 52:22; 56:5; 75:30–31).

In September 1833 he was appointed president of the Big Blue Branch in Jackson County, Missouri, and in 1834 he was called to serve on the Clay County high council. He learned by mail of his appointment to the Quorum of the Twelve Apostles.[4] As President of the Twelve, one of his first official actions was to testify of the truth of the Doctrine and Covenants (see the Testimony of the Twelve Apostles). Another important call was to serve a mission to the eastern states in 1835. Of this mission Thomas wrote, "In company with the Twelve I left Kirtland and preached through the Eastern States, holding Conferences, regulating and organizing the Churches, and returned September 25."[5]

On 23 July 1837 the Lord said in a revelation to Thomas: "I have heard thy prayers; and thine alms have come up as a memorial before me. . . . There have been some few things in thine heart and with thee with which I, the Lord, was not well pleased. . . . Be thou humble; and the Lord thy God shall lead thee by the hand, and give thee answer to thy prayers." (D&C 112:1, 2, 10.)

Thomas failed to heed the admonition. In August 1838 the oft-quoted "cream strippings" incident occurred. Thomas's wife, Elizabeth, and George W. Harris's wife, Lucinda, desired to make cheese, and, as George A. Smith explained, "neither of them possessing the requisite number of cows, they agreed to exchange milk. . . . It was agreed that they should not save the strippings, but that the milk and strippings should all go together. . . . Mrs. Marsh, wishing to make some extra good cheese, saved a pint of strippings from each cow and sent Mrs. Harris the milk without the strippings."[6]

From small beginnings the issue over the strippings escalated. Eventually a Church trial was held. The bishop concluded that Elizabeth had defrauded Lucinda. Thomas appealed to the high council. When their decision affirmed the previous decision, he appealed to the First Presidency of the Church, who affirmed that Elizabeth was guilty. George A. Smith said that "Thomas B. Marsh then declared that he would sustain the character of his wife, even if he had to go to hell for it."[7]

The Lord sought to change the course that Thomas was pursuing by giving him a revelation: "In it God told him what to do, and that was to sustain br. Joseph. . . . But no, he took a course to sustain his wife and oppose the prophet of God, and she led him away."8 After leaving the Church Thomas and Lucinda went to Richmond, Missouri, and, as Joseph Smith wrote, "made affidavit . . . to all the vilest slanders, aspersions, lies and calumnies towards myself and the Church that he could invent. . . . Now he has fallen, lied and sworn falsely, and is ready to take the lives of his best friends."9 He was excommunicated on 17 March 1839.

During the ensuing eighteen years Thomas moved from state to state, earning his living as a teacher specializing in biblical geography. John Taylor said of these years, "He has been all the time since [his apostasy] afraid of his life, afraid the 'Mormons' would kill him and he durst not let them know where he was. In meeting with some of the apostates he said to them, 'You don't know what you are about; if you want to see the fruits of apostacy, look on me.' "10

In 1857 Thomas traveled through Iowa and Nebraska. Wandle Mace described him as "an old man, a stranger carrying a satchel and wearing a black waterproof coat to shield him from the storm . . . [with a] palsied frame." He also recorded what Thomas said was his greatest desire: "I want to die in the Church. Oh, if I could see Joseph, and talk with him and acknowledge my faults to him, and get his forgiveness from him . . . then I would die happy."11

In the summer of 1857 Thomas joined the Walker company and migrated to the Rockies. He arrived in the Salt Lake Valley on 4 September 1857 and the next day visited Brigham Young, who later said, "He came into my office and wished to know whether I could be reconciled to him, and whether there could be a reconciliation between himself and the Church of the living God."12

On 6 September 1857 Thomas spoke to a congregation of Saints on Temple Square:

> My voice never was very strong, but it has been very much weakened of late years by the afflicting rod of Jehovah. He loved me too much to let me go without whipping. . . . For if he had not cared anything about me, he would not have taken me by the arm and given me such a shaking. . . .
>
> . . . I know that I was a very stiffnecked man. . . .

. . . I want your fellowship; I want your God to be my God. . . . I have learned to understand what David said when he exclaimed, "I would rather be a doorkeeper in the house of God than to dwell in the tents of wickedness."[13]

At the conclusion of his remarks President Young addressed the congregation, saying, "Brother Marsh now wishes to be received into full fellowship, and to be again baptised here. . . . I shall call a vote." All hands appeared to be raised in affirmation, and Thomas remarked, "I thank God for it."[14]

Brigham then declared, "In conversing with brother Marsh, I find that he is about the same Thomas that he always was—full of anecdotes and chit-chat. He could hardly converse for ten minutes without telling an anecdote. His voice and style of conversation are familiar to me. . . . He has told me that he would be faithful, and that he would do this and the other; but he [does not] know what he will do next week or next year."[15]

Thomas was rebaptized on 16 July 1857. By the early 1860s his health and thinking deteriorated. President John Taylor wrote, "After his arrival here, I remember hearing him talk in the Fourteenth Ward meetinghouse. It seemed to me about the most foolish and ridiculous talk, devoid of common sense, common intelligence, and common manhood, that I had heard for a long time. Said I to myself: 'There is a specimen of apostasy.' "[16]

Thomas moved to Ogden, where he died a pauper and an invalid in January 1866.

Notes

1. Thomas B. Marsh, "History of Thomas B. Marsh," *Millennial Star* 26 (4 June 1864): 360.
2. *LDS Biographical Encyclopedia* 1:74.
3. Marsh, *Millennial Star* 26 (11 June 1864): 375.
4. See Journal History, 25 April 1835.
5. Marsh, *Millennial Star* 26 (18 June 1864): 391.
6. George A. Smith, in *JD* 3:283.
7. Ibid., p. 84.
8. Journal History, 12 July 1857.
9. *HC* 3:167.
10. Journal History, 9 August 1857.

11. Journal of Wandle Mace, Archives Division, Church Historical Department, The Church of Jesus Christ of Latter-day Saints, Salt Lake City, Utah.

12. Brigham Young, in *JD* 5:206.

13. Thomas B. Marsh, in *JD* 5:206–8.

14. Young, p. 209.

15. Ibid.

16. John Taylor, *The Gospel Kingdom* (Salt Lake City: Bookcraft, 1964), p. 188.

WILLIAM E. MCLELLIN

Testimony of the Twelve Apostles,
D&C 66; 68; 75:6–8; 90:35

Birth: *18 January 1806, Smith County, Tennessee. Son of Charles McLellan.*
Death: *24 April 1883, Independence, Jackson County, Missouri.*

William E. McLellin[1] first heard the preaching of Mormonism in the summer of 1831. He wrote in his journal: "Mr. [Harvey] Whitlock . . . expounded the Gospel the plainest I thot that I ever heard in my life. . . . D[avid] Whitmer then arose and bore testimony to having seen an Holy Angel who had made known the truth of this [Book of Mormon] record to him. all these strange things I pondered in my heart."[2]

In a letter to relatives dated 4 August 1832 William wrote, "Though I had between 30 & 40 students and the people [were] generally satisfied with me as teacher, yet I closed my school on the 29th July and on the 30th left for Independence" to learn more of Mormonism.[3]

On 20 August 1831 he penned, "I rose early and betook myself to earnest prayr to God to direct me into truth; and from all the light that I could gain by examinations searches and researches I was bound as an honest man to acknowledge the truth and Validity of the book of Mormon and also that I had found the people of the Lord—The Living Church of Christ."[4]

William was baptized that day by Hyrum Smith. In the evening "the Enemy of all righteousness made a mighty struggle to persuade me that I was deceived until it seemed to me sometimes that horror would overwhelm me." William was comforted when Newel Knight "came and by the spirit of God was enabled to tell me the very secrets of my heart and in a degree to chase darkness from my mind."[5]

William journeyed to Ohio to meet the Prophet. He lived with him for about three weeks, "and from my acquaintance then and until now I can truly say I believe him to be a man of God, a prophet, a seer and revelator to The Church of Christ."[6] Desirous to receive a revelation from the Lord through his Prophet, "I went before the Lord in secret, and on my knees asked him to reveal the answer to five questions through his Prophet, and that too without his having any knowledge of my having made such request."[7] He then asked Joseph Smith to inquire of the Lord concerning him. The subsequent revelation both commended and reproved his actions (see D&C 66:1–3).[8] He wrote in response to the revelation, "I now testify in the fear of God, that every question which I had thus lodged in the ears of the Lord of Sabbath, were answered to my full and entire satisfaction."[9]

However, just one month later William criticized the language of the revelations in the proposed Book of Commandments. Through Joseph Smith the Lord challenged anyone, particularly "him that is the most wise among you," to imitate even the least of the revelations contained therein (see D&C 67:6–7). Joseph later wrote, "William E. M'Lellin, as the wisest man, in his own estimation, having more learning than sense, endeavored to write a commandment like unto one of the least of the Lord's, but failed."[10]

By winter 1832 William was serving a mission with Parley P. Pratt in Missouri and in Illinois. His success on the mission led to leadership in the Church by 1834, when he became a member of the high council in Clay County and later an assistant teacher in the School of the Elders in Kirtland. On 15 February 1835 he was called to the Quorum of the Twelve Apostles.

His faithfulness in that Quorum was short-lived. In 1835 he wrote a letter censuring the First Presidency and by 1836 had apostatized. He explained his actions in a letter to J. T. Cobb: "I left the church in Aug. 1836 . . . because the *Leading men* to a great extent left their religion and run into and after speculation, pride, and popularity! . . . I quit because I could not uphold the Presidency as men of God."[11]

On Friday, 11 May 1838, he appeared before a bishop's court in Far West, Missouri. He explained that his apostasy centered on his lack of confidence in the Presidency of the Church. He volunteered that this lack had caused him to quit praying and keeping the commandments for a time and that he had indulged in sinful lusts.[12] William was excommunicated in 1838 for "unbelief and apostasy."[13]

After his excommunication he joined mobbers in robbing and driving the Saints from Missouri. While the brethren were imprisoned at Richmond,

> McLellin, who was a large and active man, went to the sheriff and asked for the privilege of flogging the Prophet. Permission was granted on condition that Joseph would fight. The sheriff made known to Joseph McLellin's earnest request, to which Joseph consented, if his irons were taken off. McLellin then refused to fight unless he could have a club, to which Joseph was perfectly willing; but the sheriff would not allow them to fight on such unequal terms.[14]

After his separation from the Church, William resided in Hampton, Illinois, where apostates William Law and Robert Foster also lived.[15] By 23 January 1847 he was with Martin Harris in Kirtland organizing a new church—the Church of Christ. Soon after the organization began William visited David Whitmer in Richmond, Missouri, and encouraged him to lead the new church; thereafter David was considered to be the church's prophet. However, the sect apparently did not last beyond 1849.[16]

On 5 June 1869 William joined the Hedrickites, but by November he had lost interest in the religious organization. His wife joined the Reorganized Church of Jesus Christ of Latter Day Saints and encouraged their move to Independence, Missouri, in 1870.[17]

During this time of William's fickle embrace of pseudo-Mormonism, questions arose about his testimony of the Book of Mormon. Three years before his death he affirmed that testimony in his letter to J. T. Cobb:

> I have set to my seal that the Book of Mormon is a true, divine record and it will require more evidence than I have ever seen to ever shake me relative to its purity. . . .
>
> . . . When a man goes at the Book of M. he touches the apple of my eye. He fights against truth—against purity—against light—against the purist, or one of the truest, purist books on earth. . . .

Fight the wrongs of L.D.S.ism as much as you please, but let that unique, that inimitable book alone.[18]

He further advised Cobb to "cease your opposition and strife against the Book, . . . for you might just as well fight against the rocky mountains as the Book!!"[19]

During his last year William remained aloof from all churches, holding the belief that the Lord would *"establish the Church of Christ* shortly, and then if they will accept me, I'll unite with them!!!"[20] He died on 24 April 1883 in obscurity at the age of seventy-seven.

Notes

1. Surname has variant spellings: McLellan and M'Lellin.

2. William E. McLellin, *The Journals of William E. McLellin 1831–1836,* ed. Jan Shipps and John W. Welch (Provo, Utah: *BYU Studies,* Brigham Young University, 1994), p. 29.

3. Letter of William E. McLellin to relatives, 4 August 1832, typescript, pp. 1–2, RLDS Library—Archives, Reorganized Church of Jesus Christ of Latter Day Saints, Independence, Missouri.

4. McLellin, *Journals,* p.33.

5. Ibid., p. 34.

6. Letter, p. 2.

7. William E. McLellin, "History and Writings of William E. McLellin" (n.p., n.d.), p. 6, in author's possession.

8. William was scribe for the revelation concerning himself. See McLellin, "History," p. 6.

9. Ibid.

10. *HC* 1:226.

11. As cited in Larry C. Porter, "William E. McLellin's Testimony of the Book of Mormon," *BYU Studies* 10 (Summer 1970): 487.

12. See *HC* 3:31.

13. *LDS Biographical Encyclopedia* 1:83.

14. *HC* 3:215 n.

15. See the journal of Lorenzo Brown, typescript, p. 11, Special Collections, Harold B. Lee Library, Brigham Young University, Provo, Utah.

16. See Davis Bitton, "The Waning of Mormon Kirtland," *BYU Studies* 12 (Summer 1972): 459.

17. See Lyndon W. Cook, *The Revelations of the Prophet Joseph Smith* (Salt Lake City: Deseret Book Co., 1985), p. 107.

18. As cited in Porter, p. 486.

19. As cited in ibid.

20. As cited in ibid., p. 487.

DANIEL SANBORN MILES
D&C 124:138

Birth: *23 July 1772, Sanbornton, Belknap County, New Hampshire. Son of Josiah Miles and Marah Sanborn.*
Death: *12 October 1845, Hancock County, Illinois.*

Daniel Miles was a Universalist before accepting Mormonism on 22 April 1832 in Bath, New Hampshire. By 1836 he had moved his family to Kirtland to be with the Saints of God. He is first mentioned in the *History of the Church* at a priesthood meeting held in the Kirtland Temple on 24 February 1836. At the meeting he was considered worthy to be ordained to the priesthood.[1]

On 6 April 1837, when Daniel was nearly sixty-five years old, he became one of the Seven Presidents of the Seventies. He chaired a quorum meeting two weeks later in the Kirtland Temple, where the Presidents adopted a personal resolution to "discard the practice of ball-playing, wrestling, jumping and all such low and degrading amusements, and above all the use of ardent spirits of any kind."[2]

Daniel journeyed with Brigham Young to Far West, Missouri. On 29 March 1838 the Prophet Joseph Smith penned, "Brothers Brigham Young, Daniel S. Miles, and Levi Richards arrived here when we [the Smith family] did. They were with us on the last part of our journey, which ended much to our satisfaction. They also are well. They have provided places for their families, and are now about to break the ground for seed."[3] Daniel remained in Far West until mobocracy forced him to flee to Illinois for safety.

In Illinois he served as a temporary member of the Nauvoo high council and continued in his position as a President in the First Quorum of the Seventy (see D&C 124:138).[4] Little is known of the circumstances that led to his death. He attended a conference in October 1845 and "was taken sick" at one of the meetings.[5] He died on 12 October 1845 at the home of Josiah Butterfield in Hancock County, Illinois, at the age of seventy-three. Joseph Young, senior President of the Seventy, eulogized Daniel Miles as "a man of good faith, constant in his attendance at the meetings of the council, until the time of his death, which occurred at quite an advanced stage of his life."[6]

Notes

1. See *HC* 2:399–400; see also Lyndon W. Cook and Milton V. Backman Jr., eds., *Kirtland Elders' Quorum Record 1836–1841* (Provo, Utah: Grandin Book Co., 1985), p. 14.

2. *Messenger and Advocate* 3 (May 1837): 511.

3. *HC* 3:11.

4. See Lyndon W. Cook, *The Revelations of the Prophet Joseph Smith* (Salt Lake City: Deseret Book Co., 1985), p. 267.

5. Diary of Hosea Stout, 2 vols., typescript, 2:77, Special Collections, Harold B. Lee Library, Brigham Young University, Provo, Utah.

6. *LDS Biographical Encyclopedia* 1:192.

GEORGE MILLER
D&C 124:20–24, 60, 70

Birth: *25 November 1794, Orange County, Virginia. Son of John Miller and Margaret Pfeiffer.*
Death: *1856, Marengo, McHenry County, Illinois.*

During his boyhood George Miller resided in northern and central Kentucky, where he learned the carpenter trade. This skill served him well years later when he worked as a tradesman in several ports from Baltimore to New Orleans and at the University of Virginia. In 1831 George moved to Macomb Township, Illinois, and built an eight-room house, farmed three hundred acres, and attended the Presbyterian church. According to his biographer his introduction to Mormonism "came from a recruiter seeking volunteers to fight Missouri's so-called Mormon War." He dismissed Mormonism as "a humbug" but gave thousands of bushels of grain to the Mormon refugees.[1]

Among the recipients of George's generosity were the Prophet Joseph Smith and his extended family. George recorded the first time he saw the Prophet: "A large man sitting in front [in a wagon] driving seemed to be familiar to me as if I had always known him, and suddenly the thought burst on my mind that it was none other than the prophet, Joseph Smith. Indeed, my whole frame was in a tremor with the occurrence of the thought."2 George urged the Prophet to agree to preach at a later date, but Joseph was reluctant at first because he had just escaped from prison and felt like "a bird uncaged"—he wanted to spend time with his family and friends. When he finally consented, "a time and place was fixed upon" and George "went to notify the people of the appointment of the Mormon Prophet to preach."3

After listening to him George later penned, "I had no remaining doubts left in regard to the truth of the prophet."4 This experience, coupled with his receiving of a healing blessing that cured him of a dramatic, sudden paralysis, led him to enter the waters of baptism on 10 August 1839. In his journal he recorded the consequences of his baptism:

[I was] openly persecuted for my religious belief and profession. My cattle were shot on the prairies. . . . My fences [were] laid down, and the flocks and herds of the prairies turned on my grain fields. I was vexed by petty lawsuits. Men that I had never had dealings with would recover sums of money from me, by bringing into the justice's court false witnesses, and those that owed me would prove payment.5

On 19 January 1841 the Lord revealed through the Prophet that "my servant George Miller is without guile; he may be trusted because of the integrity of his heart; and for the love which he has to my testimony I, the Lord, love him" (D&C 124:20). The office of bishop was then sealed upon him (see verse 21). Following the revelation George wrote, "The poor, the blind, the lame, the widow, and the fatherless all looked to me for their daily wants. . . . My days were filled with toil and care, and my nights . . . with sleepless anxiety in waiting on the suffering poor and the sick of the city."6

In the same revelation he was also instructed to help build the Nauvoo House, which was to be "a good house, worthy of all acceptation, that the weary traveler may find health and safety while he shall contemplate the word of the Lord" (D&C 124:23). George directed the procuring of timber in Wisconsin for the construction of the Nauvoo House and the Nauvoo Temple. He also served his community as a regent of the University of Nauvoo and as a colonel and, later, as brigadier general in the Nauvoo Legion. His close association with the Prophet was the highlight of his years in Nauvoo: "I have known Joseph Smith intimately for near three & a half years," he wrote. "I unhesitatingly aver that . . . a more generous, liberal, honorable, high toned virtuous man, never existed on the footstool of the great *Jehovah*."[7]

George Miller cleaved to Mormonism as taught by Joseph Smith but clashed with Brigham Young. George wrote of their disagreements over settling the pioneering Saints among the Ponca Indians and choosing a northern route to the Rockies.[8] In March 1847 he announced his resignation from the Church in a letter to Brigham Young. He tried to justify his actions: "Although . . . in poverty and rags, I am not unwilling to undertake to do anything that this people persist in doing to build up this Kingdom. I have been as a beast of burden ever since I came into the church and I have never swerved in my actions, or feelings, to do with my might all things to push forward the cause of Zion, and am, and ever have been, willing to spend and be spent for the cause."[9]

He left the Camp of Israel and journeyed south to Texas, joining Lyman Wight and other apostates in 1848. After recognizing Wight as a pretender and a charlatan, fifty-six-year-old George journeyed to Michigan to join the Strangite movement. He fulfilled several missions for James Strang, three to Council Bluffs, Iowa, and one to the middle states. In 1854 he returned to Texas in an attempt to convert Lyman Wight. In acknowledgement of his service to Strang he was appointed "prince, privy counsellor and general in Christ in the kingdom of God."[10] George died without Church fellowship in 1856 in Marengo, Illinois, en route to California.

Notes

1. George Miller, "Journal of History," comp. H. H. Smith (n.p., n.d.), p. 22, in author's possession.
2. Ibid., p. 23.
3. Ibid., p. 24.
4. Ibid., pp. 24–25.
5. Ibid., p. 26.
6. Ibid., p. 29.
7. As cited in Lyndon W. Cook, "'A More Virtuous Man Never Existed on the Footstool of the Great Jehovah': George Miller on Joseph Smith," *BYU Studies* 19 (Spring 1979): 407.
8. See Miller, p. 29.
9. Ibid., p. 30.
10. Strangite records, in author's possession.

ISAAC MORLEY

D&C 52:23; 64:15–16, 20

Birth: 11 March 1786, Montague, Hampshire County, Massachusetts. Son of Thomas E. Morley and Editha Marsh.
Death: 24 June 1865, Fairview, Sanpete County, Utah.

At age twenty-six Isaac Morley married his classmate and childhood sweetheart, Lucy Gunn. They made their first home in the Ohio wilderness. The War of 1812 temporarily interrupted their plans of taming the wilderness as Isaac served as a captain in the Ohio militia, playing the flute in a militia band until "at the end of 3 months he was brought home ill with chills and fever."[1] After recovering from his illness he began to clear land and create a prosperous farm, and "by hard work and careful planning [he] accumulated considerable property and other assets."[2] As new settlers moved to his region the town of Kirtland was created.

In 1828 Isaac and his wife joined the Campbellites after listening to the preaching of Sidney Rigdon. Enthused by his new religious leanings, Isaac sought to combine his acquired prosperity with religion by establishing a common ownership or a communal home for believers, nicknamed "the family." Latter-day Saint missionaries to the Lamanites preached to "the family" and converted many, including forty-four-year-old Isaac and his wife.

Soon after the Morleys' baptisms the Prophet Joseph Smith moved to Kirtland and within a few weeks was residing on Isaac's property. Biographer John Clifton Moffitt writes, "Joseph Smith and wife came to Father Morleys and lived in his family through the winter, a branch of the Church was organized there, meetings held there and many of the people were baptized. [Later] a frame house was built on Father Morley's lot for Joseph Smith's family to live in (D&C 41:7)."[3]

The fourth general conference of the Church was held on Isaac's farm in June 1831. At the conference Isaac was ordained a high priest and called to be a counselor to Bishop Edward Partridge. He was asked to sell his farm and consecrate the money from the sale to the upbuilding of the Church. At first he refused the directive; however, when the Lord said through Joseph Smith, "I gave commandment that his farm should be sold," in obedience he sold his property and gave the proceeds to the Church (see D&C 64:15–16, 20).

After nineteen years of residing in the Kirtland vicinity Isaac and his family moved to Independence, Missouri. His daughter Cordelia wrote about the religious persecution in Missouri that raged against his family: "We were threatened day and night. They told us they would burn our house down over our heads. . . . The mob gave us no peace and all the while telling us we had to leave the country or they would kill us. . . . We took our things out of the house three different times, each night expecting our house would be burned to the ground."[4]

On one occasion Isaac was tried for treason, imprisoned, and sentenced to be shot in the public square. To his credit he did not falter in his faith, but is numbered among six Latter-day Saints who willingly offered their lives for their friends. Unfortunately, his bravery did not deter mobocracy. A mob threw large stones at the windows of his home, breaking panes and shattering glass on his sleeping children. Isaac was "so unnerved" by the blatant mob violence that "he hid in the corn field for about a month. His family would take him meals and necessities and visit him there."[5]

The growing tension caused him and his family to flee to safety in Clay County. Once again, mobs threatened his family. To relieve the tension he moved his family to Far West, where on 7 November 1837 he was ordained a patriarch.[6] Within the year he was captured and taken prisoner to Richmond, "amidst the crys and pleadings of his children," according to Cordelia.[7] For three weeks he languished in jail before his case came to trial. After no evidence was found against him, his case was dismissed and he was permitted to return to his family, who "hardly recognized him" because of his tattered appearance.[8]

Unable to live in safety in Missouri, Isaac and his family fled to Illinois. They lived in a tent until a cabin was built in what became known as "Morley Settlement," or Yelrome, which is Morley spelled backwards. Temporary peace pervaded the settlement and it began to flourish under Isaac's leadership as stake president. However, in 1844 a committee of five men informed him of a plan to arrest the Prophet. Isaac wrote an urgent letter to Joseph Smith, telling him that the committee had presented him with three options: The Mormons "must take up arms" and aid in the arrest, or they could move immediately to Nauvoo, or "give up our arms, and remain quiet until the fuss is over." Isaac told the Prophet that they would comply with none of the demands but would "stand in our own defense."[9]

Mobs did not strike Yelrome in 1844, but in September 1845 they began looting and burning the town. Isaac's home, cooper shop, property, and grain were burned. Heeding the advice of Brigham Young, he moved his family to Nauvoo and then in 1847 joined the pioneer exodus to the West. Isaac assumed much responsibility for the welfare of the exiled Saints. He served as a member of a high council and then as leader and patriarch of Summer Quarters, later known as Kanesville.

After completing that trek to the Salt Lake Valley he was called in October 1849 to lead 224 settlers to the Sanpete Valley. When he saw the present site of Manti he stated, "This is the place. Here I will stay."[10] Isaac plowed the first furrow and supervised the construction of the first schoolhouse and gristmill in the area. He represented the county in the state legislature from 1851 to 1855. However, as he advanced in years, "President Young thought it too much for so old a man as Father Morley (to struggle longer in this total situation) so called him back to Salt Lake City."[11] In obedience he returned to the city.

After a few years he moved to Santaquin, Utah, and then to Fairview. In 1864 "he took a severe cold, rheumatism set in and he was almost helpless for ten months."[12] Isaac died on 24 June 1865 in Fairview at the age of seventy-nine.

Notes

1. Florence Allen Cheney, "Biography of Lucy Gunn Morley" (n.p., n.d.), p. 2, in author's possession.

2. John Clifton Moffitt, "Isaac Morley on the American Frontier" (n.p., n.d.), p. 2, in author's possession.

3. Ibid., p. 4.

4. As cited in ibid., p. 9.

5. Cheney, p. 3.

6. See HC 2:524.

7. As cited in Moffitt, p. 17.

8. Ibid., p. 18.

9. *HC* 6:481–82.
10. Moffitt, p. 38.
11. Ibid., p. 47.
12. Ibid., p. 49.

JOHN MURDOCK
D&C 52:8; 99

Birth: *15 July 1792, Kortwright, Delaware County,
New York. Son of John Murdock Sr. and Eleanor Riggs.*
Death: *23 December 1871, Beaver County, Utah.*

When John Murdock was four years old his mother died and his
father remarried. He wrote, "My stepmother was a very high-spirited
woman and very partial towards her children; which was the cause of
difficulty in my father's family." He was never "content under the government of my stepmother."[1] Seeking solace from his problems, John
turned to prayer and meditation. While he meditated, "a vision passed
before my mind. . . . [A] question put to me was if I had commemo-
rated the death and sufferings of the Savior, by obeying the ordinances."[2] This query caused him to search for a religion that believed
in gospel ordinances.

He first united with the Lutheran Dutch Church, but "soon found
they did not walk according to the scriptures." He next joined the
Presbyterian Seceder Church, but "I soon became dissatisfied with
their walk, for I saw it was not according to the scriptures." He then
united with the Baptists, but "finding their walk not to agree with their
profession, I withdrew myself from them."[3] He turned to the
Methodist faith and was often asked to preach, but discovered "when I
did not please them I would have to be silent among them awhile." By
1827 he had joined the Campbellites, but as many of the members denied the "gift and power of the Holy Ghost," John lost interest and
concluded "all the sects were out of the way."[4]

Then in the winter of 1830 he heard that "four men had arrived in Kirtland from the state of New York, who were preaching, baptizing, and building up the church after the ancient order." He journeyed twenty miles to see the new preachers for himself. He arrived in Kirtland about dark and was introduced to the men and presented with a copy of the Book of Mormon. As he read the new scripture, "the spirit of the Lord rested on me, witnessing to me of the truth of the work. . . . About ten o'clock [the next] morning, being November 5th, 1830, I told the servants of the Lord that I was ready to walk with them into the water of baptism."[5] He was baptized on 5 November 1830 by Parley P. Pratt. "This was the third time I had been immersed," he wrote, "but I never before felt the authority of the ordinance, but I felt it this time and felt as though my sins were forgiven."[6]

On 30 April 1831 his wife, Julia, died, just six hours after giving birth to twins.[7] The grief-stricken father gave the surviving twins, Joseph and Julia, to Joseph and Emma Smith to rear. He then accepted the Lord's command to journey with Hyrum Smith to Missouri (see D&C 52:8–9). On the trek his feet became wet, "by which I took a violent cold by which I suffered near unto death. . . . [But] I could not die because my work was not yet done."[8]

After returning from Missouri he learned that "my little son Joseph had died." The baby, already ill, had caught cold as the result of exposure when a mob raided the John Johnson home, where Joseph and Emma were staying. He died a short time later. "But my daughter was still doing well with Bro. Joseph, the Prophet," John wrote.[9]

During the winter of 1832–33 John received a glorious vision of the Savior: "I saw the form of a man, most lovely, the visage of his face was sound and fair as the sun. His hair a bright silver grey, curled in most majestic form, His eyes a keen penetrating blue, and the skin of his neck a most beautiful white and he was covered from the neck to the feet with a loose garment, pure white, whiter than any garment I have ever before seen. His countenance was most penetrating, and yet most lovely."[10]

John served a mission with Zebedee Coltrin from April 1833 to April 1834, laboring primarily in New York, and afterward continued his faithful service in the Church as a volunteer in Zion's Camp, a high councilor in Clay County, Missouri, and the presiding officer of the Far West high council.

Mobbers in Missouri threatened John's and George M. Hinkle's families that "if we were not away . . . [mobbers] would exterminate us without regard to age or sex and throw our property into the river."[11] Some weeks later, while John was travelling with his brother-in-law, three armed men on horseback approached their wagon. Soon the men were joined by other mobocrats, who surrounded the wagon and threatened the two men. John confidently spoke to the ruffians: "Gentlemen, show me two men among you that shall be traveling the road peaceably on their own business as we were doing, and let them be attacked by 3 ruffians, as we supposed we were and if they will not defend themselves, I will show you two cowards and scoundrels."[12] Impressed by his boldness, the mobbers let him pass without further molestation to safety in Illinois.

John and his family moved to Nauvoo, where he was ordained bishop of the Nauvoo Fifth Ward in 1842. He later served in the stake presidency at Lima, Illinois. As mobocracy flared in Illinois, John joined the migrating Saints in the exodus to the Salt Lake Valley. His service in the Valley was noteworthy—he was a high councilor, bishop of the Salt Lake Fourteenth Ward, and delegate to the House of Representatives in 1849.

A mission call in 1851 ended his civic service in the Valley. He journeyed nearly eight thousand miles to preach the gospel in Australia. He became discouraged on the mission and wrote to the mission president, "I do not feel able to remain here. . . . We have experienced great inconvenience for want of Books of Mormon, Doc. and Cov., Voice of Warnings, and Hymn Books."[13] On 14 October 1852 a letter from Brigham Young released him: "Return in peace. Your Mission is accomplished and others are on the way to follow up and build upon the foundation which you have laid. . . . Therefore, rest satisfied, and come home to Zion and dwell in the midst of the people of God."[14]

After an absence of nearly two years John returned to his family in the valley of the Saints. "I find my whole system, nerves and lungs much affected. My limbs palsied and my blood cankered," said John.[15] He advised that none of his sons "be exempt from providing for me and my family; neither for any of them to be deprived of the privilege for I wanted my blessing to rest on them all, consequently I wanted them all to feel the obligation and enjoy the privilege of seeing that I was taken care of, that the blessing of the Lord and my blessing might rest on them all."[16]

On 9 April 1854 John was ordained a patriarch by Heber C. Kimball. For the next thirteen years he gave many patriarchal blessings to those residing in Utah County. While visiting his son John in Beaver

County, Patriarch Murdock became very feeble and died on 23 December 1871 at the age of seventy-nine.

Notes

1. Journal of John Murdock, typescript, pp. 1–2, Archives and Manuscripts, Harold B. Lee Library, Brigham Young University, Provo, Utah.
2. Ibid., p. 3.
3. Ibid., pp. 3–4.
4. Ibid., pp. 4–5.
5. Ibid., p. 8.
6. Ibid.
7. John married Julia Clapp on 14 December 1823 and they became the parents of five children.
8. Journal, p. 10.
9. Ibid., p. 11.
10. Ibid., p. 12.
11. Ibid., pp. 14, 18.
12. Ibid., p. 18.
13. Reva Baker Holt, "A Brief Synopsis of the Life of John Murdock" (n.p., 1965), p. 11, in author's possession.
14. Ibid., p. 12.
15. Ibid., p. 13.
16. Ibid.

NOAH PACKARD
D&C 124:136

Birth: *7 May 1796, Plainfield, Hampshire County, Massachusetts. Son of Noah Packard and Molly Hamblin.*
Death: *7 (or 17) February 1859, Springville, Utah County, Utah.*

In 1817 Noah Packard traveled on foot alone to Parkman, Ohio, where he became acquainted with Sophia Bundy. They were married on 29 June 1820, and Noah wrote, "Help-mate indeed she was during her life, and we lived an agreeable one."[1] He supported his family by farming, "tho' I frequently embarked in other business, but was generally unsuccessful."[2]

He was not a religious man, and once told a neighbor that "I would not join any Church under heaven, and that there was something wrong and that the sects of the day were not right and that they would go to meeting and put on a long face on the Sabbath, and on the next day would go home and cheat their neighbors and that such a religion I did not believe in."[3]

In 1831 he heard a rumor that "a gold Bible had been dug out of the earth." The rumor gained credence when William Jolly, a recent convert to Mormonism, moved into the neighborhood. Noah penned, "I felt in my heart to pitty them [the Jolly family], and told my wife we would go and make them a visit." It was the testimony of Mrs. Jolly that caused Noah to search the Bible and accept her invitation to read the Book of Mormon. He wrote, "I told her I would, and took it and carried it home and placing the book against my forehead asked secretly the Lord if that work was His, He would make it manifest to me."[4] He read the Book of Mormon twice, and it was during the second reading that "the Lord poured out His spirit upon" him.[5] He and Sophia were baptized in June 1832 by Parley P. Pratt.

Successive missionary labors marked Noah's first years in the Church. His first mission was to Chatham, Ohio, in January 1833. Of this experience Noah wrote, "I was greatly blessed with the Spirit of the Lord. I could stand up boldly in our meetings and bear testimony to the truth of the Book of Mormon."[6] In April 1833 he set out for the East "without purse or script to proclaim salvation, or the gospel to my fellow men." He wrote of the miracles he witnessed on this mission: "I . . . laid hands on a sister who was in great pain from a broken bone; by the blessing of God the pain immediately left her. . . . [While] preaching near the head of Seneca Lake a woman invited me to her house, she had a child that was very deaf, as I passed him standing in the yard I laid my hands upon his head and asked the Lord to heal him, which was done, for which I felt to thank the Lord."[7]

He returned to Ohio after having "traveled 1,782 miles on foot held 72 meetings, baptized 18 persons, [and] organized one branch of the church." He was then called to preside over the Parkman Branch.[8]

After he sold his Parkman farm for $2,200 he moved to Kirtland and loaned one thousand dollars to assist in building the house of the Lord. The Prophet Joseph Smith wrote of his generosity: "Oh! may God bless him a hundred fold, even of the things of the earth, for this righteous act."[9] He later gave four hundred dollars to discharge the contracted debts of the Church.[10]

Noah was ordained a high priest on 15 January 1836 and called to serve on the Kirtland high council. He signed the Kirtland Camp constitution but did not migrate with the camp to Missouri. In "consequence of poverty, I was obliged to winter at Wellsville on the Ohio River," he wrote.[11] He joined the Saints at Quincy, Illinois, in 1839.

On 7 April 1841 he was chosen as a counselor to Don Carlos Smith, president of the high priests quorum (see D&C 124:136). After the death of Don Carlos he served as counselor to George Miller, from 1841 to 1846. During these same years he fulfilled missions in several states, "having traveled in all about 15,000 miles, preached 480 times, and baptised 53 into the Church." Of these missionary labors Noah descriptively wrote, "If any of the elders of The Church of Jesus Christ of Latter-day Saints, in traveling to preach the gospel, have gone hungry, so have I; if any have traveled with sore feet, so have I; if any have been seized and put out of towns when speaking to the people, so have I."[12]

When the Saints began to flee from Nauvoo, Noah was too ill to travel. He remained in Illinois until a restoration of health enabled him to journey to Wisconsin, where he labored in the lead mines for about four years, acquiring the funding needed to purchase teams to take his family to the Salt Lake Valley. He arrived in the Valley in 1850 with the Jonathan Foote company.

By 1851 he was residing in the pioneer settlement of Springville: "After living in my wagons and tent about one year and eight months got a house built and moved into it."[13] In Springville he was prominent in ecclesiastical and civic affairs—he was a captain of the "Silver Greys" military unit, a farmer, a surveyor, and a counselor to Asahel Perry, president of the Springville Branch. According to family tradition, contention arose between the local Church authorities and Noah over the tabernacle being built in Springville. A descendant of Noah's, Michael W. P. Ball, wrote, "Noah expressed to the authorities that the Tabernacle was out of plumb and was a danger to all who enter therein. The authorities became wroth with him and even swore at him during church for suggesting that the Tabernacle was out of plumb."[14]

Unjustifiable attacks and false charges led to Noah's being dropped from the branch presidency. He continued to be vocal about the problem with the tabernacle but wrote, "Had to be on my guard lest I should say something that would displease the Bishop and his Council." He lamented, "My sorrows and afflictions were great; and my heart was grieved to the verry bottom; and I prayed unto the Lord by day and by night, and he sustained me. . . . The abuse which I have received in Springville far exceeds any which I received whilst traviling praching the Gospel among the Gentiles."[15]

He served the city as an alderman but due to the continuing difficulties chose to resign. Noah died on 7 February 1859 in Springville. One biographer wrote of him, "He died as he had lived firm and unshaken in the gospel of Christ, being in fellowship with his brethren and leaving many friends to lament his loss."[16]

Notes

1. Noah Packard, "A Synopsis of the Life and Travels of Noah Packard," typescript, p. 1, Harold B. Lee Library, Brigham Young University, Provo, Utah.

2. Ibid.

3. Ibid., p. 2.

4. Ibid., pp. 2–3.

5. Ibid., p. 3.

6. Ibid.

7. Ibid., p. 5.

8. Ibid.

9. *HC* 2:281.

10. See Packard, p. 6.

11. Ibid., p. 7.

12. Ibid., p. 9.

13. Ibid., p. 10.

14. Michael W. P. Ball, letter to author, 4 February 1994. Sometime either in the late 1960s or '70s the tabernacle was torn down because it was out of plumb.

15. Packard, pp. 12–13.

16. *LDS Biographical Encyclopedia* 2:685.

HIRAM PAGE
D&C 28

Birth: *1800, Vermont.*
Death: *12 August 1852, near Excelsior Springs, Ray County, Missouri.*

In his youth Hiram Page studied medicine and traveled extensively through Vermont, New York, and Canada practicing his profession. In his early twenties he settled in Seneca County, New York, where he became acquainted with the Whitmer family. Catherine Whitmer, the oldest daughter of Peter Whitmer, and Hiram were married on 10 November 1825. They resided on the Whitmer farm in Fayette, New York, during their early married years.

From the Whitmers, Hiram learned about the coming forth of the Book of Mormon. He was privileged to be one of the Eight Witnesses shown the plates by the Prophet Joseph Smith. He was baptized on 11 April 1830, just five days after the Church was organized.

Before the conference of 26 September 1830, Hiram found a stone five-by-three inches in length and one-half inch thick with two holes. He believed the stone possessed qualities that enabled him to be a "revelator."[1] He claimed to receive revelations through the stone identifying the location of the "American New Jerusalem" and the proper governing process of the Church.[2] The Prophet was greatly distressed over Hiram's claim and prayed for an answer. Doctrine and Covenants section 28 came in response to the prophetic pleadings. Oliver Cowdery, who had been influenced by Hiram's supposed revelations, was instructed, "Thou shalt take thy brother, Hiram Page, between him and thee alone, and tell him that those things which he hath written from that stone are not of me and that Satan deceiveth him" (D&C 28:11). It appears that Hiram accepted the rebuke and counsel, for at the September 1830 conference he renounced the stone and the spurious revelations.

In May 1831 Hiram and his family left New York and settled in Thompson, Ohio, before moving to Jackson County, Missouri. In Missouri he was "recommended to the Bishop in Zion as being worthy of inheritances among the people of the Lord according to the laws of the Church" in Zion.[3] He settled a few miles from Independence in what became known as the Whitmer settlement on land he purchased for $1.25 an acre. There he was severely persecuted for his religious beliefs. General Moses Wilson detailed the atrocities:

> I went, in company with forty others, to the house of Hiram Page, a Mormon, in Jackson county. We got logs and broke in every door and window at the same instant; and pointing our rifles at the family, we told them, we would be d—d if we didn't shoot every one of them, if Page didn't come out. At that, a tall woman made her appearance, with a child in her arms. I told the boys she was too d—d tall. In a moment the boys stripped her, and found it was Page. I told them to give him a d—d good one. We gave him sixty or seventy blows with hickory withes which we had prepared.[4]

His injuries were so severe that family members feared for his life. In November 1833 Hiram sought legal recourse from Esquire Silvers, the circuit court judge in Lexington. The judge refused to issue a warrant and advised him to "fight and kill the outlaws whenever they came upon us."[5]

Discouraged by the advice, Hiram moved to Clay County. He was commissioned by his brother-in-law David Whitmer to counteract the influence of Sally Crandall, who claimed that she could know and see men's hearts. She testified that she had seen the heart of Hiram Page and it was "not right."[6] After completing this assignment he moved to Far West, becoming one of the first property owners in the area.

In Far West, Hiram lost faith in the prophetic calling of Joseph Smith and was excommunicated. He left the community and moved to Ray County, near Excelsior Springs. In 1848 he wrote a letter to William McLellin explaining the reason for his withdrawal from the Church: "Joseph had tried to place himself above the revealed word [by] . . . presumptuously and prematurely attempting to gather the Saints to the revealed Zion," which Hiram considered "so abominable that the Lord could not suffer him to hold the keys any longer."[7]

His testimony of the Book of Mormon remained strong:

As to the book of Mormon, it would be doing injustice to myself, and to the work of God in the last days, to say that I could know a thing to be true in 1830, and know the same thing to be false in 1847. . . . [To] say that a man of Joseph's ability, who at that time did not know how to pronounce the word Nephi, could write a book of six hundred pages, as correct as the book of Mormon, without supernatural power . . . yea, it would be treating the God of heaven with contempt to deny these testimonies, with too many others to mention here.[8]

Hiram resided near Excelsior Springs the remainder of his life. The 1850 census lists him as having no real wealth, but continuing to labor as a farmer.[9] He died on 12 August 1852 on his farm.

On 2 August 1913 the First Presidency of the Church issued a statement remembering the deception of Hiram Page:

From the days of Hiram Page . . . at different periods there have been manifestations from delusive spirits to members of the Church. . . . When visions, dreams, tongues, prophecy, impressions, or an extraordinary gift of inspiration conveys something out of harmony with the accepted revelations of the Church or contrary to the decisions of its constituted authorities, Latter-day Saints may know that it is not of God, no matter how plausible it may appear.[10]

Notes

1. The stone was handed down in the Whitmer family from one generation to another and is currently held by the Reorganized Church of Jesus Christ of Latter Day Saints.

2. See Bruce G. Stewart, "Hiram Page: An Historical and Sociological Analysis of an Early Mormon Prototype," M. A. thesis, Brigham Young University, April 1987, pp. 122, 134.

3. Ibid., p. 37.

4. HC 4:394–95.

5. As cited in Stewart, p. 44.

6. HC 2:140.

7. As cited in Stewart, p. 161.

8. As cited in ibid., pp. 163–64.

9. See the Missouri federal census 1850.

10. As cited in Stewart, p. 178.

JOHN EDWARD PAGE
D&C 118:6; 124:129

Birth: 25 February 1799, Trenton Township, Oneida County, New York. Son of Ebenezer and Rachel Page.
Death: 14 October 1867, Sycamore, DeKalb County, Illinois.

John E. Page was a farmer and an avowed Methodist before being baptized a Mormon in 1833. By May 1836 he was called on a mission to Canada. He objected to the call because he was destitute of clothing. The Prophet Joseph Smith took off his coat and gave it to him and "told him to go, and the Lord would bless him abundantly on his mission."[1] On this mission John baptized 305 individuals.

On 16 February 1837 he left with his family to serve a second mission in Canada, taking "all the earthly goods I possessed, which consisted of one bed and our wearing apparel of the plainest kind, to continue my mission in the same region of country as before." During his two years of labor he baptized nearly six hundred people and traveled more than five thousand miles, "principally on foot and under the most extreme poverty, relative to earthly means, being alone sustained by the power of God and not of man, or the wisdom of the world."[2]

In 1838 John led the Canadian Saints to Missouri. In October they arrived in DeWitt, just as the Mormon community was being attacked by a ruthless mob. John's wife and two children died there as martyrs to the mob atrocities.[3] While struggling with his grief John was called to the apostleship (see D&C 118:6).[4] His first apostolic assignment was to serve a mission in England with other members of the Twelve. He failed to fulfill this responsibility. His next assignment, given in April 1840, was to accompany Orson Hyde to dedicate Palestine for the return of the Jews. He started on this mission with Orson but never left the country.[5] On 15 January 1841 the *Times and Seasons* stated, "Elders Orson Hyde and John E. Page are informed, that the Lord is not well pleased with them in consequence of delaying their mission, (Elder John E. Page in particular,) and they are requested by the First Presidency to hasten their journey towards their destination."[6] Orson soon left for Europe, leaving his obstinate companion behind.

In April 1842 John defended his failure to complete the mission: "If I have erred, I still have the truth which is this church and its doctrines. Where I have erred, I hope to find mercy, where I have done right I hope to be justified."[7] He retained his fellowship in the Twelve and soon journeyed to Pittsburgh, where in 1843 he published the newspaper *The Gospel Light* and two pamphlets: *Slander Refuted* and *The Spaulding Story*. Soon after the Martyrdom an advertisement appeared in the Pennsylvania *Argus* newspaper saying that "Elder John E. Page was out of employment, and would preach for anybody that would sustain his family."[8]

John returned to Nauvoo by December 1844, "assuring the saints that he was one with them, and gave his testimony to the present organization of the church in the most solemn manner."[9] In early 1845 he frequently met in counsel with the Twelve, but by the end of 1845 his name was conspicuously absent from Church records. One biographer explained that his absence was due to being "much disturbed that his ministry was only providing him and his family with a poverty level livelihood."[10] The seriousness of his repeated absences escalated as John began to advocate James J. Strang as the rightful successor to Joseph Smith.

On 13 January 1846 Strang issued a summons to the Twelve Apostles in Nauvoo, demanding that they come to Voree, Wisconsin, and "make satisfaction" for usurpation of power. John E. Page was the only Apostle to respond to Strang's demands. "I have looked upon the church as being like a clock without weights, or a watch without a mainspring, all stops till they are restored," said John to Strang. This public rebellion was noted and on 9 February 1846, "in consequence of his murmuring disposition, and choosing to absent himself from our Councils," John lost his apostolic authority and on 26 June 1846 was excommunicated for seeking to lure Canadian Saints to Strangism.[11]

After his excommunication he united with Strang, was ordained president of Strang's twelve apostles, and became editor of the Strangite publication *Zion's Reveille*. His ministerial theme centered on the responsibility of each member to support the ministers of God's flock. "Ministers cannot suck the wind and chew their breath and live more than others can," he said. His affiliation with Strang ended in 1849 as John was delivered "over to the buffetings of Satan until he repents."[12]

John then sought for truth in James C. Brewster's break-off faction of Mormonism. In a letter written on 19 October 1849 he encouraged "all my Friends and Acquantances [to] lay aside all prejudices" and read the *Olive Branch,* a Brewsterite newspaper.[13] By the 1850s his affiliation with Brewster had ended and he was laboring on a small farm on the weekdays in Sycamore, Illinois, and preaching at another Mormon breakaway church on Sundays. The last apostate organization he affiliated with was the Hedrickites in November 1862. He was ordained an apostle and was instrumental in securing the Independence temple lot for the Hedrickites.

John died on 14 October 1867 from complications of asthma at his rural home in Sycamore at the age of sixty-eight.

Notes

1. "History of John E. Page," *Millennial Star* 27 (18 February 1865): 103.
2. Ibid.

3. See ibid.

4. John filled the vacancy created by the apostasy of Luke S. Johnson.

5. See *LDS Biographical Encyclopedia* 1:92.

6. *Times and Seasons* 2 (15 January 1841): 287.

7. As cited in John Quist, "John E. Page: An Apostle of Uncertainty," *Journal of Mormon History* 12 (1985): 55–56.

8. "History," p. 104.

9. *HC* 7:344.

10. Nathaniel and Joanna Paige, et. al., "Page—Ekstrom Genealogy" (n.p., n.d.), p. 12, in author's possession.

11. *HC* 7:582; Quist, p. 58. Ezra Taft Benson took John's place in the Twelve.

12. Ibid., p. 62.

13. *Olive Branch* 2 (November 1849): 79, as cited in Quist, p. 63.

EDWARD PARTRIDGE

D&C 36; 41:9, 11; 42:10; 50:39; 51; 52:24, 41; 57:7;
58:14–15, 24, 62; 60:10; 64:17; 82:11; 115; 124:19, 21

Birth: *27 August 1793, Pittsfield, Berkshire County, Massachusetts. Son of William Partridge and Jemima Bidwell.*
Death: *27 May 1840, Nauvoo, Hancock County, Illinois.*

Edward Partridge learned the hatter's trade as an apprentice in a hat shop near his hometown of Pittsfield, Massachusetts. By age twenty he had completed four years of apprenticeship and was a journeyman hatter in New York. By 1830 he was the proprietor of his own hat shop and owned two lots adjoining the public square in Painesville, Ohio.

Desirous to teach his family Christianity, Edward expressed interest in Universalism and Unitarianism, while his wife, Lydia, expressed faith in the Campbellite church. Their religious allegiances changed in the fall of 1830 as they listened to Mormon missionaries. Edward's initial opinion was negative; however, he sent an employee to obtain a Book of Mormon for him. He cautiously accepted its truth but refused to be baptized.

In the winter of 1830 he traveled with Sidney Rigdon to meet the Prophet Joseph Smith in New York. After listening to a discourse by the Prophet he stated that he believed and was ready to be baptized, "if Brother Joseph will baptize me."[1] He was baptized the next day, 11 December 1830, by the Prophet. He asked the Prophet to seek the Lord's will concerning him. The answer received was, "You are blessed, and your sins are forgiven you, and you are called to preach my gospel as with the voice of a trump" (D&C 36:1).

Edward returned to Ohio and three days after his arrival was called to be the first Bishop of the Church, "and this because his heart is pure before me, for he is like unto Nathanael of old, in whom there is no guile" (D&C 41:11). At the fourth general conference he was commissioned to journey to Missouri with other Church leaders. Accordingly, on 19 June 1831 Edward bid farewell to his family and journeyed to the wilderness town of Independence, Missouri. In a letter to his wife he expressed his humility at being called as a bishop. "You know I stand in an important station," he wrote, "and as I am occasionally chastened I sometimes feel my station is above what I can perform to the acceptance of my Heavenly Father."[2]

Discontent grew between the Mormons and the Missourians in Independence, with angry Missourians threatening the Saints and doing bodily harm to Church leaders. Bishop Partridge recorded that on 20 July 1833:

> I was taken from my house by the mob, . . . who escorted me about half a mile, to the court house, on the public square in Independence; and then and there, . . . I was stripped of my hat, coat and vest and daubed with tar from head to foot, and then had a quantity of feathers put upon me; and all this because I would not agree to leave the county, and my home where I had lived two years. . . .
>
> . . . I bore my abuse with so much resignation and meekness, that it appeared to astound the multitude, who permitted me to retire in silence, many looking very solemn, their sympathies having been touched . . . ; and as to myself, I was so filled with the Spirit and love of God, that I had no hatred towards my persecutors or anyone else.[3]

On 23 July 1833, just three days after Edward was tarred and feathered, the mobocrats again gathered in Independence with intentions to further intimidate and harass the Mormons. In order to prevent threatened bloodshed, Bishop Partridge submitted to the demands of the mobs and signed an agreement to leave Jackson County. Fury continued to erupt, forcing Edward and his family to camp on the banks of the Missouri River for five days before being ferried across to Clay County. He wrote to the Prophet, "Many are living in tents and shanties not being able to procure houses."[4] The Partridge family lived in "a miserable old house" with a dirt floor and a fireplace.[5] Amid these trying times Edward journeyed throughout the county comforting the poor.

His return to Kirtland in 1835 was marked with missionary zeal. He and Thomas B. Marsh traveled through the snow, preaching across Missouri, Illinois, and Indiana on their way to Ohio. He then joined Isaac Morley preaching in the eastern states. The Lord recognized the faithful contributions of these missionaries: "Behold I am well pleased with my servant Isaac Morley, and my servant Edward Partridge, because of the integrity of their hearts in laboring in my vineyard."[6]

Edward remained in Kirtland through the spring of 1836 and attended classes in grammar, Hebrew, and gospel subjects. However, once the temple was dedicated he returned to Missouri. During his absence his family had suffered from religious persecution in Clay County. Edward settled them in Far West, hoping for a happier situation there. But Far West was also plagued with apostasy and mobocracy. Edward wrote, "The soldiers took my hay and corn. . . . They also took logs from a hovel I had been building for my cows and burnt them, . . . the town was nearly stripped of fence."[7]

He was taken prisoner in Far West before being moved to Richmond, where he joined the Prophet and other leaders to await trial. Of his incarceration he wrote, "We were confined to a large open room, where the cold northern blast penetrated freely. Our fires were small and our allowance for wood and food was scanty; they gave us not even a blanket to lie upon; our beds were the cold floor. . . . The vilest of the vile did guard us and treat us like dogs; yet we bore our oppressions without murmuring."[8] The charges against Edward were treason, arson, burglary, robbery, and larceny. His bail was set at one thousand dollars; however, he was released on 28 November 1838.

He quickly returned to Far West, where he joined his family. But continued threats against his life forced him to leave loved ones and flee to Illinois, where he assisted other Mormon refugees.

On 25 March 1839 the Prophet wrote from Liberty Jail to the Saints "and to Bishop Partridge in Particular" the stirring accounts contained in sections 121, 122, and 123 of the Doctrine and Covenants.[9]

Edward had been no stranger to personal afflictions and on 13 June 1839 penned of his own poverty and failing physical health: "I have not at this time two dollars in this world, one dollar and forty-four cents is all. I owe for my rent, and for making clothes for some of the poor, and some other things. . . . What is best for me to do, I hardly know. Hard labor I cannot perform; light labor I can; but I know of no chance to earn anything, at anything that I can stand to do. It is quite sickly here."[10]

Edward moved to Nauvoo, where he was appointed bishop of the upper ward. Unfortunately, his sevice in Nauvoo was brief. While building a home outside of town and attempting to move furniture, he collapsed from exhaustion and was forced to bed. About the same time his youngest daughter, Harriett, unexpectedly died. Edward died ten days after his daughter on 27 May 1840 at the age of forty-six. His funeral was the first of major import to be held in Nauvoo. In Doctrine and Covenants 124:19 the Lord revealed that he had received Edward Partridge "unto myself."

Notes

1. As quoted in Lucy Mack Smith, *History of Joseph Smith by His Mother,* ed. Preston Nibley (Salt Lake City: Bookcraft, 1954), p. 192.

2. Edward Partridge Jr., "Biography and Family Genealogy, Unpublished Journal" (Salt Lake City: n.p., 1878), pp. 6–7.

3. *HC* 1:391.

4. Partridge, p. 9.

5. Albert Robison Lyman, "The Edward Partridge Family" (n.p., 1954), p. 22, Archives Division, Church Historical Department, The Church of Jesus Christ of Latter-day Saints, Salt Lake City, Utah.

6. *HC* 2:302.

7. Partridge, p. 57.

8. Ibid., pp. 52–53.

9. See *HC* 3:289.

10. Journal History, 13 June 1839.

DAVID W. PATTEN

Testimony of the Twelve Apostles,
D&C 114:1; 124:19, 130

Birth: *14 November 1799, Theresa, near Indian River Falls, New York. Son of Benoni Patten and Edith (Abigail) Cole.*
Death: *25 October 1838, Battle of Crooked River, Missouri.*

In his youth David W. Patten journeyed alone from New York to southeastern Michigan, where he made himself a home in the woods. He attended Methodist meetings even though "I was looking for the Church of Christ to arise in its purity, according to the promise of Christ, and [believed] that I should live to see it."[1] A letter from his brother John Patten conveyed information about the restoration of the gospel. David traveled over three hundred miles to Indiana to converse with John about the new religion. Convinced of its truth, he was baptized by his brother. At the time of his baptism he stood six feet, one inch in height and weighed over two hundred pounds.

David was ordained an elder on 17 June 1832 and immediately began serving a mission in Michigan. On the mission he discovered his gift of healing: "The Lord did work with me wonderfully, in signs and wonders following them that believed in the fulness of the Gospel of Jesus Christ, insomuch that the deaf were made to hear, the blind to see, and the lame were made whole. Fevers, palsies, crooked and withered limbs, and in fact all manner of diseases common to the country, were healed by the power of God, that was manifested through his servants."[2]

By the fall of 1833 he had completed three missions and was residing in Kirtland until the Prophet asked him to serve the brethren in Missouri. The Prophet hoped that David would prove to be a blessing to the Saints, and wrote, "O, may God grant it a blessing for Zion, as a kind angel from heaven."[3] David reached Clay County in March 1834 and spent his days and nights ministering to the exiled Saints.

On one occasion an enraged mobber threatened him with a bowie knife, swearing, "You d—d Mormon, I'll cut your d—d throat." David calmly responded, "My friend, do nothing rash."[4] His gentle composure caused the mobber to assume that David was carrying a concealed weapon, and he fled.

David left Missouri to journey to the southern states, where again he preached the gospel and healed the sick. While on this mission David laid his hands on the head of Johnston F. Lang's wife, who had been ill for eight years. She was instantly healed.

On 15 February 1835 David was ordained to the Quorum of the Twelve Apostles and blessed, "O God, give this, Thy servant, a knowledge of Thy will; may he be like one of old, who bore testimony of Jesus; may he be a new man from this day forth."[5] In May 1835 he joined his brethren of the Twelve in missionary service in the eastern states, traveling through New York, Canada, Vermont, and Maine. His next mission was to the southern states.

In Tennessee he was arrested for promising the Holy Ghost to those who accepted baptism. He and his companion were held under a two thousand dollar bond until their trial on 22 June 1835. According to Wilford Woodruff, "They plead their own cause. Although men came forward and testified they did receive the Holy Ghost after they were baptized, the brethren were condemned; but were finally released by paying the expenses of the mob court."[6]

Feeling the injustice of the court, David "arose to his feet and delivered a speech of about twenty minutes, holding them spell-bound while he told them of their wickedness and abominations that they were guilty of, also of the curse of God that awaited them, if they did not repent, for taking up two harmless, inoffensive men for preaching the Gospel of Christ." The judge exclaimed, "You must be armed with secret weapons, or you would not talk in this fearless manner to an armed court." David replied, "I have weapons that you know not of, and they are given me of God." After the court session David was "warned in a dream to get up and flee, as the mob would soon be there."[7]

As he was leaving Tennessee he "suddenly became aware that a person [Cain] on foot by his side was keeping pace with the mule on which he rode."[8] Abraham O. Smoot recorded from memory David's description of the wandering traveler:

His head was about even with my shoulders as I sat in my saddle. He wore no clothing, but was covered with hair. His skin was very dark. I asked him where he dwelt and he replied that he had no home, that he was a wanderer in the earth and traveled to and fro. He said he was a very miserable creature, that he had earnestly sought death during his sojourn upon the earth, but that he could not die, and his mission was to destroy the souls of men. About the time he expressed himself thus, I rebuked him in the name of the Lord Jesus Christ and by virtue of the Holy Priesthood, and commanded him to go hence, and he immediately departed out of my sight."[9]

After a two-year absence David returned to Kirtland, where he witnessed apostasy and experienced personal sorrow and inward struggles as his brother-in-law, Warren Parrish, sought to destroy his faith. It is believed that David made known to the Prophet that he wished to die a martyr's death. The Prophet responded, "When a man of your faith asks the Lord for anything, he generally gets it."[10]

The fulfillment of the Prophet's rejoinder was in October 1838. Violent mob action was taking place in Missouri, and bands of lawless men roamed the country, destroying homes, burning crops, and ravishing women. For his defense of the Saints, David was known as "Captain Fearnot." On 24 October 1838, when news reached Far West that mobbers had taken prisoners near Crooked River, David responded, and about midnight seventy-five men volunteered to serve under his command. It was near Crooked River that a shot was fired and the battle ensued. Biographer Lycurgus A. Wilson wrote: "With the watch-word 'God and Liberty,' on his lips, David, ordering a charge, ran forward. The mob fled in confusion before the rush that followed . . . but as David led the pursuit down the river bank, a mobber who had taken refuge behind a tree for a momentary pause before taking to the river, turned and shot him in the abdomen."[11] The brethren rallied around their wounded leader and carried him to the home of Stephen Winchester.

David's dying words were, "I feel that I have kept the faith, I have finished my course, henceforth there is laid up for me a crown, which the Lord, the righteous Judge, will give me." To his wife he said, "Whatever you do else, O do not deny the faith." He prayed, "Father, I ask Thee in the name of Jesus Christ, that thou wouldst release my spirit, and receive it unto Thyself." He then said, "Brethren, you have held me by your faith, but do give me up, and let me go, I beseech you."[12] David Patten died at 10:00 P.M. on 25 October 1838 at the age of thirty-eight.

Of his martyrdom the Prophet Joseph wrote: "Brother David W. Patten was a very worthy man, beloved by all good men who knew him. He was one of the Twelve Apostles, and died as he lived, a man of God and strong in the faith of a glorious resurrection, in a world where mobs will have no power or place."[13]

At his funeral on 27 October 1838 the Prophet, while pointing to David's lifeless body, stated, "There lies a man that has done just as he said he would—he has laid down his life for his friends."[14] His remains were laid to rest with military honors at Far West, and his grave is now unmarked and unknown.

Of his noble spirit the Lord stated, in a revelation to the Prophet, "David Patten I have taken unto myself; behold, his priesthood no man taketh from him" (D&C 124:130). He assured the Prophet, "My servant David Patten . . . is with me at this time" (D&C 124:19).

Notes

1. *Millennial Star* 26 (25 June 1864): 406.
2. As quoted in Lycurgus A. Wilson, *Life of David W. Patten: The First Apostolic Martyr* (Salt Lake City: Deseret News, 1904), p. 16.
3. As quoted in ibid., p. 28.
4. As quoted in ibid., p. 29.
5. As quoted in ibid., p. 33.
6. As quoted in ibid., pp. 43–44.
7. As quoted in ibid., pp. 44–45.
8. Ibid., p. 45.
9. As quoted in ibid., p. 46.
10. As quoted in ibid., p. 53.
11. Ibid., p. 67.
12. As quoted in ibid., p. 69.
13. As quoted in ibid., p. 70.
14. As quoted in ibid., p. 71.

ZIBA PETERSON
D&C 32; 58:60

Death: *1849, Placerville, Eldorado County, California.*

It is believed that Ziba Peterson was in his late teens or early twenties at the time of his baptism on 18 April 1830.[1] He was ordained an elder by June 1830 and was one of six elders present when, as Joseph Smith described it, "the Holy Ghost was poured upon us in a miraculous manner—many of our number prophesied, whilst others had the heavens opened to their view."[2]

In October 1830 the Lord recognized the "great interest and desires . . . felt by the elders [including Ziba] respecting the Lamanites, of whose predicted blessings the Church had learned from the Book of Mormon." The elders desired to know the will of the Lord "as to whether elders should be sent at that time to the Indian tribes in the West." (D&C 32: Introduction.) Ziba Peterson was one of four elders called to be a missionary to the Lamanites; the others were Oliver Cowdery, Parley P. Pratt, and Peter Whitmer Jr. (see D&C 32:1–3).

"As soon as this revelation was received," wrote Mother Smith, "Emma Smith, and several other sisters, began to make arrangements to furnish those who were set apart for this mission, with the necessary clothing."[3] Ziba left for the mission from Fayette, New York, on 17 October 1830. He and his companions began their fifteen-hundred-mile journey on foot preaching to the Catteraugus Indians near Buffalo, New York; the Wyandots in Sandusky, Ohio; and settlers in the Kirtland area.

Fifty miles west of Kirtland the missionaries visited the home of Simeon Carter. When a warrant was served against Elder Pratt in the Carter home, Ziba accompanied him to the courtroom. Near midnight Parley invited Ziba to sing the hymn "Oh How Happy Are They" with him to the judge. The exasperated judge jailed Parley but allowed Ziba to rejoin the other missionaries.

The missionaries continued their journey to the western frontier and arrived in Independence, Missouri, in December 1830. Ziba and Peter Whitmer preached to the Indians across the Missouri River on 8 April 1831. Ziba preached with Oliver Cowdery in Lafayette County, where Ziba met and may have converted his future wife, Rebecca Hooper. In the summer of 1831 he also preached in Lone Jack, a frontier community in southeastern Missouri.

On 1 August 1831 the Lord chastened him for trying to hide his sins: "Let that which has been bestowed upon Ziba Peterson be taken from him; and let him stand as a member in the church, and labor with his own hands, with the brethren, until he is sufficiently chastened for all his sins; for he confesseth them not, and he thinketh to hide them" (D&C 58:60). Three days later he confessed his faults, "which was satisfactory to the Church."[4] However, in May 1833 he withdrew from Church fellowship and on 25 June 1833 was excommunicated and delivered "over to the buffetings of Satan."[5]

Ziba continued to reside in the Independence area after the expulsion of the Saints from Jackson County. By 1833 he was teaching school in Lone Jack and by 1840 was residing in Lafayette County, next door to his father-in-law, Thomas Hooper.

In May 1848 Ziba journeyed with his family to California. His daughter, Mary, related the circumstances of their departure: "Although at that time only a little child of six years of age, the sadness of that parting has remained with me through life. . . . The captain giving his orders, teamsters yoking their oxen. . . . Many relatives travelled with us yet for several hours, delaying till the last moment the parting."[6]

Ziba and his family arrived in the California mining town of Dry Diggins in October 1848. He gained prominence among the miners and was elected sheriff. The *Alta California* carried an account of his apprehension and hanging of three desperadoes who had stolen six hundred dollars and threatened to kill the proprietor of a gambling house.[7] Their hanging, the first "legal" hanging in California, led to renaming Dry Diggins "Hangtown."

Ziba died soon after the hangings. The cause of his death is unknown. His widow moved the family to Napa Valley and purchased a lot in Sonoma from former Missouri governor Lilburn W. Boggs.

Notes

1. See Irene Johnson and Kahlile Mehr, "The Other Missionary—Ziba Peterson" (n.p., 10 July 1991), p. 2, in author's possession.

2. *HC* 1:85.

3. Lucy Mack Smith, *History of Joseph Smith by His Mother*, ed. Preston Nibley (Salt Lake City: Bookcraft, 1954), p. 190.

4. Donald Q. Cannon and Lyndon W. Cook, eds., *Far West Record: Minutes of The Church of Jesus Christ of Latter-day Saints, 1830–1844* (Salt Lake City: Deseret Book Co., 1983), p. 9.

5. *HC* 1:367.

6. Marjorie C. Pitts, "The Story of Mary Peterson Clark," as cited in Johnson and Mehr, p. 10.

7. *Alta California*, 8 February 1849.

WILLIAM WINES PHELPS

D&C 55; 57:11–12; 58:40–41; 61: Introduction; 67: Introduction; 70:1; 85: Introduction

Birth: *17 February 1792, Dover, Morris County, New Jersey. Son of Enon Phelps and Mehitabel Goldsmith.*

Death: *6 March 1872, Salt Lake City, Salt Lake County, Utah.*

William W. Phelps was first introduced to the Church when he purchased a Book of Mormon on 9 April 1830 from Parley P. Pratt. He "sat up all night to compare the Book of Mormon with the Bible." The following morning William exclaimed, "I am going to join that church; I am convinced that it is true."[1] In a letter to Oliver Cowdery that was printed in the *Messenger and Advocate* he wrote, "From the first time I read this volume of volumes, even till now, I have been struck with a kind of sacred joy at its title page. . . . What a wonderful volume!"[2]

On 11 May 1831 the *Ontario Phoenix*, one of three newspapers for which William had served as an editor, contained his valedictory announcing his removal from New York.

He moved to Kirtland to offer his time and talents to the Church. In June 1831 the Prophet received a revelation for William: "Thou art called and chosen; and after thou hast been baptized by water, . . . then thou shalt be ordained by the hand of my servant Joseph Smith, Jun., to be an elder unto this church. . . . And on whomsoever you shall lay your hands, if they are contrite before me, you shall have power to give the Holy Spirit." (D&C 55:1–3.) He was baptized on 10 June 1831 and ordained an elder by Joseph Smith.

He accompanied the Prophet on his journey from Kirtland to Missouri. On 20 July 1831 the Prophet received a revelation directing that "William W. Phelps be planted in this place, and be established as a printer unto the church" (D&C 57:11). One of the most famous publications printed on his press was the Book of Commandments. He also printed the first newspaper of the Church, *The Evening and the Morning Star.* The article that elicited the most negative response among Missourians was "respecting free people of color, who may think of coming to the western boundaries of Missouri as members of the church."[3] Although the article was composed mainly of quotes from Missouri law and the Missouri constitution and was primarily meant to serve as a caution to missionaries, many Missourians viewed it as an open invitation to free blacks to gather with the Saints in Jackson County. It inflamed the old settlers of the state and was one of the causes for the Mormons' expulsion.[4]

In July 1833, as William was in the process of printing the Book of Commandments, a mob attacked his house. He offered himself as ransom to the mob and was willing to be scourged or even put to death if the mob would cease their destruction and abuses. The offer was not accepted. "I know it was right that we should be driven out of the land of Zion," wrote William to Church leaders in Kirtland, "but, brethren, if the Lord will, I should like to know what the honest in heart shall do?"[5] The Prophet sent William a written rebuke for his pride and for the false insinuations contained in his letter.[6]

Humbled by the rebuke, he journeyed to Kirtland. There he helped prepare the 1835 edition of the Doctrine and Covenants and the first Church hymnbook and served as a scribe to Joseph Smith for the writings of Abraham. The Prophet wrote, "The principles of astronomy as understood by Father Abraham and the ancients unfolded to our understanding."[7]

William also turned his heart to the temple, and contributed five hundred dollars toward completing it. At the temple dedication he reported seeing heavenly personages in the upper story of the temple.[8] All six verses of William's hymn "The Spirit of God Like a Fire Is Burning" were sung at the dedication, including:

We'll wash and be washed, and with oil be anointed,
Withal not omitting the washing of feet:
For he that receiveth his penny appointed
Must surely be clean at the harvest of wheat.

After these glorious events William returned to Missouri and settled in Far West. With money collected from the Saints, William purchased the northern half of Far West and John Whitmer purchased the southern half. It appeared to many that "these two brethren . . . seemed to be conducting matters with a high hand, also in their own interests—for personal gain."[9] In April 1837 the high council investigated their financial dealings. With an agreement reached that the land be transferred to Bishop Edward Partridge and that all proceeds from land sales be appropriated to the upbuilding of Zion, William and John were exonerated.[10] However, on 1 November 1837 the Lord in a revelation to the Prophet Joseph Smith stated, "John Whitmer and William W. Phelps have done those things which are not pleasing in my sight."[11] In March 1839 William and John were excommunicated from the Church.

William "was among the most bitter enemies of the Prophet."[12] However, by 1840 he had repented and wrote to Joseph Smith: "I am as the prodigal son, though I never doubt or disbelieve the fulness of the Gospel. I have been greatly abused and humbled. . . . I have done wrong and I am sorry. The beam is in my own eye. I have not walked along with my friends according to my holy anointing."[13]

The Prophet responded, "It is true, that we have suffered much in consequence of your behavior—the cup of gall, already full enough for mortals to drink, was indeed filled to overflowing when you turned against us. . . . 'Had it been an enemy, we could have borne it.' . . . 'Come on, dear brother, since the war is past, For friends at first, are friends again at last.'"[14]

The breach between the Prophet and William mended quickly and William was again appointed to publishing tasks and asked to serve as a spokesman for the Prophet on several occasions. In 1844 he was appointed to the Nauvoo City Council. He was with the Prophet as he rode to Carthage on 24 June 1844, and he visited him on the morning of the twenty-seventh in Carthage Jail.[15] After the Martyrdom William stated, "We have hitherto walked by sight, and if a man wanted to know anything he had only to go to Brother Joseph. Joseph has gone, but he has not left us comfortless. . . . If you want to do right, uphold the Twelve. . . . I will sustain the Twelve as long as I have breath."[16]

In accordance with his resolve, William migrated with the persecuted Saints to Iowa Territory and then to the valley of the Great Salt Lake. He first camped in the old Salt Lake fort and then constructed a brick home in the area that he occupied until his death.

In civil affairs William was a prominent figure in Utah—a member of the constitutional convention, surveyor general and chief engineer of the Great Salt Lake Valley, speaker of the House of Representatives, and member of the board of regents for the University of Deseret. He also served as an ordinance worker in the Endowment House. William died on 6 March 1872 at the age of eighty.

Notes

1. Alice Phelps, letter to Walter Dean Bowen, as cited in Bowen, "The Versatile W. W. Phelps—Mormon Writer, Educator, Pioneer," M. S. Thesis, Brigham Young University, August 1958, p. 23.

2. *Messenger and Advocate* 1 (February 1835): 177.

3. *The Evening and the Morning Star* 2 (July 1833): 109.

4. See *Church History in the Fulness of Times* (Salt Lake City: The Church of Jesus Christ of Latter-day Saints, 1989), p. 132.

5. *HC* 1:457.

6. Oliver Cowdery Letter Book, as cited in Bowen, p. 59.

7. *HC* 2:286.

8. See Journal History, 8 November 1857.

9. *CHC* 1:423.

10. See *HC* 2:483–84.

11. *HC* 2:511.

12. *HC* 3:359.

13. *HC* 4:141–42.

14. *HC* 4:163–64.

15. See Bowen, p. 118.

16. As cited in ibid., p. 121.

ORSON PRATT

Testimony of the Twelve Apostles,
D&C 34; 52:26; 75:14; 124:129; 136:13

Birth: *19 September 1811, Hartford, Washington County, New York. Son of Jared Pratt and Charity Dickinson.*
Death: *3 October 1881, Salt Lake City, Salt Lake County, Utah.*

Of his early youth Orson Pratt penned, "From the age of ten to nineteen I saw much of the world, and was tossed about without any permanent abiding-place; but through the grace of God I was kept from many of the evils to which young people are exposed. The early impressions of morality and religion instilled into my mind by my parents, always remained with me, and I often felt a great anxiety to be prepared for a future state."[1]

It was the Book of Mormon that brought stability to Orson's life. "Such a revelation is the Book of Mormon," he wrote; "the most infallible certainty characterizes every ordinance and every doctrinal point revealed in that book."[2] He was baptized on his nineteenth birthday by his brother Parley and was soon called to preach the gospel with Parley in Missouri (see D&C 34; 52:26). After the mission Orson became the first man in this dispensation to serve as an elders quorum president.

He set the example for priesthood brethren by serving another mission (see D&C 75:14), for which he traveled "on foot near 4,000 miles, attended 207 meetings . . . baptized 104 persons and organized several new branches of the church."[3] After returning to Kirtland he worked on the limestone foundation of the temple before joining Zion's Camp (see D&C 103:40). He recorded his experience in the camp in biblical terms: "Behold the presence of the Lord was with us by day and by night and his Angel went before us to prepare the way. Joseph often spake unto us from the mouth of the Lord. . . . The promises of the Lord were verified . . . we were blessed and counseled from on high throughout our Journey."[4]

While reading the *Messenger and Advocate* Orson learned that he was requested to be in Kirtland for a meeting on 26 April 1835. Within two days of reading the notice he arrived at the temple site and was ordained to the Quorum of the Twelve Apostles.[5] During the time of his service in the Quorum he earned a "Certificate of Proficiency" in Hebrew and taught English grammar. He earned a certificate qualifying him to teach Hebrew as well.

Orson had begun his teaching career in December 1835. It was interrupted as religious persecution drove the Saints from Ohio to Missouri and from there to Illinois. In Illinois he led the department of literature and mathematics at the University of Nauvoo. Unfortunately, as his educational abilities soared, his faith wavered. John Taylor wrote, "When I saw that he was very severely tried . . . I talked with him for nearly two hours, to prevent, if possible, his apostasy."[6] He was excommunicated on 20 August 1842. Wilford Woodruff wrote the reason for the apostasy: "John C. Bennett was the ruin of Orson Pratt."[7] Orson "confessed his sins and manifested deep repentance."[8] He was rebaptized by the Prophet on 20 January 1843 and "received the Priesthood and the same power and authority as in former days."[9]

After the Martyrdom Orson was confident in the leadership of Brigham Young and followed him to the temporary encampments of Iowa Territory and on to the Rockies (see D&C 136:13). Orson kept a meticulous log of the miles traveled and astronomical and other scientific observations, and he calculated the latitude and longitude of prominent sites. He was one of two Latter-day Saints to first view the Salt Lake Valley: "We could not refrain from a shout of joy."[10]

After traversing Emigration Canyon he dedicated the Valley and then helped plat the city of the Great Salt Lake. He returned to the Camps of Israel in Iowa and from there journeyed east to England. His literary contributions in England include a booklet, "The Kingdom of God," and a pamphlet, "New Jerusalem, or the Spirit of Modern Prophecy," and he served as editor of the newspaper *The Millennial Star*. Even though he returned to America in the 1850s, Orson crossed the Atlantic Ocean sixteen times to share the gospel with those in the British Isles.

His Church service dramatically changed when he publicly announced the doctrine of plural marriage in 1852. His remaining years were spent defending the doctrine, and Mormonism in general. His philosophical writings led to tension between himself and Brigham

Young. For Orson this was most disturbing, as writing was not always joyous to him: "Writing has always been tedious to me, but seeing the good that may be accomplished, I have whipped my mind to it, till I am nearly baldheaded, and grey-bearded, through constant application. I almost envy the hours as they steal away. . . . I wish to accomplish something ere I die, that shall not only be esteemed great by good and holy men, but that shall be considered great in the sight of God."[11]

Brigham Young chose to differ, saying to Orson, "You have been like a mad stubborn mule."[12] He counseled, "I want you to do just as you have done in your Apostleship, but when you want to teach new doctrine, to write those ideas, and submit them to me, and if they are correct I will tell you."[13] In spite of strong counsel, Brigham was very supportive of Orson Pratt. Upon overhearing another deride the Apostle he remarked, "If Brother Orson were chopped up in inch pieces, each piece would cry out Mormonism was true."[14]

The goodness that Orson accomplished in his life proclaimed his testimony. He presided over the territorial legislature, served as a regent of the University of Deseret, and debated the Reverend John Phillip Newman, chaplain of the United States Senate and pastor of the Metropolitan Church of Washington, D. C.; and he and his family were baptized over twenty-six hundred times for deceased kindred dead. In 1874 he was appointed historian and general Church recorder, which position he held at the time of his death.

In 1875 when President Young reorganized the Quorum of the Twelve according to seniority in service, Orson, who had been ranked second in the Quorum, was now ranked fifth. John Taylor became the senior Apostle. Orson later published an affidavit in the *Deseret News* affirming his support for the change: "I unreservedly endorse John Taylor."[15]

Near the end of his life he suffered from severe diabetes. On 19 September 1880 he announced in a Tabernacle address that it was fifty years to the day since he had joined the Church. After the speech was concluded, Wilford Woodruff addressed the congregation: "We are not in the habit of flattering any man, but I want to say a few words concerning Brother Pratt. . . . I never saw a man in my life that I know of that has spent as few moments idly as he has. I have never seen a storm at sea so heavy—even when shipping seas over the bow, side and stern—but what he would read his book. . . . He has improved his time. . . . I feel to thank God that we can still hear his voice."[16]

Orson's last speech was given in the Tabernacle on 18 September 1881. "Tomorrow—if I live till tomorrow—I shall be seventy years of age," he said. ". . . They are the years appointed to man. . . . I know what my hopes are. I know the plan of salvation."[17] Orson Pratt was the last surviving member of the original Council of the Twelve Apostles.

On 3 October 1881, after telling Joseph F. Smith the inscription he wanted on his tombstone—"My body sleeps for a moment, but my testimony lives and shall endure forever"—Orson died.[18]

Notes

1. Orson Pratt, "History of Orson Pratt," *Millennial Star* 27 (28 January 1865): 55.

2. Orson Pratt, *Divine Authenticity of the Book of Mormon* (Liverpool: Orson Pratt, 1851), p. 83.

3. Orson Pratt diaries, 2 February 1833, as cited in Breck England, *The Life and Thought of Orson Pratt* (Salt Lake City: University of Utah Press, 1985), p. 31.

4. Orson Pratt diaries, 6 May 1834, as cited in England, pp. 35, 36.

5. See England, p. 39.

6. John Taylor, "Succession in the Priesthood," p. 18, Utah Historical Society Library, as cited in England, p. 81.

7. Wilford Woodruff journals, August 1842, as cited in England, p. 81.

8. Brigham Young, *Manuscript History of Brigham Young, 1801–1844* (Salt Lake City: Elden J. Watson, 1968), p. 126, as cited in England, p. 84.

9. "Minutes of the Council of Twelve," 20 January 1843, as cited in England, pp. 84–85.

10. Orson Pratt, extracts from journal, in *Millennial Star* 12 (15 June 1850): 178.

11. Orson Pratt letter to Parley P. Pratt, 2 November 1853, as cited in England, pp. 197–98.

12. As cited in England, p. 210.

13. "Historian's Office Minutes," 5 April 1860, as cited in England, p. 215.

14. "Young Office Journal," 1 October 1860, as cited in England, p. 217.

15. *Deseret News,* 1 October 1877.

16. Wilford Woodruff, in *JD* 21:314, 315.

17. Journal History, 18 September 1881.

18. Orson F. Whitney, in Conference Report, October 1911, p. 68.

PARLEY P. PRATT

Testimony of the Twelve Apostles,
D&C 32; 49; 50:37; 52:26; 97:3–5; 103:30, 37; 124:129

Birth: *12 April 1807, Burlington, Otsego County, New York. Son of Jared Pratt and Charity Dickinson.*
Death: *13 May 1857, near Van Buren, Crawford County, Arkansas.*

Parley P. Pratt's early schooling was limited. "But I always loved a book," wrote Parley. "If I worked hard, a book was in my hand in the morning. . . . A book at evening, . . . a book at every leisure moment of my life."[1] While preaching in western New York he visited an old Baptist deacon who told him of a new book, "a very strange book!"[2] The next day he read that strange book—the Book of Mormon: "I read all day; eating was a burden, I had no desire for food; sleep was a burden when the night came, for I preferred reading to sleep. . . . I esteemed the Book, or the information contained in it, more than all the riches of the world."[3]

Parley was baptized in early September 1830 by Oliver Cowdery and was ordained an elder shortly thereafter. He immediately began to preach and converted his brother Orson Pratt. In October 1830 Parley was called to be a missionary to the Lamanites (see D&C 32:1–2). With his companions, Oliver Cowdery, Peter Whitmer, and Ziba Peterson, he traveled to Buffalo and from there to Ohio. The news they brought about the Book of Mormon caused such excitement in Ohio that "people thronged us night and day, insomuch that we had no time for rest and retirement."[4] Taking an affectionate leave of the Saints in Ohio, the missionaries proceeded on to Independence, Missouri, about fifteen hundred miles from where they had started. On this mission they preached to three Indian tribes: the Catteraugus Indians, near Buffalo, the Wyandots of Ohio, and the Delawares of Missouri.[5]

Parley served many missions before becoming a recruiting officer for Zion's Camp in February 1834 (see D&C 103:30). One day around noon in the camp, he was exhausted and had slept but a few moments when he heard a loud voice say, "Parley, it is time to be up and on your journey." After relating the incident to Joseph Smith, the Prophet bore testimony that it was "the angel of the Lord who went before the camp."[6]

Parley was ordained an Apostle on 21 February 1835. In his blessing of ordination the Lord was petitioned to "increase [Parley's] love for thee and for thy cause; increase his intelligence, communicate to him all that wisdom, that prudence and that understanding which he needs as a minister of righteousness, and to magnify the apostleship whereunto he is called."[7] Parley then served successive missions to Pennsylvania, New York, New England, Canada, and New York again before settling in Missouri in 1838. In Far West he and five other men, including the Prophet Joseph Smith, were betrayed and taken captive. The Prophet comforted the other prisoners, saying, "Be of good cheer, brethren; the word of the Lord came to me last night that our lives should be given us, and that whatever we may suffer during this captivity, not one of our lives should be taken."[8]

They suffered imprisonment in Independence and Richmond. In November 1838, after listening to the guards in Richmond recount their deeds of rape, murder, and robbery against the Mormons, Parley heard the Prophet speak "in a voice of thunder, or as the roaring lion, uttering, . . . 'Silence, ye fiends of the infernal pit. In the name of Jesus Christ I rebuke you, and command you to be still. . . . Cease such talk, or you or I die this instant!'" The guards were instantly contrite and begged his pardon.[9]

After a mock trial Parley was committed to jail in Richmond for the "alleged crime of murder."[10] In prison he became discouraged, but in response to his query "Shall I ever be at liberty again?" his first wife, Thankful, who had passed away two years before, appeared to him in a vision and reassured him that he would escape.[11] On 4 July 1839 he and fellow prisoners, who were now incarcerated in Columbia, hung a flag from a window with the word *liberty* in large letters. This flag caused much merriment for the townspeople, as the prisoners were deprived of their liberty.[12] However, they escaped by overpowering the jailor. In the excitement Parley lost contact with his friends and also lost his horse. Yet he felt joyous and exclaimed aloud, "Thank God for this hour, it is the happiest of my life; I am free, although lost in the wilderness, and if I cannot find myself, thank God nobody else can find me."[13] After days of wandering he arrived among friends in Illinois, where he was finally able to see the Prophet again: "Neither of us could refrain from tears as we embraced each other once more as free men. . . . He blessed me with a warmth of sympathy and brotherly kindness which I shall never forget."[14]

In the 1840s Parley served a mission in England, where he was editor and publisher of the *Millennial Star.* The first edition of the periodical contained his hymn "The Morning Breaks, the Shadows Flee."[15] While serving another mission to the United States he "had been constrained by the Spirit to start prematurely for home." Along his route he learned of the deaths of Joseph and Hyrum Smith: "I felt so weighed down with sorrow and the powers of darkness that it was painful for me to converse or speak to any one, or even to try to eat or sleep. I really felt that if it had been my own family who had died, and our beloved Prophet been spared alive, I could have borne it. . . . I had loved Joseph with a warmth of affection indescribable."[16]

Parley wondered, "How shall I meet the aged and widowed mother of these two martyrs? How shall I meet an entire community bowed down with grief and sorrow unutterable?" His answer came from the Spirit of the Lord: "Lift up your head and rejoice; for behold! it is well with my servants Joseph and Hyrum. . . . Go and say unto my people in Nauvoo, that they shall . . . make no movement in Church government to reorganize or alter anything until the return of the remainder of the Quorum of the Twelve."[17]

Because of this divine answer Parley was instrumental in blessing the people in Nauvoo and England and the pioneers in the Salt Lake Valley. In describing what would appear for many to be a busy time he wrote, "Lest any time should run to waste, I filled up the interstices not otherwise occupied, in the study of the Spanish language." This studying proved beneficial, for Parley was next called on a "General Mission to the Pacific," which led him not only to the islands but also to South American countries. "Priestcraft reigns triumphant in all these countries," wrote Parley. "I feel as though the Book of Mormon . . . should be translated into Spanish and printed, and then the key be turned to these nations." He had a great desire to translate the Book of Mormon "as soon as I have the language sufficiently perfect."[18]

His final mission was to the States. On 7 September 1856 he wrote in his journal, "I preached my farewell discourse in the Tabernacle, in which I bore testimony to the Book of Mormon and of the calling of Joseph Smith, and of his Presidency and Apostleship."[19] It was near Van Buren, Arkansas, that fifty-year-old Parley was murdered in May 1857. He is viewed by the Church as a martyr.

Notes

1. Parley P. Pratt, *Autobiography of Parley P. Pratt,* ed. Parley P. Pratt Jr. (Salt Lake City: Deseret Book Co., 1985), p.2.

2. Ibid., p. 2.

3. Ibid., pp. 20, 22.

4. Ibid., p. 36.

5. See ibid., pp. 40, 44.

6. Ibid., p. 94.

7. Ibid., p. 97.

8. As quoted in ibid., p. 164.

9. Ibid., pp. 179–80.

10. Ibid., p. 183.

11. See ibid., pp. 204–5.

12. See ibid., p. 210.

13. Ibid., pp. 210–11.

14. Ibid., pp. 253–54.

15. See ibid., p. 264.

16. Ibid., pp. 292, 293.

17. Ibid., pp. 293, 294.

18. Ibid., pp. 342, 363, 369.

19. Ibid., p. 400.

ZERA PULSIPHER

D&C 124:138

Birth: *24 June 1789, Rockington, Windham County, Vermont. Son of John Pulsipher and Elizabeth Dutton.*

Death: *1 January 1872, Hebron, Washington County, Utah.*

"I married a very agreeable companion," wrote Zera (or Zerah) Pulsipher of his wife, Mary. "Lived with her about one year when she died leaving one child which we named Harriett." A few weeks after her death, "she came to me in vision and appearing natural looked pleasant as she ever did and sat by my side and assisted me in singing a hymn—beginning thus: 'That glorious day is dawning nigh when Zions Light Shall Shine.'" Years later he concluded that the hymn they sang was to prepare him for the message of the Restoration.[1]

Zera was a Baptist minister in Onondaga County, New York. In the summer of 1831 he "heard a minister [speak of] an ancient record or Golden Bible in Manchester near Palmyra which remark struck me like a shock of electricity at the same time thought it might be something that would give light to my mind upon principles that I had been thinking of for years."[2]

Several months later Jared Carter came to preach in the area. One evening after Elder Carter had addressed a large congregation, Zera rose to his feet and said to the crowd that "we had been hearing strange things and if true they were of the utmost importance to us. If not true it was one of the greatest impositions." Anxious to know the truth, Zera fervently prayed for an answer. The answer came as he was threshing in his barn: "All at once there seemed to be a ray of light from heaven which caused me to stop work for a short time, but soon began it again. Then in a few minutes another light came over my head which caused me to look up. I thought I saw the Angels with the Book of Mormon in their hands in the attitude of showing it to me and saying 'this is the great revelation of the last days in which all things spoken of by the prophets must be fulfilled.'" Zera rejoiced, crying, "Glory Hal-la-lu-ya to the God and the Lamb forever."[3]

Wanting to share his new religious views with his Baptist congregation he proposed a special meeting. At the meeting he announced to the surprised worshippers "my determination to join the Church of Latter Day Saints, which I did and a large body of my church went with me."[4] His desire to be a missionary was strong. According to one account, he asked his wife one day for a clean shirt and a pair of socks.

"Where on earth are you going?" she asked.

"I don't know, only that I'm going to preach the gospel. The Lord will show me where to go. I am going where He guides me."

"How long will you be gone?" she inquired.

"I don't know. Just long enough to do the work the Lord has for me to do."[5]

While preaching in the vicinity he baptized Wilford Woodruff, a future prophet of God. Wilford recorded his initial impression of Zera's preaching: "After singing, he preached to the people for an hour and a half. The spirit of God rested mightily upon him and he bore a strong testimony of the divine authenticity of the Book of Mormon and of the mission of the Prophet Joseph Smith. I believed all that he said. The spirit bore witness of its truth."[6]

In the spring of 1835 Zera gathered with the Saints in Ohio. During the ensuing years he served a mission to Canada and later to New York before being ordained one of the Seven Presidents of the Seventies on 6 March 1838 (see D&C 124:138). In this position he helped the Kirtland poor journey to Missouri. "They wanted to join us and get out of that Hell of persecution," he wrote. ". . . We could not neglect them, for . . . they were poor and could not help themselves."[7] On the arduous trek "we suffered the perils of a hard journey for near one thousand miles among a hostile people, but the Lord had brought to try us to see what our faith was made of."[8]

Zera was instructed by the Prophet to settle in Adam-ondi-Ahman. His stay in that area was brief:

> The people being much opposed to our faith decided to drive us out of the country. . . . They began to burn their houses and then go to the governor and swear that we had drove them out of their settlements and burned their buildings. . . .
>
> There we stayed about a month, being continually annoyed by mobs and thieves stealing everything that they could lay their hands upon that belonged to people of our church. . . . I think I never slept many nights while I was there without having my sword and pistols by my bed and frequently called by the sound of the Bugle to defend the people from mobs.[9]

Struggling with religious persecution, Zera cried, "Lord what does all these things mean?" The divine answer: "Be still and know that I am God."[10]

Zera fled with his family from Missouri to Illinois and then to the territory of Iowa. His observation of the Winter Quarters encampment was, "There were not well people enough to take care of the sick and dying."[11] In the spring of 1847 he started for the Salt Lake Valley in a company of fifty wagons. With ten of the wagons he went ahead of the company to assist in making roads.[12] Of the first winter in the Valley he penned, "I have seen the hand of God in preserving ourselves and cattle."[13]

At the October 1856 general conference Zera was startled to hear Heber C. Kimball call him "in public to awake to my duty. . . . I soon saw that Brother Kimball was right and that I was holding a high and responsible station in the church as asleep with many others." Immediately he and other Presidents of the Seventies told Brigham Young that "if he knew of any others that would take our places better, magnify it for the interest of the kingdom than we could, he was perfectly at liberty to do so." Young assured them that they were to continue in the Presidency of the Seventy but that they needed to magnify their callings.[14]

Responding to the challenging directive, Zera exerted greater religious zeal. "I was frequently out four or five evenings a week besides day meetings," he wrote. Zera continued to be a leader among the Saints until he "transcended the bounds of the Priesthood in the ordinance of sealing, for which he was cited to appear before the First Presidency of the Church April 12 1862."[15] He was released as a General Authority.

He served as a patriarch for the next ten years in southern Utah. He found delight in knowing "we were a great distance from the abode of the white men, in the very midst of the roving red men."[16] He resided in Santa Clara, Washington County, before pioneering the town of Hebron. Zera died on 1 January 1872 at the age of eighty-two.

Notes

1. Zera Pulsipher, "History of Zera Pulsipher as Written by Himself," typescript, p. 4, Special Collections, Harold B. Lee Library, Brigham Young University, Provo, Utah.

2. Ibid., p. 5.

3. Ibid., p. 6.

4. Ibid., p. 7.

5. Milton V. Backman Jr., *The Heavens Resound: A History of the Latter-day Saints in Ohio, 1830–1838* (Salt Lake City: Deseret Book Co., 1983), p. 104.

6. Matthias F. Cowley, *Wilford Woodruff: History of His Life and Labors* (Salt Lake City: Bookcraft, 1964), p. 33.

7. Pulsipher, p. 8.

8. Ibid., pp. 11–12.

9. Ibid., p. 12.

10. Ibid., pp. 12, 13.

11. Ibid., p. 21.

12. See ibid., p. 22.

13. Ibid., p. 24.

14. Ibid., pp. 24–25.

15. John Van Cott was chosen as his successor in the Council of the Seventies. *LDS Biographical Encyclopedia* 1:194.

16. Pulsipher, p. 26.

Charles C. Rich

D&C 124:132

Birth: *21 August 1809, Campbell County, Kentucky. Son of Joseph Rich and Nancy O'Neal.*
Death: *17 November 1883, Paris, Bear Lake County, Idaho.*

In 1829 Charles C. Rich was a cooper and a schoolteacher in Tazewell County, Illinois. "Charles was [an] . . . honest young man but made no pretensions to religion," a neighbor, Hosea Stout, recalled.[1] A letter to Morris Phelps from a relative, which announced the Book of Mormon, was shared with Charles and awakened his religious curiosity. Two missionaries "presented me a book of Mormon which I read and advocated."[2] "I studied carefully, anxiously, and prayerfully, that I might know if it were the Church of Jesus Christ. . . . The spirit would then whisper, you have not been baptized, you have not obeyed the Gospel; but when I had complied with the law, then I . . . obtained a perfect knowledge of the truth, and could then bear a testimony of it to all the world."[3]

He was baptized in April 1832 in Tazewell County. He volunteered to march with Zion's Camp to Missouri and was elected captain of the Pontiac Michigan branch of the camp. When the march ended Charles journeyed to Kirtland, where he was ordained a high priest and given his patriarchal blessing, which promised that "Satan would have no power over him. . . . He would gather thousands to Zion . . . like Nathaniel of old."[4]

As his Church responsibilities heightened, Charles had little time for romance. A few friends recommended Sarah DeArmon Pea, living in southern Illinois, as a young woman to consider courting. On their recommendation twenty-seven-year-old Charles wrote to Sarah on 23 March 1837:

> Miss Sarah Pea. It is with pleasure that I at this time pen a few lines to you, although a perfect stranger to you however I trust that these few lines may be received by you and may be the beginning of a happy acquaintance with you. I will now let you know the reason of my boldness in writing to you. It is because Elder G. M. Hinkle and others have highly recommended you as a Saint of the Last Days as being worthy of my attention. I think I should be happy to get a good companion such a one as I could take comfort with through life and such a one as could take comfort with me. . . . If these lines is received with the same feeling that I write them I trust that you may be single and unengaged. . . . So no more at present but I remain yours with the best of respects
>
> from Charles C. Rich[5]

This beginning of their courtship matured to marriage eleven months later on 11 February 1838 in Far West.

In Far West, Charles served on the high council and was elected president of the high priests quorum.[6] When mobocracy threatened the Saints he defended the communities of Far West and DeWitt, but to no avail. He estimated his personal losses in Missouri to be $3,450.[7]

In Illinois, Charles again took an active role in ecclesiastical and civil affairs, serving on the Nauvoo high council, the Nauvoo stake presidency, and the Nauvoo City Council and as captain and then brigadier general in the first regiment of the Nauvoo Legion and as a regent of the University of Nauvoo. In 1846 he left Illinois in the Mormon exodus to the West. In the temporary encampment of Mount Pisgah he was the presiding elder and spent much of his time visiting the sick. "Ague and fever and chill and fever is the great difficulty with the saints," wrote William Huntington.[8]

He led a company of Mormon pioneers to the Salt Lake Valley in 1847 and served as a counselor in the Salt Lake Stake presidency until 12 February 1849, when he was called to the Council of the Twelve

Apostles. In his apostolic blessing he was promised he would be "mighty & great & thy wisdom expand, increase & grow until thou shalt understand the things of God & magnify his name."[9]

His service as an Apostle for thirty-four years was filled with varied assignments. He is perhaps best remembered for pioneering San Bernardino, California. Charles was ill for seven weeks of the journey to California, suffering from the "bloody flux." The illness reduced his weight from 192 to 137 pounds and he was unable to sit up without fainting. Yet through the blessings of the Lord, his health was restored and he was able to serve as mayor of San Bernardino.

After returning to the Salt Lake Valley, Charles was a general in the Nauvoo Legion, represented Davis County in the territorial legislature from 1858 to 1860, and accepted the assignment to preside over the European Mission. In Europe he counseled with Saints in England, Norway, Sweden, Ireland, Germany, and France before returning to the United States in 1862.

In 1864 he led settlers to the Bear Lake region. Charles was honored when the settlers named the newly formed county "Rich" and the new settlement "St. Charles." Continual pressure to transform the wilderness into a productive civilization took its toll on his health. "You will probably learn after awhile," Brigham Young wrote, "if you have not learned it already, that you can not endure everything, and to live out your days you must take more care of yourself than you have been doing of late."[10]

After six years of faithful service to the communities in the Bear Lake region Charles was released and invited to return to Salt Lake City. He chose instead to live his remaining years among his friends in the Bear Lake region. Unfortunately, in October 1880 he suffered a paralyzing stroke, the first in a series that lasted for more than three years. The continuing strokes led to his loss of speech and use of his legs. Charles died in November 1883 at his home in Paris, Idaho, at the age of seventy-four.

Notes

1. Autobiography of Hosea Stout, p. 244, as cited in Leonard J. Arrington, *Charles C. Rich, Mormon General and Western Frontiersman* (Provo, Utah: Brigham Young University Press, 1974), p. 14.

2. Charles C. Rich, "History of Charles C. Rich," as cited in Arrington, p. 17.

3. Charles C. Rich, in *JD* 19:250.

4. Book of Patriarchal Blessings Index 2:70; 1:37, Archives Division, Church Historical Department, The Church of Jesus Christ of Latter-day Saints, Salt Lake City, Utah.

5. Letter of Charles Rich to Sarah Pea, 23 March 1837, as cited in Arrington, p. 56.

6. See Donald Q. Cannon and Lyndon W. Cook, eds., *Far West Record: Minutes of The Church of Jesus Christ of Latter-day Saints, 1830–1844* (Salt Lake City: Deseret Book Co., 1983), p. 119.

7. See Arrington, p. 68.

8. Journal of William D. Huntington, 27 July 1856, as cited in Arrington, p. 105.

9. As cited in Arrington, p. 134.

10. Letter of Brigham Young to Charles C. Rich, 18 November 1866, as cited in Arrington, p. 269.

WILLARD RICHARDS
D&C 118:6; 124:129; 135:2

Birth: *24 June 1804, Hopkinton, Middlesex County, Massachusetts. Son of Joseph Richards and Rhoda Howe.*
Death: *11 March 1854, Salt Lake City, Salt Lake County, Utah.*

Acknowledging Divine Providence for his preservation from childhood accidents, Willard Richards turned to religious studies. In Richmond, Massachusetts, he attended revivals until becoming convinced at age seventeen that his sins were unpardonable. He attempted to unite with the local Congregational church, but his request for admission was disregarded. Frustrated by the religionists of his day, he concluded that all sects were wrong and decided that he would wait for God to establish his true church upon the earth.[1]

His interests turned from religion to academics, and he began teaching in Massachusetts and New York. By 1827 he was lecturing on electricity and other scientific subjects throughout New England. His initial interest in a wide variety of scientific studies narrowed to medicine by 1834. He attended the Thomsonian Infirmary in Boston and studied the worth of herbs in curing the sick. By the summer of 1835 Willard had established a medical practice near Boston.[2]

That summer he acquired a copy of the Book of Mormon. He had heard of the restored Church from reading slanderous newspaper reports about "a boy named Jo Smith, some where out west, [who] had found a Gold Bible," but he had never studied its doctrine.[3] While reading in the Book of Mormon he discovered the profound truth of man's purpose on earth: "Adam fell that men might be; and men are, that they might have joy" (2 Nephi 2:25).[4] Willard declared that "God or the devil has had a hand in that book, for man never wrote it." Within ten days he had read the book twice, settled his accounts, and freed himself from every incumbrance to journey seven hundred miles to Kirtland to further investigate the Church.[5] He firmly believed that if the doctrine was true, "God has something greater for me to do than peddle pills."[6]

In October 1836 he arrived in Kirtland and accepted the hospitality of his cousin Brigham Young. After a year and a half of investigating the new religion a hole was cut in the ice of the Chagrin River and there Brigham baptized thirty-two-year-old Willard on the last day of December 1836.

On 13 June 1837 Willard was numbered among the missionaries leaving Kirtland to share the gospel in the British Isles. His preaching in Preston, Bedford, Manchester, Bolton, and the surrounding countryside led many to the waters of baptism. In 1838, while walking with a recent convert, Jennetta Richards, and her friend, "I remarked, 'Richards was a good name—I never want to change it, do you, Jennetta?' 'No, I do not,' was her reply, and I think she never will."[7]

Willard and Jennetta were married on 24 September 1838. "Most truly do I praise my Heavenly Father for his great kindness in providing me a partner according to his promise," wrote Willard. "I pray that he may bless us forever."[8]

Just seven months after his marriage he was appointed first counselor to Joseph Fielding, president of the British mission. In 1840, when members of the Twelve arrived in England, he learned of his apostolic call (see D&C 118:6).[9] He was ordained on 14 April 1840, being the first and only Apostle ordained outside the United States.

In April 1841, after serving in the English mission for nearly four years, Willard returned to the United States. He stayed with Brigham

Young and then the Prophet in Nauvoo. His move to the Prophet's residence was to facilitate the rapidly escalating clerical and literary work of the Church. Willard was appointed private secretary to Joseph Smith, Church recorder, clerk, and historian. In November 1841 Joseph wrote in his journal, "I have been searching all my life to find a man after my own heart whom I could trust with my business in all things, and I have found him.—Doctor Willard Richards is the man."10

More than a year before the Martyrdom the Prophet prophesied that "the time would come that the balls would fly around [Willard] like hail, and he should see his friends fall on the right and on the left, but that there should not be a hole in his garment."11 On 27 June 1844 at Carthage Jail this prophetic statement was literally fulfilled. When the jailor suggested that the imprisoned men would be safer in the jail cell, Joseph turned to Willard and asked, "If we go into the cell, will you go in with us?" He replied, "Brother Joseph you did not ask me to cross the river with you—you did not ask me to come to Carthage—you did not ask me to come to jail with you—and do you think I would forsake you now? But I will tell you what I will do; if you are condemned to be hung for treason, I will be hung in your stead, and you shall go free."12

Willard remained with the Prophet in Carthage Jail and was a witness to the Martyrdom (see D&C 135:2). His written account "Two Minutes in Jail" descriptively details the murders.13

The same loyalty he had given to Joseph Smith was willingly shared with Brigham Young. He faithfully wrote, revised, and preserved Church historical records at Brigham's direction. He accompanied his cousin to the Great Salt Lake Valley in 1847 and returned with him to Winter Quarters. It was in Winter Quarters that Brigham selected Willard Richards to be the Second Counselor in the First Presidency. He faithfully fulfilled the calling from 1847 to 1854.

After suffering from debilitating health problems for eighteen years, Willard succumbed to dropsy on 11 March 1854 in Salt Lake City at age forty-nine. He was the first Apostle of this dispensation to die a natural death. Brigham Young praised his honorable life: "He was as true and unwavering in his course as the sun is to the earth. . . . There is not a shade of deviation . . . from the principles of righteousness."14

Notes

1. See *LDS Biographical Encyclopedia* 1:53.
2. See Willard Richards, "History of Willard Richards," *Millennial Star* 27 (25 February 1865): 119–20.
3. *LDS Biographical Encyclopedia* 1:53.
4. See Lawrence R. Flake, *Mighty Men of Zion* (Salt Lake City: Karl D. Butler, 1974), p. 124.
5. *LDS Biographical Encyclopedia* 1:53.
6. As cited in Flake, p. 124.
7. Richards, "History," *Millennial Star* 27 (11 March 1865): 151.
8. Ibid., 24 September 1838.
9. The Lord reaffirmed his confidence in the Twelve on 19 January 1841 (see D&C 124:128–29).
10. Journal History, 21 November 1841.
11. *HC* 6:619.
12. *HC* 6:616.
13. See *Times and Seasons* 5 (1 August 1844): 598–99; *HC* 6:619–21.
14. *Deseret News*, 16 March 1854, as cited in Flake, p. 124.

SIDNEY RIGDON

D&C 35; 36:2; 37; 40; 41:8; 44; 49; 52:3, 41; 58:50, 57; 61:23, 30; 63: Introduction, 55–56; 70:1; 71; 73; 76; 90:6; 93:44, 51; 100; 103:29; 111: Introduction; 115:13; 124:103–10, 126

Birth: *19 February 1793, near St. Clair Township, Allegheny County, Pennsylvania. Son of William Rigdon and Nancy Galliger (Gallaher).*
Death: *14 July 1876, Friendship, Allegheny County, New York.*

In the fall of 1830 Sidney Rigdon was introduced to the restored Church by his friend Parley P. Pratt. Being a former Baptist preacher and one of the founders of the Campbellite movement, he was initially skeptical of the new religious thinking. However, when he read the Book of Mormon he recognized truth and was baptized on 14 November 1830. Sidney became a key figure in the Church from 1830 to 1838. He dedicated Independence, Missouri, as the land of Zion, pronouncing "this land consecrated and dedicated to the Lord for a possession and inheritance for the Saints"[1] (see D&C 58:57). He was a scribe for the Prophet Joseph Smith for much of the translation of the Bible. He shared many revelations with the Prophet, including the vision of the degrees of glory (see D&C 76). He was a spokesman for Joseph and a powerful speaker, and was known as a "defender of the truth."

Sidney was persecuted for his valiant testimony of the truth of the restored gospel. On 24 March 1832 he was tarred and feathered in Hiram, Ohio. "I saw Elder Rigdon stretched out on the ground, whither they had dragged him by his heals," wrote Joseph after this abuse. "I supposed he was dead." Two days later Joseph visited him and discovered that "his head [was] highly inflamed, . . . and when he saw me he called to his wife to bring him his razor. She asked him what he wanted of it; and he replied, to kill me. . . . He continued delirious some days."[2]

For years Sidney suffered from delusions and disturbing rantings and ramblings. Nevertheless, on 18 March 1833 he became a member of the First Presidency (see D&C 90:6). "Brother Sidney is a man whom I love," wrote the Prophet, "but he is not capable of that pure and steadfast love for those who are his benefactors that should characterize a President of the Church of Christ. . . . But notwithstanding these things, he is a very great and good man. . . . He is a man whom God will uphold, if he will continue faithful to his calling."[3]

Sidney's love of the Prophet and Mormonism was severely tested in Missouri. When he was taken as a prisoner to Richmond, Parley P. Pratt "saw S. Rigdon taking leave of his wife and daughters, who stood at a little distance, in tears of anguish indescribable."[4] According to Lyman Wight, when Sidney and his brethren had been taken by the mob he "received a slight shock of apoplectic fits, which excited great laughter and much ridicule in the guard and mob-militia."[5] The conditions of his imprisonment led to depression and his claim that "the sufferings of Jesus Christ were a fool to his."[6] At a court hearing he defended himself while lying on a cot placed in the courtroom because he was too weak to sit in a chair. Alexander Doniphan recorded, "Such a burst of eloquence it was never my fortune to listen to, at its close there was not a dry eye in the room, all were moved to tears." One of the listeners stated, "We came here determined to do injury to this man. He is innocent of crime. . . . And now, gentlemen, out with your money and help the man to return to his destitute family."[7] The audience raised one hundred dollars for Sidney.

From this moment on Sidney played only a minor role in the Church. Although he was on important Church councils, he had little influence on the Prophet or the citizens of Nauvoo. On 19 January 1841 the Lord affirmed Sidney's position in the First Presidency (see D&C 124:103–10). However, by 1842 a personal conflict developed between Sidney and Joseph after the Prophet asked Sidney's daughter Nancy to enter into plural marriage with him. Nancy refused, and the false rumors that ensued caused damage to Sidney and Joseph's relationship that was never fully repaired.

The Prophet wrote to Sidney on 27 March 1843, "I believe and am laboring under the fullest convictions that you are actually practicing deception and wickedness against me and the Church of Jesus Christ of Latter-day Saints." He concluded, "I must, as a conscientious man, publish my withdrawal of my fellowship from you to the Church."[8] He was cut off from the Church on 13 August 1843 for plotting with apostates, but was later reinstated. At a special Church conference in October 1843, Joseph attempted to have Sidney removed as his counselor. However, Church members rallied behind Sidney and voted that he be retained in his position. Joseph angrily declared, "I have thrown him off my shoulders, and you have again put him on me. You may carry him, but I will not."[9]

Fearful that his family would be harmed if the mobocrats attacked Nauvoo, Sidney moved to Pittsburgh, Pennsylvania. One day before the Martyrdom Joseph said, "Poor Rigdon, I am glad he is gone to Pittsburg out of the way; were he to preside he would lead the Church to destruction in less than five years."[10]

After the Martyrdom Sidney returned to Nauvoo offering himself as a "guardian" of the Church. He claimed that he had received a vision on the day Joseph was martyred instructing him to press his claim for guardianship.[11] Brigham Young said, "Here is President Rigdon, who was counselor to Joseph. I ask, where are Joseph and Hyrum? They are gone beyond the veil; and if Elder Rigdon wants to act as his counselor, he must go beyond the veil where he is. . . . I tell you, in the name of the Lord that no man can put another between the Twelve and the Prophet Joseph."[12] The Church membership rejected Sidney's claims and supported the Twelve.

In September 1844 a Church court was held and fellowship was withdrawn from Sidney and he was "delivered over to the buffetings of Satan until he repents."[13]

Rigdon returned to Pittsburgh and organized the Church of Christ on 6 April 1845. His following failed to grow. At age sixty Sidney was forced to live on the charity of his family. During the last years of his life he resided in Friendship, New York, where it was reported he visited the post office each day to get the paper, read, and converse with neighbors. Sidney died on 14 July 1876.

Notes

1. John Whitmer, *An Early Latter Day Saint History: The Book of John Whitmer,* ed. F. Mark McKiernan and Roger D. Launius (Independence, Mo.: Herald Publishing House, 1980), p. 79.

2. *HC* 1:265.

3. *HC* 1:443.

4. Parley P. Pratt, *Autobiography of Parley P. Pratt,* ed. Parley P. Pratt Jr. (Salt Lake City: Deseret Book Co., 1985), p. 162.

5. As cited in John Jaques, "The Life and Labors of Sidney Rigdon," *Improvement Era* 3 (February 1900): 265–66.

6. As cited in ibid.

7. *Saints' Herald,* 2 August 1884, as cited in F. Mark McKiernan, "Sidney Rigdon's Missouri Speeches," *BYU Studies* (Autumn 1970): 91.

8. *HC* 5:313.

9. *HC* 6:49.

10. *HC* 6:592–93.

11. See *HC* 7:229.

12. *HC* 7:233, 235.

13. *Times and Seasons* 5 (15 October 1844): 686.

Burr Riggs
D&C 75:17

Birth: *17 April 1811, New Haven, New Haven County, Connecticut. Son of Gideon Riggs and Susan Pitcher.*
Death: *8 June 1860, Mt. Pleasant, Henry County, Iowa.*

After being baptized and ordained an elder Burr Riggs served an unofficial mission with his friends in 1831. Levi Hancock recorded:

> Three good looking young men . . . inquired for me. I never had seen them to my knowledge before. They asked how I did and told me they were preachers belonging to the Church of Christ. I learned their names were "Edson Fuller, Heamon Bassett and Burr Riggs." . . .
>
> Those elders ran into all manner of doings, receiving revelations and seeing angels. Falling down frothing at the mouth. One of them who acted the worst was Burr Riggs. I have seen him jump up from the floor, strike his head against the joist in the Baldwins new house and swing some minutes, then fall like he was dead. After an hour or two he would come to. He would prophesy and tell what he had seen. At other times he appeared to be so honest and sincere I was led to believe all said, but concluded that all could not be blessed and perhaps I was not as pure as those young men. What I had received was enough for me.[1]

It appears that despite these unusual manifestations of false spirits, Burr clung to his Church membership. He was ordained a high priest on 25 October 1831 and appointed by revelation to preach with Major Ashley in the "south country" (D&C 75:17). It appears that this mission assignment was not fulfilled.

On 13 February 1833 a council of high priests in Kirtland investigated charges against Burr Riggs. On 26 February they excommunicated him for not magnifying his calling. He repented and marched with the faithful in Zion's Camp to Missouri. On the march he was with Joseph Smith when the Prophet discovered "stones which presented the appearance of three altars having been erected one above the other, according to the ancient order. . . . The brethren procured a shovel and a hoe, and removing the earth to the depth of about one foot, discovered the skeleton of a man, almost entire, and between his ribs the stone point of a Lamanitish arrow." Burr retained the arrowhead, which, as Joseph learned through revelation, had killed "a white Lamanite, a large, thick-set man, and a man of God. His name was Zelph."[2]

Burr returned to Kirtland after the encampment and married Lovina Williams, the daughter of Frederick G. Williams, and began his practice as a medical doctor. By 1836 he had moved with his family to Far West, Missouri, and purchased two hundred acres and a "Lot on which I erected a dwelling home Stable &c and commencd improving my land and had at the time I was drove away about forty acres of Corn vegetable &c."[3] He signed a redress petition seeking compensation for atrocities he suffered in Missouri: "In the year of 1836 when moving to the State of Missouri . . . was met in Ray County in Said State by a Mob of 114 armed men and commanded us not to proced any fur ther but to return or they would take our lives and the Leader Stepped forward and kocked his peace at the Same time we turned around with our team and the mob followed us about Six miles and Left us."[4]

By 1839 Burr Riggs had lost faith in Mormonism and was numbered among the apostates.[5] Little is known of his life from 1840 to 1850 except that he was residing in Adams County, Illinois. He died in 1860 at Mt. Pleasant, Iowa, at the age of forty-nine.

Notes

1. Autobiography of Levi Ward Hancock, typescript, p. 27, Special Collections, Harold B. Lee Library, Brigham Young University, Provo, Utah.

2. *HC* 2:79.

3. As cited in Clark V. Johnson, ed., *Mormon Redress Petitions: Documents of the 1833–1838 Missouri Conflict* (Provo, Utah: Religious Studies Center, Brigham Young University, 1992), p. 330.

4. Ibid.

5. See Anson Call, "Autobiography of Anson Call," typescript, p. 16, Special Collections, Harold B. Lee Library, Brigham Young University, Provo, Utah.

SAMUEL JONES ROLFE
D&C 124:142

Birth: *26 August 1794 (1796), Concord, Merrimack County, New Hampshire. Son of Benjamin Rolfe and Mary Swett.*
Death: *July 1867, Lehi, Utah County, Utah.*

Samuel Rolfe, a resident of Maine from 1810 to 1830, moved to Kirtland soon after his baptism in 1835. He became a carpenter on the Kirtland Temple and was remembered by the Prophet for giving him $1.25. Joseph wrote of his gratitude for Samuel and others who "opened their hearts in great liberality, and paid me."[1]

At a priesthood meeting held in the Kirtland Temple on 15 January 1836, Samuel was appointed to be an assistant doorkeeper of the House of the Lord.[2] Later that year he located in Caldwell County, Missouri. His name appears on the "list of land holdings" signifying that he lawfully possessed ownership of his land but was "compelled by the Exterminating order . . . to leave the same in the hands of the mob."[3]

Samuel settled in Illinois and became a member of the Nauvoo First Ward. In a revelation given to the Prophet Joseph Smith in 1841 he was appointed to preside over the priests quorum (see D&C 124:142). He was also called to be a carpenter on the Nauvoo Temple: "A few days ago the Twelve and the Trustees counseled together on the propriety of employing a suitable number of carpenters this winter to prepare the timbers for the Temple, so as to have them all ready when the stone work was finished. . . . The names of the carpenters selected as steady hands are as follows. . . . Samuel Rolfe. . . ."[4]

Samuel received an unusual blessing on 13 December 1841 at the baptismal font in the Nauvoo Temple. He "was seriously affected by a felon," meaning an acute and painful inflammation of the deeper tissues of a finger, and was told to "dip his finger in the font and be healed and he was healed."[5]

In February 1844, as Joseph Smith sought volunteers for an exploring expedition to California and Oregon, Samuel was among the few who volunteered. None of the volunteers ventured west at that time due to problems that eventually led to the Martyrdom. When Samuel did go west in 1846, he served as a bishop in Winter Quarters before being selected as a captain in the Abraham O. Smoot pioneering company.

In 1851 he migrated to San Bernardino, California, where he was elected county treasurer and called to be a counselor in the stake presidency in Sycamore Grove. Samuel returned to Utah, where he died in July 1867 at the age of seventy-two.

Notes

1. *HC* 2:327.

2. See *HC* 2:371.

3. As cited in Clark V. Johnson, ed., *Mormon Redress Petitions: Documents of the 1833–1838 Missouri Conflict* (Provo, Utah: Religious Studies Center, Brigham Young University, 1992), pp. 743–44.

4. *HC* 7:326.

5. Edward Stevenson, *Selections from the Autobiography of Edward Stevenson, 1820–1897 (1820–1846)*, ed. Joseph Grant Stevenson (Provo, Utah: Stevenson's Genealogical Center, 1986), p. 83.

MARION G. ROMNEY
Official Declaration—2

Birth: *19 September 1897, Colonia Juarez, Mexico. Son of George Samuel Romney and Artemesia Theresa Redd.*
Death: *20 May 1988, Salt Lake City, Salt Lake County, Utah.*

Eight days after Marion G. Romney's birth, his father left the family to serve a mission in the Chicago area. During his absence Marion became seriously ill and did not recover until a priesthood blessing promised that "his life would be spared for the purpose of accomplishing [a great] mission."[1]

His youth in the Mexican colonies was simple but happy. The

colonists lived by the adage "Eat it up, wear it out, make it do, do without." Marion was baptized at age eight and given his patriarchal blessing by his grandfather Lemuel Redd at age twelve. In the blessing he was promised, according to biographer F. Burton Howard, that "if he would be faithful, he would become mighty in expounding the scriptures."[2]

When Marion was fourteen years old a rebellion in Mexico forced him to flee with his family to the United States. They resided temporarily in Texas and then California before moving to Idaho in 1913. In 1917 he moved with his family to Rexburg, Idaho, where he enrolled in Ricks Academy, excelling in debate, drama, and athletics. At the Academy he met a teacher—his future bride, Ida Jensen. Their friendship was interrupted when Marion accepted a mission call to Australia. To finance the mission he secured a loan cosigned with his father to supplement his savings. As he prepared to leave his father told him, "My son, we will miss you. We will be glad to welcome you back, but I would like you to know that we would rather come to the train and take you off in a coffin than for you to disgrace yourself and the Church by any immoral act which you might commit while you are away."[3]

On the mission Marion was recognized as a gospel scholar and scriptorian, and he was successful in sharing the gospel with many. He wrote in his journal, "I honestly feel that [the Lord] has blessed me far beyond my merits."[4]

Returning to the United States, he pursued an education at Brigham Young University, where Ida was completing her graduate work in teaching. Their relationship matured and they were married on 12 September 1924 in the Salt Lake Temple. The young couple resided in Salt Lake City and Marion continued his studies at the University of Utah, graduating with a bachelor's degree in political science and history. In the fall of 1926 he enrolled in law school and passed the rigorous bar exam in 1929. As he opened his legal practice in Salt Lake City, he resolved to arrive at the office thirty minutes earlier than his associates to read, pray, and ponder the scriptures.

In addition to his scriptural emphasis and growing legal practice, Marion expanded his interest in politics. In 1934 he was elected to the Utah House of Representatives. He resigned in April 1935, viewing his call as bishop of the Thirty-Third Ward in the Liberty Stake as more important. On 15 May 1938 he was sustained as president of the Bonneville Stake. Less than two years later, while attending the April 1941 general conference, Marion was startled to hear his name proposed and unanimously accepted as one of five Assistants to the Quorum of the Twelve Apostles. One of his legal associates asked, "Are you going to accept?" "Yes," Marion replied. When asked what the position would pay, he responded, "I don't know." At the conclusion of their conversation his associate told him, "Marion, you are a fool."[5]

Marion's responsibility as an Assistant to the Twelve was to be the assistant managing director of the welfare department of the Church. At this time the Church was small enough that he "could call every stake president in the Church by name, and was acquainted with every one of its welfare projects."[6] In comparing the LDS welfare program with accepting government aid he said, "There are some things to which we have a legal right but which we cannot afford, and the acceptance of public relief is one of them."[7]

In October 1951 Marion was sustained as a member of the Quorum of the Twelve. "There is no man among my associates," said Harold B. Lee, "who more closely emulates the life of the Savior than does my beloved brother, friend, and confidant, Marion G. Romney."[8]

In the privacy of a Quorum meeting eighteen months after receiving the call, Marion confessed: "I hope I can be true to the gospel and to you Brethren. I have been one that could see weaknesses in other men, but they are getting a little dimmer." In 1956 he again expressed his personal feelings about the apostleship to the brethren: "I am grateful that ever since I became a member of the General Authorities, I have never closed a day with less to do than I had at the beginning of the day. I don't worry about the policies of the Church over which I have no jurisdiction. I am too busy. I am however, concerned about three things: keeping myself worthy, first; my strength, second; and third, my ability to fulfill the assignments which come to me."[9]

His devotion to the work was intense and total and his loyalty to the Lord transcended all personal concerns: "I don't remember in my life of ever being in doubt about the truthfulness of the gospel. I cannot remember, at least, a time when I didn't know that the Lord lives. My testimony has changed in that today it is much easier to get an answer from the Lord. His presence is nearer. I know him much better now than I did fifty years ago."[10]

He was ordained as Second Counselor to President Harold B. Lee on 7 July 1972 and as Second Counselor to President Spencer W. Kimball on 30 December 1973. On 2 December 1982 he was called to be First Counselor. Sustaining him in these pressing leadership assignments was his wife, Ida, of whom Marion said, "She took over where Mother left off and has made me what I am."[11]

As Marion neared the end of his life he became partially blind and suffered from Parkinson's disease. Despite his deteriorating health, in 1985 he was sustained as President of the Quorum of the Twelve Apostles. Three years later he died on 20 May 1988 at the age of ninety.

Notes

1. F. Burton Howard, *Marion G.Romney, His Life and Faith* (Salt Lake City: Bookcraft, 1988), p. 25.
2. Ibid., p. 34.
3. As quoted in ibid., p. 65.
4. Ibid,. p. 80.
5. Ibid., pp. 115–16.
6. Ibid., p. 123.
7. Ibid., p. 120.
8. As quoted in ibid., pp. 168–70.
9. Ibid., p. 184.
10. Ibid., p. 230.
11. Ibid., p. 145.

SHADRACH ROUNDY
D&C 124:141

Birth: *1 January 1789, Rockingham, Windham County, Vermont. Son of Uriah Roundy and Lucretia Needham.*
Death: *4 July 1872, Salt Lake City, Salt Lake County, Utah.*

Shadrach Roundy, a prominent member of the Board of Trustees of the Free Will Baptist Church in Spafford Corners, New York, became curious about Mormonism when local pastor John Gould encouraged the Free Will congregation to investigate the new religion. Shadrach journeyed on horseback to converse with Joseph Smith in Fayette, New York, in the winter of 1830. Acknowledging young Joseph as a Prophet, Shadrach embraced the gospel. He soon sold his interest in Spafford Corners and by 1834 was residing near Willoughby, Ohio.

According to family tradition, the Prophet frequently visited him at his Ohio home. A friendship developed as Shadrach found occasions to visit the Prophet in Kirtland. Joseph wrote, "A few days since, Elder Shadrach Roundy brought me a quarter of beef. . . . I invoke the blessings of the Lord to be poured out upon him."[1] Shadrach contributed not only sustenance to the Prophet but financial aid and physical labor to build the Kirtland Temple.

Hoping to flee from the religious injustice in Ohio, Shadrach moved his family to Far West, Missouri, in 1836. Again raging mobs forced his removal. Before fleeing he made arrangements for his "available property, to be disposed of by . . . providing means for the removing from this State of the poor and destitute."[2]

Shadrach and other exiled Saints located temporarily in Warsaw, Illinois, before moving to Nauvoo in 1840. In Nauvoo he supported his family as a merchant; however, he is most remembered for being a bodyguard for the Prophet, a member of the Nauvoo Legion, and a lieutenant and later a captain of the Nauvoo police force. To protect the Prophet and the citizens of Nauvoo, Shadrach often was on duty for many days and nights at a time without sleep or rest. On one occasion he was credited with "saving the Prophet from being kidnapped and probably from being murdered."[3]

On 19 January 1841 the Prophet received a revelation calling Shadrach to the bishopric with Vinson Knight and Samuel H. Smith (see D&C 124:141). In 1842 he was a temporary member of the Nauvoo high council. After the Martyrdom he helped the Saints cross from Nauvoo to Iowa Territory en route to the Rockies. He viewed his assignment as captain of a hundred as part of the fulfillment of a prophecy given by Joseph Smith. "There are some men here," Joseph had said, pointing to Shadrach, "who shall do a great work in that land [the Rockies]."[4]

Before trekking to the Salt Lake Valley, Shadrach was bishop of the Winter Quarters Fifth Ward. At age fifty-eight he was invited by Brigham Young to join the vanguard pioneer company of 1847. This was the first of his five crossings of the plains. After reaching the Salt Lake Valley in July 1847 he was one of three men to plow the first furrow.

In February 1849 Shadrach became responsible for supervising the construction of the Salt Lake Fort. Two months later he was ordained the bishop of the Salt Lake Sixteenth Ward. From 1849 to 1856 he served as bishop and as a member of the first territorial legislature. He gave valuable service as captain of the Silver Greys. He was a successful businessman, as evidenced by the Utah federal census, which showed that in 1850 he had accumulated a real wealth (land) of four hundred dollars, in 1860 a real wealth of two thousand dollars and a personal wealth (personal belongings, cash, et cetera) of one thousand dollars and in 1870 a real wealth of four thousand dollars and a personal wealth of two hundred dollars.[5]

In his later years Shadrach was ordained a patriarch. He enjoyed retelling the stirring scenes of the Mormon expulsion from Missouri to young and old. Shadrach died in 1872 at the age of eighty-three. His obituary in the *Deseret Evening News* stated that he died "of old age, at 7:00 yesterday (4th of July) at his residence in the city. . . . For some years his health had been feeble; but, though weak in body, he was always strong and cheerful in spirit. . . . Thinking himself stronger than he was, [he] exerted himself in his garden, caught cold and was prostrated."[6]

Notes

1. As cited in Shadrach Roundy, "Great and Obvious Travails of Shadrach Roundy in the Church of Jesus Christ of Latter-day Saints" (n.p., n.d.), p. 1, in author's possession.

2. Everette Ellsworth Roundy, comp., *The Roundy Family in America, from the Sixteen-Hundreds* (Dedham, Mass.: n.p., 1942), p. 220.

3. Roundy, p. 222.

4. *HC* 5:86.

5. See the Utah federal census 1850, 1860, 1870.

6. *Deseret Evening News*, 5 July 1872.

SYMONDS RYDER
D&C 52:37

Birth: *20 November 1792, Hartford, Windsor County, Vermont. Son of Joshua and Marilla Ryder.*
Death: *1 August 1870, Hiram, Portage County, Ohio.*

Symonds[1] Ryder's father was a man of considerable influence and property for several years. However, when his fortunes were reversed, young Symonds obtained work with Elijah Mason in Hartford, Vermont. After accruing $133 during his six years of employment Symonds left Vermont, bound for the wilderness of Ohio. He arrived on horseback in January 1814 in Hiram, Ohio. He purchased 115 acres, which left him, as Charles H. Ryder wrote, "rather short of funds so he boarded with Orrin Pitkin and gave him two days work out of a week for his board and worked the other four days on his own land."[2] Symonds returned to Vermont and in the spring of 1816 brought his father's family to Hiram. The family prospered in Ohio and increased the size of their farm to over four hundred acres.

Symonds's name appears prominently on Hiram historical records. He was elected to the board of trustees of the Western Reserve Eclectic Institute and was the fourth corporal in the militia company in Garrettsville, a small community near Hiram. For several years he was the treasurer of Hiram College and for fifty-one years was an overseer or elder of the Nelson-Hiram branch of the Campbellites.

His continual service to the Campbellites was interrupted for three months in the summer of 1831. Ezra Booth's testimony of the Prophet Joseph Smith so impressed Symonds that he sought an audience with the Prophet in Kirtland. He joined the Church in early June 1831. His ordination as an elder occurred on 6 June, and two days later he was called to the ministry in the place of Heman Basset (see D&C 52:37).[3] His ministerial call was signed by the Prophet Joseph Smith and Sidney Rigdon. According to historian James B. Holm, "both in the letter he received and in the official commission to preach, however, his name was spelled R-i-d-e-r, instead of R-y-d-e-r. . . . He thought if the 'Spirit' through which he had been called to preach could err in the matter of spelling his name, it might have erred in calling him to the ministry as well."[4]

Ryder's later apostasy may have been influenced by more than the misspelling of his name. He wrote of his misunderstanding of the law of consecration and stewardship: "When they went to Missouri to lay the foundation of the splendid city of Zion, and also of the temple, they left their papers behind. This gave their new converts an opportunity to become acquainted with the internal arrangement of their church, which revealed to them the horrid fact that a plot was laid to take their property from them and place it under the control of Joseph Smith the prophet."[5]

Whatever his reasons, Symonds not only left the Church but carried an intense determination to eradicate Mormonism. In late summer of 1831 he united with his mentor Ezra Booth in planting the seeds of hatred toward Joseph and Mormonism in Hiram.

Even as Symonds and Ezra were trying to rid Hiram of Mormonism, John Johnson was extending hospitality to the Prophet, Sidney Rigdon, and others. Soon after his arrival at the Johnson farm, Rigdon challenged Symonds in the *Ohio Star* to a debate on the authenticity of the Book of Mormon. Symonds published his refusal, citing as his excuse Rigdon's "irascible temper, loquacious extravagance, impaired state of mind, and want of due respect to his superiors."6 Sidney reacted to this indictment by claiming that Symonds "presented himself before the public as an accuser; he has been called upon before the same public, to support his accusations; and does he come forward and do it? nay, but seeks to hide himself behind a battery of reproach, and abuse, and low insinuations. . . . He could blow like a porpoise when there was no person to oppose him."7

The name-calling and haranguing further sparked the smoldering fuels of mobocracy. It reached its apex on 24 March 1832, when the Prophet and Rigdon were tarred and feathered. Symonds Ryder and Ezra Booth are reported in Mormon historical records as being apostate leaders of the mob. Joseph Smith stated that as he was attacked,

> One said, "Simonds, Simonds," (meaning, I supposed, Simonds Ryder,) "pull up his drawers, pull up his drawers, he will take cold." Another replied: "Ain't ye going to kill 'im? ain't ye going to kill 'im?" when a group of mobbers collected a little way off, and said: "Simonds, Simonds, come here;" and "Simonds" charged those who had hold of me to keep me from touching the ground (as they had done all the time), lest I should get a spring upon them. . . . One cried, "Simonds, Simonds, where's the tar bucket?"8

Sidney Rigdon recorded in 1836, "To the credit of Simonds, we will say that since that time he has been silent on the subject, in this he has displayed more honesty than some others of his brethren."9 But Sidney did not let the issue pass, and Symonds threatened him with a lawsuit. Sidney wrote, "I do not want to be sued for the terrible crime of telling the truth about a man."10

According to Symonds's son, Hartwell, his father was not involved in the tarring and feathering, nor did he preach on the following Sunday in the south schoolhouse on Ryder road and glory in the belief that he had been an instrument of the Lord in driving the Mormons out of Hiram. Instead, Hartwell wrote, his father was "ill in bed at the time."[11]

With contrition and meekness, Symonds Ryder returned to his Campbellite church in September 1831. He regained the confidence of the Campbellites and once again became their overseer or elder. From 1829, the year in which he was first elected, until 1852, he was the only elder of the Campbellite Church in Hiram. His congregation was at its largest in 1849, when 121 individuals were listed as members.

Symonds died on 1 August 1870 in Hiram at the age of seventy-seven. In a eulogy given in the Hiram church, B. A. Hinsdale said, "God grant that we may do our work as well as he did his; then we may go to our graves in equal peace."[12] A large stained-glass window in the church bears the inscription "In Memory of Symonds Ryder."

Notes

1. Although sometimes rendered as *Simonds,* the correct spelling of the name is *Symonds.*

2. Charles H. Ryder, "History of Hiram" (n.p., 1846), p. 6, in author's possession.

3. Seventeen-year-old Heman Basset was a participant in the abnormal spiritual activities of 1831 and was one of the earliest converts to withdraw in Ohio.

4. James B. Holm, ed., *Portage Heritage* (Portage, Ohio: The Portage County Historical Society, 1957), p. 171. Another historian claimed that when Joseph Smith "misspelled" Ryder's first name *Simon* instead of *Symonds,* Ryder lost faith in him, feeling that if the Lord really did speak to Smith, he would spell his name "correctly."

5. Letter of Symonds Ryder to A. S. Hayden, as cited in Max H. Parkin, *Conflict at Kirtland: A Study of the Nature and Causes of External and Internal Conflict of the Mormons in Ohio Between 1830 and 1838* (Salt Lake City: Max Parkin, 1966), p. 91.

6. *Ohio Star* 2 (29 December 1831).

7. *Ohio Star* 3 (12 January 1832).

8. *HC* 1:262–63.

9. *Messenger and Advocate* 2 (January 1836): 243.

10. *Messenger and Advocate* 2 (June 1836): 334.

11. As cited in Doris Messenger Ryder, "A History of Simonds Ryder," Ohio Genealogical Society *Report* 9 (April 1969), pp. 1–2.

12. Ibid.

JACOB SCOTT
D&C 52:28

Birth and death: *Unknown.*

Jacob Scott attended the fourth general conference of the Church in June 1831 in a schoolhouse on Isaac Morley's farm in Kirtland. At the conference he became one of the first men in this dispensation to be ordained a high priest by the Prophet.[1]

One day after the conference Jacob was called by revelation to serve a mission: "Let my servants Edson Fuller and Jacob Scott also take their journey" (D&C 52:28). However, Jacob Scott apostatized after receiving the command and refused to go.[2]

George A. Smith said that Jacob and his apostate friends "became more violent, more cruel, and manifested a greater spirit of persecution than any other enemies."[3]

Notes

1. See autobiography of Levi Ward Hancock, typescript, p. 33, Special Collections, Harold B. Lee Library, Brigham Young University, Provo, Utah.

2. See John Whitmer, *An Early Latter Day Saint History: The Book of John Whitmer,* ed. F. Mark McKiernan and Roger D. Launius (Independence, Mo.: Herald Publishing House, 1980), p. 73 n. 2.

3. George A. Smith, in *JD* 11:4–5.

LYMAN ROYAL SHERMAN
D&C 108

Birth: *22 May 1804, Monkton, Addison County, Vermont. Son of Elkanah Sherman and Asenath Hulbert.*
Death: *27 January 1839, Far West, Caldwell County, Missouri.*

Lyman R. Sherman's early interest in the Book of Mormon was mentioned by his brother-in-law, Benjamin Johnson: "My mother, brother Seth, sister Nancy, and Lyman R. Sherman, with some of the neighbors, . . . would meet together to read the Book of Mormon. . . . Their reading soon led to marveling at the simplicity and purity of what they read, and at the spirit which accompanied it, bearing witness to its truth."[1] Soon Lyman was baptized and blessed with the gift of tongues. Benjamin Johnson wrote, "The spirit came upon Brother Sherman in mighty power, and he opened his mouth in an unknown tongue, to the great surprise and joy of all, . . . being the first known to have spoken in the gift of tongues by the power of God in this dispensation."[2]

In April 1835 Lyman received his patriarchal blessing from Joseph Smith Sr. and was told that since his father had passed away, "God shall be thy father and he shall comfort thee."[3]

Lyman was called to be a President of the Seventies; however, because of his previous ordination to the office of high priest, he was released.[4] On 26 December 1835 he said to the Prophet Joseph Smith, "I have been wrought upon to make known to you my feelings and desires, and was promised that I should have a revelation which should make known my duty."[5] The Prophet received a revelation that very hour:

> Verily thus saith the Lord unto you, my servant Lyman: Your sins are forgiven you, because you have obeyed my voice in coming up hither this morning to receive counsel of him whom I have appointed. . . .
>
> Wait patiently until the solemn assembly shall be called of my servants, then you shall be remembered with the first of mine elders, and receive right by ordination with the rest of mine elders whom I have chosen.

Behold, this is the promise of the father unto you if you continue faithful.

And behold, and lo, I am with you to bless you and deliver you forever. Amen. (D&C 108:1, 4–5, 8.)

In 1836 Lyman participated in the Kirtland Temple dedication. On 8 January 1837 he met with others in the temple to worship, and after the sacrament had been administered, according to Wilford Woodruff, "Elder Sherman sung in the gift of tongues & proclaimed great & marvelous things while clothed upon by the power & spirit of God."[6] On 10 October 1837 he was selected to be a member of the Kirtland high council.

When dissenters in Kirtland sought to use the printing office to "bolster up a church organization opposed to the Prophet," it was reported that Lyman set fire to the building to thwart the plans of Joseph's enemies.[7] The blaze destroyed the printing office and scorched the temple and other buildings.

Lyman journeyed from Kirtland to Missouri and on 13 December 1838 was called to the Far West high council in "the place of Newell Knight untill he returns."[8] His call to the apostleship came in a letter written on 16 January 1839 by Joseph Smith, Sidney Rigdon, and Hyrum Smith while confined in Liberty Jail.[9] Lyman Sherman was to replace Orson Hyde in the Twelve.

Lyman was never ordained to the apostolic priesthood, as he died on 27 January 1839 at the age of thirty-four. Of his death Heber C. Kimball said, acording to Wilford Woodruff, that it "was not the will of God for a man to take Brother Hyde's place."[10]

Notes

1. Benjamin F. Johnson, *My Life's Review* (Independence, Mo.: Zion's Printing and Publishing Co., 1947), p. 11.

2. Benjamin Johnson, letter to George S. Gibbs, 1903, as cited in E. Dale LeBaron, "Benjamin Franklin Johnson: Colonizer, Public Servant, and Church Leader," M.A. thesis, Brigham Young University, 1967, p. 344.

3. Book of Patriarchal Blessings Index, Archives Division, Church Historical Department, The Church of Jesus Christ of Latter-day Saints, Salt Lake City, Utah.

4. See *LDS Biographical Encyclopedia* 1:191.

5. *HC* 2:345.

6. Wilford Woodruff, "The Kirtland Diary of Wilford Woodruff," ed. Dean C. Jessee, *BYU Studies* 12 (Summer 1972): 382.

7. Johnson, pp. 29–30.

8. Donald Q. Cannon and Lyndon W. Cook, eds., *Far West Record: Minutes of The Church of Jesus Christ of Latter-day Saints, 1830–1844* (Salt Lake City: Deseret Book Co., 1983), p. 223.

9. See Lyndon W. Cook, "Lyman Sherman—Man of God, Would-Be Apostle," *BYU Studies* 19 (Fall 1978): 124.

10. As cited in ibid. n. 27.

HENRY GARLIE SHERWOOD
D&C 24:81, 132

Birth: *20 April 1785, Kingsbury, Washington County, New York. Son of Newcomb Sherwood.*
Death: *24 November 1862 (or 1867), San Bernardino, San Bernardino County, California.*

Henry Sherwood was baptized and ordained an elder in August 1832. By 1834 he was residing in Kirtland and was working on the temple. After receiving his elder's license on 5 April 1836 he preached in Ohio, Kentucky, and Tennessee. A brief report of his mission appeared in the *Messenger and Advocate,* in which he stated, "I travelled among the several branches, endeavoring with my best ability to set in order the things then wanting, and to teach the ways of God more perfectly."[1] On 3 September 1837 Henry was appointed to the Kirtland high council, the first of three councils on which he served.

He suffered with the Saints from threats of mobocracy in Ohio and later in Missouri. By the summer of 1839 he was residing in Illinois, where Wilford Woodruff recorded that Henry was stricken with malaria and was "nigh unto death." He was miraculously healed on 22 July 1839 as the Prophet Joseph Smith "stood in the door of his tent and commanded him in the name of Jesus Christ to arise and come out of his tent, and he obeyed him and was healed."[2]

Henry's renewal of health led to new vigor in gospel service. His name appears on many historical entries during the Nauvoo era, for he served as clerk for the Nauvoo high council from 1839 to 1840 and was a member of that council from 1839 to 1846 (see D&C 124:132). He also served on a committee to build houses for the wives of the Twelve and was invited to purchase stock in the Nauvoo House (see

D&C 124:81). In addition to these varied assignments he was elected the first Nauvoo marshal, selected as a delegate to a political convention, and authorized to compile a city directory. His community service was temporarily interrupted when he accepted a mission call to New Orleans. His continual service was recognized by the Prophet Joseph, who commented about him and other brethren, "My heart feels to reciprocate the unwearied kindnesses that have been bestowed upon me by these men."[3]

While at Henry's home Lorenzo Snow received his now-famous revelation which he described as follows: "The eyes of my understanding were opened, and I saw as clear as the sun at noonday, with wonder and astonishment, the pathway of God and man. I formed the following couplet which expresses the revelation, as it was shown to me. . . . As man now is, God once was: As God now is, man may be."[4]

On 24 June 1844 the Prophet exclaimed to Henry and others, "I am going like a lamb to the slaughter, but I am calm as a summer's morning."[5] Just three days later Joseph and his brother Hyrum were martyred.

Henry's faithful service continued after the Martyrdom. He was in the vanguard pioneer company of 1847 and served as commissary general of the camp. He is most remembered as the man who made the drawing of the first survey of Salt Lake City. Lacking paper of suitable size, he drew the survey on sheepskin.

In September 1852 Henry left Salt Lake City to survey a ranch purchased by the Church in San Bernardino, California. His twenty-three years of unmarred Church service appeared to end when a conflict arose between Henry and Church leaders in 1855. According to family records, Henry apostatized from the Church.

In the late 1850s Henry was employed as an agent for the Pony Express Company in Salt Lake City. He returned to San Bernardino by the 1860s and died on 24 November 1862.

Notes

1. *Messenger and Advocate* 3 (August 1837): 550.
2. *HC* 4:4 n.
3. *HC* 5:109.
4. Eliza R. Snow Smith, *Biography and Family Record of Lorenzo Snow* (Salt Lake City: Deseret News Co., 1884), p. 46.
5. *HC* 6:555.

ALVIN SMITH

D&C 137:5

Birth: *11 February 1798 (or 1799), Tunbridge, Orange County, Vermont.*
Son of Joseph Smith Sr. and Lucy Mack.
Death: *19 November 1823, Manchester, Ontario County, New York.*

Little is known of Alvin Smith's childhood until his family was residing in Lebanon, New Hampshire. In that town the dreaded disease of typhus fever "raged tremendously," according to Lucy Mack Smith, Alvin's mother. The fever spread from one child to another in the Smith household: "Among the number seized with this complaint were, first, Sophronia; next Hyrum, who was taken while at school and came home sick; then Alvin."[1] He was not permanently damaged by the disease.

Lucy wrote of Alvin's assistance to the family. In 1816 she and the children, with the aid of teamster Caleb Howard, were traveling from Vermont to the town of Palmyra, New York. Joseph Smith Sr. had gone ahead a short time earlier to help secure their situation. One morning as the family was preparing for the day's journey, Alvin noticed that Mr. Howard was stealing the team. "Mother," he cried, "Mr. Howard has thrown the goods out of the wagon, and is about starting off with the team." His alertness to the impending theft helped prevent the loss of their property.[2]

Alvin's work ethic helped "pay for one hundred acres of land for which Mr. Smith contracted with a land agent." When the second payment was due he worked outside the home to raise the money, "and after much hardship and fatigue, returned with the required amount."[3]

On the morning of 22 September 1823 Alvin's younger brother Joseph, who had conversed with the angel Moroni throughout the previous night, was attempting to work in the family's wheat field. Lucy wrote that as he and Alvin were reaping, "Joseph stopped quite suddenly, and seemed to be in a very deep study. Alvin, observing it, hurried him, saying, 'We must not slacken our hands or we will not be able to complete our task.'" Their father, assuming that Joseph was ill, instructed him to return to the house.[4] On the way home Joseph, overcome with weariness, fell to the ground. He lay there for a time until he was again met by the angel, who "commanded me to go to my father and tell him of the vision and commandments which I had received" (Joseph Smith—History 1:49).

When the messenger departed Joseph returned to the field. Finding his father gone, he asked Alvin "to go straightway and see his father," according to Lucy, "and inform him that he had something of great importance to communicate to him, and that he wanted him to come out into the field. . . . Alvin did as he was requested." That evening the family conversed of the heavenly visitation to young Joseph. When Alvin observed how fatigued his brother was becoming, he kindly remarked, "Now, brother, let us go to bed, and rise early in the morning, in order to finish our day's work at an hour before sunset, then, if mother will get our suppers early, we will have a fine long evening, and we will all sit down for the purpose of listening to you while you tell us the great things which God has revealed to you."[5] This was the beginning of many evenings in which the Smith family would gather to listen to young Joseph.

As the Prophet was preparing to receive the fulness of the gospel, Alvin was anxious to see "his father and mother once more comfortable and happy. He would say, 'I am going to have a nice, pleasant room for father and mother to sit in, and everything arranged for their comfort, and they shall not work any more as they have done.' "[6] He made arrangements to build a comfortable house for his parents across the street from their log cabin. By November 1823, less than two months after the angel Moroni's appearance, the home was partially completed.

Unfortunately, on the fifteenth of that month, at about ten o'clock in the morning, Alvin became very ill with bilious colic.[7] Lucy wrote: "He came to the house in much distress, and requested his father to go immediately for a physician. He accordingly went, obtaining one by the name of Greenwood, who, on arriving, immediately administered to the patient a heavy dose of calomel. . . . Alvin at first refused to take the medicine, but by much persuasion, he was prevailed on to do so." The calomel "lodged in his stomach, and all the medicine afterwards freely administered by four very skillful physicians could not remove it."[8] By the third day of the illness he was convinced the medicine would take his life.

He called his brother Joseph to him and said, "I am now going to die, the distress which I suffer, and the feelings that I have, tell me my time is very short. I want you to be a good boy, and do everything that lies in your power to obtain the Record. Be faithful in receiving instruction, and in keeping every commandment that is given you."9

The last words of Alvin Smith were, "Father, mother, brothers, and sisters, farewell! I can now breathe out my life as calmly as a clock." He died on 19 November 1823. In remembrance of her son, Mother Smith penned, "Alvin was a youth of singular goodness of disposition—kind and amiable, so that lamentation and mourning filled the whole neighborhood in which he resided."10 His young brother Joseph said he had "pangs of sorrow that swelled my youthful bosom and almost burst my tender heart."11

Adding to the grief of the family were rumors that his remains had been removed from their interment. To stop the rumors Joseph Smith Sr. wrote for the 25 September 1824 *Wayne Sentinel:*

> Whereas reports have been industriously put in circulation that my son, Alvin, had been removed from the place of interment and dissected, which reports, every person possessed of human sensibility must know, are peculiarly calculated to harrow up the mind of a parent and deeply wound the feelings of relations; therefore, for the purpose of ascertaining the truth of such reports, I, with some of my neighbors, this morning repaired to the grave, and removing the earth, found the body, which had not been disturbed.12

Alvin was never forgotten by his family. When Joseph explained to his parents his desire to marry Emma, he confessed, "I have been very lonely ever since Alvin died and I have concluded to get married." While Mother Smith lived in the frame home in Palmyra she observed to Oliver Cowdery, "There is scarcely anything which I here see [in her home] that has not passed through the hands of that faithful boy." Father Smith, when told of the doctrine of baptism for the dead, was "delighted to hear and requested that Joseph should be baptized for Alvin immediately." On 14 September 1840, as Father Smith neared death, he paused "for some time, being exhausted." He then remarked, "I can see and hear, as well as ever I could. . . . I see Alvin."13

On 21 January 1836 in the Kirtland Temple the Prophet had a vision of his brother, who had died more than twelve years before: "I beheld the celestial kingdom of God, and the glory thereof. . . . I saw . . . my brother Alvin, that has long since slept; and marveled how it was that he had obtained an inheritance in that kingdom, seeing that he had departed this life before the Lord had set his hand to gather Israel the second time, and had not been baptized for the remission of sins" (D&C 137:1, 5–6).

On 22 August 1842 the Prophet expressed his admiration and love for his brother Alvin: "He was the oldest and noblest of my father's family. He was one of the noblest of the sons of men. . . . In him there was no guile. He lived without spot from the time he was a child. From the time of his birth he never knew mirth. He was candid and sober and never would play; and minded his father and mother in toiling all day. He was one of the soberest of men, and when he died the angel of the Lord visited him in his last moments."[14]

Notes

1. Lucy Mack Smith, *History of Joseph Smith by His Mother,* ed. Preston Nibley (Salt Lake City: Boocraft, 1954), pp. 51–52.

2. Ibid., pp. 62–63.

3. Ibid., pp. 64, 65.

4. Ibid., p. 79.

5. Ibid., pp. 80–81.

6. Ibid., p. 85.

7. According to B. H. Roberts, "An anti-Mormon writer in *Littell's Living Age* (Vol. xxx—of the whole series—p. 429, Aug. 1851) refers to this sad experience of the Smith family in these terms: 'Alvah [Alvin], however spiritual he may have been, had a carnal appetite; ate too many green turnips, sickened, and died.' " *CHC* 1:33 n. 7.

8. Smith, p. 86.

9. Ibid., p. 87.

10. Ibid., p. 88.

11. Ibid., p. 333.

12. Ibid., pp. 331–32.

13. Ibid., pp. 93, 140, 308, 313.

14. *HC* 5:126–27.

Don Carlos Smith
D&C 124:133

Birth: *25 March 1816, Norwich, Windsor County, Vermont. Son of Joseph Smith Sr. and Lucy Mack.*
Death: *7 August 1841, Nauvoo, Hancock County, Illinois.*

Perhaps because he was her youngest son Mother Smith referred to Don Carlos Smith as "Little Carlos." The Prophet Joseph Smith wrote of him, "[Don Carlos] was one of the first to receive my testimony."[1] He was baptized about 9 June 1830 in Seneca Lake, New York, by David Whitmer.

He soon migrated to Kirtland with his family. The day after he arrived in Ohio a meeting was held at Isaac Morley's home. The Smith family were "very much fatigued from their journey, and during the meeting Don Carlos fell asleep in his chair, and after several had spoken he awoke and arose and bore as strong a testimony as I ever heard, of the truth of the work."[2]

At age nineteen Don Carlos was ordained a high priest and appointed president of the high priests quorum in Kirtland. In 1837 he became editor of the *Elders' Journal,* until a fire destroyed the printing office. When mobocracy flared in Ohio, handbills accusing him of illegally solemnizing marriages advertised a reward for his capture. He fled with his family from Kirtland to the small town of New Portage.

In the spring of 1838 Don Carlos journeyed to Virginia and Pennsylvania, soliciting needed funds to remove his own and his parents' families to Missouri. On 7 May 1838 they began the difficult journey to Missouri. After days of arduous travel Don Carlos remarked to his father, "This exposure is too bad, and I will not bear it any longer; the first place that I come to that looks comfortable, I shall drive up and go into the house, and do you follow me." He then went to the nearest farmhouse and said to the landlord, "I do not know but that I am trespassing, but I have with me an aged father, who is sick, besides my mother, and a number of women with small children. We have traveled two days and a half in this rain, and if we are compelled to go much further, we shall all of us die. If you will allow us to stay with you over night, we will pay you almost any price for our accommodation."[3] The landlord cordially offered his hospitality.

Don Carlos served a four-month mission in 1838 to Tennessee and Kentucky with his cousin George A. Smith and others, for the purpose of collecting funds to buy out land claims of non-Mormons in Daviess County. When they heard of the increasing persecutions of the Saints in Missouri they returned to Far West. Joseph wrote, "During his absence, [Don Carlos's] wife and two little children were driven by the mob from his habitation, and she was compelled to carry her children three miles, through snow three inches deep, and wade through Grand river, which was waist deep, during the inclement weather."[4]

Don Carlos joined his family in Illinois. There, in July 1839, Joseph told Don Carlos and George A. Smith to administer to the many Saints who had fallen ill. The Prophet admonished them to "visit all the sick, exercise mighty faith, and administer to them in the name of Jesus Christ, commanding the destroyer to depart, and the people to arise and walk." They administered to over sixty people, who praised the Lord for their miraculous healing.[5]

During his Nauvoo years Don Carlos edited thirty-one issues of the *Times and Seasons* from 1839 to 1841. He was appointed president of the high priests quorum of Nauvoo (see D&C 124:133). His responsibilities heightened within the first week of February 1841 when he was elected to the Nauvoo City Council, selected as brigadier-general in the second cohort of the Nauvoo Legion, and appointed regent of the University of Nauvoo.

According to one account, "Don Carlos Smith was the handsomest man [his sister Catherine] ever saw when dressed in his uniform as an officer of the Nauvoo legion and riding his charger on parade."[6] Norton Jacob shared the opinion, "There was a splendid military parade and review of the Nauvoo Legion. . . . There was . . . present in command Brigadier Don Carlos Smith, a noble looking young man."[7] The Prophet Joseph wrote of him, "He was six feet four inches high, was very straight and well made, had light hair, and was very strong and active. His usual weight when in health was two hundred pounds. He was universally beloved by the Saints."[8]

One of his choice experiences in Nauvoo was receiving a blessing from his father shortly before his father's death. In the blessing he was told: "You shall be great in the sight of the Lord, for he sees and knows the integrity of your heart, and you shall be blessed; all that know you shall bless you. Your wife and your children shall also be blessed, and you shall live to fulfill all that the Lord has sent you to do."[9]

In August 1841 Don Carlos became ill. On the morning of 7 August 1841 at 2:20 A.M. he died at the age of twenty-five. The cause of death was presumed to be either tuberculosis, pneumonia, or "quick consumption." According to one source "his funeral obsequies took place on the 9th inst. amid a vast concourse of relatives and friends. He was buried with military honors."[10] The Prophet named his seventh child Don Carlos after his brother. He wrote, "Don Carlos Smith . . . was a noble boy; I never knew any fault in him. . . . He was a lovely, a good-natured, a kind-hearted and a virtuous and a faithful upright child; and where his soul goes, let mine go also."[11]

Notes

1. *HC* 4:393.
2. Autobiography of James Rollins, typescript, p. 2, Special Collections, Harold B. Lee Library, Brigham Young University, Provo, Utah.
3. Lucy Mack Smith, *History of Joseph Smith by His Mother*, ed. Preston Nibley (Salt Lake City: Bookcraft, 1954), p. 295.
4. *HC* 4:394.
5. *HC* 4:398–99.
6. H. S. Salisbury, "Prophet's Sister," typescript, p. 1, Archives Division, Church History Department, The Church of Jesus Christ of Latter-day Saints, Salt Lake City, Utah.
7. Autobiography of Norton Jacob, typescript, p. 6, Special Collections, Harold B. Lee Library, Brigham Young University, Provo, Utah.
8. *HC* 4:399.
9. Smith, p. 311.
10. Lyman Omer Littlefield, *Reminiscences of Latter-day Saints* (Logan, Utah: The Utah Journal Co., 1888), p. 155.
11. *HC* 5:127.

EDEN SMITH
D&C 75:36; 80:1–5

Birth: *1806, Indiana. Son of John and Sarah Smith.*
Death: *7 December 1851, Vermillion County, Indiana.*

Eden Smith's missionary labors in 1831–32 were of short duration and were performed within five to fifteen miles of his home. For example, his mission with Micah Welton began in Northampton, Ohio, on 10 December 1831 and ended in Northampton nine days later (see D&C 75:36).[1] He kept a journal of his missionary activities from 25 September 1831 to 21 August 1832. A typical entry reads: "I went to Stow and preachd in the fore noon and did tonight and then attended in the afternoon and preachd and then returned home and Laboured for the support of my familey."[2]

In March 1832 at Hiram, Ohio, the Prophet received a revelation directing Eden to serve a mission with Stephen Burnett (see D&C 80:1–2). According to Eden's journal, they served in eastern Ohio on a number of missionary trips during the following months into the surrounding country; he held many meetings and baptized a few.[3] He later joined Charles C. Rich in preaching near Eugene, Ohio, and served as the president of the branch there.

A letter from Joseph Smith and Frederick G. Williams dated 2 July 1833 to Eden's father, John Smith, reveals the contentious spirit of Eden and his father: "God withdrew His Spirit from you, and left you in darkness. . . . It seems also that your son Eden is confederate with you, and needs to be reproved, together with yourself, in all humility before the Lord, or you must expect to be dealt with according to the laws of the Church."[4]

The First Presidency also addressed a letter to the Church at Eugene, Ohio: "Dear Brethren: . . . You have authority to call a conference, and sit in judgment on Eden's case, and deal with him as the law directs. . . . You have authority to sit in council on the Smiths; and if found guilty, to deal with them accordingly."[5]

Eden was disfellowshipped on 2 July 1833. He repented and was restored to fellowship.

He joined the Saints in Missouri and later in Nauvoo, Illinois, where he was a lieutenant in the Nauvoo Legion. He served a mission with Benjamin Leland to Erie County, Pennsylvania, in April 1843. By 1846 he was residing in Kanesville, Iowa. According to one source Eden journeyed from Kanesville to the Salt Lake Valley but returned to Kanesville by 1848.[6] By 1850 he was residing in Pottawattamie County, Iowa.[7] He died on 7 December 1851 at the age of forty-five.

Notes

1. See journal of Eden Smith, typescript, p. 1, Special Collections, Harold B. Lee Library, Brigham Young University, Provo, Utah.

2. Ibid., p. 1.
3. See ibid., p. 4.
4. *HC* 1:370.
5. *HC* 1:371.
6. Letter of Earl T. Peterson to author, 19 December 1978, in author's possession.
7. See the Iowa federal census 1850.

EMMA HALE SMITH
D&C 25; 132: 51–56

Birth: *10 July 1804, Harmony, Susquehannah County, Pennsylvania. Daughter of Isaac Hale and Elizabeth Lewis.*
Death: *30 April 1879, Nauvoo, Hancock County, Illinois.*

Emma Smith stood about five feet, nine inches tall, had dark hair and brown eyes, and was described as "well-turned, of excellent form . . . with splendid physical development."[1] Her father wrote of Joseph Smith's courting of Emma: "Smith made several visits at my house, and at length asked my consent to his marrying my daughter Emma. This I refused."[2] Emma, without the approval of her father, was married to Joseph in January 1827 in South Bainbridge, New York. She wrote of her elopement, "I had no intention of marrying when I left home; but [Joseph] . . . urged me to marry him, and preferring to marry him to any other man I knew, I consented."[3] On 22 September 1827 Emma was privileged to be the first to know that Joseph had acquired the plates from the angel Moroni. The plates "lay in a box under our bed for months," she said, "but I never felt at liberty to look at them."[4] Emma was a scribe for the Book of Mormon translation, and said of her experience, "It is marvelous to me. . . . when acting as his scribe, [he] would dictate to me hour after hour; and when returning after meals, or after interruptions, he could at once begin where he had left off, without either seeing the manuscript or having any portion of it read to him."[5] She bore a continuing testimony, even in her seventy-fourth year, of her husband's prophetic calling: "I believe he was everything he professed to be."[6]

Emma was baptized on 28 June 1830 by Oliver Cowdery. Section 25 in the Doctrine and Covenants is addressed to her: "Behold, thy sins are forgiven thee, and thou art an elect lady, whom I have called" (D&C 25:3). The word *elect* was defined by Joseph Smith on 17 March 1842 in Nauvoo, when he told the sisters that "elect meant to be elected to a certain work . . . and that the revelation was then fulfilled by Sister Emma's election to the Presidency of the [Relief] Society."[7]

Emma was admonished to develop her talents, which included selecting sacred hymns (see D&C 25:7–8, 11). She compiled a pocket-sized hymnbook titled "A Collection of Sacred Hymns for the Church of the Latter-day Saints," which contained ninety hymns, the first being "Know This, That Every Soul Is Free."

Her calling was to be "a comfort unto" the Prophet (see D&C 25:5). Joseph loved Emma, for she was faithful in fulfilling this calling. He pleaded with the Lord on behalf of her and their children: "Have mercy, O Lord, upon [my] wife and children, that they may be exalted in thy presence, and preserved by thy fostering hand" (D&C 109:69).

Emma was also loved by Mother Smith, who wrote of her concern at her enduring willingness to be charitable:

> A revelation was given, commanding Parley P. Pratt, Ziba Peterson, Peter Whitmer, and Oliver Cowdery, to take a mission to Missouri, preaching by the way. As soon as this revelation was received, Emma Smith, and several other sisters, began to make arrangements to furnish those who were set apart for this mission, with the necessary clothing, which was no easy task, as the most of it had to be manufactured out of the raw material.
>
> Emma's health at this time was quite delicate, yet she did not favor herself on this account, but whatever her hands found to do, she did with her might, until so far beyond her strength that she brought upon herself a heavy fit of sickness, which lasted four weeks.[8]

Mother Smith described her daughter-in-law's fortitude:

> I have never seen a woman in my life, who would endure every species of fatigue and hardship, from month to month, and from year to year, with that unflinching courage, zeal, and patience, which she has ever done. . . .

... How often I have parted every bed in the house for the accommodation of the brethren, . . . while Joseph and Emma slept upon the . . . floor with nothing but their cloaks for both bed and bedding.[9]

While reaching out to serve others, Emma quietly endured her own personal sufferings. Of the nine children she bore, only four grew to maturity. This, together with religious persecution, bigotry, and the incarceration of her husband, led her to pen in a letter to Joseph, "No one but God, knows the reflections of my mind and the feelings of my heart when I left our house and home, and almost all of everything that we possessed excepting our little children, and took my journey out of the State of Missouri, leaving you shut up in that lonesome prison."[10]

Emma's concern was always for her husband and children. Brief historical entries in Joseph's journal reflect his caring for her: "Emma began to be sick with fever; consequently I kept in the house with her all day. . . . Emma is no better. I was with her all day. . . . Emma was a little better. I was with her all day. . . . Emma is very sick again. I attended with her all the day, being somewhat poorly myself."[11]

Emma was promised in a patriarchal blessing that her diligence would lead to great blessings: "For thy faithfulness and truth, thou shalt be blessed with thy husband and rejoice in the glory which shall come upon him. . . . Thou shalt be blessed with understanding, and have power to instruct thy sex, teach thy family righteousness, and thy little ones the way of life, and the holy angels shall watch over thee: and thou shalt be saved in the kingdom of God."[12]

Emma has been criticized for not following the leadership of Brigham Young and coming west with the Saints after the death of Joseph. Criticism led her to exclaim, "I have no friend but God, and no place to go but home."[13] She married Major Lewis Bidamon and was his wife for thirty-two years. On one occasion she said, "I have always avoided talking to my children about having anything to do in the church, for I have suffered so much I have dreaded to have them take any part in it."[14]

Her health failed rapidly in April 1879. Her family rallied to her side the evening of 29 April 1879. Her son Alexander recalled hearing his mother call, "Joseph, Joseph, Joseph." Joseph Smith III reported seeing his mother extend her left arm and hearing her say, "Joseph! Yes, yes, I'm coming."[15] Emma Smith Bidamon died at 4:20 A.M. on 30 April 1879 in Nauvoo at the age of seventy-four. She is buried next to the remains of her husband, the Prophet Joseph Smith.

Notes

1. Inez A. Kennedy, *Recollections of the Pioneers of Lee County* (Dixon, Ill.: n.p., 1893), p. 96, as cited in Linda King Newell and Valeen Tippetts Avery, *Mormon Enigma: Emma Hale Smith* (New York: Doubleday, 1984), p. 1.

2. Emily C. Blackman, *History of Susquehanna County, Pennsylvania* (Philadelphia: Claxton, Remsen, and Haffelfinger, 1873), p. 578, as cited in Susan Easton Black, "Isaac Hale: Antagonist of Joseph Smith," *Regional Studies in Latter-day Saint Church History, New York* (Provo, Utah: Department of Church History and Doctrine, Brigham Young University, 1992), p. 100.

3. Milton V. Backman Jr., *Eyewitness Accounts of the Restoration* (Orem, Utah: Grandin Book Co., 1983), p. 54, as cited in ibid., p. 101.

4. Interview of Emma Smith Bidamon by Nels Madson and Parley P. Pratt Jr., 1877, Archives Division, Church Historical Department, The Church of Jesus Christ of Latter-day Saints, Salt Lake City, Utah.

5. "Last Testimony of Sister Emma," *Saints' Herald* 26 (1879): 290.

6. Interview of Emma Smith Bidamon.

7. *HC* 4:552–53.

8. Lucy Mack Smith, *History of Joseph Smith by His Mother,* ed. Preston Nibley (Salt Lake City: Bookcraft, 1954), p. 190.

9. Ibid., pp. 190–91, 231–32.

10. Emma Smith to Joseph Smith, 9 March 1839, as cited in Newell and Avery, p. 79.

11. *HC* 5:166, 167.

12. Patriarchal blessing, as cited in Newell and Avery, pp. 54–55.

13. Vesta Crawford notes, Marriott Library, University of Utah, as cited in Newell and Avery, p. 243.

14. Edmund C. Briggs, "A Visit to Nauvoo in 1856," *Journal of History* 9 (October 1916): 446–62, as cited in Newell and Avery, p. 269.

15. *Zion's Ensign,* 31 December 1903, as cited in Newell and Avery, p. 304.

GEORGE A. SMITH
D&C 124:129; 136:14

Birth: *26 June 1817, Potsdam, St. Lawrence County, New York. Son of John Smith and Clarissa Loomis Lyman.*
Death: *1 September 1875, Salt Lake City, Salt Lake County, Utah.*

When George A. Smith was nine years old he sustained a severe blow to the head that, in his words, "rendered me insensible for three weeks." A group of physicians diagnosed him with a skull fracture and determined that surgery was necessary. George's father, however, "being a man of faith," dismissed the physicians, and in a matter of weeks George's health was restored.[1]

Crediting his restored health to divine intervention, George embraced the Congregational faith of his parents; yet he struggled to comply with the doctrine. He attended revivalist meetings searching for greater truth, but instead was "sealed up" by a preacher to "eternal damnation" for not being publicly converted.[2]

In August 1830 his uncle Joseph Smith Sr. and cousin Don Carlos brought a Book of Mormon to his home. After reading the text George was baptized on 10 September 1832. In 1833 he moved with his family from New York to Kirtland, where he "was on hand for any duty required, and spent many nights guarding the house of the brethren who were in much danger from mobs."[3] At age sixteen he volunteered to march with Zion's Camp and served as the armor bearer and personal guard for the Prophet Joseph Smith.

His mission call came soon after he returned from Zion's Camp. His cousins Joseph and Hyrum Smith gave him gray cloth for a coat, Brigham Young gave a pair of shoes, and his father gave a pocket Bible. The Prophet also gave him a Book of Mormon and some advice: "Preach short sermons. Make your prayers short and deliver your sermons with a prayerful heart."[4] George journeyed 1,850 miles on foot, held seventy-five meetings, and baptized eight persons on his first mission.

After he returned to Kirtland he became afflicted with inflammatory rheumatism and grew discouraged. The Prophet admonished, "You should never get discouraged, whatever your difficulties may be. If you are sunk in the lowest pit in Nova Scotia and all the Rocky Mountains piled on top of you, you ought not to be discouraged but to hang on, exercise faith and keep up good courage, and you will come out on top of the heap."[5]

His second mission was to the southern states, where he became acquainted with Bathsheba Bigler, whom he courted through letters for the next few years. Returning from this mission he joined the Saints in Missouri and endured with them abuse, religious bigotry, and mobocracy. However, it was in Missouri that his service to the Church was greatly magnified—he was called to the Quorum of the Twelve Apostles (see D&C 124:129).

As a member of the Twelve he desired to join his brethren in their missionary labors in England. After beginning the journey, his poor health forced him to stop at the Prophet's home to rest. Upon seeing him Joseph Smith Sr. asked, "Who's been robbing the burying yard?" George replied, "I am determined to go to England." The aged patriarch gave him a blessing promising that he would go to England and his health would be restored. The promise was literally fulfilled.[6] Biographer Merlo J. Pusey writes that on his twenty-third birthday "people came to him inquiring about the restored gospel at all hours of the day and often kept him busy until 2 o'clock in the morning. It was not unusual for him to baptize five or six persons in a day."[7]

When he returned to Nauvoo he married Bathsheba Bigler: "[We] dedicated ourselves to God, for life, praying for His blessings to rest upon us during life and that prosperity might crown our labors."[8] His devotion led the Prophet to state on 15 May 1843, "George A., I love you as I do my own life." George replied, "I hope, Brother Joseph, that my whole life and actions will ever prove my feelings and affection toward you."[9]

After the Martyrdom George continued his faithful service. He helped complete the beautiful Nauvoo Temple, and after the laying of the capstone he penned, "My feelings were such that I could not suppress a flood of tears."[10] He joined Brigham Young in the vanguard company traveling to the Salt Lake Valley in 1847. On the journey he "narrowly escaped death when he slipped in the mud and the horse he had been watering stepped on George's foot and then twice on his chest."[11] While riding in the wagon he displayed an inclination to read, which led Brigham Young to refer to him as "a walking encyclopedia."[12]

George returned to Winter Quarters to guide other Saints as they migrated to the Salt Lake Valley (see D&C 136:14). He was then given responsibility for the settlement in southern Utah which was named St. George in his honor. He later served as historian and general Church recorder, traveling extensively through Mormon settlements to gather information. One humorous series of events occurred in 1864 as he journeyed to the Bear Lake Valley. Two vehicles were reported to have broken down under George's weight of more than three hundred pounds, much to the amusement of his less hefty brethren. He attempted to finish the journey on horseback, but his horse stalled from fatigue, and it was said that his companions had "to build a scaffold to get him onto another one."[13]

From 1868 to 1875 George served as First Counselor in the Presidency of the Church. One assignment he fulfilled in the Presidency was to rededicate the Holy Land for the return of the Jews.[14] On the Mount of Olives he prayed that Palestine "might become fertile, and the early and late rains descend upon it, and the prophecies and promises unto Abraham and the prophets be fulfilled." After leaving the Middle East he stopped in Toppesfield, England, where he visited ancestral lands. "I have encountered nothing that gives me more satisfaction," he said, "than being here in the graveyard of my ancestors, on the ground where they walked and lived and labored 300 years ago."[15]

When he returned to the United States, George was suffering from a lung ailment. He died on 1 September 1875 at the age of fifty-eight. President Young penned, "The death of Pres. George A. Smith has cast a gloom over the entire community. . . . He has gone with as good a record, I believe, as any man who ever lived upon this earth."[16]

Notes

1. See *Millennial Star* 27 (1865): 406.
2. *LDS Biographical Encyclopedia* 1:38.
3. Ibid., p. 39.
4. Merlo J. Pusey, *Builders of the Kingdom: George A. Smith, John Henry Smith, George Albert Smith* (Provo, Utah: Brigham Young University Press, 1981), p. 19.
5. Ibid, p. 21.
6. Ibid., p. 37.

7. Ibid, p. 41.

8. Journal of George A. Smith, as cited in ibid., p. 45.

9. History of George A. Smith, p. 154, as cited in ibid., p. 47.

10. As cited in ibid., p.56.

11. Ibid., p. 67.

12. Ibid., p. 68.

13. Preston Nibley, comp., *Pioneer Stories* (Salt Lake City: Deseret Book Co., 1940), pp. 115–16.

14. Orson Hyde fulfilled a similar mission in 1840–42.

15. *Contributor* 4 (1883): 2, as cited in Pusey, p. 121.

16. Dean C. Jessee, ed., *My Dear Son: Letters of Brigham Young to His Sons* (Salt Lake City: Deseret Book Co., 1974), pp. 219–20, as cited in ibid., p. 123.

Hyrum Smith

D&C 11; 23; 52:8; 75:32; 94: Introduction; 111:
Introduction; 115:1, 5, 6, 13; 124:15, 91–96, 124;
135:1, 6; 138:53

Birth: *9 February 1800, Tunbridge, Orange County, Vermont. Son of Joseph Smith Sr. and Lucy Mack.*
Death: *27 June 1844, Carthage, Hancock County, Illinois.*

In 1823 Hyrum Smith's older brother Alvin said to him, "Hyrum, I must die. . . . Take care of [our parents] in their old age, and do not any more let them work hard."[1] True to his brother's trust, Hyrum not only cared for his parents but exercised a special watch care over all family members, and was ever mindful of the needs of his brother Joseph. It was Hyrum who brought a wooden chest to Joseph in 1827 that was used to hide the Book of Mormon plates.

It is not surprising that the Lord gave a revelation through the Prophet Joseph to his brother Hyrum: "Behold thou art Hyrum, my son; seek the kingdom of God, and all things shall be added according to that which is just" (D&C 11:23). Hyrum was a diligent seeker after truth. He became one of the Eight Witnesses to the Book of Mormon and helped preserve the printer's copy. According to typesetter John H. Gilbert, "Hyrum Smith brought the first installment of manuscript, of 24 pages, closely written on common foolscap paper—he had it under his vest, and vest and coat closely buttoned over it. At night Smith came and got the manuscript, and with the same precaution carried it away. . . . This was kept up several days."[2]

Hyrum was baptized in June 1829 at Seneca Lake by his brother Joseph. On 6 April 1830 he became one of the original six members of the Church. On 9 June 1830 he was ordained a priest and given responsibilities over a branch of the Church at Waterloo, New York. On 31 March 1831 the Prophet Joseph wrote to him from Kirtland, "My dearly beloved brother Hyrum, I have had much concern about you, but I always remember you in prayers, calling upon God to keep you safe in spite of men or devils. I think you better come to this country immediately."[3]

In compliance Hyrum moved his family to Kirtland, where he was ordained an elder and later a high priest. On 14 June 1831 he left on his first extended mission from Ohio to Missouri, traveling through Michigan, Indiana, and Illinois. After returning to Ohio he accepted the responsibility of serving on the finance committee and the Kirtland Temple building committee.

While faithfully completing his many Church responsibilities, he did not neglect Alvin's admonition to care for the Smith family. When a dispute arose between his brothers Joseph and William, Hyrum interceded. Joseph recognized his peaceful mediation and wrote of him, "I could pray in my heart that all my brethren were like unto my beloved brother Hyrum, who possesses the mildness of a lamb, and the integrity of a Job, and in short, the meekness and humility of Christ; and I love him with that love that is stronger than death, for I never had occasion to rebuke him, nor he me."[4]

In 1836–37 Hyrum was called to the Kirtland high council, appointed Assistant Counselor to the First Presidency, and set apart as Second Counselor in the First Presidency. While faithfully serving in these capacities he heard rumors in Far West of "mob action but couldn't believe them because we had broken no law."[5] Of the religious persecution and later incarceration that he and others experienced, Hyrum said, "We endeavored to find out for what cause; but all that we could learn was, because we were 'Mormons.'"[6]

Hyrum was imprisoned in Liberty Jail from November 1838 to

April 1839—five and a half months of hardship, privation, and insult. "Many call to see us out of curiosity to view us as they would an elephant."[7] His struggle after his escape with his brother Joseph was seen by his mother in a night vision: "They were on the prairie traveling, and seemed very tired and hungry. . . . They looked so pale and faint that it distressed me. . . . My soul was grieved; I rose from my bed and spent the remainder of the night in walking the floor. The next day I made preparations to receive my sons."[8] They returned as their mother had envisioned.

Hyrum settled with his family in Nauvoo, where on one occasion he told members of the Quorum of the Twelve and Quorum of the Seventies who had been called on missions: "Never trifle and take lightly your office and calling and hold strictly to the importance of your mission. At all times remember your position before the Lord and hold in high esteem and respect the priesthood you bear."[9]

Hyrum is perhaps best remembered as the Patriarch to the Church, being sustained on 24 January 1841. Joseph Smith Sr., Hyrum's father, had laid his hands on Hyrum's head before his death and pronounced, "You shall be as firm as the pillars of heaven unto the end of your days. I now seal upon your head the patriarchal power, and you shall bless the people."[10] The Lord confirmed that blessing, saying in a revelation given to Joseph Smith: "Whoever he blesses shall be blessed, and whoever he curses shall be cursed; that whatsoever he shall bind on earth shall be bound in heaven; and whatsoever he shall loose on earth shall be loosed in heaven. And from this time forth I appoint unto him that he may be a prophet, and a seer, and a revelator unto my church, as well as my servant Joseph." (D&C 124:93–94.)

The Prophet wrote of his brother:

Brother Hyrum, what a faithful heart you have got! Oh may the Eternal Jehovah crown eternal blessings upon your head, as a reward for the care you have had for my soul!

O how many are the sorrows we have shared together; and again we find ourselves shackled with the unrelenting hand of oppression. Hyrum, thy name shall be written in the book of the law of the Lord, for these who come after thee to look upon, that they may pattern after thy works.[11]

Hyrum died a religious martyr in Carthage Jail on 27 June 1844, when a ball struck him on the left side of the nose. He fell backward to the floor, exclaiming, "I am a dead man!" (D&C 135:1.) As he fell to the floor, another bullet from outside the building entered his left side. At the same instant a bullet from the door grazed his breast and entered his head by the throat. A fourth ball entered his left leg. John Taylor, a witness to this barbaric scene, wrote that Joseph and Hyrum

> will be classed among the martyrs of religion; and the reader in every nation will be reminded that the Book of Mormon, and this book of Doctrine and Covenants of the church, cost the best blood of the nineteenth century to bring them forth for the salvation of a ruined world. . . . They lived for glory; they died for glory; and glory is their eternal reward. From age to age shall their names go down to posterity as gems for the sanctified. (D&C 135:6.)

Notes

1. Lucy Mack Smith, *History of Joseph Smith by His Mother,* ed. Preston Nibley (Salt Lake City: Bookcraft, 1954), p. 87.

2. Wilford Wood, *Joseph Smith Begins His Work* (Wilford Wood, 1958), as cited in Pearson H. Corbett, *Hyrum Smith—Patriarch* (Salt Lake City: Deseret Book Co., 1963), p. 54.

3. Letter of Joseph Smith to Hyrum Smith, Harpersville, Broome County, New York, as cited in Corbett, p. 81.

4. *HC* 2:338.

5. Journal History, 1838.

6. *HC* 3:420.

7. Hyrum Smith, "Daily Record of H. Smith," 29 October 1838—18 April 1839, as cited in Davis Bitton, Guide to Mormon Diaries and Autobiographies, 1977, p. 321.

8. Lucy Mack Smith, p. 301.

9. Corbett, p. 225.

10. Lucy Mack Smith, p. 309.

11. *HC* 5:107–08.

JOHN SMITH

D&C 102:3

Birth: *16 July 1781, Derryfield, Rockingham County, New Hampshire. Son of Asael Smith and Mary Duty.* **Death:** *23 May 1854, Salt Lake City, Salt Lake County, Utah.*

In the fall of 1828 Joseph Smith wrote in a letter to his grandfather Asael Smith that "the sword of vengeance of the Almighty hung over this generation, and that except they repented and obeyed the gospel, and turned from their wicked ways, humbling themselves before the Lord, it would fall upon the wicked and sweep them from the earth as with the bosom of destruction."[1] Commenting on the letter, John said, "Joseph writes like a prophet."[2]

In August 1830 Joseph Smith Sr. visited his brother John and shared with him the Book of Mormon. Reading the book caused a "small explosion within the Potsdam First Congregational Church," as John and his wife lost interest in congregational teachings.[3] John was expelled from worship services in early January 1832 and on 9 January was baptized into the Mormon faith. His son George wrote of the baptism:

> My father had been for several years very feeble in health and for about six months previous to his baptism had not been able to visit his barn. The neighbors all believed that baptism would kill him. I cut the ice in the creek and broke a road for 40 rods through the crust of two feet of snow and the day was very cold. The neighbors looked on with astonishment expecting to see him die in the water, but his health continued improving from that moment.[4]

The scoffing of neighbors led John to pen in 1833, "It seems that God hath said they are joined to their idols Let them alone."[5] After being threatened for his adherence to Mormonism, John sold his farm, settled his debts, and moved his family from New York to Ohio.

His arrival in Kirtland in May 1833 was greeted with joy by the Prophet Joseph Smith, for John was the first of his father's family to accept the gospel. On 17 February 1834 Uncle John, as he was affectionately known by the Saints, was called to the Kirtland high council (see D&C 102:3). In a letter to a nephew written eight months after his call to the council, John confirmed his faith:

> I tell you in the fear of God that these things are true as the Lord lives, and I would that you would search out these things for yourself, for I know that it is within your reach if you are willing to humble yourself before the Lord. . . . It is because I love you and seek your best good that I tell you these things. . . . The Church of Jesus Christ of Latter Day Saints will prosper in spite of wicked men and devils until it fills the whole earth.[6]

John received his patriarchal blessing on 26 September 1835 from his brother Joseph Smith Sr.[7] Less than one year later the two men served a mission to the East and strengthened the Saints from New York to Pennsylvania, "confer[ring] on the brethren their patriarchal blessings."[8] On this mission they confronted Alexander Campbell, leader of the Disciples of Christ, and "told him to repent and washed our feet against him."[9]

When John returned to Kirtland he was appointed an Assistant Counselor to the Prophet in September 1837. His service was brief, as mobs forced him to flee from Kirtland. "What the Lord will do with us I know not, altho he slay me I will trust in him," wrote John. "We are like the ancients wandering from place to place in the wilderness."[10]

On the advice of the Prophet he settled with his family in Adam-ondi-Ahman and became president of the local stake. His tenure ended abruptly as mobs drove him from the region. Forced to live in the wilderness without proper shelter, he suffered from frostbite and starvation: "We have had but little bread save what we obtained by rubbing corn on [a] grate as to get meal. . . . I was very low."[11] Although impoverished and discouraged, his spirit brightened when the Prophet "took the shoes from his feet and gave to me."[12]

After his sorrows in Missouri, John was given many other leadership assignments, serving as president of the Zarahemla Stake, patriarch, and president of the Nauvoo Stake. When religious persecution heightened in Illinois, sixty-five-year-old John joined the exodus of the Saints to the West. He was the first president of the Salt Lake Stake and was responsible for the initial settlement of the Valley. At the October

1848 general conference he was released as stake president and sustained as the fifth Patriarch of the Church. He was ordained in January 1849. In his journal he wrote of the welcome change in his responsibilities: "Since that time my burden has been lighter and I have been regaining my health since, but I find that I am about wore out with excessive labour."[13]

Uncle John gave 5,560 patriarchal blessings in ten years. He died in 1854 at the age of seventy-two. At his side was his son, John Lyman Smith, who had conveyed this message to the brethren: "Father John Smith Patriarch does not wish the brethren who meet in the Council to pray for him to live for I know it is the will of the Lord to take me to himself when he pleases & I want him to do it in the best possible manner for my ease and comfort."[14]

Notes

1. As cited in Irene M. Bates, "Uncle John Smith, 1781–1854: Patriarchal Bridge," *Dialogue* 20 (Fall 1987): 80.

2. Merlo J. Pusey, *Builders of the Kingdom: George A. Smith, John Henry Smith, George Albert Smith* (Provo, Utah: Brigham Young University Press, 1981), p. 3.

3. Ibid., p. 4.

4. As cited in Bates, p. 80.

5. As cited in ibid.

6. As cited in ibid., p. 81.

7. See Book of Patriarchal Blessings Index 2:143; 7:1, Archives Division, Church Historical Department, The Church of Jesus Christ of Latter-day Saints, Salt Lake City, Utah.

8. *HC* 2:446.

9. Journal of John Smith, as cited in Davis Bitton, Guide to Mormon Diaries and Autobiographies, 1977.

10. Journal of John Smith, 23 April 1838, George A. Smith Family Papers, Manuscripts Division, Special Collections, Marriott Library, University of Utah, Salt Lake City, Utah.

11. Journal of John Smith, as cited in Davis Bitton.

12. Ibid., 21 September 1839, as cited in Bates, p. 83.

13. As cited in ibid., p. 85.

14. As cited in ibid., p. 87.

JOSEPH SMITH JR.

Birth: *23 December 1805, Sharon, Windsor County, Vermont. Son of Joseph Smith Sr. and Lucy Mack.*
Death: *27 June 1844, Carthage, Hancock County, Illinois.*

In the early nineteenth century in western New York, religious revivalists shouted, "Lo here, lo there." The contest that ensued led young Joseph to say to himself, "What is to be done? Who of all these parties are right; or, are they all wrong together? If any one of them be right, which is it, and how shall I know it?" (Joseph Smith—History 1:10). One day while reading in the Epistle of James, first chapter and fifth verse, he read, "If any of you lack wisdom, let him ask of God, that giveth to all men liberally, and upbraideth not; and it shall be given him." He later wrote, "Never did any passage of scripture come with more power to the heart of man than this did at this time to mine" (Joseph Smith—History 1:12). He desired wisdom, and so, on a beautiful clear day in the spring of 1820, he asked God in prayer.

The answer he received and the vision he saw of "two Personages, whose brightness and glory defy all description," brought joy to him (Joseph Smith—History 1:17). However, after sharing his answer he was treated with contempt by many and was told that all visions and revelations had "ceased with the apostles" (Joseph Smith—History 1:21). Despite the ridicule and persecution which followed, he continued to declare, "I had actually seen a light, and in the midst of that light I saw two Personages, and they did in reality speak to me. . . . I knew it, and I knew that God knew it, and I could not deny it" (Joseph Smith—History 1:25).

Three and a half years after the first vision, the angel Moroni, an ancient prophet who had once lived in America, appeared to Joseph. The angel told him of a book "written upon gold plates, giving an account of the former inhabitants of this continent" (Joseph Smith—History 1:34).

In 1829 Joseph was privileged to translate the ancient writings, known as the Book of Mormon. The contents of this book were shared with family, friends, and newfound acquaintances from New England to the frontier of the United States.

On 6 April 1830 a few believers gathered in Fayette, New York, to organize a church, today known as The Church of Jesus Christ of Latter-day Saints. From small beginnings the Church grew rapidly despite mounting persecution against Joseph Smith and his followers in New York, Ohio, Missouri, and Illinois. The growth led Josiah Quincy, the mayor of Boston from 1845 to 1849, to write: "It is by no means improbable that some future textbook . . . will contain a question something like this: What historical American of the nineteenth century has exerted the most powerful influence upon the destinies of his countrymen? And it is by no means impossible that the answer to that interrogatory may be thus written: Joseph Smith, the Mormon Prophet."[1]

Joseph did not seek for fame but sought to do the will of God. The Lord blessed his quest. Revelations, translations, covenants, and eternal truths were the fruits of his life's labor.

Joseph's devotion to God was noted by faithful contemporaries such as John Taylor. After the martyrdom of the Prophet, John Taylor wrote that he "left a fame and name that cannot be slain" (D&C 135:3). He also said, "I think he was one of the greatest Prophets that ever lived, Jesus himself excepted."[2]

Notes

1. *CHC* 2:349–50.
2. In *JD* 18:327.

JOSEPH SMITH SR.
D&C 4; 23; 90:20; 102:3; 124:19

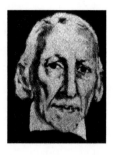

Birth: *12 July 1771, Topsfield, Essex County, Mass-achusetts. Son of Asael Smith and Mary Duty.*
Death: *14 September 1840, Nauvoo, Hancock County, Illinois.*

At age twenty-four Joseph Smith Sr. married Lucy Mack and settled on a farm in Tunbridge, Vermont. Five years later the couple rented out the farm and opened a mercantile business. Being somewhat of an entrepreneur, Joseph became excited about selling crystallized ginseng root for a high price in faraway China. He invested all of his means to export the root. The financial venture failed miserably, leaving the Smiths destitute and with the burden of indebtedness. To meet his financial obligations Joseph sold his farm in Tunbridge.[1]

Hoping for more prosperous circumstances, the family moved to farmlands in Vermont. In Sharon, Windsor County, Joseph cultivated a rented farm during the summer and taught school in the winter. It was on this farm that the Prophet Joseph Smith was born. For a number of years the family moved from one farm to another in Vermont and New Hampshire, seeking the best location for farming, but they never found the desired prosperity.

The move to Palmyra, New York, in 1816 did not provide the monetary income that Joseph Sr. had wanted, but that move changed the course of his religious life. Knowledge of the gospel was given to "Father Smith," as he was affectionately known, by his namesake, Joseph Smith Jr. As the young boy followed the directive of the angel Moroni to tell his father of the message he had received, he was promised, "He will believe every word you say to him."[2] Why the surety of the promise? Joseph Smith Sr. was known by name millennia before his birth and had been foreordained to a great work in the latter days (see 2 Nephi 3:15). After hearing his son's remarkable recitation he declared, "My son, be not disobedient to this heavenly vision!"[3]

Where many fathers might have lacked the humility to follow their sons, Joseph Smith Sr. never sought prominence over young Joseph. He was supportive of his son's prophetic calling and even suffered persecution for his beliefs. He was privileged to be one of the Eight Witnesses of the Book of Mormon who saw the plates and the engravings on them, "all of which has the appearance of ancient work, and of curious workmanship" (The Testimony of Eight Witnesses).

Father Smith's testimony was tested when he was imprisoned for a note of indebtedness against him for fourteen dollars. He was promised he could go free if he renounced the Book of Mormon. "How much better it would be for you to deny that silly thing," he was told, "than to be disgraced and imprisoned, when you might not only escape this, but also have the note back, as well as the money which you have paid on it."[4]

To this Father Smith made no reply. His thoughts turned to the Apostle Paul: "I was not the first man who had been imprisoned for the truth's sake; and when I should meet Paul in the Paradise of God, I could tell him that I, too, had been in bonds for the Gospel which he had preached."[5]

On the day the Church was organized Father Smith was baptized. His prophetic son took him by the hand and exclaimed, "Praise to my God! that I lived to see my own father baptized into the true Church of Jesus Christ!"[6] Of his testimony Father Smith declared, "I have never denied the Lord. . . . The Lord has often visited me in visions and dreams, and has brought me, with my family, through many afflictions, and I this day thank his holy name."[7]

On 18 December 1833 he received a glorious promise in his patriarchal blessing pronounced by his son Joseph: "Blessed of the Lord is my father, for he shall stand in the midst of his posterity . . . and shall be numbered among those who hold the right of Patriarchal Priesthood."[8] That day he was ordained the first Patriarch in this dispensation. Lorenzo Snow was privileged to hear several of the patriarchal blessings pronounced by Father Smith. "I was convinced that an influence, superior to human prescience, dictated his words," he wrote.[9]

At age sixty-four Father Smith served a mission with his brother John. They traveled nearly twenty-four hundred miles throughout the East, strengthening the Saints, pronouncing patriarchal blessings, and sharing the gospel with relatives. His love for his family in the East and for his immediate family on the western frontier was unabated. His fatherly bond to his son Joseph was often noted. When Joseph was taken prisoner at Far West, Father and Mother Smith heard him scream. "Not knowing the cause, we supposed they were murdering him," Lucy Mack Smith wrote. "Soon after the screaming commenced, five or six guns were discharged. At this, Mr. Smith, folding his arms tight across his heart, cried out, 'Oh, my God! my God! they have killed my son! they have murdered him! and I must die, for I cannot live without him!'" His agony was so great over the presumed loss that he immediately became ill and "never afterwards entirely recovered, yet he lived about two years and was occasionally quite comfortable, and able to attend meetings."[10]

In Nauvoo Father Smith was physically weak and suffered from continual coughing. Before he died he invited family members to receive a blessing at his hands. "To Joseph he said: . . . 'You shall even live to finish your work.' At this Joseph cried out, weeping, 'Oh! my father, shall I?' 'Yes,' said his father, 'you shall live to lay out the plan of all the work which God has given you to do. This is my dying blessing upon your head in the name of Jesus.'"[11]

After blessing his wife he paused momentarily and then announced, "I can see and hear, as well as ever I could." After a long pause he added, "I see Alvin. . . . I shall live seven or eight minutes." Lucy wrote, "In about eight minutes his breath stopped, without even a struggle or a sigh, and his spirit took its flight for the regions where the justified ones rest from their labors. He departed so calmly, that, for some time, we could not believe but that he would breathe again."[12]

Where is this noble man who so faithfully fulfilled his role in the latter days? The Lord through his anointed Prophet revealed that Father Smith is in a celestial realm and sits "with Abraham at his right hand, and blessed and holy is he, for he is mine" (D&C 124:19).

Notes

1. See Mark L. McConkie, *The Father of the Prophet* (Salt Lake City: Bookcraft, 1993), pp. 150–52.

2. Lucy Mack Smith, *History of Joseph Smith by His Mother*, ed. Preston Nibley (Salt Lake City: Bookcraft, 1954), p. 79.

3. As cited by Orson Pratt, in *JD* 15:184.

4. Smith, p. 185.

5. Ibid.

6. Ibid., p. 168.

7. Book of Patriarchal Blessings Index 1:1, Archives Division, Church Historical Department, The Church of Jesus Christ of Latter-day Saints, Salt Lake City, Utah.

8. Joseph Smith, *Teachings of the Prophet Joseph Smith,* comp. Joseph Fielding Smith (Salt Lake City: Deseret Book Co., 1976), p. 38.

9. As cited in McConkie, p. 41.

10. Smith, pp. 289–90.

11. Ibid., pp. 309–10.

12. Ibid., pp. 313–14.

JOSEPH F. SMITH
D&C 138

Birth: *13 November 1838, Far West, Caldwell County, Missouri. Son of Hyrum Smith and Mary Fielding.*
Death: *19 November 1918, Salt Lake City, Salt Lake County, Utah.*

When Joseph F. Smith was two months old, mobbers ransacked the family home while his mother, Mary Fielding Smith, was visiting her husband, Hyrum, in Liberty Jail: "I, being an infant, and lying on the bed, another bed being on the floor, was entirely overlooked by the family . . . during the fright and excitement. So when the mob entered the room where I was, the bed on the floor was thrown on to the other completely smothering me up."[1] Miraculously, he survived. He was taken by his mother first to Illinois; then, after the assassination of his father, to Iowa Territory; and then on to the Salt Lake Valley.

At age fifteen Joseph was called to labor as a missionary in the Hawaiian Islands. While on his mission he penned, "I well know that I am young and inexperienced at present, therefore I wish to be humble, prayerful before the Lord, that I may be worthy of the blessings and love of God to protect me at all times."[2] His prayer was answered. When journeying with missionary companions, drunken men confronted him swearing that they would kill any Mormons. "Are you a Mormon?" one of the men asked. Without hesitation Joseph boldly replied, "Yes, siree; dyed in the wool; true blue, through and through." The surprised man said, "Well, you are the —— pleasantest man I ever met! Shake, young fellow, I am glad to see a man that stands up for his convictions."[3]

After an absence of nearly four years Joseph returned to Salt Lake City unharmed: "The day following my arrival home I reported myself to President Young and immediately enlisted in the legion (militia) to defend ourselves against the encroachment of a hostile and menacing army. From that time until the proclamation of peace . . . I was constantly in my saddle."[4] When the threat of war abated, Joseph remained in Utah for a season and served as sergeant of arms of the territorial legislature and as a high councilor in the Salt Lake Stake. A mission call to the British Isles and then again to the Hawaiian Islands prompted further journeys.

On 1 July 1866 Brigham Young said, "Hold on, shall I do as I feel led? I always feel well to do as the Spirit constrains me. It is my mind to ordain Brother Joseph F. Smith to the Apostleship, and to be one of my counselors."[5] At the age of twenty-seven Joseph F. Smith joined the Quorum of the Twelve Apostles and the First Presidency. He served as a counselor to Brigham Young, John Taylor, Wilford Woodruff, and Lorenzo Snow.

During these years he was also active in civil affairs. For seven consecutive terms he was elected to the House of Representatives, acted as president of the Constitutional Convention in 1882, and served on the Salt Lake City Council for several terms. His civil service ended when a federal government crusade against the doctrine of plural marriage forced him to go into exile. From 1884 to 1891 he hid from federal officers and polygamy hunters who sought his arrest. He wrote of his frustrations: "I cannot conceive of anything more contemptible or more execrable than the present and continued attempts of the Federal Officials to blast the peace and break up the sacred relations of husbands and wives, parents and children!"[6]

On 10 September 1891 President Benjamin Harrison of the United States granted amnesty to Joseph F. Smith. "I thank God and am grateful to the President of the United States," wrote Joseph. For the first time in seven years he was able to speak in the tabernacle: "I spoke briefly, for I was so overcome by my feelings that I could scarcely restrain them."[7]

Joseph F. Smith became the President of the Church in 1901 and served until his death in 1918. For him, the most difficult personal experience of his administration was the death of his son, Hyrum M. Smith, a member of the Quorum of the Twelve: "My soul is rent asunder. My heart is broken, and flutters for life! O my sweet son, my joy, my hope! O I love him still."[8] Perhaps to console the bereaved father, on 3 October 1918 he received a vision of the Savior's visit to the spirits of the dead. This vision was "submitted to the counselors in the First Presidency, the Council of the Twelve, and the Patriarch, and it was unanimously accepted by them" on 31 October 1918 (D&C 138: Introduction).

President Joseph F. Smith died nineteen days after the unanimous affirmation of his vision. His death followed an attack of pleurisy that grew in intensity until he developed pleuropneumonia. A public funeral was not held for the prophet because of an influenza epidemic in Salt Lake City. Funeral services were conducted near the open grave. Bishop Charles W. Nibley eulogized, "As a preacher of righteousness, who could compare with him? He was the greatest that I ever heard—strong, powerful, clear, appealing."[9]

Notes

1. Joseph Fielding Smith, comp., *Life of Joseph F. Smith*, 2nd ed. (Salt Lake City: Deseret Book Co., 1969), p. 124.

2. Ibid., pp. 180–81.

3. Ibid., p. 189.

4. Ibid., p. 195.

5. Ibid., p. 227.

6. Ibid., p. 258.

7. Ibid., pp. 299–300.

8. Ibid., p. 474.

9. Ibid., p. 433.

SAMUEL HARRISON SMITH
D&C 23; 52:30; 61:35; 66:8; 75:13; 102:3; 124:141

Birth: *13 March 1808, Tunbridge, Orange County, Vermont. Son of Joseph Smith Sr. and Lucy Mack.*
Death: *30 July 1844, Nauvoo, Hancock County, Illinois.*

When the Smith family moved to Palmyra, Samuel was nine years old. At age thirteen he joined the local Presbyterian church, but his membership was short-lived, as he, like other members of his family, believed in the visions of his brother Joseph. Samuel was baptized on 25 May 1829 by Oliver Cowdery, becoming the third person baptized in this dispensation. After his baptism "he returned to his father's house, greatly glorifying and praising God, being filled with the Holy Spirit."[1]

Samuel was privileged to be one of the Eight Witnesses of the Book of Mormon and one of the six original members of the Church. At the first conference of the Church, Samuel, six feet in height and athletic in nature, was ordained an elder. He is traditionally recognized as the first missionary of the Church. Although he was discouraged with his initial missionary labors, his mission helped lead to the baptisms of Brigham Young and Heber C. Kimball.

During the next two years Samuel preached from Maine to Missouri, journeying over four thousand miles, mostly on foot. His call to serve with William McLellin had an unusual beginning (see D&C 66:8). According to his mother, Lucy Mack Smith, Samuel "heard a voice in the night, which said, 'Samuel, arise immediately, and go forth on the mission which thou wast commanded to take. . . .' He arose from his bed and took what clothing he had in readiness, and set off without further delay."[2]

He served his most challenging mission with Orson Hyde (see D&C 75:13). This eastern mission lasted eleven months and included meetings and baptisms from Ohio to Maine. "This was one of the most arduous and toilsome missions ever performed in the Church," Orson wrote. "To travel two thousand miles on foot, . . . often sleeping in school houses after preaching—in barns, in sheds, by the way side . . . was something of a task."[3] Samuel wrote, "Went from House to House and many during that day rejected us we shook off the dust from our feet as a testimony against them."[4]

From 1832 to 1836 Samuel resided in the Kirtland vicinity, laboring with his hands as a farmer. However, the Kirtland years were filled with added Church responsibilities, as he was appointed an agent for the Church's Literary Firm, which was established to print Church publications, and as he served as a member of the Kirtland high council (see D&C 102:3). His father gave him a blessing two days after he was appointed to the high council: "Samuel, I lay my hands upon thy head, and pronounce the blessings of thy progenitors upon thee, that thou mayest remain a Priest of the Most High God, and like Samuel of old, hear His voice, saying, Samuel, Samuel. Amen."[5]

Samuel received his patriarchal blessing from his father in December 1834 and was promised, "The just shall rise up and call thee, a perfect man. . . . The testimony which thou hast borne and shall bear, shall be received by thousands, and thou shalt magnify thy calling and do honor to the Holy Priesthood."[6]

In January 1836 Samuel and his family moved to Missouri and were subjected to mob violence. His wife was "taken by the mob from her house (they took her by picking up the feather bed and carried her with her babe out into the sleet and rain and placed the bed on the ground). [Then they] burned the house down to the ground."[7] His wife never fully recovered from the effects of the persecution, and it was said that "she never spoke above a whisper" following the experience.[8]

Samuel fled with his family from Missouri and was one of the first to seek refuge in Quincy, Illinois, before settling in Nauvoo. The last blessing he received from his father was in Nauvoo. He was told, "The Lord has seen your diligence, and you are blessed, in that he has never chastised you, . . . and there is a crown laid up for you, which shall grow brighter and brighter unto the perfect day."[9]

In Nauvoo his responsibilities increased. He was an alderman; chairman of the committee of improvement, formed to construct and repair roads; associate justice of the municipal court; captain in the Nauvoo Legion; and a regent of the University of Nauvoo. In January 1841 he was called to be a counselor to Vinson Knight, Presiding Bishop of the Church (see D&C 124:141). He was later called as bishop of the Nauvoo Ward.

In 1844 the events that led to the martyrdom of Samuel's brothers impacted his own life. When he learned of the imprisonment of his brothers in Carthage, he attempted to aid them. He was met by a mob who intercepted him and prevented his traveling to Carthage. He returned home and purchased a horse noted for its speed, and rode toward Carthage again. As he neared the town the second time, he learned that his brothers were dead. His daughter, Mrs. M. B. S. Norman, wrote, "The terrible shock was too much for him, and for an instant he reeled in his saddle and they expected him to fall. . . . He steadied himself, saying, 'God help me! I must go to them.' "[10]

The mob hid in a thicket, and as they saw him approach they gave chase. Samuel managed to stay out of the range of their bullets and arrived in Carthage.[11]

The next day he escorted the bodies of his brothers back to Nauvoo. After Mother Smith had viewed the bodies and retired to her room, Samuel said to her, "Mother, I have had a dreadful distress in my side ever since I was chased by the mob, and I think I have received some injury which is going to make me sick."[12] He suffered from bilious fever until his death on 30 July 1844. His obituary stated, "If ever there lived a good man upon the earth, Samuel H. Smith was that person."[13]

Notes

1. *HC* 1:44.

2. Lucy Mack Smith, *History of Joseph Smith by His Mother*, ed. Preston Nibley (Salt Lake City: Bookcraft, 1954), p. 217.

3. Orson Hyde, "History of Orson Hyde," *Millennial Star* 26 (3 December 1864): 776.

4. "Events in the Life of Samuel Harrison Smith Including His Missionary Journal for the Year 1832," Archives Division, Church Historical Department, The Church of Jesus Christ of Latter-day Saints, Salt Lake City, Utah.

5. *HC* 2:32.

6. As cited in Ruby K. Smith, *Mary Bailey* (Salt Lake City: Deseret Book Co., 1954), pp. 41–42, as cited in Dean Jarman, "The Life and Contributions of Samuel Harrison Smith," M. S. thesis, Brigham Young University, June 1961, pp. 67–68.

7. Letter of Mary B. Norman to Sue Beattie, 21 October 1915, as cited in Jarman, p. 78.

8. Interview with Sue Beattie, granddaughter of Samuel H. Smith, 28 July 1959, as cited in Jarman, p. 79.

9. Smith, p. 310.

10. Journal History, 25 July 1844.

11. See ibid.

12. Smith, p. 325.

13. *HC* 7:222.

SYLVESTER SMITH

D&C 75:34; 102:3, 34

Birth: *1805.*

Sylvester Smith, a resident of Amherst, Ohio, was ordained a high priest on 25 October 1831 by Oliver Cowdery and three months later was appointed by revelation to preach the gospel (see D&C 75:34). "I have traveled about five hundred miles in about six weeks, and held fifteen meetings," he wrote, "and I trust that I shall continue to receive the grace of God to support me even to the end."[1]

Sylvester is remembered for his quarrelsome spirit on the march with Zion's Camp. His criticism of camp leaders for the way in which they prepared for the journey, and his complaints about the strain on the men and teams pulling the heavy wagons, sparked dissension. The Prophet confronted him about "sowing the seed of discord." Sylvester defiantly replied that "if Joseph was a prophet he was not afraid and would contradict him in the face of all present."[2] The most retold incident of discord occurred when Sylvester and his company approached camp marching to the music of a fife. James L. Bradley writes: "Lunging to his feet, snarling through large, barred, white teeth, with saliva dripping from sagging jowls, the Prophet's bulldog rushed toward the marching men. Fortunately, Prophet Joseph Smith called off the dog before he bit Sylvester Smith, or caused bodily harm to the other men. The rush of the attacking dog enraged Sylvester Smith. . . . [His] verbal attack was of such a nature that Joseph Smith recorded it as 'the first outbreak of any importance since the beginning of the journey.' "[3]

Sylvester was so angry that he threatened to kill the dog. According to George A. Smith, "Joseph reproved him sharply, showing him that such a spirit would not conquer or control the human family, that he must get rid of it, and predicted that if he did not get rid of it, the day would come when a dog would gnaw his flesh, and he not have the power to resist it."[4] Sylvester defiantly yelled, "You are prophesying lies in the name of the Lord."[5]

The contention between the two men did not end in Zion's Camp. When Sylvester returned to Kirtland he publicly denounced the

Prophet's conduct. Joseph wrote, "I was met in the face and eyes, as soon as I had got home, with a catalogue of charges as black as the author of lies himself; and the cry was Tyrant—Pope—King—Usurper—Abuser of men—Angel—False Prophet—Prophesying lies in the name of the Lord—Taking consecrated monies—and every other lie to fill up and complete the catalogue."[6] A court verdict overwhelmingly favored the Prophet. Sylvester admitted his error and confessed his faults.[7]

From 17 February 1835 to 13 January 1836 he served on the Kirtland high council (see D&C 102:3, 34). For a short time he was a President of the Seventies. In the weeks preceding the Kirtland Temple dedication he received a remarkable manifestation of the power of the Lord. Joseph Smith wrote, "The heavens were opened unto Elder Sylvester Smith, and he, leaping up, exclaimed, 'The horsemen of Israel and the chariots thereof.'"[8] According to George A. Smith, "In his exertion and excitement it seemed as though he would jump through the ceiling."[9] Several days later in a meeting with Church leaders he "saw a pillar of fire rest down and abide upon the heads of the quorum [of the Seventy]."[10] Sylvester was released from the Presidency of the Seventy on 6 April 1837.[11] He had withdrawn from Church affiliation by 1838.

Notes

1. *HC* 1:388.
2. Autobiography of Levi Ward Hancock and journal of Wilford Woodruff, as cited in James L. Bradley, *Zion's Camp 1834: Prelude to the Civil War* (Logan, Utah: James L. Bradley, 1990), pp. 62–63.
3. Ibid., p. 128.
4. George A. Smith, in *JD* 11:7.
5. George A. Smith journal, as cited in Bradley, p. 129.
6. *HC* 2:144.
7. See *Messenger and Advocate* (October 1834): 10–11.
8. *HC* 2:383.
9. Smith, p. 10.
10. *HC* 2:386.
11. John Gaylord was chosen to fill the vacancy that resulted in the Council of the Seventy.

WILLIAM SMITH
Testimony of the Twelve Apostles,
D&C 124:129

Birth: *13 March 1811, Royalton, Windsor County,*
Vermont. Son of Joseph Smith Sr. and Lucy Mack.
Death: *13 November 1893, Osterdock, Clayton*
County, Iowa.

"Whenever the neighbors wanted a good days work done," wrote William Smith, "they knew where they could get a good hand," until Joseph had his visions.[1] "Our creditors then came upon us, . . . and stripped us of every cent and left us houseless and homeless, and almost friendless."[2] According to his mother, Lucy Mack Smith, when William returned home one day to find angry men demanding payment of a debt from Lucy, he yelled, "'What is this host of men doing here? Are they robbing or stealing?' . . . [He] seized a large handspike, sprang up stairs, and, in one instant, cleared the scoundrels out of the chamber . . . exclaiming, 'Away from here, you cut-throats, instantly, or I will be the death of every one of you.'"[3]

He was asked if he had doubted "Joseph's testimony sometimes." "No," was the reply. "We all had the most implicit confidence in what he said. He was a truthful boy. Father and Mother believed him. Why should not the children?"[4]

On 9 June 1830 William was baptized in Seneca Lake by David Whitmer. He labored as a missionary in New York, Ohio, and Pennsylvania before being ordained an elder. Two years after his marriage to Caroline Amanda Grant he became a member of the Quorum of the Twelve Apostles.

His zeal for the work faltered, and his love of the Prophet wavered to a brutal degree. With uncontrolled anger he once attacked his brother Joseph so savagely that the Prophet was not able to sit or rise without help. Grieved by his actions, Joseph wrote of "the wickedness of his brother, who Cain like had sought to kill him."[5] William pleaded, "You know my passions and the danger of falling from so high a station."[6] Joseph immediately forgave his brother and advised him to magnify his apostolic calling.

The brotherly reconciliation did not resolve William's weakness. On 3 November 1835 the Prophet received a revelation prophesying of William's great potential if he would repent: "I will yet make him a polished shaft in my quiver, in bringing down the wickedness and abominations of men; and there shall be none mightier than he, in his day and generation, nevertheless if he repent not speedily, he shall be brought low, and shall be chastened sorely for all his iniquities he has committed against me."[7]

He did not hearken to the warning.

Despite his known contentious attitude, William retained his standing in the Quorum of the Twelve (see D&C 124:129). However, on 4 May 1839 a resolution passed at a general conference requested that he "give an account of [his] conduct; and that in the meantime [he] be suspended from exercising the functions of [his] office."[8] The suspension ended and William was called to join with the Twelve in missionary labors in England. He failed to respond to the call, excusing himself because of poverty: "I do not wish to exonerate myself from all blame, but merely wish to state the circumstances in which I have been placed. . . . I can assure you, that it is not because I have any doubts respecting the work of the last days. . . . Unfortunately for me, poverty has been my lot, ever since I was called to the ministry."[9]

In April 1841 he journeyed to the East to gather funds for building the Nauvoo Temple. He pocketed the collected funds for his own use.

In 1842 William was elected to the Nauvoo City Council and to the Illinois House of Representatives on the Democratic ticket. This public vote of confidence did not change his chameleon-like character or his animosity toward his brother Joseph. The last time he saw the Prophet alive, he physically threatened him.

After his brothers' martyrdom William enthusiastically rallied support for the leadership of the Twelve: "My advice to all, . . . uphold the proper authorities of the church. . . . I mean the whole, and not a part: the twelve . . . the whole twelve."[10] In October 1844 Brigham Young announced that William had the right to be ordained the Patriarch to the Church. "I must say I am very thankful . . . the legal right rests upon me," said William.[11] He was not ordained until 24 May 1845.

Just five days after his ordination President Young "prayed that the Lord would overrule the movements of Wm. Smith who is endeavoring to ride the Twelve down."[12] William was asserting that his ordination to the office of Patriarch entitled him to be the President of the Church. On 5 October 1845 the apostolic calling of William was revoked.

Three days later he wrote, "I have only one word to say do you think it right for any man to rob a <u>little</u> fatherless boy of his office in the <u>church</u> of <u>christ</u>."[13] He was excommunicated on 12 October 1845 for appropriating "public funds of the Church to his own private use— for publishing false and slanderous statements concerning the Church: and for a general looseness and recklessness of character which ill comported with the dignity of his high calling."[14]

Reacting to the excommunication, William wrote, "I Know them to be wicked men and infernal *Scoundrells* and they Cut me off."[15] To Emma Smith he penned, "I am determined never to speak to a *woman* . . . untill I can see the Smith family standard raised in majesty and glory to *us all*."[16]

His deviation from the truth led him to apostate factions. By May 1846 he was recognized as a Strangite apostle and patriarch. In Palestine Grove, Illinois, and again at Covington, Kentucky, he attempted to organize his own church. Failing to attract a following, William quelled his aspirations for nearly a decade.[17]

At the outbreak of the Civil War he enlisted in the Union Army. After the war he returned to his residence in Elkader, Iowa, and again sought leadership in an apostate faction. He wrote to Joseph Smith III, president of the Reorganized Church of Jesus Christ of Latter Day Saints, requesting an appointment as a counselor in the first presidency. Even though the request was denied, William joined his nephew's church.[18]

William wrote of his experience with the Church, *William Smith on Mormonism*, in 1883. Seven years later he moved to Osterdock, Iowa, where he died in 1893 at the age of eighty-two.

Notes

1. *Deseret Evening News*, 20 January 1894, p.11.

2. William Smith, *William Smith on Mormonism*, pp. 12–13, as cited in "Background and Early Life of William Smith" (n.p., n.d.), p. 11.

3. Lucy Mack Smith, *History of Joseph Smith by His Mother*, ed. Preston Nibley (Salt Lake City: Bookcraft, 1954), pp. 183–84.

4. *Deseret Evening News*, 20 January 1894, p. 11.

5. "Manuscript History of the Church," Book FA-1, p. 150, as cited in "Background," p. 44.

6. *HC* 2:339.

7. *HC* 2:300.

8. *HC* 3:345.

9. *Times and Seasons* 2 (15 December 1840): 252.

10. *CHC* 2:433.

11. Letter of William Smith to Brigham Young, 16 October 1844, Archives Division, Church Historical Department, The Church of Jesus Christ of Latter-day Saints, Salt Lake City, Utah.

12. *HC* 7:420.

13. Letter of William Smith to Brother Rodgers, Galena, Ill., 8 October 1845, Archives Division, Church Historical Department, The Church of Jesus Christ of Latter-day Saints, Salt Lake City, Utah.

14. *The Frontier Guardian*, 6 February 1850.

15. Letter of William Smith to Lewis Robbins, St. Louis, Mo., 7 November 1845, Archives Division, Church Historical Department, The Church of Jesus Christ of Latter-day Saints, Salt Lake City, Utah.

16. Letter of William Smith to Emma Smith, St. Louis, Mo., 1845, Archives Division, Church Historical Department, The Church of Jesus Christ of Latter-day Saints, Salt Lake City, Utah.

17. He was rebaptized in 1860 by J. J. Butler. See Lyndon W. Cook, *The Revelations of the Prophet Joseph Smith* (Salt Lake City: Deseret Book Co., 1985), p. 276.

18. See *The History of the Reorganized Church of Jesus Christ of Latter Day Saints*, 4 vols. (Independence, Mo.: Herald Publishing House, 1896), 4:212.

JOHN SNIDER

D&C 124:22–24, 62, 70

Birth: 11 February 1800, Pleasant Valley, New Brunswick, Nova Scotia, Canada. Son of Martin Snider Sr. and Sarah Armstrong.
Death: 18 December 1875, Salt Lake City, Salt Lake County, Utah.

John Snider (or Snyder) united with "a Society [that] . . . met together twice a week for the purpose of discussing topics of religion." Leading the religious discussion was John Taylor, a former Methodist preacher. At one discussion Taylor spoke of Philip's journey to Samaria (see Acts 8) and asked a series of questions: "Where is our modern Philip? . . . Where moreover, is the ancient church with Apostles and Prophets inspired by Heaven?"[1] Listening to his queries was Parley P. Pratt, who spoke with definitive clarity of the apostasy from the primitive Church and of the Restoration.

John was converted to Mormonism and baptized in June 1836 by Elder Pratt. By 1837 he was serving his first mission in the British Isles. Despite considerable opposition, he was successful in sharing the gospel. By the spring of 1838 he had journeyed to Far West, Missouri, and purchased a farm.

As mobocracy escalated in Missouri and the Saints were expelled, John sold his farm and moved to Springfield, Illinois. When traveling to Washington to seek redress of the Saints' grievances the Prophet Joseph Smith stayed in the Snider home in Springfield: He wrote to Emma on 9 November 1839, "This morning we are under the nesesity of leaveing [Sidney Rigdon] at Brother Snyders and pesueing our Journy [to Washington, D.C.] without him."[2]

By 1840 John had joined the Saints in Nauvoo and by 1841 was serving on the personal staff of the Prophet as an assistant aide-de-camp in the Nauvoo Legion. In 1843 he was privileged to be "appointed to administer baptism for the dead in the river while the font could not be used."[3] On 19 January 1841 he was called by revelation to help build the Nauvoo House, to "build a house unto my name" (D&C 124:22). In a revelation dated 22 December 1841 John was instructed to journey to England to collect funds and materials for the construction of the Nauvoo House and the Nauvoo Temple and to "speedily return with means to strengthen the hands of the laborers, and adorn and beautify the Tabernacle of Jehovah."[4] He was delayed in fulfilling this mission assignment because of poverty and the need he felt to have the Twelve pay his passage to the British Isles.[5]

After being told by the Prophet that he needed to obtain his own passage, John left Nauvoo on 26 March 1842. Although the British Saints were poor, they "donated various small sums between May and December, 1842, as contributions for building the Temple, and paid over nine hundred and seventy-five dollars and four cents. The names of the donors and amounts are recorded in the 'Law of the Lord.'"[6]

John sailed from Liverpool to New Orleans with 157 Saints, arriving in Nauvoo on 23 January 1843.

On the return of the martyred Joseph's body to Nauvoo, John Snider was one of the bodyguards.[7] According to family tradition he did not remain long in Illinois before returning to Toronto in 1844, "the object being to give the sons . . . a chance to learn the Mason's trade," a skill John had learned in his youth. In 1847 he left Toronto and journeyed to Bonapart, Iowa, and then to Nauvoo, where he assisted in disposing of Mormon properties after the exodus of the Saints.[8]

In 1850 he left his family to search for gold in California. His wife and two sons joined the Lorin W. Babbitt company bound for the Salt Lake Valley. Soon after their arrival in the Valley they were joined by John, who supported them by building homes. According to his biographer, Edwin Snider, John's death on 18 December 1875 in Salt Lake City was caused by "over exertion after eating a hearty meal."[9]

Notes

1. As quoted in Edwin G. Snider, "John Snider" (n.p., n.d.), p. 1.

2. Joseph Smith, *The Personal Writings of Joseph Smith,* comp. Dean C. Jessee (Salt Lake City: Deseret Book Co., 1984), p. 448.

3. *HC* 5:350.

4. *HC* 4:561.

5. See *HC* 4:504.

6. *HC* 5:438.

7. See *HC* 7:135.
8. Snider, p.2.
9. Ibid.

ERASTUS SNOW
D&C 136:12

Birth: *9 November 1818, St. Johnsbury, Caledonia County, Vermont. Son of Levi Snow and Lucina Streeter.*
Death: *27 May 1888, Salt Lake City, Salt Lake County, Utah.*

The youthful years of Erastus Snow were spent on a family farm in Vermont. There he began to develop his propensity to ponder the Savior's teachings, repeating them again and again until he knew them by memory. Upon first hearing Orson Pratt and Luke S. Johnson speak of Mormonsim, fourteen-year-old Erastus was anxious to be baptized. From the day of his baptism in 1833 he was desirous to preach the gospel; hence he was ordained a teacher. He met regularly with the Saints on Sundays and visited them in their homes.

In 1835 he moved to Kirtland, where he lived with the Prophet Joseph Smith for several weeks. During the winter he attended the Elders School and received a blessing from Joseph Smith Sr. The Patriarch prophesied: "You have desired to preach the Gospel, even when you knew it not. Therefore, thou shalt preach it to the ends of the earth."[1] Around this time he was ordained a member of the Second Quorum of the Seventy.

On his first mission east in 1836 he traveled sixteen hundred miles, preached 220 sermons, and baptized fifty persons. Missionary zeal led him from Missouri to Ohio, Pennsylvania, Maryland, and Virginia. As he journeyed from state to state he found many seeking religious truth and the blessings of the priesthood. Brief journal entries reveal his willingness to bless the Saints: "Prayed and rebuked the disease and it departed. This being in the evening, she arose and next morning dressed herself . . . much to the surprise of her physicians and the joy of her family."2

After each mission Erastus returned to Kirtland, until mobocracy forced his removal to Missouri. In Far West, Erastus distinguished himself by defending Church members in skirmishes. The Saints being forced to leave Missouri, Erastus and his family arrived in Quincy, Illinois, in April 1839.

Erastus settled with his family in Montrose, Iowa, where he served on the high council. Later he moved his family across the Mississippi River to Nauvoo. He served several missions and was in Massachusetts engaged in that work when he learned of the Martyrdom. Back in Nauvoo, anxious to see justice prevail, he attended a "mock trial" for the accused assassins of the Prophet and the Patriarch. Of the trial he wrote: "A more ridiculous legal farce never was played by any officers in any county than was there exhibited. I need not add that the guilty wretches were acquitted."3

His attention next turned to completing and then serving within the Nauvoo Temple. All too soon the mob-enforced exodus was upon them, and the Snows joined the exiled Saints in the temporary encampments in Iowa Territory, leaving behind their property in Nauvoo, which they sold for about one-fourth of its value. From Winter Quarters Erastus trekked in the vanguard company. On the trek Brigham Young noted Erastus's neglect of the cattle. It was the first time Erastus had been rebuked since joining the Church nearly fifteen years before, and he hoped "it may last me for the next fifteen years."4

Erastus is remembered as being one of the first Latter-day Saints to gaze upon the Salt Lake Valley. His journal entry of 21 July 1847 reads, "This morning I started on horseback, and leaving Canyon Creek I ascended westward five miles to the summit of the Mountain Pass." As twenty-eight-year-old Erastus and his companion, Orson Pratt, alternately walked and rode slowly through the thickets (having only one horse), they climbed the butte and at "the first glimpse of the blue waters of the Great Salt Lake, swung our hats and shouted, 'Hosannah!'"5

Anxious to bring his family and other Saints to the Valley, Erastus returned to Winter Quarters, arriving there 31 October 1847. He and a few other elders were then sent to the eastern states to solicit aid for the poor Saints in Winter Quarters. This took three or four months. Upon their return the Saints began preparing for the trek to Salt Lake, where Erastus and his family arrived on 20 September 1848.

Erastus was called as a counselor in the Salt Lake Stake presidency in October 1848 and was ordained an Apostle on 12 February 1849. For nearly forty years he was a pillar of missionary, emigration, and colonizing work.

His missionary labors took him to the Scandinavian countries in 1850. Within two years he had supervised the Danish translation and publication of the Book of Mormon, the Doctrine and Covenants, and a hymnal. He also published a newspaper, *Scandinavian Sterne,* seven pamphlets, and the book *Rise in History and Doctrines of the Church.*

Upon his return to the United States in 1852 he was assigned to preside over the Iron Mission in southern Utah. Then, as the pioneering settlements were beginning to prosper, Erastus was called to the St. Louis area in 1853. In St. Louis he organized a stake, supervised the emigration of crossing the plains, and published the newspaper *St. Louis Luminary.* Letters to family and friends reveal his firm conviction of the gospel: "I feel strong and fearless, resolute and dauntless in facing an unbelieving, cold-hearted world in preaching or writing in behalf of the Kingdom of God."[6]

At the urgent request of President Brigham Young, Erastus returned to the Rockies to help prepare for war against an encroaching army. As the threat dissipated he was called to preside over the "Dixie Mission." He helped strengthen struggling communities throughout southern Utah, Arizona, Nevada, and New Mexico. The Mormon community of Snowflake, Arizona, was named in honor of Elder Snow and its founder, William J. Flake. His great joy in these southern settlements was anticipating and then officiating in the St. George Temple.

From 1884 to 1888 the life of Erastus Snow took a dramatic turn. Government officials, seeking to imprison him for practicing plural marriage, forced his exile. To avoid arrest he journeyed to Mexico, where he strengthened Saints in the Mormon colonies of Chihuahua. At great danger to himself he returned to Salt Lake City, where he died on 27 May 1888.

President Joseph F. Smith said of the departed Apostle: "As an orator and profound reasoner, I always felt impressed that he had no superior, especially when he warmed up to his subject, and entered into his discourse with the full force and energy of his active and vigorous mind."[7]

Notes

1. As cited in Andrew Karl Larson, *Erastus Snow: The Life of a Missionary and Pioneer for the Early Mormon Church* (Salt Lake City: University of Utah Press, 1971), p. 25.

2. As cited in Larson, p. 74.

3. As cited in Bess Snow, "History of Levi and Lucina Streeter Snow" (n.p., 1950), p. 93.

4. As cited in ibid., p. 148.

5. As cited in ibid., pp. 160–61.

6. Erastus Snow, personal family letter, in author's possession.

7. Joseph F. Smith, *Gospel Doctrine* (Salt Lake City: Deseret Book Co., 1977), p. 199.

DANIEL STANTON
D&C 75:33

Birth: *28 May 1795, Manlius, Onondaga County, New York. Son of Amos Stanton and Elizabeth Wyman.*
Death: *26 October 1872, Panaca, Lincoln County, Nevada.*

Daniel Stanton, a veteran of the War of 1812, migrated to Ohio in 1819. He was baptized on 3 November 1830 in Kirtland by Parley P. Pratt. When he was ordained a high priest by Oliver Cowdery he said "he had a long time since covenanted to do the will of God in all things, and also said that it was his desire to be sealed with the Holy Spirit of promise."[1]

He served a mission with Seymour Brunson before settling his family in Jackson County, Missouri (see D&C 75:33). He presided over Branch Number Two in the county before being called as a counselor to Bishop John Corrill. Religious persecution in the area forced him to flee to Clay County. Amid personal affliction he volunteered to serve a mission and labored in Missouri, Illinois, and Indiana.

By 1838 Daniel had returned to Missouri, where he was appointed to serve on the Adam-ondi-Ahman high council. After assisting suffering Saints in the region, he fled from Missouri to Quincy, Illinois. Ezra T. Benson recorded an incident involving Daniel in Quincy:

> On Sunday the 19th of July, we [he and his wife] went to the meeting in the afternoon. . . . During the meeting Sylvester B. Stoddard raised

a quarrel over the communion table with Daniel Stanton, the president of the branch. My wife inquired what I thought of that. I answered that I thought it did not alter the truth of the work. At the close of the meeting we repaired to the Mississippi River and were baptized therein by Elder Daniel Stanton.[2]

Daniel served as the stake president in Quincy before moving to Lima, Illinois, where he again served on a high council.

He journeyed in the Mormon exodus from Illinois to the Salt Lake Valley. He was one of the earliest settlers in Springville, Utah. By 1860 he was in the small Utah community of Fairfield, and by 1870 in Panea.[3] He relocated in Panaca, Nevada, not long before his death in 1872 at the age of seventy-seven.

Notes

1. Donald Q. Cannon and Lyndon W. Cook, eds., *Far West Record: Minutes of The Church of Jesus Christ of Latter-day Saints, 1830–1844* (Salt Lake City: Deseret Book Co., 1983), p. 21.
2. Autobiography of Ezra Taft Benson, *Instructor* 80 (March 1845): 102.
3. See the Utah federal census 1860, 1870.

NORTHROP SWEET
D&C 33

Birth: *1802, New York.*

A few days after Northrop Sweet's baptism in October 1830, the Prophet Joseph Smith received a revelation for him:

> Behold, I say unto you, my servants Ezra [Thayre] and Northrop, open ye your ears and hearken to the voice of the Lord your God, whose word is quick and powerful, sharper than a two-edged sword, to the dividing asunder of the joints and marrow, soul and spirit; and is a discerner of the thoughts and intents of the heart.
>
> For verily, verily, I say unto you that ye are called to lift up your voices as with the sound of a trump, to declare my gospel unto a crooked and perverse generation. (D&C 33:1–2.)

It appears that Northrop accepted the revelation and was faithful during the early New York era. He joined with the Saints in moving to Kirtland.

However, in 1831 Northrop apostatized and formed a religion called "The Pure Church of Christ" with Wycam Clark and four others. They claimed "they could carry the whole world with them by preaching 'Mormon' principles. They had two or three meetings; but the society would never have been known in the world, had not a few of us remembered the circumstances and told of it."[1] The church was "composed of six members . . . but that was the extent of the growth of this early schism."[2] When the newly formed church failed to prosper, Northrop moved from Kirtland to Lake County, Ohio. He remained a resident of Ohio until about 1845, when he moved to Batavia, Michigan. He was living with his son Hezekiah in Bethel, Michigan, in 1880 at the age of seventy-eight.

Notes

1. George A. Smith, in *JD* 7:114.
2. George A. Smith, in *JD* 11:4.

NATHAN ELDON TANNER
Official Declaration—2

Birth: *9 May 1898, Salt Lake City, Salt Lake County, Utah. Son of Nathan William Tanner and Sarah Edna Brown.*
Death: *27 November 1982, Salt Lake City, Salt Lake County, Utah.*

Waiting to assist in the birth of N. Eldon Tanner, should that prove necessary, was his fourteen-year-old uncle, Hugh B. Brown, who recalled: "My first recollection of Eldon was his birth cry, as I waited to help if needed. Ever since that time there has been a bond between us, as I instinctively recognized a child of promise."[1]

When Eldon was six weeks old he journeyed to Canada with his mother. En route his mother was robbed. "The robbers took everything valuable except the baby," she reported.[2] He grew to manhood in the small farming community of Aetna, Alberta. There he assisted his father with dry-farming wheat and oats and learned the meaning and value of long days, hard work, and the proper use of time.

Schooling was always second to harvesting and other farm labors. Diligent with his studies, Eldon completed nine school grades in Aetna before moving with his family to Cardston. While waiting to register for classes, he remembered, "I saw in the far corner of the room two girls talking. I asked my friend Ken Woolf who the beautiful girl was. He said it was Sally Merrill (nickname Sara). I said, 'Someday I'm going to marry her.'"[3]

That revealing insight took time to come to fulfillment. During those years Eldon was employed as a principal of a three-room school, and as fate would have it Sara was hired to be a teacher in the school. "That's where I fell in love with Sara and actually tried to get her to marry me." he remembered. After the courtship had blossomed into marriage Sara wrote, "I have been so much more fortunate in my marriage than nearly anyone I know that I feel very thankful."[4]

Eldon provided for his bride by following his academic interest as a principal and teacher. One of his students, Heber Wolsey, said of him that he "ruined me for ever settling for less than my best."[5] Outside the classroom Eldon served his community as a health officer, a Scoutmaster, and for a time a constable. He further diversified his professional career by opening a small general store. The complexity of operating the business increased as Eldon added a gas station, a butcher shop, and a farm implement business. To spend the time necessary to make his business successful he left academia until he sold his interest in the business. He moved his young family to Cardston in 1927 and became principal of Cardston High School.

In 1928 Eldon was called to the bishopric of the Cardston First Ward and in November 1933 ordained bishop. As his Church responsibilities increased, so did his desire to give greater service to the community. The beginning of his political career was in 1933 as an elected member of the Cardston City Council. Later he was named a delegate to the 1935 provincial election. He won a landslide victory, with twenty-two of the twenty-five precincts supporting him.

Once elected, he was invited by the Social Credit Party to be the speaker of the Alberta Legislature. On the opening day of the legislative session he borrowed a chair and a "gown" to officiate in the prestigious position. After the second session of the legislature he was invited to join the executive council as minister of lands and mines, and later to head both the Department of Lands and Forests and the Department of Mines and Minerals. In accepting these cabinet positions N. Eldon Tanner became the first Latter-day Saint in the British Commonwealth to become a cabinet member.

As such, he is credited with developing a system of leasing oil lands that benefitted the oil companies but also the province of Alberta. The incentives he organized led to Alberta being recognized as the fastest-growing oil producer in the world. His leadership caused one journalist to quip, "In Alberta, the government, for all practical purposes involving oil, is Tanner."[6]

After ten years of valuable service in the cabinet, Eldon resigned. He had been elected to represent Cardston four times and had served in the Alberta government for nearly seventeen years. Returning to the private sector in 1952, he became president of Merrill Petroleums, a merged company of three oil firms in Calgary. Two years later he was named executive vice president of Trans-Canada Pipelines Company. His main responsibility with this company was to resolve the economic and political issues involved in constructing a pipeline extending twenty-three hundred miles. For moving the pipeline forward he was recognized by the *Journal of Trade and Commerce* in western Canada as the man of the year. Soon after its completion he resigned from Trans-Canada Pipelines with hopes of retiring on his three-hundred-acre ranch on the outskirts of Calgary.

In 1953 Eldon was called as president of the Calgary Stake. The stake had twenty-four hundred members and covered 21,600 square miles. Eldon's motto as president was "one person, one job."[7]

In 1960 a visit with his uncle Hugh B. Brown revealed that President David O. McKay wanted to see him. The next day, at age sixty-two Eldon was called as an Assistant to the Council of the Twelve Apostles. Two years later he became a member of the Council. And on 3 October 1963, one year after his call to the Twelve, he became Second Counselor in the First Presidency of the Church. "I feel that I have been in a state of shock all day," wrote Eldon that evening.[8]

This was the beginning of long service in the First Presidency as he served as Counselor to four Presidents: David O. McKay, Joseph Fielding

Smith, Harold B. Lee, and Spencer W. Kimball. He wrote, "I have not words to express my deep love for the Lord and my gratitude to him for his many blessings unto me and mine, and I sincerely pray for his continued guidance and strength, as I try to serve him."[9] President Kimball described Eldon Tanner: "As approachable as a child, as wise as a father, and as loving as a gentle brother. . . . Certainly Nathan Eldon Tanner is a man to match our mountains: tall, rugged, unyielding, immeasurable."[10]

During his years as Counselor he saw great expansion in Church membership, a rapid increase in meetinghouse and temple building, and the construction of the new Church Office Building. His leadership was central in the rejuvenating of the business district adjoining Temple Square in Salt Lake City. In the late 1970s a deteriorating health condition diagnosed as Parkinson's disease necessitated curtailing his rigorous and demanding schedule. N. Eldon Tanner died on 27 November 1982 at his home in Salt Lake City at the age of eighty-four.

At his death the First Presidency issued the following statement: "With the passing of President N. Eldon Tanner the entire Church feels a tremendous loss. . . . His unflinching testimony of God the Eternal Father and of the Risen Lord Jesus Christ has been a strength to millions over the earth."[11]

Notes

1. Hugh B. Brown, "President N. Eldon Tanner, a Man of Integrity," *Ensign* 2 (November 1972), pp. 13–14.

2. As quoted in G. Homer Durham, *N. Eldon Tanner, His Life and Service* (Salt Lake City: Deseret Book Co.), 1982, p. 10.

3. Durham, p. 21.

4. As quoted in Durham, p. 25.

5. Heber Wolsey, "Memorandum to G. Homer Durham," March 1981, as cited in Durham, p. 31.

6. *Colliers,* 9 August 1952, pp. 68–69, as cited in Durham, p. 86.

7. Durham, p. 171.

8. N. Eldon Tanner diary, as cited in Durham, p. 198.

9. N. Eldon Tanner, *Seek Ye First the Kingdom of God* (Salt Lake City: Deseret Book Co., 1973), p. 291.

10. *Deseret News,* 30 March 1978.

11. "President N. Eldon Tanner Dies," *Ensign* 13 (January 1983), p. 9.

JOHN TAYLOR

D&C 118:6; 124:129; 135; 138:53

Birth: 1 November 1808, Milnthorpe, Westmoreland County, England. Son of James Taylor and Agnes Taylor.
Death: 25 July 1887, Kaysville, Davis County, Utah.

John Taylor was reared in the English countryside and attended a common school near his father's farm in Hale, Westmoreland, England. At age fourteen he became apprenticed to a cooper in Liverpool, later taking up the turner's trade in Penrith, Cumberland.

His quest for religious truth began in his youth, when "he saw, in vision, an angel . . . holding a trumpet to his mouth, sounding a message to the nations. The import of this vision he did not understand until later in life," but it resulted in a quest for greater truth. Perceiving "more spiritual light" in the Methodist dogma, when about sixteen he left the Church of England. A year or so later he was recognized as a Methodist exhorter or local preacher, a distinction he continued when he migrated to Canada.[1]

His unusual perceptions of the Methodist faith led to his dismissal as an exhorter and to the formation of Bible study classes. Meantime Elder Parley P. Pratt, an Apostle, had come to Toronto. Having begun to investigate Elder Pratt's teachings, John said: "If I find his religion true, I shall accept it, no matter what the consequences may be; and if false, then I shall expose it." He carefully compared Elder Pratt's teachings with the scriptures: "I made a regular business of it for three weeks, and followed Brother Parley from place to place." On 9 May 1836 John Taylor was baptized by Elder Pratt. Much later in life, he said, "I have never doubted any principle of Mormonism since."[2]

His testimony for the work was evident in his ordinations as an elder and as a high priest, and in the fall of 1837 notification of his call to the Quorum of the Twelve Apostles (see D&C 118:6). Of the apostolic appointment he commented, "I felt my own weakness and littleness; but I felt determined, the Lord being my helper, to endeavor to magnfy it."[3]

Undaunted by poverty, John crossed the ocean to Britain, where he was instrumental in opening the mission in Ireland, in assisting migrating Saints to Nauvoo, and in baptizing literally hundreds. Returning to Nauvoo he became prominent in civic affairs, being elected to the Nauvoo City Council and being named a regent of the Nauvoo University and judge advocate with the rank of colonel in the Nauvoo Legion. He was also associate editor of the *Times and Seasons* and proprietor of the *Nauvoo Neighbor.*

As regards the Nauvoo era, John Taylor is most remembered as one who was with the Prophet Joseph Smith and his brother Hyrum in the Carthage Jail on 27 June 1844 (see D&C 135). In the afternoon in the loathsome jail he sang "A Poor Wayfaring Man of Grief." At 5:15 P.M. a scene of terror filled the room. While his beloved Prophet and Hyrum Smith were murdered, John Taylor was severely wounded with four bullets penetrating his body and a fifth that would have hit his heart if it had not struck the watch in his vest pocket. "I felt," said Elder Taylor, "a dull, lonely, sickening sensation at the news [that the Prophet was dead]. . . . Oh, how lonely was that feeling! How cold, barren and desolate!"[4]

John was taken to the Hamilton Hotel, but it was not until the following day that his wounds could be dressed.

Although he was a victim of religious bigotry, his faithful obedience did not end. He followed the leadership of the Twelve from Nauvoo to Iowa Territory, willingly leaving behind his property worth ten thousand dollars with little hope of recompense. With the same resoluteness he served another mission to the British Isles. He gathered many of the English Saints with him in the valley of the Great Salt Lake before accepting another mission assignment to France.

In Paris he dramatically conflicted with impudent Protestant ministers. Undaunted, he continued to spread the gospel by making arrangements for the translation of the Book of Mormon into French and by publishing a monthly periodical, *Etoile du Deseret,* and the book *The Government of God.* Determined to share the gospel with others in the European continent, he traveled to Germany, where he supervised the translation of the Book of Mormon into German. In Hamburg he published a monthly periodical, *Zion's Panier.*

After an absence of three years he returned to the United States and was again called on a mission. This time he presided in the eastern states, where he supervised immigration and published the newspaper *The Mormon*. In the first edition of the paper he wrote, "We are Mormon, inside and outside; at home or abroad, in public and private— everywhere." His defense of the religious beliefs of the Church was noted by Brigham Young: "I can say, as to its editorials, that it is one of the strongest papers ever published."[5]

In May 1857 John Taylor left his positions in the East and returned to the Salt Lake Valley to prepare for the Utah War. He said: "If the earthquake bellows, the lightnings flash, the thunders roll and the powers of darkness are let loose, and the spirit of evil is permitted to rage and an evil influence is brought to bear on the Saints, and my life with theirs, is put to the test—let it come."[6]

As the threat of war abated, John actively served in the development of the pioneer settlements. From 1857 to 1876 he served in the territorial legislature, the first five sessions as speaker of the House of Representatives. From 1868 to 1870 he was the probate judge of Utah County, and in 1877 he served as superintendent of district schools.

His civic service ended at the death of President Brigham Young. As leader of the Latter-day Saints, his energy focused on building the kingdom. With increased zeal he pushed forward the work on the temples. Regular priesthood meetings and conferences began to be held in all the stakes of Zion. At a jubilee conference in April 1880 President Taylor said: "It occurred to me, that we ought to do something, as they did in former times, to relieve those that are oppressed with debt, to assist those that are needy, to break off the yoke of those that may feel themselves crowded upon, and to make it a time of general rejoicing."[7]

The rejoicing ended with the passage of the Edmunds Bill outlawing plural marriage. President Taylor warned the Saints that the storm was coming and that it would break in its fury upon them: "Let us treat it the same as we did this morning in coming through the snowstorm—put up our coat collars and wait till the storm subsides. After the storm comes sunshine. While the storm lasts it is useless to reason with the world; when it subsides we can talk to them."[8]

In February 1885 he preached his last public sermon: "You will see trouble! *trouble!* TROUBLE enough in these United States. And as I have said before, I say today—I tell you in the name of God, WOE! to them that fight against Zion, for God will fight against them!"[9] That night he went into self-imposed exile to escape the ruthless persecution aimed at him by unrelenting and hate-blinded enemies of the Church.

He wrote from exile: "We are engaged in a great work, and laying the foundation thereof—a work that has been spoken of by all the holy prophets since the world was. . . . I pray God the Eternal Father that when we have all finished our probation here, we may be presented to the Lord without spot or blemish, as pure and honorable representatives of the Church and kingdom of God."[10]

At the home of Thomas F. Rouche of Kaysville about 7:55 P.M. on 25 July 1887 at the age of seventy-eight, President Taylor died. Engraved on a silver plate on his coffin are the words: "Holiness to the Lord. Rest in Peace."

Notes

1. B. H. Roberts, *The Life of John Taylor* (Salt Lake City: Bookcraft, 1963), pp. 26, 28.
2. Ibid., p. 38.
3. Ibid., pp. 47, 48.
4. Ibid., pp. 134–35, 140.
5. Ibid., pp. 249, 271.
6. Ibid., p. 273.
7. Ibid., p. 333.
8. Ibid., p. 360.
9. Ibid., pp. 383–84.
10. Ibid., pp. 394, 398.

EZRA THAYRE
D&C 33; 52:22; 54: Introduction; 56:5, 8–9; 75:31

Birth: *14 October 1791, Randolph, Windsor County, Vermont. Son of Ezra Thayer and Charlotte French.*

Ezra Thayre (or Thayer), a bridge, dam, and mill builder in the Palmyra, New York, area, wrote of his conversion to the Book of Mormon through the preaching of Hyrum Smith:

When Hyrum began to speak, every word touched me to the inmost soul. I thought every word was pointed to me. . . . The tears rolled down my cheeks. . . . When Hyrum got through, he picked up a book and said, "Here is the book of Mormon." I said, "Let me see it." I then opened the book, and I received a shock with such exquisite joy that no pen can write and no tongue can express. I shut the book and said, "What is the price of it?" "Fourteen shillings," was the reply. I said, "I'll take the book." I opened it again, and I felt a double portion of the Spirit, that I did not know whether I was in the world or not. I felt as though I was truly in heaven.[1]

Ezra was baptized in October 1830 by Parley P. Pratt. After his baptism he experienced opposition from friends and family, but the appearance of an angel and other signs from heaven convinced him of the correctness of his religious choice.[2]

A few days after Ezra's baptism the Prophet Joseph Smith received a revelation directing him and Northrop Sweet to serve a mission (see D&C 33:1–2). Ezra accepted this directive as a revelation from God. En route from New York to Ohio he preached at several houses and baptized many into the Church.

Ezra was present at the fourth general conference of the Church, held in Kirtland, where he was ordained a high priest. Four days later, on 7 June 1831, the Prophet received a revelation calling Ezra to serve a mission with Thomas B. Marsh (see D&C 52:22). He failed to serve this mission. The reason for this failure seems to have been his role in the controversy over Leman Copley's consecrating his farm for an inheritance of the Saints and later breaking that agreement. An exact determination of Ezra's transgressions is difficult; however, "it is evident that selfishness and rebellion" were the root of his problems.[3] The Lord revealed:

My servant Ezra Thayre must repent of his pride, and of his selfishness, and obey the former commandment which I have given him concerning the place upon which he lives.

And if he will do this, as there shall be no divisions made upon the land, he shall be appointed still to go to the land of Missouri;

Otherwise he shall receive the money which he has paid, and shall leave the place, and shall be cut off out of my church, saith the Lord God of hosts. (D&C 56:5, 8–10.)

Apparently Ezra repented, for on 25 January 1832 he was again appointed to serve a mission with Thomas B. Marsh (see D&C 75:31). He was faithful to this charge. One year later he was appointed to negotiate the purchase of land in Kirtland for the Church, including 103 acres of the Peter French Farm. On this land the Kirtland Temple was built.

Ezra is most remembered for bringing the first case before a high council, in Kirtland. He preferred charges against Elder Curtis Hodges Sr. on 19 February 1834, claiming that Hodges erred in spirit and erred in loud speaking and unclear articulation. Viewing Brother Hodges's behavior as "unbecoming in an Elder in this Church," he requested a hearing before the council. Elder Hodges pleaded not guilty to the charges. Reputable elders substantiated Ezra's complaint. "Brother Story testified that Elder Hodges talked so loud at a prayer meeting that the neighbors came out to see if some one was hurt." The decision of the council was that Hodges was guilty.[4]

Following the decision Ezra volunteered to march with Zion's Camp. On 16 May 1834 as the camp approached Dayton, Ohio, the Prophet "felt much depressed in spirit" and told his traveling companions "there had been a great deal of bloodshed in that place" at some time. Soon Ezra, George A. Smith, and others who were riding with the Prophet arrived at a sixty-feet-high mound that contained human bones.[5] On 29 May 1834, when the horses became ill and some died because of the moldy corn they had eaten, Ezra concocted a home remedy he called his "18x24" formula. Most of the animals recovered after taking it.[6] When the camp arrived at Fishing River on 22 June 1834, Ezra was attacked with the cholera. Lucy Mack Smith explained his process of recovery: "He went to the river and commenced dipping himself, and finding that it helped him, he continued until he was quite restored."[7]

Ezra's Church membership was suspended in May 1835 for impropriety, based on a complaint signed by Oliver Granger.[8] In September that year the Prophet Joseph Smith wrote of his love for Ezra: "This day my soul has desired the salvation of Brother Ezra Thayer."[9]

Apparently the complaint was settled. Ezra moved to Missouri and resided in Adam-ondi-Ahman, where he served on the high council. After the Saints were expelled from Missouri, Ezra moved to Rochester, New York. On 9 July 1840 Heber C. Kimball wrote to the Prophet about staying one night with Ezra in Rochester, "He was glad to see me, and inquired much about you and the rest of the brethren: he seemed to be firm in the faith of the gospel and has much love for his brethren."[10] Jonathan Crosby had a differing opinion of Ezra's faithfulness. He had found him in Rochester also, and said, "He treated us well, but was dead spiritually."[11]

After the Martyrdom Ezra refused to follow the leadership of the Quorum of the Twelve. He was living in Michigan in 1860 and was a high priest in the Reorganized Church of Jesus Christ of Latter Day Saints.[12]

Notes

1. *Saints' Herald*, July 1862, as cited in Lyndon W. Cook, *The Revelations of the Prophet Joseph Smith* (Salt Lake City: Deseret Book Co., 1985), pp. 47–48.

2. See Ezra Thayre autobiography, as cited in Davis Bitton, Guide to Mormon Diaries and Autobiographies, 1977.

3. *HC* 1:180.

4. *HC* 2:33–34.

5. *HC* 2:66.

6. See James L. Bradley, *Zion's Camp 1834: Prelude to the Civil War* (Logan, Utah: James L. Bradley, 1990), p. 98.

7. Lucy Mack Smith, *History of Joseph Smith by His Mother*, ed. Preston Nibley (Salt Lake City: Bookcraft, 1954), p. 229.

8. See *HC* 2:221.

9. *HC* 2:281.

10. *Times and Seasons* (1 April 1845): 6:861.

11. Jonathan Crosby autobiography, Utah State Historical Society, Salt Lake City, Utah, pp. 23–24.

12. See Susan Easton Black, *Early Members of the Reorganized Church of Jesus Christ of Latter Day Saints,* 6 vols. (Provo, Utah: Religious Studies Center, Brigham Young University, 1993), 5:777.

ROBERT BLASHEL THOMPSON
D&C 124:12–14

Birth: *1 October 1811, Great Driffield, Yorkshire, England.*
Death: *27 August 1841, Nauvoo, Hancock County, Illinois.*

Robert Thompson received his education and developed an interest in religion in Dunnington, Yorkshire, England. He joined the Methodists and was a preacher for some years before immigrating to

Upper Canada in 1834. It was the preaching of Parley P. Pratt that led Robert to become a member of the Church in May 1836.

Anxious to join with the Saints, he journeyed to Kirtland in May 1837, but within the year he had returned to Upper Canada to serve a mission. After baptizing many Canadians he once again attempted to settle in Kirtland, but the persecution against the Saints had increased, so Robert joined his brother-in-law Hyrum Smith and journeyed to Far West, Missouri. Escalating persecution led to open confrontation in Missouri. Robert fought in the Battle of Crooked River in defense of the Saints; consequently his enemies swore they would kill him. He suffered from exposure and lack of food as he attempted to avoid their clutches.

He temporarily settled in Quincy, Illinois, and was employed as a writer for the *Argus* newspaper and as a courthouse clerk. When he moved to Nauvoo he served as a scribe for the Prophet and also gathered libelous reports and publications against the Church at the Prophet's request. He was appointed general Church clerk, colonel and aide-de-camp of the Nauvoo Legion, Nauvoo city treasurer, and a regent of the University of Nauvoo.

On 19 January 1841 Robert was called by the Lord to assist the Prophet in writing a proclamation to the kings, presidents, and governors of the earth. "Let my servant Robert B. Thompson help you to write this proclamation, for I am well pleased with him" (D&C 124:12).[1] In the revelation the Lord promised: "I will bless him with a multiplicity of blessings; let him be faithful and true in all things from henceforth, and he shall be great in mine eyes; but let him remember that his stewardship will I require at his hands" (D&C 124:13–14).

From May to August 1841 he worked with Don Carlos Smith as an associate editor of the *Times and Seasons*. On 16 August 1841 he was seized with the same disease that had caused the death of Don Carlos the week before. "The attachment between them was so strong, it seemed as though they could not long be separated." Robert died on 27 August 1841 at his residence in Nauvoo at the age of twenty-nine. The Prophet said that he died "in full hope of a glorious resurrection."[2]

The *Times and Seasons* gave notice of his death: "With feelings, too pungent to be expressed, we have to record the death of our esteemed and much beloved BROTHER ROBERT BLATSELL THOMPSON." It editorialized:

For the last five or six years he has been a faithful and an efficient Elder of this church; laboring incesantly for the cause of truth. . . . He departs this life in the triumphs of faith, bearing testimony, in his dying moments of the truth of the fullness of the gospel of Jesus Christ, and of the faith of the new and everlasting covenant; rejoicing greatly, that his time had come, when he too could go, and be at rest in the paradise of God.[3]

Years later his widow recalled: "This indeed was a time of sorrow, but I can never forget the tender sympathy and brotherly kindness [Joseph Smith] ever showed toward me and my fatherless child. When riding with him and his wife Emma in their carriage I have known him to alight and gather prairie flowers for my little girl."[4]

Notes

1. Robert's premature death precluded his assistance with this project.
2. *HC* 4:411–12.
3. *Times and Seasons* 2 (1 September 1841): 519.
4. Mercy Thompson, "Recollections," *Juvenile Instructor* 27 (1 July 1892): 399.

JOSEPH H. WAKEFIELD
D&C 50:37; 52:35

Birth: *About 1792.*

Joseph Wakefield, a known resident and property owner in Watertown, New York, was baptized either in or before 1831. He moved from the East to Kirtland, Ohio, where through the Prophet Joseph Smith the Lord appointed him to preach with Parley P. Pratt in the Western Reserve (see D&C 50:37). Elder Pratt recorded a few of their missionary experiences:

In obedience . . . Joseph Wakefield and myself visited the several branches of the Church, rebuking the wrong spirits which had crept in among them, setting in order things that were wanting; ordaining Elders and other officers; baptizing such as believed and repented of their sins. . . . On some occasions we assembled fifty or sixty little children in one circle, in the midst of the assembly of the saints, and laid our hands upon them all, and prayed for them, and blessed them in the name of Jesus.[1]

After the mission Joseph was ordained a high priest on 3 June 1831 by Lyman Wight. Four days later the Prophet received another revelation appointing him to preach with Solomon Humphrey in the East (see D&C 52:35). They preached in St. Lawrence County, New York, where Joseph baptized George A. Smith, a future Apostle, "in the presence of [his] father and mother, and many of [his] neighbors," in September 1832.[2]

After completing this mission Joseph Wakefield returned to Kirtland, where subsequently he joined with dissident Mormons. George A. Smith reported that after his apostasy Joseph "announced to the astonished world the fact that, while he was a guest in the house of Joseph Smith, he had absolutely seen the Prophet come down from the room where he was engaged in translating the word of God, and actually go to playing with the children! This convinced him that the Prophet was not a man of God, and that the work was false, which, to me and hundreds of others, he had testified that he knew came from God."[3]

This apostate, of whom the Lord had said in 1831, "Joseph Wakefield, in whom I am well pleased," by 1834 was attempting to defame Joseph Smith and prove the Book of Mormon was written by Solomon Spaulding. He was duly excommunicated. George A. Smith said his attacks on the Church led to mobocracy: "He afterwards headed a mob meeting, and took the lead in bringing about a persecution against the Saints in Kirtland and the regions round about."[4]

Notes

1. Parley P. Pratt, *Autobiography of Parley P. Pratt,* Parley P. Pratt Jr., ed. (Salt Lake City: Deseret Book Co., 1985), p. 51.
2. George A. Smith, "Auto-Biography of George Albert Smith," *Millennial Star* 27 (15 July 1865): 438.
3. George A. Smith, in *JD* 7:112.
4. Ibid.

MICAH BALDWIN WELTON
D&C 75:36

Birth: *13 August 1792, Watertown, Litchfield County, Connecticut.*[1] *Son of Eliakim Welton and Loly Barnes.*
Death: *9 August 1861, Knox County, Illinois.*

The lure of the Ohio frontier in 1820 led Micah Welton to abandon his interest in medicine in favor of becoming a millwright and a farmer.[2] His belief in God during the early Ohio years was recorded by his biographer: "He was a firm believer in God and a great bible student. If anyone asked him a question he could quote the bible chapter and verse."[3]

Micah was baptized on 23 June 1831 at Northampton, Ohio, by John Smith. He was ordained a priest, then an elder, and then called by revelation to labor as a missionary in eastern Ohio with Eden Smith (see D&C 75:36). They began their mission from Northampton on 10 December 1831 and preached in several small communities before returning to Northampton nine days later. They started again on a mission but had returned to Northampton a second time on 4 February 1832.[4]

In May 1833 a council held in Norton Township, Ohio, considered the standing of "Baldwin Welton" and other elders. The decision of the council was that "their ordinations were illegal, and that the churches should not receive them in their several offices."[5] It is assumed that "Baldwin Welton" is Micah Baldwin Welton. The legality of his missionary license was established on 31 March 1836, five days after he attended the Kirtland temple dedication.[6] Later that year he was residing in Clay County, Missouri.

As persecution raged against the Saints in Missouri, Micah moved his family to Pike County, Illinois. He was ordained a seventy in 1839 at Quincy, Illinois, and was a member of the Third Quorum of Seventy in Nauvoo. He was a property owner in Nauvoo from 1839 to 1844 and faithfully lived the gospel, being appointed to serve a mission in Kentucky in 1844 and laboring as a carpenter on the Nauvoo Temple.

After 1846, however, Church records do not mention Micah Welton. He did not migrate to Iowa Territory or to the Rockies with the Saints. He died in August 1861 at Knox County, Illinois, at the age of sixty-eight.

Notes

1. Handwritten entries in Sarah Elizabeth Welton family Bible, in author's possession.

2. "History of Appanoose County," p. 554, in author's possession; see also the Ohio federal census 1820.

3. Nina K. Wolff, "Micah Baldwin Welton" (n.p., n.d.), p. 1, in author's possession.

4. Journal of Eden Smith, typescript, p. 1, Special Collections, Harold B. Lee Library, Brigham Young University, Provo, Utah.

5. HC 1:343.

6. Wolff, p. 1.

HARVEY G. WHITLOCK
D&C 52:25

Birth: *1809, Massachusetts.*

On 3 June 1831, at the fourth general conference, Harvey Whitlock was ordained a high priest by Joseph Smith. Levi Hancock wrote:

> Joseph put his hands on Harvey Whitlock and ordained him to the high priesthood. He turned as black as Lyman [Wight] was white. His fingers were set like claws. He went around the room and showed his hands and tried to speak; his eyes were in the shape of oval O's. Hyrum Smith said, "Joseph, that is not of God." . . . Joseph bowed his head, and in a short time got up and commanded Satan to leave Harvey, laying his hands upon his head at the same time. . . .
>
> . . . Harvey Whitlock [said] when Hyrum Smith said it was not God, he disdained him in his heart and when the Devil was cast out he was convinced it was Satan that was in him.[1]

From this time forward Harvey preached the good news of the gospel. He labored with David Whitmer in Illinois, Indiana, Michigan, Ohio, and Missouri (see D&C 52:25). He attended several conferences in Missouri from 1831 to 1833. At the conference in August 1831 he "made remarks upon the second coming of Christ."[2] At the conference on 24 August 1832 he proposed four questions:

1st. Can a man in the Church of Christ walk by faith without law?
2nd. Was the law given to bring men to faith?
3rd. Was the law added because of transgression?
4th. Was the law given because it was asked for?[3]

He was expelled from Jackson County in 1833 by mobbers.

Harvey lost his fellowship among the Saints in 1835. He wrote to the Prophet Joseph Smith on 28 September that year: "I have fallen from that princely station whereunto our God has called me. . . . I have sunk myself . . . in crimes of the deepest dye." He declared himself to be "a poor, wretched, bewildered, way-wanderer to eternity."

In Joseph's response on 16 November 1835 he wrote:

> I have received your letter . . . and I have read it twice, and it gave me sensations that are better imagined than described, let it suffice that I say that the very flood gates of my heart were broken up—I could not refrain from weeping. I thank God that it has entered into your heart to try to return to the Lord, and to this people, if it so be that He will have mercy upon you. I have inquired of the Lord concerning your case; these words came to me . . . [If you repent and remain faithful you will] be counted worthy to stand among princes, and shall yet be made a polished shaft in my quiver for bringing down the strongholds of wickedness.[4]

Harvey returned to Kirtland, and on 30 January 1836 the First Presidency authorized his rebaptism and his ordination to the office of a high priest.[5] In 1838 he forsook the Church during the Missouri difficulties.

In 1840 he was residing in Cedar County, Iowa. By 1850 he had moved to the Rockies and was living among the Saints in Utah County, where he had a household of ten and had accumulated a real wealth (land) worth one hundred dollars as the result of his practice as a doctor.[6] In 1851 he was arrested as an accessory to theft. Thereafter he denied the faith but, typical of his previous actions, was again rebaptized about 1858.[7]

By 1864 Harvey had moved to Northern California. He joined the Reorganized Church of Jesus Christ of Latter Day Saints. In 1866 he was appointed to serve a mission for the RLDS church.[8]

Notes

1. Autobiography of Levi Ward Hancock, typescript, pp. 33–34, Special Collections, Harold B. Lee Library, Brigham Young University, Provo, Utah.

2. Donald Q. Cannon and Lyndon W. Cook, eds., *Far West Record: Minutes of The Church of Jesus Christ of Latter-day Saints, 1830–1844* (Salt Lake City: Deseret Book Co., 1983), pp. 13–14.

3. Ibid., p. 53.

4. *HC* 2:314–15.

5. See *HC* 2:388.

6. See the Utah federal census 1850.

7. See Lyndon W. Cook, *The Revelations of the Prophet Joseph Smith* (Salt Lake City: Deseret Book Co., 1985), p. 81.

8. Susan Easton Black, *Early Members of the Reorganized Church of Jesus Christ of Latter Day Saints,* 6 vols. (Provo, Utah: Religious Studies Center, Brigham Young University, 1993), 6:223.

DAVID WHITMER
D&C 14; 17–18; 30:1–2; 52:25

Birth: *7 January 1805, a small trading post near Harrisburgh, Dauphin County, Pennsylvania. Son of Peter Whitmer Sr. and Mary Musselman.*
Death: *25 January 1888, Richmond, Ray County, Missouri.*

During his infancy David Whitmer's family moved to a wooded farmland adjoining Seneca Lake in western New York. There David grew to manhood. At age twenty he was elected sergeant in a newly organized militia company, the "Seneca Grenadiers," his first public position of trust.[1]

In 1828 he heard rumors of a "gold Bible." Written letters from the young schoolmaster Oliver Cowdery confirmed these rumors. David first met Joseph Smith when he conveyed the Prophet and his wife, Emma, and Oliver Cowdery by team and wagon from Pennsylvania to the Whitmer home in Fayette. David readily accepted Joseph's prophetic calling and was privileged to be one of the Three Witnesses to see the plates and behold "a dazzlingly brilliant light that surpassed in brightness even the sun at noonday and . . . a personage clothed in white and near him a table containing" the ancient artifacts.[2]

Sure of his testimony of the Book of Mormon, David was one of the first baptized in this dispensation. He is numbered among the six original members of the Church and was ordained an elder the day the Church was organized. After his marriage to Julia Ann Jolly on 9 January 1831, he moved with his young bride to Ohio and then to the frontier of Missouri to be with the Saints of God. In Missouri, mobs terrorized the Whitmer settlement, burning homes and brutally whipping men. Despite David's attempt to organize a resistance, mobbers forced the Saints from their homes across the river to the swamplands of Clay County.

On 3 July 1834 he was appointed president of the Clay County high council, and on 7 July President of the Church in Missouri. His leadership over the exiled refugees from Jackson County was laudatory. His diligence in service was recognized. But after becoming general agent for the Church's Literary Firm in September 1835, and attending the Kirtland Temple dedication in March 1836, he succumbed to smoldering apostate sentiments in Kirtland.

In 1837 he associated with a small but influential group of Kirtland Saints who rebelled against the Prophet's leadership. He later declared that under Joseph Smith's leadership the Church had "abandoned the primitive faith" and "drifted into error and spiritual blindness" by developing "an obsession with earthly power and station."[3] For these reasons, for violating the Word of Wisdom, and for possessing the same spirit as the dissenters he was excommunicated on 13 April 1838 in Far West.

Feeling betrayed by the verdict, David turned for support to his extended family. The Whitmers left the Church and David settled in Richmond, Ray County, Missouri. He remained aloof from the Saints for the next fifty years.

He avoided any religious society until being persuaded by William McLellin in 1846–47 to join his reorganized church. David soon confessed his association with McLellin was emotionally based, not divinely directed.[4]

After the brush with religiosity he confined himself to community and business ventures for the next two decades. He was elected to the city council of Richmond several times and filled the unexpired term of mayor from 1867 to 1868. In the Ray County atlas of 1877 David was featured as one of twenty influential individuals in the county.

For nearly a quarter of a century he operated the "Livery and Feed Stable" of "D. Whitmer & Son" or "Whitmer & Co." of Richmond. His advertisements promised, "Customers may rely on promptness, good turnouts, safe horses, and moderate charges." The *Richmond Conservator* reported that "the forty six years of private citizenship on the part of David Whitmer, in Richmond, [was] without stain or blemish. . . . If a life of probity, of unobtrusive benevolence and well doing for well nigh a half century, marks a man as a good citizen, then David Whitmer should enjoy the confidence and esteem of his fellow men."[5]

In the 1870s at the insistence of his family he organized the Church of Christ, whose congregation consisted of his extended family and a handful of friends. In 1887 at the age of eighty-two he wrote and published a seventy-five-page pamphlet titled "An Address to all Believers in Christ." It is poorly organized and sentimental but does express his religious views and his rejection of Mormonism as defined by Brigham Young.

During his years in a non-Mormon society David tenaciously held to his testimony of the Book of Mormon. He was widely known as "the last surviving witness" and was interviewed far more extensively than the other witnesses. He said that thousands came to inquire, and over fifty of these conversations are reported in reasonable detail in contemporary diaries, letters, and newspapers.

Just before his death David called his family and a few friends to his bedside. Turning to his attending physician, he said, "Dr. Buchanan, I want you to say whether or not I am in my right mind, before I give my dying testimony." The doctor answered, "Yes, you are in your right mind." David then bore testimony: "I want to say to you all, the Bible and the record of the Nephites (Book of Mormon) is true, so you can say that you have heard me bear my testimony on my death-bed."[6]

David died on 25 January 1888 in Richmond at the age of eighty-three. The *Richmond Democrat* eulogized his life: "No man ever lived here, who had among our people, more friends and fewer enemies. Honest, conscientious and upright in all his dealings, just in his estimate of men, and open, manly and frank in his treatment of all, he made lasting friends who loved him to the end."[7]

Notes

1. *Seneca Farmer,* 23 March 1825, as cited in Richard Lloyd Anderson, *Investigating the Book of Mormon Witnesses* (Salt Lake City: Deseret Book Co., 1981), p. 68.

2. Lyndon W. Cook, ed., *David Whitmer Interviews, a Restoration Witness* (Orem, Utah: Grandin Book Co., 1991), p. xiv.

3. David Whitmer, *An Address to All Believers in Christ* (Richmond, Mo.: n.p., 1887).

4. See Anderson, p. 70.

5. *Richmond Conservator,* 9 January 1885, as cited in Anderson, p. 74.

6. *LDS Biographical Encyclopedia* 1:270.

7. *Richmond Democrat,* 26 January 1888, as cited in Anderson, p. 76.

JOHN WHITMER
D&C 15; 26; 30; 47; 69:1–8; 70:1

Birth: *27 August 1802, Fayette Township, Seneca County, New York. Son of Peter Whitmer Sr. and Mary Musselman.*
Death: *11 July 1878, Far West, Caldwell County, Missouri.*

It was on the family farm in Fayette that John Whitmer learned the art of husbandry. He also learned the value of religious worship in his youth by attending the German Reformed Church. His religious life dramatically changed in June 1829 when Joseph Smith accepted the hospitality of the Whitmers. John readily received the prophetic calling of Joseph and his message of the Restoration. He assisted the young Prophet as a scribe for the translation of the Book of Mormon before being baptized by Oliver Cowdery.

Sacred events in holy writ witness of his devotion and the Lord's love for him (see D&C 15). He remembered with gratitude his privilege to be one of the Eight Witnesses to the Book of Mormon. John was an influence for good during the early days of the Church in New

York. He did as directed by divine revelation: "Let your time be devoted to the studying of the scriptures, and to preaching, and to confirming the church at Colesville" (D&C 26:1). He strengthened the Colesville Saints and acted as a scribe for the Bible translation in its early stages. Following the September 1830 Church conference in Fayette he was told, "My servant John, . . . thou shalt commence from this time forth to proclaim my gospel, as with the voice of a trump" (D&C 30:9).

From Fayette, New York, to Kirtland, Ohio, John shared news of the Restoration, but not all were pleased with his message. "A young man by the name of Whitmer arrived here last week . . . with a new batch of revelations from God, as he pretended, which have just been communicated to Joseph Smith," announced the *Painesville Telegraph*.[1] Undaunted by mockery, John unflinchingly asserted the truthfulness of the gospel.

When not proselytizing he continued to share his scribal talents with the Prophet, and the Lord called him to write the history of the Church (see D&C 47:1). He initially fulfilled this assignment with faithfulness. His ninety-six written pages are considered by some historians to be the most authoritative history of the Church before 1838.

John Whitmer and Oliver Cowdery hand-carried the scribed revelations to Independence, Missouri. There W. W. Phelps began the typesetting and printing, but mob action prevented their intended publication as the Book of Commandments. John remained in Missouri in a small Mormon colony near the Little Blue River. He played a leading role in the Jackson County conflict and is remembered for willingly offering himself to the mob as a hostage to prevent further violence.

He also was a leader in Clay County and his name appears on several important documents. By 1834 some of the Saints viewed him as second only to David in prominence and ability among the Whitmer brothers. On 3 July 1834 he became a member of the Church presidency in Missouri. Using legal sources he actively sought redress and protection against mob violence. Perhaps because of his diligent response to duty, the Lord commanded him to return to Kirtland to accept an endowment of the Spirit "with power from on high and proclaim the everlasting gospel."[2]

John remained in Kirtland from 1835 to 1836. On 18 May 1835 he was appointed editor of the Mormon newspaper. He wrote, "This day held a council and contrary to my feelings or expectations I was appointed to edit the *Messenger and Advocate*."[3] His last editorial contained his testimony: "I know that the Bible, book of Mormon and book of Doctrine and Covenants of the church of Christ of Latter Day Saints, contain the revealed will of heaven."[4]

Upon returning to Missouri he aided the Saints by purchasing tracts of land in Caldwell County that later became known as Far West. However, financial irregularities in the purchase led to allegations and an investigation of his actions. Angered by directives to account for his use of Church funds, he declined to disclose the records. John was excommunicated on 10 March 1838 "for persisting in unchristian-like conduct" and for refusal to return to the Prophet the historical writings of the Church. His public reaction to the excommunication was anger, but privately he wrote in his history asking that "I may be forgiven of my faults, and my sins be blotted out, and in the last day be saved in the kingdom of God, notwithstanding my private situation, which I hope will soon be bettered, and I find favor in the eyes of God, all men and his Saints."[5]

John remained in Missouri during the atrocities arising from the Extermination Order of 1838, free from persecution because of his disassociation with the Saints. When the Saints fled from their homes and property in Far West he returned and took advantage of cheap prices for land and succeeded in purchasing much of the abandoned town. He resided in Far West for the remainder of his life.

During the next forty years he wrote the final chapters of his history, revealing his bitterness toward Joseph Smith and Mormonism. He had brief religious encounters with William E. McLellin in 1847, and later a sympathetic leaning to the Strangites and then the leadership of his brother David.

After 1856 John Whitmer was the sole survivor of the Eight Witnesses. His testimony of the Book of Mormon was told again and again with strong emotions. "Old Father John Whitmer told me last winter, with tears in his eyes, that he knew as well as he knew he had an existence that Joseph translated the ancient writing which was upon the plates which he 'saw and handled.'"[6]

John died on 11 July 1878 in Far West. His estate at death consisted of 625 acres of prime farmland near Far West, livestock, farm machinery, and a two-story home. A eulogy in the *Kingston Sentinel* praised him. "Mr. Whitmer remained at Far West and has since been a highly respected and law abiding citizen."[7]

Notes

1. *Painesville (Ohio) Telegraph,* 18 January 1831, as cited in John Whtmer, *An Early Latter Day Saint History: The Book of John Whitmer,* F. Mark McKiernan and Roger D. Launius, eds. (Independence, Mo.: Herald Publishing House, 1980), p. 13.

2. "The Conference Minutes and Record Book of Christ's Church of the Latter-day Saints, Far West Record," p.41, as cited in ibid., p. 16.

3. Journal of John Whitmer, as cited in Davis Bitton, Guide to Mormon Diaries and Autobiographies, 1977.

4. *Messenger and Advocate* 2 (March 1836): 287.

5. Whitmer, p. 20.

6. Myron Bond letter, *Saints' Herald,* 15 August 1878, p. 254.

7. *Kingston (Missouri) Sentinel,* as cited in Whitmer, p. 21.

PETER WHITMER JR.
D&C 16, 30

Birth: *27 September 1809, Fayette Township, Seneca County, New York. Son of Peter Whitmer Sr. and Mary Musselman.*
Death: *22 September 1836, Liberty, Clay County, Missouri.*

Some time before his birth Peter Whitmer's family moved from Pennsylvania to the farmlands of Fayette, where they resided in a one-and-a-half story, twenty-foot-square log house. In that log cottage Peter was reared by a hard-working, God-fearing father who valued strict discipline.

He and his family worshiped with the German Reformed congregation of Zion's Church, just south of the Whitmer farm, until 1829. In the summer of 1829 young Peter became acquainted with Joseph Smith. Their friendship grew as the Prophet resided in the family home in Fayette. Peter was privileged to assist him sometimes as scribe in the translation of the Book of Mormon and to be one of Eight Witnesses who saw and handled the Book of Mormon plates.

In June 1829 the Prophet was given a revelation of what would "be of the most worth" to Peter: "The thing which will be of the most worth unto you will be to declare repentance unto this people, that you may bring souls unto me, that you may rest with them in the kingdom of my Father. Amen." (D&C 16:1, 3–6.)

The first soul Peter brought to the Lord was his own. He was baptized by Oliver Cowdery and ordained an elder in June 1830. According to the testimony of his brother David, given in 1881, Peter was one of the first seven elders ordained in the latter days.

In September 1830 he was called by revelation to preach the gospel with Oliver Cowdery: "Behold, I say unto you, Peter, that you shall take your journey with your brother Oliver; for the time has come that it is expedient in me that you shall open your mouth to declare my gospel. . . . to build up my church among the Lamanites. . . . Be diligent in keeping my commandments, and you shall be blessed unto eternal life." (D&C 30:5–6, 8.)

One month later Peter was directed to accompany Parley P. Pratt, Oliver Cowdery, and Ziba Peterson "into the wilderness among the Lamanites" (D&C 32:2).

The missionaries to the Lamanites, as they became known, began their journey in October 1830 to the frontier to share the Book of Mormon with Indian tribes. They trekked near Buffalo, New York, where they preached to the Catteraugus Indians. From Buffalo they traveled to Mentor, Ohio, where they baptized Sidney Rigdon and many of his congregation. Convert Lyman Wight recalled hearing young Peter testify that he had seen the plates. Peter's terse diary entry announced, "We declared the Book of Mormon."[1]

They then journeyed to Sandusky, Ohio, to preach to the Wyandot Indians. From Sandusky they traveled to Cincinnati and then two hundred miles to St. Louis. For the last three hundred miles they trudged through trackless wastes of snow to Independence, Missouri, about fifteen hundred miles from where they had started.

In the frontier town of Independence Peter became an accomplished tailor. One of his clients was General Alexander Doniphan, who hired him to make a suit. He remained in Independence until August 1831 when he joined other elders in returning to Ohio. At a Church conference in Ohio on 25 October 1831 he was ordained a high priest by Oliver Cowdery. Brief notes from the conference include excerpts from a speech given by Peter: "My beloved brethren ever since I have had an acquaintance with the writing of God I have [viewed] eternity with perfect confidence."[2]

He soon returned to Missouri and supported his family by continuing his trade as a tailor. Mary Elizabeth Lightner became his employee: "I went to work for Peter Whitmer, who was a tailor by trade, and just married. He was crowded with work, and Lilburn W. Boggs offered him a room in his house, as he had just been elected lieutenant governor, and wanted Peter to make him a suit for his inauguration ceremonies. Peter did make [the suit], and I stitched the collars and faced the coat. Mr. Boggs often came in to note the progress of the work."[3]

Peter and his family suffered from mobocracy and religious persecution in 1833 before fleeing to Clay County. Residing in temporary shelters on the disease-ridden swamplands of Clay proved distressing for Peter's health. Nevertheless, he extended hospitality to the sick of Zion's Camp. One of the afflicted, Heber C. Kimball, recalled his kindness: "I went to Liberty, to the house of brother Peter Whitmer, which place I reached with difficulty, being much afflicted myself with the disease that was among us. I stayed there until I started for home. I received great kindness from them."[4]

It is assumed that Peter also extended kindness to his oldest brother, Christian. Unfortunately, in 1835 Christian died. Although Peter suffered from consumption and infection at this time, his problems did not preclude his service on the local high council in 1836.

However, ten months following the death of Christian, on 22 September 1836, Peter died near Liberty, Clay County. He was buried by the side of his brother. Their brother-in-law Oliver Cowdery wrote in eulogy of the faithful brothers:

> By many in this church, our brothers were personally known: they were the first to embrace the new covenant, on hearing it, and during a constant scene of persecution and perplexity, to their last moments, maintained its truth—they were both included in the list of the eight witnesses in the Book of Mormon, and though they have departed, it is with great satisfaction that we reflect, that they proclaimed to their last moments, the certainty of their former testimony.[5]

Notes

1. As cited in Richard Lloyd Anderson, *Investigating the Book of Mormon Witnesses* (Salt Lake City: Deseret Book Co., 1981), p. 126.

2. Donald Q. Cannon and Lyndon W. Cook, eds., *Far West Record: Minutes of The Church of Jesus Christ of Latter-day Saints, 1830–1844* (Salt Lake City: Deseret Book Co., 1983), p. 21.

3. Mary Elizabeth Rollins Lightner, autobiography, *Utah Genealogical and Historical Magazine* 17 (July 1926): 196.

4. Heber Kimball, "Extract from Journal," *Times and Seasons* 6 (15 March 1845): 839.

5. Oliver Cowdery, "The Closing Year," *Messenger and Advocate* 3 (December 1836): 426.

PETER WHITMER SR.
D&C 14: Introduction; 21: Introduction; 34: Introduction; 128:21

Birth: *14 April 1773, Pennsylvania.*
Death: *12 August 1854, Richmond, Ray County, Missouri.*

Peter Whitmer Sr. married Mary Musselman and they became the parents of eight children. Three of the children are mentioned by name in the Doctrine and Covenants—David, Peter Jr., and John. By 1809 the family had settled on farmland in the German-extraction township of Fayette, New York. Peter was elected an overseer of district highways in 1826 and a local school trustee in 1827.

Among his contemporaries he was known as a hard-working, God-fearing man. He attended worship services in a log structure known as Zion's Church, located a mile south of his farm. His German Reformed pastor, Diedrich Willers Sr., described him as "a quiet, unpretending, and apparently honest, candid, and simple-minded man." The pastor's son Diedrich Willers Jr. wrote of Peter Whitmer Sr. as being "spoken of by old Fayette residents as a worthy and industrious citizen."[1]

On his property, deeded to him in four transactions between 1819 and 1827, Peter built a one-and-a-half-story log home.[2] The home played such a significant role in the early days of Mormonism that it often surpassed its owner. In 1829 the Prophet completed the translation of the Book of Mormon in the home; on the Peter Whitmer property three witnesses beheld the angel and saw the Book of Mormon plates; and on 6 April 1830 the Church was organized in the home. The first three conferences of the Church also were held there.

Peter embraced the wonderful truths that were unfolding in his home. Just twelve days after the Church was organized, on 18 April

1830, he and his wife were baptized in Seneca Lake by Oliver Cowdery. In obedience to the Lord's command, the following year he moved his family to Kirtland. By 1832 they were residing in Jackson County, Missouri. The Zion existence they had hoped to establish there ended as mobbers drove the Whitmers to the swamplands of Clay County. Father Whitmer, as he was affectionately known, suffered from religious persecution with other righteous Saints.

His faithfulness to the restored gospel and the Prophet Joseph Smith remained strong until he relocated with his family in Far West. In 1838 he turned from the truth he had avowed for nine years and joined his apostate sons Jacob, John, and David in rebellion against the Prophet. Joseph Smith wrote that Father Whitmer and others "said I was a fallen Prophet, and they were capable of leading the people."[3] Peter relocated among dissenters in Richmond, Missouri. He died on 12 August 1854 in Richmond at the age of eighty-one.

Notes

1. As cited in Richard Lloyd Anderson, *Investigating the Book of Mormon Witnesses* (Salt Lake City: Deseret Book Co., 1981), p. 125.

2. Anderson, p. 125. The house no longer stands, but a replica has been built on the foundation stones. On 26 September 1926 the Church purchased from Joseph H. Manges and his wife what was known as the "Peter Whitmer Farm."

3. *HC* 5:217.

NEWEL K. WHITNEY

D&C 63:42–46; 64:26; 72:8; 84:112, 114; 93:50; 96:2;
104:39–42; 117:1, 4, 11

Birth: *5 February 1795, Marlborough, Windham County, Vermont. Son of Samuel Whitney and Susanna Kimball.*
Death: *23 September 1850, Salt Lake City, Salt Lake County, Utah.*

At age nineteen Newel K. Whitney entered merchandising in the village of Plattsburg, New York, on the western shore of Lake Champlain. In September 1814 he fought to save Plattsburg from the British forces. Fortunately, the British fleet had already been defeated on the lake and the British land troops were so discouraged that Plattsburg was saved without much of a fight.

Even though this was a strategic victory for the United States, through the war Newel lost most of his personal possessions. He left Plattsburg and moved to Green Bay on Lake Michigan, where he set up as an Indian trader, buying and selling furs for an eastern market. A skirmish with an enraged, drunken Indian caused Newel to abandon the Indian trade.

He settled in Ohio, on the shores of Lake Erie, where he accepted employment with Sidney Gilbert as a clerk and bookkeeper. His business success was described by his wife, Elizabeth: "We prospered in all our efforts to accumulate wealth, so much so, that among our friends it came to be remarked that nothing of Whitney's ever got lost on the lake, and no product of his exportation was ever low in the market; always ready sales and fair prices."[1]

Amid their prosperity Newel and Elizabeth began to examine religious creeds. About midnight one evening they prayed to know how to receive the Holy Ghost. Elizabeth said: "The Spirit rested upon us and a cloud overshadowed the house. It was as though we were out of doors. The house passed away from our vision. . . . A solemn awe pervaded us. We saw the cloud and felt the Spirit of the Lord. Then we heard a voice out of the cloud saying 'Prepare to receive the word of the Lord, for it is coming.'"[2]

The word of the Lord came with the missionaries who had been called to take the gospel to the Lamanites and were proselytizing en route. In November 1830 Newel and Elizabeth were baptized.

The Prophet Joseph Smith saw a vision in which Newel was pleading with the Lord that the Prophet would come to Kirtland. On or about 1 February 1831 he arrived at the Whitney store:

> "Newel K. Whitney! Thou art the man!" he exclaimed, extending his hand cordially, as if to an old and familiar acquaintance.
>
> "You have the advantage of me," replied the one addressed, as he mechanically took the proffered hand—a half-amused, half mystified look overspreading his countenance—"I could not call you by name, as you have me."
>
> "I am Joseph Smith, the Prophet," said the stranger, smiling. "You've prayed me here; now what do you want of me?"[3]

Elizabeth wrote of this event, "I remarked to my husband that this was the fulfillment of the vision we had seen of a cloud, as of glory, resting upon our house."[4]

The Prophet and his wife resided with the Whitneys for several weeks. Newel's call to the bishopric would require that he open his home to many others (see D&C 72:1–8). One historical account states: "Newel K. Whitney, staggering under the weight of the responsibility that was about to be placed upon him, said to the Prophet: 'Brother Joseph, I can't see a Bishop in myself.' . . . The Prophet answered: 'Go and ask the Lord about it'. And Newel did ask the Lord, and he heard a voice from heaven say, 'Thy strength is in me.'"[5]

Joseph loved Bishop Whitney. In June 1832 he wrote to Emma, "He is chearful and patient and a true Brother to me."[6] On 7 October 1835 Joseph received a blessing for Newel through the Urim and Thummim: "Blessed of the Lord is Brother Whitney, even the bishop of the Church of Latter-day Saints, for the Bishopric shall never be taken away from him while he liveth. . . . He shall deal with a liberal hand to the poor and the needy, the sick and afflicted, the widow and the fatherless."[7]

In partial fulfillment of the blessing, Newel held a three-day feast in January 1836 for the poor Saints in the Kirtland vicinity. The Prophet wrote of this event: "Attended a sumptuous feast at Bishop

Newel K. Whitney's. This feast was after the order of the Son of God—the lame, the halt, and the blind were invited, according to the instructions of the Savior. . . . We . . . received a bountiful refreshment, furnished by the liberality of the Bishop. The company was large."[8]

Joseph's feeling for this faithful man was one of profound gratitude: "Thou art a faithful friend in whom the afflicted sons of men can confide, with the most perfect safety. Let the blessings of the Eternal also be crowned upon his head. How warm that heart! how anxious that soul! for the welfare of one who has been cast out, and hated of almost all men. Brother Whitney, thou knowest not how strong those ties are that bind my soul and heart to thee."[9]

After Joseph's death Newel was called as the Presiding Bishop of the Church. He and his family journeyed to the Salt Lake Valley in 1848.

On Saturday, 21 September 1850, he returned home from his labors in the bishopric, complaining of a severe pain in his left side. By Monday, 23 September, his condition had become worse. President Brigham Young, Heber C. Kimball, and other Church leaders gathered at his home. He passed away at 11:00 A.M. His obituary stated: "Thus, in full strength, and mature years, has one of the oldest and most exemplary and useful members of the Church fallen suddenly; leaving a large family to mourn the loss of an affectionate husband, and a kind and generous father."[10]

Notes

1. Edward W. Tullidge, *The Women of Mormondom* (New York: Tullidge and Crandall, 1877), p. 34. The Kirtland Land and Tax Records graphically portray Newel's economic prosperity. His name is found eighteen times as the taxpayer for the "Whitney Company," five times as "Whitney N. & Miller G. Trustee," and forty-eight times as an individual.

2. *LDS Biographical Encyclopedia* 1:223.

3. Orson F. Whitney, "Newel K. Whitney," *Contributor* 6 (1885): 125.

4. *LDS Biographical Encyclopedia* 1:224.

5. Roy W. Doxey, *Latter-day Prophets and the Doctrine and Covenants*, 4 vols. (Salt Lake City: Deseret Book Co., 1978), 2:434.

6. Joseph Smith, *The Personal Writings of Joseph Smith*, comp. Dean C. Jessee (Salt Lake City: Deseret Book Co., 1984), p. 239.

7. *HC* 2:288.

8. *HC* 2:362.

9. *HC* 5:108.

10. *Deseret News*, 23 September 1850.

LYMAN WIGHT

D&C 52:7, 12; 103:30; 124:18–19, 22–24, 60, 62, 70

Birth: *9 May 1796, Fairfield Township, Herkimer County, New York. Son of Levi Wight and Sarah Corbon.*
Death: *31 March 1858, Dexter, Medino County, Texas.*

Lyman Wight enlisted in the military during the War of 1812 and was stationed at Sackets Harbor, New York, until the conflict ended. He moved to Ohio about 1826 and by 1829 had joined the Campbellite-based "Common Stock Family" on the Isaac Morley farm. Like others in the "Family," he discarded his Campbellite leanings in favor of the truths preached by the missionaries, being baptized by Oliver Cowdery 14 November 1830.

At the fourth general conference of the Church he was ordained by the Prophet Joseph Smith to the office of high priest, the first man so designated in this dispensation. A few days later he was called to serve a mission to Missouri and was warned, "Let my servant Lyman Wight beware, for Satan desireth to sift him as chaff" (D&C 52:7, 12). Several months after reaching Missouri he and others went to Cincinnati, Ohio, where he was so powerful in his discourses that a hundred people were baptized.

Lyman resided in Jackson County, Missouri, until mobs forced him to flee to Clay County. He volunteered to go and inform the Prophet in Kirtland of the suffering of the Missouri Saints, although he had only three days' provisions for the journey; and he went with Parley P. Pratt. The answer to the problems of the Saints in Missouri was to raise a potential military force, Zion's Camp, to march from Kirtland in the redemption of Zion (see D&C 103:30). Lyman journeyed to Pennsylvania, New York, Indiana, Illinois, and Michigan mustering volunteers for Zion's Camp. He marched as second only to Joseph Smith in the camp, walking from Michigan to Clay County, Missouri, without stockings on his feet.

According to Benjamin F. Johnson, "By Apostle Lyman Wight we were taught to 'pray for our enemies,' that God would damn them, and 'give us power to kill them.' " [1] Lyman's bold statements such as "Boys, eat, drink and be merry for to-morrow we—fight" caused him to be greatly feared by the Missourians.[2] His explosive expressions of retaliation brought difficulties to the Saints as tempers flared.

His loudly proclaimed false doctrine brought difficulties to himself. A Church court was held on 21 August 1834 to investigate charges of Lyman preaching that "all disease in this Church is of the devil, and that medicine administered to the sick is of the Devil, for the sick in the Church ought to live by faith." Another charge made against him, in a Church court on 24 April 1837, was that he taught "the Church were under a telestial law, because God does not whip in a Celestial. . . . And that the Book of Covinants and Doctrine was a telestial law and the Book of Commandments were a Celestial law."[3] Lyman sought forgiveness and it was granted, but remarks were heard among the Saints such as "Lyman Wight, as a bull in the net, is in danger of apostasy, but the Prophet holds on to him."[4]

Nevertheless, on 28 June 1838 he was appointed second counselor to John Smith, president of the Adam-ondi-Ahman Stake. Four months later he was a captive of the mob militia and was charged with treason and murder. Missourian General Wilson confided: "Col. Wight, we have nothing against you, only that you are associated with Joe Smith. He is our enemy and a damned rascal. . . . If you will come out and swear against him, we will spare your life."

Lyman defiantly replied: "Joseph Smith is not an enemy to mankind, he is not your enemy, and is as good a friend as you have got. Had it not been for him, you would have been in hell long ago, for I should have sent you there, by cutting your throat, and no other man but Joseph Smith could have prevented me, and you may thank him for your life."

Wilson responded, "Wight, you are a strange man; but if you will not accept my proposal, you will be shot tomorrow morning at 8."

Lyman said, "Shoot and be damned."[5]

His life was spared, yet his imprisonment had just begun. Lyman was chained to the Prophet in the squalor of Richmond Jail and then confined with him in inhumane conditions in Liberty Jail. It was not until October 1839 that he enjoyed a brief season of peace, when he again served as a counselor to John Smith, but this time in the Zarahemla Stake presidency.

On 8 April 1841 Lyman was ordained to the apostleship. His first apostolic assignment was strengthening the Saints in the East and collecting funds for building the Nauvoo Temple and the Nauvoo House. He successfully fulfilled these assignments and in the process baptized about two hundred individuals in Kirtland referred to as "dead members of the Church, and brought many of them to Nauvoo."[6] From Nauvoo he journeyed up the Mississippi River to Black River, Wisconsin, in February 1844, to help supervise the cutting of timber in the pineries for the temple and the Nauvoo House.

In Wisconsin he first expressed his desire to preach to the Indians in Texas. Fulfillment of this desire did not materialize until after the martyrdom of Joseph Smith. Contrary to apostolic counsel he stubbornly held the view that Joseph Smith had called him to establish a mission in Texas among the Lamanites. His adamant, persuasive stance caused nearly 150 Saints in Wisconsin to journey with him to Texas. They established a small Mormon-breakaway colony, building mills near the present site of Austin before moving to the Perdinales River Valley.

In his tract "An Address by Way of an Abridged Account and Journal of My Life . . . with an Appeal to the Latter Day Saints, Scattered Abroad in the Earth . . ." Lyman wrote of his opposition to Brigham Young's leadership of the Church: "Notwithstanding their long ears and slanderous tongue, they will find them too short and too feeble to compete with a man who has gained his right and inheritance by passing through the sufferings which I have passed through."[7] He then invited all the earth to gather to Texas in preparation for Zion's redemption.

Lymanism, as his apostate doctrine was known, had its greatest impact among the Saints scattered in Iowa and Missouri in 1848. Two Apostles wrote: "A number of the persons affected with the 'Texas Epidemic' are busy visiting remote branches and instilling into the minds of the people the ideas that the authorities dare not interfere with Lyman in his course for he was right, however much they might say against him they would take no public action."[8] Public action was taken, however, in the Great Salt Lake City fort on 3 December 1848, as fellowship was withdrawn from Lyman Wight. That disciplinary act cured the "Texas Epidemic."

Lyman resided in Texas for the remainder of his life. In 1850 he was elected chief justice of Gillespie County. By 1851 his religious leanings had turned to thoughts of Joseph Smith III taking "his father's place in the flesh!"[9] Lyman died suddenly of epileptic fits at Dexter on 31 March 1858, having been sick only five hours.

Notes

1. Benjamin F. Johnson, letter to George S. Gibbs, as cited in E. Dale LeBaron, "Benjamin Franklin Johnson: Colonizer, Public Servant, and Church Leader," M.A. Thesis, Brigham Young University, 1967, pp. 325–46.

2. Lyman Omer Littlefield, *Reminiscences of Latter-day Saints* (Logan, Utah: The Utah Journal Co., 1888), p. 61.

3. *HC* 2:147, and Donald Q. Cannon and Lyndon W. Cook, eds., *Far West Record: Minutes of The Church of Jesus Christ of Latter-day Saints, 1830–1844* (Salt Lake City: Deseret Book Co., 1983), p. 111.

4. Edward Stevenson, *Selections from the Autobiography of Edward Stevenson, 1820–1897 (1820–1846),* ed. Joseph Grant Stevenson (Provo, Utah: Stevenson's Genealogical Center, 1986), p. 60.

5. *LDS Biographical Encyclopedia* 1:95.

6. Ibid. 1:96.

7. Lyman Wight, "An Address by Way of an Abridged Account and Journal of my Life From February 1844 up to April 1848 With an Appeal to the Latter-day Saints . . . ," p. 13, Archives Division, Church Historical Department, The Church of Jesus Christ of Latter-day Saints, Salt Lake City, Utah.

8. Letter of George A. Smith and Ezra T. Benson to Brigham Young, 7 October 1848, in Brigham Young Papers, as cited in Richard E. Bennett, "Lamanism, Lymanism, and Cornfields," *Journal of Mormon History* 13 (1986–1987): 58 n. 36.

9. As cited in Susan Easton Black, *Early Members of the Reorganized Church of Jesus Christ of Latter Day Saints,* 6 vols. (Provo, Utah: Religious Studies Center, Brigham Young University, 1993), 2:791. Many of Lyman's early followers joined the RLDS church.

FREDERICK G. WILLIAMS

D&C 64:21; 81: Introduction; 90:6, 19; 92:1; 93:41–43,
52–53; 102:3; 104:27, 29

Birth: 28 October 1787, Suffield, Hartford County,
Connecticut. Son of William (or Warren) Williams
and Ruth Granger.
Death: 25 (or 10) October 1842, Quincy, Adams
County, Illinois.

During his early youth Frederick G. Williams had a near-fatal accident one winter as he and his friends attempted to walk across frozen
Lake Erie. The ice broke, leaving them helpless on a floating block
until the next day, when they were sighted by a boat captain and rescued. Frederick was never robust after the incident.

Perhaps the persistence of health problems into maturity led him
to study medical books and proclaim himself a doctor. He advocated
the herb-based Thompsonian system of medicine before becoming
eclectic in his practice. His medical career temporarily halted at the
outbreak of the War of 1812, as he entered the fight against the British
near Lake Erie. After the war he became a boat pilot, navigating the
waters from Buffalo to Detroit. One passenger aboard his vessel, Rebecca Swain, caught his fancy and they later married.

By 1816 the young couple were residing in Warrensville, Ohio,
where Frederick again practiced medicine. As his financial situation
improved he moved to a farm in Chardon, Ohio, where he attended a
local congregation of Campbellites. Learning from coreligionists of encouraging economic opportunities in Kirtland, he and Rebecca located
there on a 144-acre farm.

Frederick was serving as a justice of the peace in Kirtland when he
met the missionaries sent to the Lamanites. Rebecca readily received
their message of the gospel and the Book of Mormon. Before Frederick
was converted he carefully weighed the truthfulness of their preaching
by comparing the Book of Mormon with the teachings of the Bible. In

October 1830 he was baptized, confirmed, and ordained an elder. As the missionaries contemplated continuing their journey to the western frontier, they invited their new convert to join them. Frederick was acquainted with the frontier and his insights proved helpful on the journey. After a ten-month absence he returned to his family in Kirtland.[1]

In March 1832 the Lord called him to be a counselor to the Prophet Joseph Smith (see D&C 81:1–3, 6). The love of the Prophet for his counselor is best illustrated by Joseph's naming his newborn son "Frederick Granger Williams Smith."[2] The Prophet trusted him with myriad responsibilities. He was a personal scribe, an organizer of the printing firm F. G. Williams and Company, and an editor of the *Northern Times*. Joseph Smith penned:

> Brother Frederick G. Williams is one of those men in whom I place the greatest confidence and trust, for I have found him ever full of love and brotherly kindness. He is not a man of many words, but is ever winning, because of his constant mind. He shall ever have place in my heart. . . . God grant that he may overcome all evil. Blessed be Brother Frederick, for he shall never want a friend; and his generation after him shall flourish.[3]

In May 1834 Frederick deeded his farm to the Prophet and joined Zion's Camp with the hope of redeeming Zion. He served as paymaster of the camp until the men were discharged. Upon returning to Kirtland he continued to faithfully demonstrate his love of the gospel and the latter-day work. Perhaps because of his unwavering faith he was privileged to witness an angel enter the Kirtland Temple on the day of dedication. He testified that the angel sat "between Father Smith and himself, and remained there during the prayer."[4] He further testified that "the Savior, dressed in his vesture without seam, came into the stand and accepted of the dedication of the house, that he saw him, and gave a description of his clothing and all things pertaining to it."[5]

Unfortunately Frederick did not maintain his attitude of devotion. Detailed accounts of his fall are sparse and confusing. On 29 May 1837 a Church court was held and five members of the high council expressed their grievances over his actions and those of four others and requested an investigation of their conduct: "We, the undersigned, feeling ourselves aggrieved with the conduct of . . . Frederick G. Williams, . . . believing that [his] course for some time past has been injurious to the Church of God, . . . We should have an investigation of [his] behavior, believing it to be unworthy of [his] high calling."[6]

The court did not come to a conclusion on the charges. After this Frederick's name was not mentioned in the Prophet's writings until the conference of 3 September 1837. At that time, when his name was presented as a counselor in the Presidency it was rejected. Family tradition and historical records conflict over whether he also lost his membership. The answer may be found in the Prophet's writing of 5 August 1838: "Frederick G. Williams . . . had recently been re-baptized."[7]

By 1838 Frederick had joined the Saints in Missouri. In writing a Missouri redress petition on 17 March 1840 he claimed that he was "redused and Left myself and family in a state of poverty with a delicate state of health in an advanced stage of life."[8] On 6 April 1840 he spoke to an assembly of Saints, humbly seeking forgiveness for his former wrongdoings in Missouri and expressing his determination to do the will of God. He was forgiven and received back into Church fellowship.

During the remaining two years of his life he was a frequent visitor in the Prophet's home. One night the Prophet said to him, "Brother Frederick, I don't like to see you leave. You are going home to die." He answered, "I am already a dead man."[9] He died in October 1842 in Quincy from a lung hemorrhage at the age of fifty-four. Many descendants believe he died of a broken heart.

Notes

1. Nancy Clement Williams, *After 100 Years! Meet Frederick Granger Williams* (Independence, Mo.: Zion's Printing and Publishing Co., 1951).
2. This child of Joseph's was born 20 July 1836.
3. As cited in Williams, p. 77.
4. *HC* 2:427.
5. George A. Smith, in *JD* 11:10.
6. *HC* 2:484–85.
7. *HC* 3:55.
8. As cited in Clark V. Johnson, ed., *Mormon Redress Petitions: Documents of the 1833–1838 Missouri Conflict* (Provo, Utah: Religious Studies Center, Brigham Young University, 1992), p. 377.
9. Williams, pp. 126–27.

SAMUEL WILLIAMS
D&C 124:137

Birth: *22 March 1789, Russell, Hampden County, Massachusetts. Son of Samuel Williams and Azubah Warner.*
Death: *10 November 1855, Ogden, Weber County, Utah.*

Samuel Williams, a resident of Kirtland, was baptized a member of the Church before migrating with the Saints to Missouri. He suffered from religious bigotry in Missouri and was forced to flee the state. He made a solemn covenant to assist other suffering Saints as they also journeyed from Missouri to Illinois.[1]

In Nauvoo, Samuel lived near the temple site from 1839 to 1846 and attended the Nauvoo Second Ward.[2] On 19 January 1841 he was appointed by revelation to be a counselor to the elders quorum president, John Hicks: "And again, I say unto you, I give unto you John A. Hicks, Samuel Williams, and Jesse Baker, which priesthood is to preside over the quorum of elders" (D&C 124:137).

After the apostasy of Hicks, Samuel served as the elders quorum president and retained Jesse Baker as a counselor.[3] Not much is written of their quorum meetings. It is assumed that Samuel's faithful adherence to duty contrasted with his predecessor, John Hicks, as he was also called to be a temporary member of the Nauvoo high council.

As persecution mounted, Samuel fled from Illinois with the migrating Saints to the frontier of Iowa. He was ordained a high priest on 24 December 1846 in Winter Quarters, where he remained until the summer of 1849. In the Utah federal census of 1850 he was listed as a stonecutter in Salt Lake City with a household of five and a real wealth (land) of $75.[4] He died on 10 November 1855 in Ogden, Utah, at the age of sixty-six.

Notes

1. See *HC* 3:252.
2. See Lyman Platt, *Nauvoo Early Mormon Record Series* (Highland, Utah: L. De Platt, 1980).
3. See *HC* 7:297.
4. See the Utah federal census 1850.

CALVES WILSON
D&C 75:15

Birth and death: *Unknown.*

Calves Wilson was baptized before 25 October 1831 and ordained a priest on that date in Orange County, Ohio, by Oliver Cowdery. Three months later he was called by revelation to proclaim the gospel: "And again, I say unto my servant Asa Dodds, and unto my servant Calves Wilson, that they also shall take their journey unto the western countries, and proclaim my gospel, even as I have commanded them" (D&C 75:15).

It is not known whether the mission was fulfilled by either man.

In the spring of 1832 Calves accompanied Lyman Wight on a mission to Cincinnati, Ohio. According to a biographer, "[Lyman] delivered a series of lectures and built up a branch of the Church, and baptized upwards of one hundred."[1] It is assumed that Calves participated in the successful preaching in the Cincinnati area.

Notes

1. *LDS Biographical Encyclopedia* 1:93.

LEWIS DUNBAR WILSON
D&C 124:132

Birth: *2 June 1805, Milton, Chittenden County, Vermont. Son of Bradley Wilson and Mary (Polly) Gill.*
Death: *11 March 1856, Ogden, Weber County, Utah.*

Lewis Wilson was a resident of Richland County, Ohio, in 1830. He was baptized on 23 May 1836 in Green Township, Richland County. A notice of his priesthood ordination appeared in the November 1836 *Messenger and Advocate*.[1] He served a short mission with his brother, George Wilson, in May 1837. His missionary license was recorded in the "License Records, in Kirtland, Ohio, by Thomas Burdick, Recording Clerk."[2]

Lewis moved from Ohio to Far West, Missouri, in the fall of 1837. The extermination order in Missouri forced his removal from the state. He itemized his losses in Missouri in a redress petition:

> I hereby certify that I purchased from Congress Two hundred and forty acres of land lying in Caldwell County and State of Missouri and Was compelled to leave the same on acount of the order of the executive of the State.
>
> When the Malitia came to Far West they took from me a valuable Horse which broke up my team I made extertions to obtain it again but without success. I was obliged to part with my land (in order to make up my team and for means to get me conveyed out of the State) for one sixth of the value.[3]

In Illinois, Lewis served on the Nauvoo high council from 1839 to 1846 (see D&C 124:132). In July 1843 he and others volunteered to rescue the Prophet Joseph Smith from the Missourians, and he was blessed for his courage by Hyrum Smith. Hyrum told the group that "if any persons were running Brother Joseph down the river, under any pretext whatever . . . [they] were to rescue Joseph, at all hazards and bring him to Nauvoo."[4] When Joseph was rescued, Lewis continued his watchcare of the Prophet as one of his bodyguards.

Lewis left Nauvoo in 1846 in the great Mormon exodus. He located in Garden Grove and later in Kanesville, Iowa Territory, before migrating to the Salt Lake Valley in 1853. He settled with his family in Ogden, Utah, where he again served on a high council. Lewis died in March 1856 in Ogden at the age of fifty.

Notes

1. See *Messenger and Advocate* 3 (November 1836): 415.

2. Ibid. 3 (June 1837): 528.

3. As cited in Clark V. Johnson, ed., *Mormon Redress Petitions: Documents of the 1833–1838 Missouri Conflict* (Provo, Utah: Religious Studies Center, Brigham Young University, 1992), p. 554.

4. *HC* 5:482.

WILFORD WOODRUFF
D&C 118:6; 124:129; 136:13; 138:53;
Official Declaration—1

Birth: *1 March 1807, Farmington, Hartford County, Connecticut. Son of Aphek Woodruff and Beulah Thompson.*
Death: *2 September 1898, San Francisco, San Francisco County, California.*

Wilford Woodruff's youth was marred by several accidents. In his words: "I have been numbered with those who are apparently the marked victims of misfortunes. It has seemed to me at times as though some invisible power were watching my footsteps in search of an opportunity to destroy my life."[1] In pondering the severity of the mishaps, he wrote, "The repeated deliverances from all these remarkable dangers I ascribe to the mercies of my Heavenly Father."[2]

While religious subjects occupied his mind at an early age, Wilford did not profess religion until age twenty-three. However, he was strongly influenced by the elderly Robert Mason—or Father Mason, as he was known—whom many called a prophet. Mason told Wilford that the Lord would establish his church and that Wilford would "become a conspicuous actor in that kingdom."[3] In preparation for these future events Wilford began to read the scriptures and participated in "earnest prayer before God day and night as far as I could. . . . I had pleaded with the Lord many hours in the forest, among the rocks, and in the fields, and in the mill—often at midnight for light and truth and for His Spirit to guide me in the way of salvation."[4]

That guidance came in the winter of 1833 as he learned of the restored gospel. He listened to the preaching of Zera Pulsipher. "I believed all that he said," Wilford later wrote. "The spirit bore witness of its truth." When he began to read the Book of Mormon, "the spirit bore witness that the record which it contained was true."[5]

On 31 December 1833 he was baptized by Zera Pulsipher. "The

snow was about three feet deep, the day was cold, and the water was mixed with ice and snow, yet I did not feel the cold."

Not long thereafter Wilford made his way to Kirtland, Ohio, where on 25 April 1834 he met the Prophet Joseph. When the Zion's Camp march began a week or so later, Wilford was a part of it. From Missouri he went on a mission to the southern states. In 1836 he was back in Kirtland.

On 15 April 1837 he received his patriarchal blessing from Joseph Smith Sr., informing him that he would bring his father's household into the kingdom of God. Within the month he left on a mission to the East to share the gospel with family and friends. On this mission he organized a branch of the Church at Fox Island before receiving word that he had been appointed to the Quorum of the Twelve Apostles (see D&C 118:6). Wilford was ordained to that calling on 26 April 1839 at Far West, Missouri.

As an Apostle his first assignment was to fulfill a mission to England. Feeble from an illness contracted along the Mississippi River, Wilford lay by a local post office in Illinois. Observing his condition, the Prophet remarked, "Well, Brother Woodruff, you have started upon your mission."

"Yes," Wilford said, "but I feel and look more like a subject for the dissecting room than a missionary."

Joseph replied: "What did you say that for? Get up, and go along; all will be right with you."[6]

Parley P. Pratt, noting that Wilford was proceeding on the mission, hailed him, saying, "Brother Woodruff, I have no money, but I have an empty purse, which I will give you." A little further on, Heber C. Kimball said to him, "As Parley has given you a purse, I have got a dollar I will give you to put in it." With these gifts Wilford left the Nauvoo area for the East and then voyaged across the Atlantic Ocean. In about three months after arriving on British shores he had baptized over two hundred people at the Benbow farm in Herefordshire. This was the beginning of his successful labor, which "enabled me to bring into the Church, through the blessings of God, over eighteen hundred souls during eight months."[7]

Upon returning to Nauvoo, at Christmas time of 1841 he visited with other Apostles in the Prophet's home. His biographer wrote: "Elder Woodruff says in his journal that the Prophet showed him and others for the first time the Urim and Thummim."[8]

In 1844 the opportunity for missionary service came again. The

Prophet admonished, "Brother Woodruff, I want you to go, and if you do not you will die." While Wilford was serving a mission in the east, the Prophet was martyred. Still sorrowing over the tragedy, in Boston on 17 July 1844 Wilford Woodruff and Brigham Young called upon Sister Vose. "Brother Young took the bed and I the armchair, and then we veiled our faces and gave vent to our grief. Until now I had not shed a tear since the death of the Prophet. My soul had been nerved up like steel."[9]

Wilford soon returned to Nauvoo, and by the end of August he was making preparations to leave for yet another mission to England. Among his preparations was a visit to the widows of the martyrs, Emma Smith and Mary Fielding Smith. Emma gave him a piece of oak for a staff, taken from Joseph's coffin. Mary gave him locks of hair from the heads of Joseph, Hyrum, Samuel, and Don Carlos Smith. He then obtained strands of hair from members of the Quorum of the Twelve Apostles. These were placed "in the knob of my staff as a relic of those noble men, the master spirits of the nineteenth century."[10]

As British Mission president, Wilford preached the gospel and published the good news. When he returned to the United States the Saints had begun their exodus to Iowa Territory. He joined them in their temporary encampments and helped organize a company to cross the plains (see D&C 136:13).

For the remaining decades of his life he played a vital role in the frontier settlements of the West. However, his main assignment for two decades was to accompany Brigham Young. "Some day," said President Young, "I shall look to you for my journal."[11] He wrote a journal for sixty-three years and a history of the leading men in the Church. In referring to his writings, Wilford wrote: "I seem to be a marked victim of the adversary. I can find but one reason for this: the devil knew if I got into the Church of Jesus Christ of Latter-day Saints, I would write the history of that Church and leave on record the works and teachings of the prophets, of the apostles and elders."[12]

In 1877 he gave the dedicatory prayer on the St. George Temple and at the close of the services was appointed to preside over the temple. In 1879 religious persecution against plural marriage caused Wilford to go into exile. "For the first time in my life I have had to flee from my enemies for the gospel's sake. . . . They are trying to arrest me for obeying the law of God in reference to Plural Marriage."[13]

At the death of President Taylor, Wilford Woodruff became the leader of the Church: "It is a position I have never looked for. . . . I pray God . . . to give me grace equal to my day." At the April conference in 1889 he was sustained as President of the Church. On that occasion he said, "I pray God to protect me and give me power to magnify my calling to the end of my days."[14]

Those were difficult days as persecution against polygamy raged. However, on 6 October 1890 the prophet had the Manifesto presented to the assembled Saints in the Tabernacle (Official Declaration—1). "I want to say to all Israel that the step which I have taken in issuing this Manifesto has not been done without earnest prayer before the Lord," said the prophet.[15]

During his presidency many noteworthy events occurred—the dedication of the Salt Lake Temple, the granting of general amnesty to Church members, and statehood for Utah. At the celebration of his ninetieth birthday a banner written with the words "We honor the man so honored of God" epitomized the life of the prophet. As he neared the end of his life he summarized his journals and concluded that from 1834 to 1895 he had traveled 172,269 miles, held 7,555 meetings, attended 75 semi-annual general conferences of the Church and 344 quarterly conferences, preached 3,526 discourses, established seventy-seven preaching places in missions, organized fifty-one branches, received 18,977 letters, written 11,519 letters, assisted in confirming 8,952 Saints, labored 603 days in the Endowment House, traveled through England, Scotland, Wales, six islands of the sea, and twenty-three states and five U.S. territories in the cause of righteousness.[16]

At his beside in San Francisco on 2 September 1898 was one of his counselors, George Q. Cannon. He wrote of President Woodruff's last moments: "I arose about 6 o'clock. The nurse told me he had been sleeping in the same position all the time. I took hold of his wrist, felt his pulse and I could feel that it was very faint. While I stood there it grew fainter and fainter until it faded entirely."[17]

The remains of the deceased leader were conveyed from San Francisco to Salt Lake City by rail. He was buried on 8 September 1898 in Salt Lake City.

Notes

1. Matthias F. Cowley, *Wilford Woodruff, History of His Life and Labors* (Salt Lake City: Bookcraft, 1964), p. 5.

2. Ibid., p. 11.

3. Ibid., p. 16.

4. Ibid., p. 18.
5. Ibid., pp. 33–34.
6. Ibid., p. 109.
7. Ibid., pp. 109–10, 119.
8. Ibid., p. 157.
9. Ibid., pp. 204, 208.
10. Ibid., pp. 227–28.
11. Ibid., pp. 346–47.
12. Ibid., p. 477.
13. Ibid., p. 506.
14. Ibid., pp. 560, 565.
15. Ibid., p. 570.
16. *LDS Biographical Encyclopedia* 1:26.
17. Cowley, p. 621.

BRIGHAM YOUNG

Testimony of the Twelve Apostles,
D&C 124:127; 126; 136; 138:53

Birth: *1 June 1801, Whittingham, Windham County, Vermont. Son of John Young and Abigail Howe.*
Death: *29 August 1877, Salt Lake City, Salt Lake County, Utah.*

Few men of the nineteenth century match the caliber and dogged determination of Brigham Young. From humble beginnings in an obscure village in Vermont he rose to the applause of thinking men; but more important, he grew in favor with God. Although some would contend that the laborious toils of farm labor and unwelcome poverty dominated his early years, it was his unwavering search for eternal truth that permeated his thoughts.

Reading the Book of Mormon, listening to missionaries, and baptism brought answers to Brigham's search: "When I saw a man without eloquence, or talents for public speaking, who could only say, 'I know, by the power of the Holy Ghost, that the Book of Mormon is true, that Joseph Smith is a Prophet of the Lord,' the Holy Ghost proceeding from that individual illuminated my understanding, and light, glory, and immortality were before me."[1]

Anxious to learn more about his new religion, Brigham journeyed to Kirtland to meet the Prophet Joseph Smith: "When I went to Kirtland I had not a coat in the world," he said. . . . "Neither had I a shoe to my feet, and I had to borrow a pair of pants and a pair of boots."[2] Of his initial meeting with Joseph he recalled: "Here my joy was full at the privilege of shaking the hand of the Prophet of God, and receiving the sure testimony, by the spirit of prophecy, that he was all that any man could believe him to be as a true Prophet."[3]

On 14 February 1835 Brigham Young was ordained a member of the Quorum of the Twelve Apostles. As an Apostle he was zealous in defense of the Prophet. One evening in Kirtland, overhearing a man loudly rail against Joseph Smith, Brigham reacted: "I put my pants and shoes on, took my cowhide, went out, and laying hold on him, jerked him round, and assured him that if he did not stop his noise and let the people enjoy their sleep without interruption, I would cowhide him on the spot, for we had the Lord's Prophet right here, and we did not want the devil's prophet yelling round the streets. The nuisance was forthwith abated."[4]

To the faithful, Brigham was a compassionate friend. Having witnessed Mary Pitt, an English woman who had suffered from crippling lameness for eleven years, being carried to her baptism, he pronounced a healing blessing. He "rebuked her lameness in the name of the Lord, and commanded her to arise and walk. The lameness left her, and she never afterwards used a staff or crutch."[5]

Brigham marveled at the miraculous healing and the thousands of converts in the British Isles that embraced the gospel: "It truly seemed a miracle. . . . We landed in the spring of 1840, as strangers in a strange land and penniless. But through the mercy of God we have gained many friends, established churches . . . and have left sown in the hearts of many thousands the seeds of eternal truth."[6]

The darkest day of his life was 27 June 1844, the day of the martyrdom of Joseph Smith: "Spent the day in Boston with brother Woodruff. . . . In the evening, while sitting in the depot waiting, I felt a heavy depression of Spirit, and so melancholy I could not converse with any degree of pleasure. . . . I could not assign my reasons for my peculiar feelings."[7]

Twelve days later he learned of the tragic deaths of the Prophet Joseph and his brother Hyrum: "The first thing I thought of was whether Joseph had taken the keys of the kingdom with him from the earth. . . . Bringing my hand down on my knee, I said, 'The keys of the kingdom are right here with the Church.'"[8]

With renewed conviction he returned to Nauvoo, where he resolutely declared, "The Twelve are appointed by the finger of God . . . an independent body who have the keys of the priesthood—the keys of the kingdom of God to deliver to all the world."[9] The authority of the Twelve was challenged on 8 August 1844 by Sidney Rigdon. With characteristic resolution and steadfastness Brigham met the challenge. He seemed to appear to an assembled multitude like the Prophet Joseph Smith in physical stature and in speech. William C. Staines wrote, "I thought it was he and so did thousands who heard it."[10]

Determined to carry forward the Lord's plans as implemented by Joseph Smith, Brigham encouraged the completion of the Nauvoo Temple. "We want to build the Temple in this place," he said, "if we have to build it as the Jews built the walls of the Temple in Jerusalem, with a sword in one hand and the trowel in the other."[11] Yet as the temple neared completion, threatened violence became unrestrained and a forced exodus was imminent.

In February 1846 Brigham Young cried, "Flee Babylon by land or by sea." Thousands of obedient Saints responded and fled from the comforts of Nauvoo to the rigors of Iowa's wilderness. Their sacrifice and suffering, from the loess hills of Iowa to the barren plains of Nebraska and the rigors of the Rockies, is a historic migration without parallel.

"This is the right place, drive on," Brigham said on 24 July 1847 as he looked over the semi-arid desert of the Great Salt Lake Valley.[12] These words were echoed in correspondence to Charles C. Rich: "Let all the brethren and Sisters cheer up their hearts, and know assuredly that God has heard and answered their prayers and ours, and led us to a goodly land."[13]

Leaving only a handful of Saints in the Valley, Brigham returned to the bluffs of the Missouri River to bring his leadership to the many Saints there and guide them to their new home of safety in the Rockies. There in Winter Quarters, he was sustained in December 1847 as prophet and President of The Church of Jesus Christ of Latter-day Saints, fulfilling the prophecy given by Joseph Smith many years before in Kirtland that "the time will come when Brigham Young will preside over this church."[14]

President Young served faithfully in that capacity for thirty years. His contributions to the Church and kingdom of God are unequaled. As President he faced multiple problems of emigration, settling, and religious persecution. Yet he never swerved in his conviction to the faith. "We have been kicked out of the frying-pan into the fire," said Brigham, "out of the fire into the middle of the floor, and here we are and here we will stay." He knew that God had revealed to him "that this is the spot to locate his people, and here is where they will prosper."[15]

His courageous steadfastness earned for him the title "Lion of the Lord." Even President Abraham Lincoln recognized that Brigham was not someone to offend. He told T. B. H. Stenhouse, a Mormon journalist, "You go back and tell Brigham Young that if he will let me alone I will let him alone."[16] Brigham was a man with a mission and vision of what the future would hold for the Latter-day Saints:

> It has been asked if we intend to settle more valleys. Why certainly we expect to fill the next valley and then the next, and the next, and so on. It has been the cry of late, through the columns of the newspapers, that the "Mormons" are going into Mexico! That is quite right, we calculate to go there. Are we going back to Jackson County? Yes. When? As soon as the way opens up. . . . We intend to hold our own here, and also penetrate the north and the south, the east and the west, there to make others and to raise the ensign of truth. . . . We will continue to grow, to increase and spread abroad, and the powers of earth and hell combined cannot hinder it.[17]

Brigham Young died at 4 P.M. on 29 August 1877 in Salt Lake City, after calling "Joseph, Joseph, Joseph." In life he had been separated from his beloved friend, the Prophet Joseph Smith, yet with Brigham's death they were united again. Like Joseph, Brigham had fulfilled the measure of his creation. And he advised that at his interment there should be "no crying or mourning with anyone as I have done my work faithfully and in good faith."[18]

Notes

1. Brigham Young, in *JD* 1:90.
2. Brigham Young, in *JD* 2:128.
3. *CHC* 1:289.
4. Brigham Young, *Manuscript History of Brigham Young, 1801–1844*, ed. Elden Jay Watson (Salt Lake City: Elden Jay Watson, 1968), pp. 17–18.

5. Matthias F. Cowley, *Wilford Woodruff, History of His Life and Labors* (Salt Lake City: Bookcraft, 1964), p. 120.

6. *CHC* 2:86.

7. Young, *Manuscript History*, p. 169.

8. James R. Clark, comp., *Messages of the First Presidency*, 6 vols. (Salt Lake City: Bookcraft, 1965–75), 1:233.

9. *HC* 7:233.

10. As cited in Francis M. Gibbons, *Brigham Young, Modern Moses, Prophet of God* (Salt Lake City: Deseret Book Co., 1981), p. 104.

11. *HC* 7:256.

12. *CHC* 3:224.

13. Letter of Brigham Young to Charles C. Rich, 2 August 1847, as cited in Leonard J. Arrington, *Charles C. Rich, Mormon General and Western Frontiersman* (Provo, Utah: Brigham Young University Press, 1974), p. 118.

14. *CHC* 1:289.

15. As cited in Milton R. Hunter, in Conference Report, April 1947, p. 68.

16. As cited in Leonard J. Arrington, *Brigham Young, American Moses* (New York: Alfred A. Knopf, 1985), p. 295.

17. Brigham Young, in *JD* 18:355–56.

18. As cited in Preston Nibley, *Brigham Young: The Man and His Work* (Salt Lake City: Deseret News Press, 1936), p. 537.

JOSEPH YOUNG
D&C 124:138

Birth: *7 April 1797, Hopkinton, Middlesex County, Massachusetts. Son of John Young and Nabbie Howe.*
Death: *16 July 1881, Salt Lake City, Salt Lake County, Utah.*

Joseph Young was reared in the wilderness of the eastern states, amid trees and woods, flowers and streams. He attended various denominational services with his family in small communities from Vermont to New York. Although he practiced the trade of painting and glazing, he preferred being an itinerant preacher, traveling through the forest preaching the message of Jesus Christ.

In 1818 he left his parental home to further his quest for eternal truth. "I was anxious about this period, to know something of the future existence, beyond this mortal life and labored for the knowledge of it incessantly."[1] In June 1830 he traveled with his brother Phineas to Canada: "On our way thence, we stopped in the town of Lyons, at the house of a J. Green. Here I think we remained one night. It was at this place, I first had sight of the Book of Mormon. It was shown to us [by] a Solomon Chamberlain. Nothing could have been more acceptable to my famishing soul. I hailed it as my Spiritual Jubilee a deliverance from a long night of darkness and bondage."[2]

Joseph and Phineas left Upper Canada and journeyed to Pennsylvania to visit a small branch of the Church. In Columbia, Pennsylvania, Joseph was baptized on 6 April 1832 and ordained an elder a few days later. He soon began missionary labors in New York and Upper Canada, among friends and relatives. When sharing the new doctrine with his brother John, he met opposition: "Joseph, you have received a new doctrine, and another spirit from what you have had heretofore, and I fear it is a delusion; for the scriptures say that many false spirits have gone out into the world, and this is one of them."[3]

Joseph penned his immediate reaction to these words: "My spirit sunk within me; and darkness profound gathered thick like a cloud, covering my mind and spirit so densely, that I was in great mental agony. However I did [not] remain long in this sad condition; for I prayed earnestly to the Lord for deliverance, and it came as suddenly as if I had been led from a dungeon, into the sunlight of heaven."[4]

His brother was seized with severe pains in his head, and returning to his home he "threw himself on the hearth . . . wrestling under excruceeding [sic] agonies." He requested, "Joseph, you profess to have the priesthood of an institution that heals the sick. If you have received such a gift as that, I wish you would lay your hands on me." Joseph agreed to bless him if he promised to not persecute or speak against the doctrine again. The afflicted brother consented and Joseph prayed for him. "My prayer was heard in a moment or two and he was perfectly healed."[5] Six months later Joseph baptized his brother John.

By 1834 Joseph was residing in Kirtland and had responded to the call to march with Zion's Camp to Missouri. The Prophet promised that if he would keep his counsel on the march, "not a hair of his head would be hurt."[6] Of that arduous journey Joseph wrote: "I never went through a more severe trial of my faith. It was as much as we all could bear. We walked one hundred miles in three days in the hottest weather."[7]

In February 1835 the Prophet confided in him his intention to organize the Quorum of the Seventy, and revealed, "Brother Joseph, the Lord has made you president of the Seventies" (D&C 124:138–39).[8] For the next forty-six years he presided as one of the seven Presidents. One of his first assignments was to help the Kirtland poor remove to Far West, Missouri. En route they stopped at Haun's Mill, where many suffered in the terrible massacre. According to family tradition, about 4:00 P.M. Joseph sat in the doorway of a cabin with his young son Seymour on his knee and his wife next to him. He saw armed men on horses riding toward the mill at great speed: "Joseph latched the door of the cabin where they were, and faced his wife. She raised her arms and cried to God to protect her husband, and then begged him to try to escape to the woods. He hated to leave her but she insisted, and he climbed out a window and escaped into the heavy brush."[9]

When the massacre ended he returned to help bury the bodies in an old abandoned well.

Joseph and his family fled from the atrocities in Missouri to Quincy, Illinois. They eventually settled in Nauvoo, where they built an attractive red brick home. Joseph supported his family by painting and glaz-ing. He was privileged to preside at the dedication of the temple, and on 10 February 1846 he was appointed to preside over the Saints still residing in Nauvoo. However, before the year ended he fled from rising mobocracy. His wife wrote of their departure: "We are leaving our homes today to cross the frozen river. We must not look back, but plac-ing our faith in God, we must leave our destiny in His hands. Joseph appears to be cheerful, but the little children cry much of the time. They suffer with the cold, and the fires are cheerless."[10]

In 1850 they trekked to the Valley of the Great Salt Lake. Living in the desert near the Salt Lake was not easy for Joseph. He wrote: "We have had nothing to eat for three days. My brother Lorenzo sent us a small piece of venison tonight, which he had obtained from a trapper. We all relished it much. . . . It may please God to send us bread again. We must not falter in our faith, but sing always to the Glory of God."[11]

From 1856 to 1872 Joseph's family resided near Temple Square in the Salt Lake Twelfth Ward. During these years Joseph's valuable ser-vice was noteworthy. On 30 April 1860 he led a "Church train" to the East, consisting of thirty-six wagons loaded with Utah-grown prod-ucts. In 1862 he gave a series of lectures at the Deseret Theological In-stitute in Salt Lake City on "Travels of the Children of Israel." In 1870 Joseph fulfilled a mission to the British Isles, there preaching the good news of the Restoration. After returning to the Valley he journeyed to pioneer settlements in Utah, Arizona, Idaho, and New Mexico to orga-nize quorums of the seventies.

In 1881 Joseph Young succumbed to general weakness and debil-ity incident to old age. He died on 16 July 1881 at the age of eighty-four. His funeral was held in the Salt Lake Tabernacle on 19 July 1881 and was attended by thousands of Latter-day Saints.[12]

Notes

1. Joseph Young, "Autobiographical Sketch of Joseph Young," comp. Merrill S. Lofthouse (n.p., n.d.), pp. 5–6, in author's possession.

2. Ibid., p. 6.

3. Ibid., p. 9.

4. Ibid., pp. 9–10.

5. Ibid., pp. 10–12.

6. James L. Bradley, Zion's Camp 1834: Prelude to the Civil War (Logan, Utah: James L. Bradley, 1990), p. 26.

7. As cited in Lucille Young Nelson, "Joseph Young" (n.p., n.d.), p. 107, in author's possession.

8. *HC* 2:181 n.

9. Nelson, p. 111.

10. As cited in ibid., p. 116.

11. As cited in ibid., p. 118.

12. Joseph Young's son Seymour Young added six pages to his father's autobiographical sketch, in author's possession.